Robin Williams
cool
Mac apps
Third Edition

D0731159

John Tollett with Robin Williams

Peachpit Press • Berkeley • California

Ron Grand

Robin Williams Cool Mac Apps, Third Edition: Twelve apps to enhance creativity and productivity
©2008 John Tollett and Robin Williams

Cover design: John Tollett
Production: John Tollett and Robin Williams
Prepress: David Van Ness

Peachpit Press
1249 Eighth Street
Berkeley, California 94710
510.524.2178 voice
510.524.2221 fax

Find us on the World Wide Web at **www.peachpit.com**
To report errors, please send a note to errata@peachpit.com
Peachpit Press is a division of Pearson Education

ISBN-13: 978-0-321-50896-6
ISBN-10:   0-321-50896-3

10 9 8 7 6 5 4 3 2 1

Printed and bound in the United States of America

Contents

3 *iDVD*

4 iTunes

199

5 *Mail*

6 Address Book 349

7 iChat AV and Bonjour 373

8 Safari

9 *iCal*   445

Not just cool, *amazingly cool.*

You might have noticed that the name of this book is *Cool Mac Apps,* not *Every Mac App.*

When writing a book about the many cool apps that come bundled with a Mac, you basically have to decide if it's going to be a 1,000-page book that covers most (not all) apps, or a 500-page book that covers your favorite apps—the ones that you use most and that are most useful.

Well, obviously, we chose the 500-page version, partly because we wanted to make the book available before Apple does something crazy, like change all the apps to the next versions that are bound to be even more amazingly cool than they already are. That makes right now a perfect time to jump in and learn as much as you can, because these apps aren't getting smaller and less loaded with features. They certainly are, however, getting easier, more intuitive, and more versatile. Part of Apple's genius is in making incredibly complex tasks as easy as clicking a button.

We're constantly amazed at how often dedicated Mac users neglect some of the fabulous apps that are on their Macs. The reason is always the same—once you learn how to use a program just well enough to do the basics (like a message to your email list, or visit web sites), you tend to stay in that comfort zone rather than experiment with a scary new feature or an unfamiliar application, like iCal, iMovie, or iDVD. Even applications that are familiar to you probably have features that you'd love if you knew they were there. Well, get over it and start having fun.

This book is divided into two sections:

Section One: The coolest Mac apps for creativity
In this section we cover the three iLife apps that Mac users are most likely to use: iPhoto, iMovie, and iDVD.

The iLife suite also includes two other apps that we didn't include: Garage-Band and iWeb. GarageBand is a great app for creating soundtracks (or podcasts). We use it, love it, and are amazed at what non-musicians, like us, can do with it. However, we'd rather use the space for other apps that are more useful to most people. iWeb is also an amazing app. You use it to create and publish wonderful web sites, blogs, and podcasts. But most Mac users we know prefer to use the publishing features found in iPhoto and iMovie, so we've reluctantly excluded that chapter.

Before we had access to these iLife apps, we just occasionally used our digital camera and our video camera and we never showed our movies to anyone (too boring); we seldom bought music—our music collection consisted of dust-covered, scratched CDs scattered around the house. Now we shoot photos of everything, edit movies into masterpieces that people love to watch, and create DVD projects that contain slideshows and movies, and listen to our online collection of music in iTunes.

Section Two: The coolest Mac apps for productivity. This section explains in detail our favorite productivity apps that are included as part of Mac OS X—Mail, Address Book, iChat, Bonjour, Safari, iCal, and Dashboard.

We've also included iTunes and Photo Booth, even though they're not productivity applications in the strictest sense. But iTunes adds so much to the digital lifestyle, and has so many features, we couldn't leave it out. And Photo Booth is too fun to ignore.

We included Time Machine because it doesn't matter how productive you are if you lose an important file. You no longer have to worry about making regular backups of your most important files. Time Machine takes care of that for you. Speaking from lost-file experience, Time Machine is the coolest app of them all.

We don't just write about these apps, we love them, and we use them every day. They're not just cool—they're amazingly cool.

Enjoy,

John & Robin

Section One

The coolest Mac apps for creativity

The collection of Mac software known as *iLife* includes five applications: iPhoto, iMovie, iDVD, GarageBand, and iWeb. All five are incredibly powerful and wonderfully creative. However, we've narrowed the focus in this book to our favorite three that we find most useful, versatile, and fun: iPhoto, iMovie, and iDVD.

We find that we spend most of our creative time in one or all three of these apps. With iPhoto you can manage a large library of photos; create slideshows, books, calendars, cards, and much more; iMovie awakens your creative potential and you can share your movies in a variety of ways—just click a button to send your movie to YouTube. Then use iDVD to burn your project to a DVD, complete with menus that include motion graphics.

If you have a .Mac account, you can upload movies and photos to your own personal web gallery with the click of a button. It's all too much fun.

iPhoto

iPhoto makes managing, sharing, and enhancing your digital photos both easy and fun. Effortlessly import photos from a digital camera, digital memory card reader, CD, DVD, Zip disk, or from any location on your Mac's hard disk.

Organize your photos, expertly retouch blemishes, remove red-eye, adjust contrast and brightness, make other adjustments, then share your photos with friends, family, or business associates in a number of different ways.

If you have a .Mac account, use iPhoto to create online photo albums and screen saver slideshows, order custom prints, greeting cards, calendars or photo albums, using your favorite digital photos.

The Source list lets you choose how to view your photos—as Events, Photos, Recent photos, Subscriptions, Albums, Projects, etc. This example shows Events, collections of photos taken within a specified time frame that you set in iPhoto Preferences.

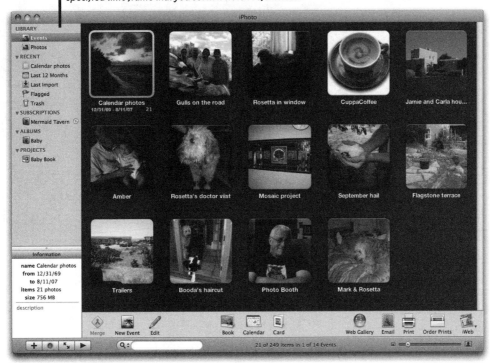

The iPhoto Window

Choose a mode to view your photos—as Events or as Photos. In the Source list, click the "Events" icon or the "Photos" icon. Actually, both modes are Events (a collection of photos grouped by date taken), but the way each mode behaves and displays photos is a little different.

About Events

Photos are often shot in groups of related subject matter during a short time period. For instance, today you might take a dozen photographs of a road trip, a week later you photograph your dog's vet visit, and several days later you photograph the new landscaping at your house. When you import these photos, they're imported as three different Events, because they were shot on three different days—and iPhoto treats each *day* as a separate Event. You can change the time frame of Events in the Events pane of iPhoto's Preferences (page 47). From the "Autosplit into Events" pop-up menu, you can choose "One event per day," "One event per week," "Two-hour gaps," or "Eight-hour gaps." So, if you shoot an event in the morning and another three hours later, iPhoto will treat them as separate events if you change the Autosplit preference to "Two-hour gaps."

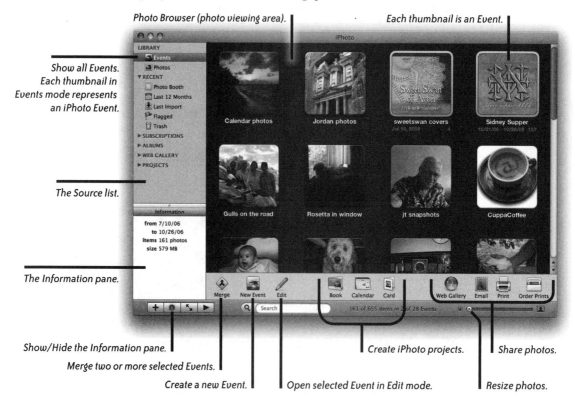

Photo Browser (photo viewing area).

Each thumbnail is an Event.

Show all Events. Each thumbnail in Events mode represents an iPhoto Event.

The Source list.

The Information pane.

Show/Hide the Information pane.

Merge two or more selected Events.

Create a new Event.

Open selected Event in Edit mode.

Create iPhoto projects.

Share photos.

Resize photos.

Events mode

iPhoto organizes photos into Events. By default, iPhoto considers all photos shot in a one-day period to be a single Event. Click "Events" in the sidebar to show all Events in the photo browser pane as thumbnail images (previous page). Each Event thumbnail usually represents a group of photos that were imported at the same time.

View the Library in Events mode.

When you move your pointer across an Event thumbnail, all the photos that belong to the Event "skim" through the thumbnail image area, providing a quick glimpse of the Event's contents. Another way to "skim" through Event photos is to hover the pointer over an Event thumbnail, then tap the left and right Arrow keys on your keyboard.

The single photo that represents an entire Event is called the Key Photo. By default, the first photo in an Event is the Key Photo. To designate a particular photo as the Key Photo, double-click the Event (to show all its photos), then select the photo you want to use. Then, from the Events menu, choose "Make Key Photo."

To show the photos in an Event, double-click the Event thumbnail. The viewing area changes to show all photos that belong to that Event (below).

To open an Event in a separate window, Command-double-click the Event. **Or** from the Events menu, choose "Open Event in Separate Window." **Or** Control-click an Event, then choose "Open Event in Separate Window."

Show all Events.   *Click title to rename Event.*   *Previous and Next Events.*

To customize which tools appear in this toolbar, from the View menu, choose "Show in Toolbar."

Create a New Event

Events are automatically created when you import photos from a camera, media card, CD, or from a location on your hard disk (see pages 12–15). But you can also *manually* create a new Event, then add photos to it.

To manually create a new Event:

Do one of the following:

▼ With "Events" selected in the Source list, click "New Event" in the toolbar. An *empty*, untitled Event is placed in the viewing area.

▼ With "Events" selected in the Source list, select "Create Event" in the Events menu. An *empty,* untitled Event is placed in the viewing area.

▼ With "Events" selected in the Source list, select two or more existing Events, then choose "Create Event" in the Events menu. iPhoto creates an untitled Event that contains the photos of the selected Events. The original Events are deleted.

This is similar to "Merge Events," except that a merged Event keeps the name of the first Event selected.

▼ With "Events" selected in the Source list, double-click an Event in the viewing area to show the Event's photos in the viewing area. Select one or more photos in the Event, then from the Events menu, choose "Create Event."

▼ With "Photos" selected in the Source list, select one or more photos, then from the Events menu, choose "Create Event…." In the dialog sheet that slides down, click "Create."

A photo can only appear in one Event at a time. If you create a new Event from existing selected photos, the photos are moved out of their original Event and into the new one.

Add Photos to an Event

An empty, New Event.

When you create an empty, new Event (by using one of the top two bulleted items listed above), it shows in Events mode as a blank thumbnail, and it doesn't appear in Photos mode at all, until after you manually add photos to it.

There are a couple of ways to add photos to an empty Event, explained on the following page.

Drag photos between Events

You can drag photos from one Event to another Event. As mentioned previously, this removes the photo from its original Event.

To move photos between Events:

1. Select an Event into which you want to move photos.

2. Double-click the Event to make it appear in the Source list as the most recently viewed Event (right). If you've changed the Events Preferences, as explained on the next page, click the "Show Photos" button that appears in the Event thumbnail. In the example below, an Event named "Buddy Icons" has been selected and is shown as the most recently viewed Event in the Source list (right).

3. Click "Photos" in the Source list. In the viewing area, select the photo or photos you want to move.

4. Drag the selected photos to the Event you just listed as a "Recent" item in the Source list. A blue border highlights the Recent Event when you drag the photo selelction on top of it (shown below).

The most recently viewed Event shows at the top of the "Recent" list.

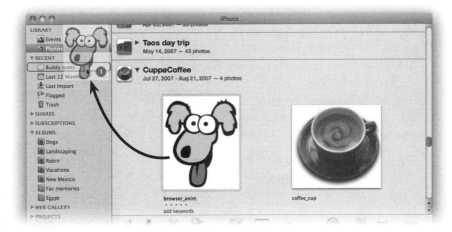

Drag photos from albums to Events

When you drag an Event from an existing album or Smart Album in the Source list to an Event listed as "Recent" in the Source list, the photo is copied to the Event, and remains in its original location (Albums, Smart Albums, or Events).

1. Repeat Steps 1 and 2 above, then select an existing album from the "Albums" catergory in the Source list. The album's photos are displayed in the viewing area.

2. Drag photos from the album to the "Recent" Event in the Source list.

Make the Events mode more useful

No doubt about it, the Events mode is beautiful. Watching photos fly through the thumbnail placeholder when you move your pointer across an Event (skimming) provides a snazzy preview of photos in the Event. But you can make it even more useful and versatile by modifying its behavior in iPhoto Preferences.

This small change makes the Events mode our preferred way of viewing the iPhoto Library.

To modify Events behavior:

1. From the iPhoto menu, choose "Preferences...."
2. Click "Events" in the toolbar to show the "Events" pane (below).
3. Change the "Double-click Event" selection to "Magnifies photo."

This preference determines what happens when you double-click an Event in the photo browser. With the first item, "Shows Event photos," double-clicking an Event shows all photos contained in the Event. The second option, "Magnifies photo," lets you skim across the Event thumbnail until you see the photo you want, then double-click to fill the viewing area with that particular photo.

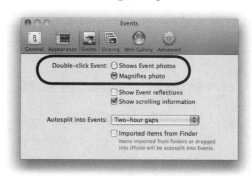

But that's not all you get with this preference. Now each Event thumbnail reveals a "Show Photos" button when your pointer is over the Event (right). Move your pointer on top of the button and the Event thumbnail changes to show an index sheet of photos from the Event. To show all photos in the Event, click the "Show Photos" button.

An Event shown as an index sheet of photos.

Delete an Event

To delete an Event, select it, then press Command-Delete. **Or,** drag the Event to the Trash icon in the Sources list.

Merge or split Events

It's possible that several different Events could contain photos that should be grouped together instead of in separate Events. Or photos that don't really belong together could end up in a single Event. iPhoto lets you reorganize the photos by *merging* or *splitting* Events.

To merge two Events:

1. In Events mode, select two or more Events.
2. Click the Merge icon in the toolbar.
3. A sheet slides down from the title bar and asks you to confirm that you want to merge these events. Click the "Merge" icon (below).

   Or, drag an Event on top of another Event to merge the two Events.

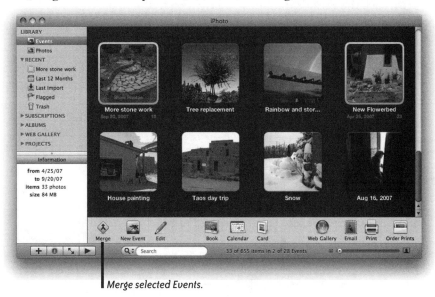

Selected Events are highlighted with a golden-yellow border.

Merge selected Events.

To split one Event into two Events:

1. Double-click an Event to show its collection of photos.
2. Select the photos (or photo) you want to split away from the current Event.
3. Click the "Split" icon in the toolbar. iPhoto creates a new, untitled Event that contains the selected photos.

4. Click "Untitled Event" (below-left) in the viewing area, then type a custom name for the Event (below-right).

View the Library in Photos mode.

Photos mode

For another way to view your Library, choose "Photos" in the Source list. Your photo collections are still organized as Events, but now each Event is shown in the Viewer as an item in a list (below).

To hide or show the photos in an Event, click the disclosure triangle next to the thumbnail image.

To open or close all Events at once, Command-click the disclosure triangle.

To rename an Event, double-click the Event title, then type a new name.

To rename a photo, click the photo's title, then type a new name.

To select all the photos in an Event, click the Event title.
Or, click the Event's thumbnail image next to the title.

To delete an Event, Command-click the Event. **Or,** drag the Event to the Trash icon in the Source list.

Hide/Show photos in this Event.

To rename an Event, click its title.

Click "Photos" to view all Events in the format shown here.

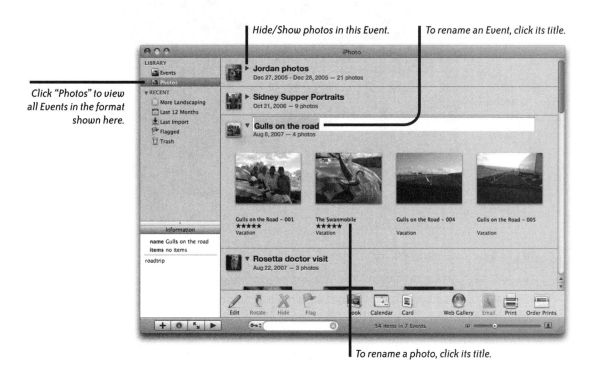

To rename a photo, click its title.

The Source List

In addition to the Events and Photos view listed under the "Library" category in the sidebar, iPhoto's Source list provides other ways to view and organize photos. In the example shown, an *item count* appears in parentheses to the right of each album, showing how many photos the album contains. To show item counts in the sidebar, go to the General pane of iPhoto Preferences, then select the "Show item counts" checkbox.

Recent albums

The Recent category lists several automatically generated albums (collections of photos). The first album in the list shows the currently selected Event. Click the album to show the photos in that Event.

The **Last 12 Months** album shows all photos that were imported in the last year. In the General pane of iPhoto's Preferences, you can change this to any time period between one and 18 months.

The **Last Import** album shows photos from the most recent import session.

The **Flagged** album shows photos that you've marked with a flag icon. To flag a photo, select a photo (or multiple photos), then from the Photos menu, choose "Flag Photo."

The **Trash** album shows photos you've deleted. To permanently delete the photos, Control-click the Trash album, then choose "Empty Trash."

Other album categories

As you use iPhoto's cool features, other categories appear in the Source list, with albums listed under them. When you create and publish a .Mac Web Gallery, a **Web Gallery** category is added to iPhoto's Source list. If you sub- scribe to someone else's Web Gallery, the subscribed albums are shown in a **Subscriptions** category. When you create new, custom albums, the albums appear in an **Albums** category. A **Projects** category shows Book, Calendar, or Card projects that you've created in iPhoto, and a **Slideshows** category shows slideshows created in iPhoto. If you and another Mac user on a local network both have Sharing enabled in iPhoto's Preferences, a **Shares** cat- egory shows the shared Libraries and albums.

The Information pane

The Information pane located below the Source list shows information about anything that's selected in iPhoto—an album, a photo, multiple photos, an Event, multiple Events, or any item in the Source list.

The Source list is organized into categories. Click the disclosure triangle next to a category name to hide or show the albums in it.

Click here to show the Information pane and see information about any selected item.

Import Photos

When a digital camera or a memory card reader is connected to your Mac with a USB cable and recognized by iPhoto, the "Import" view automatically opens. The next few pages explain how to import your photos directly from a camera, a media card reader, a CD, or a location on your hard disk.

Import photos from a camera or media card

Import photos from a device, such as a digital camera or a digital memory card reader (remove the media card from a camera and insert it in a media card reader).

1. If importing directly from a camera, turn your camera off before connecting it to the computer. To conserve the camera's battery power, connect the camera's AC power adapter to the camera, then plug it into a power outlet.

2. Connect the camera (or the card reader) to the computer's USB port.

3. Connect the USB cable that came with the camera or card reader to your Mac's USB port. If importing directly from a camera, turn it on.

   ▼ An icon representing the memory card or your camera (left) appears on the Desktop, indicating it has been mounted.

   ▼ iPhoto opens in Import view (shown below) to show all photos on the memory card or in the camera.

JT IMAGES

A mounted media card.

The Information pane shows how many photos are selected for import, the overall size of selected photos, and when the photos were shot.

Show/Hide the Information pane.

4. Click the "Import All..." button to import all photos.

To import just *selected* photos, make a multiple selection of the photos you want, then click "Import Selected."

To select multiple photos, click on the first selection, then Command-click additional photos to add them to the selection.

5. After import, click the Eject button in the Source list (below).

 *Eject the mounted device.*

6. Disconnect the device from your computer.

Autosplit events after importing. Select this checkbox (circled below) to group photos into separate *Events* during import, based on the time frame in which they were shot.

When you shoot photos, you usually shoot a group of related photos, a birthday, for example. Then a day or two later you shoot another group of photos for another event, such as a friend's visit. When you're ready to import your photos, iPhoto splits the photos into separate events, based on when they were shot. By default, iPhoto considers each day an event. You can change the time frame of an event in the Events pane of iPhoto Preferences. Event time frames can be defined by day, week, two-hour gaps, or eight-hour gaps.

Hide photos already imported. Select this checkbox to hide photos that you've already imported, but haven't erased from the camera or digital media card. This makes it easier to find photos that haven't been imported yet.

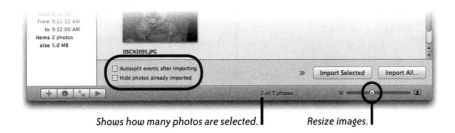

Shows how many photos are selected.   *Resize images.*

After you click the "Import" button, this dialog lets you choose to erase or keep the photos on the camera (or media card).

Import photos from your hard disk or a CD

You can import photos that you already have on your hard disk or stored on a CD.

1. If you have a CD that contains photos you want to import, insert the CD in your optical drive.
2. From the File menu, select "Import to Library...."
3. The "Import Photos" window opens, shown below. In the Sidebar, select the CD icon (if you inserted a CD), or choose a folder on your computer where photos are stored.
4. Select an entire folder of photos, an individual photo, or multiple photos, then click "Import."

iPhoto creates a New Event, named the same as the folder of imported photos. If you import a selection of individual photos that are not in a folder, iPhoto creates an untitled Event.

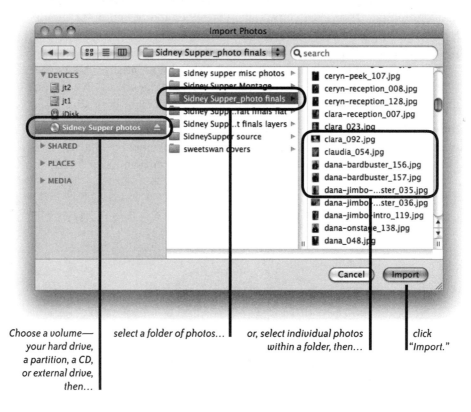

Choose a volume—
your hard drive,
a partition, a CD,
or external drive,
then...

select a folder of photos...

or, select individual photos
within a folder, then...

click
"Import."

Here's an even easier way to import photos from a location on your hard disk or a CD: drag a photo, a multiple-selection of photos, or a folder of photos to the viewing area of the iPhoto window (shown below).

Or drag the item (or items) to the "Photos" icon in the Library section of the sidebar, as shown below.

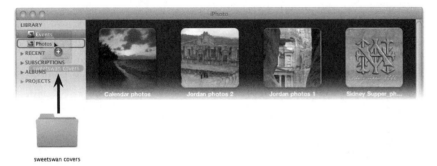

Or drag photos to an existing album in the Source list. The imported photos are added to the Library as an Event, and to the album.

To import photos *and* mark them as flagged, drag a selection of photos to the "Flagged" folder in the Source list.

A progress bar at the bottom of the window shows how many photos remain to be imported. To stop the import process, click the "Stop Import" button.

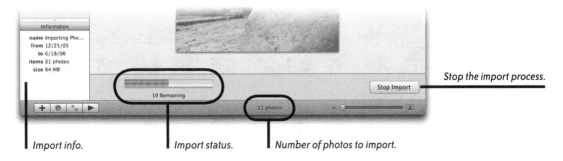

Stop the import process.

Import info.   Import status.   Number of photos to import.

The View Menu

The selections you make in the View menu determine what information is shown with Event and photo previews (Titles, Ratings, and Keywords), how events and photos are sorted (by Date, Keyword, Title, Rating, or Manually), what buttons are shown in the toolbar, and some special options for Full Screen previewing.

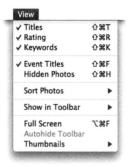

The top three items in the menu (left) affect both view modes—Events and Photos. Click an item in the View menu to checkmark it and display that information beneath photo previews (shown on the right).

The Swan Mobile arrives
★★★★★
Mary Sidney Society

The next item in the menu affects the Photos view mode. Checkmark **Event Titles** to show an Event title and thumbnail image that visually separates one Event from another (below-top). If you choose *not* to checkmark "Event Titles," the Photos view mode shows all photos of all Events as one large collection (below-bottom).

When "Event Titles" is checkmarked in the View menu, the Photos view mode shows each Event separated by a title and a thumbnail image.

A small dot in a bar always indicates that the pane is resizable. Press and drag the dot up or down.

When "Event Titles" is not checkmarked in the View menu, photos of all Events appear together.

Checkmark the **Hidden Photos** item to show any photos that you've marked as "Hidden." Photos that are hidden become visible, marked with a red X, as shown on the right. To learn more about Hidden Photos, see page 36.

Sort Photos lets you choose how photos are arranged in the window—by Date, Keyword, Title, Rating, or Manually. You can also choose to have any of these arrangements sorted in ascending or descending order (below-left).

Hidden photos are marked with a red X.

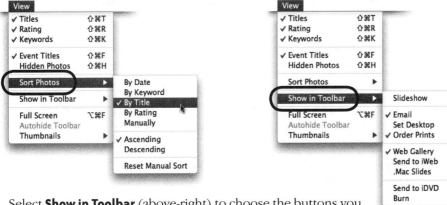

Select **Show in Toolbar** (above-right) to choose the buttons you want to place in the toolbar (below). Learn all about these buttons and what they do on pages 22–31.

Choose **Full Screen** in the View menu to preview photos in Full Screen mode (pages 33–35).

The last two items in the View menu relate to Full Screen mode. **Autohide Toolbar** keeps the toolbar hidden until you move your pointer over the bottom edge of the screen.

The **Thumbnails** options are available only when "Full Screen" is checkmarked. Click the **Always Show** submenu item to make the Full Screen toolbar always visible. When you choose "Always Show," the menu item changes to say **Autohide Thumbnails.** Click that item to hide the Thumbnails pane automatically. Move your pointer near the top edge of the screen to show the Thumbnails pane. The other submenu items let you set the position of the thumbnails palette (Top, Left, or Right), and set the layout of the thumbnails pane (number of rows).

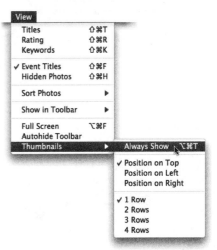

Create an Album

Create **albums** to organize your photos into custom collections for various uses, such as for slideshows, online Web Gallery presentations, Books, Calendars, photos you want to transfer to others or burn to a disc, etc.

You can put the same photo in any number of albums because iPhoto just *references* the original photo stored in the Library. This means you won't end up with multiple copies of the same photo on your computer, taking up space on your hard disk.

To create an album:

1. Click the Add (+) button, circled below.

2. In the sheet that drops down, choose "Album" from the toolbar. Type a name for the new album, then click "Create." The new album appears in the Source list, under the "Albums" category.

   You can choose to select photos *before* you click the Add button, then automatically add the selected photos to the new album. Click the "Use selected items in new album" checkbox.

3. Click "Create." The new album appears under the "Albums" category in the sidebar, as shown on the left.

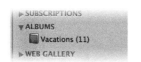

A new album in the Source list.

Photos that you delete go to the Trash.

To empty the Trash: *Control-click the Trash icon, then choose "Empty Trash."*

Or, from the iPhoto menu, choose "Empty Trash."

Albums you create appear in the "Albums" category.

Click the Add (+) button to open a dialog sheet (top of window), then choose an item from the dialog toolbar you want to add to the Source list.

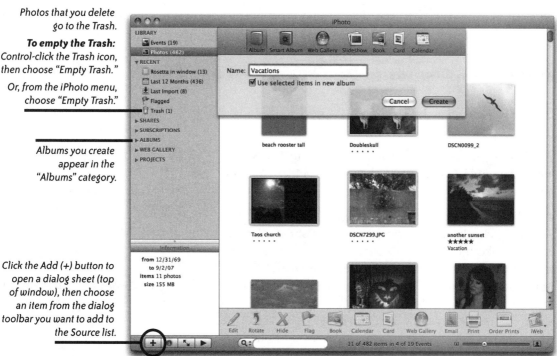

To create an Album from selected photos:

1. Select one or more photos in the photo browser.

2. From the File menu, choose "New Album From Selection...."

3. Name the album in the sheet that drops down,
   as shown on the previous page.

To add photos to an album:

Drag a photo, or multiple photos, from any Event or album onto an album icon in the Source list (the sidebar). You can even drag an entire Event from the main viewing area to an album in the sidebar.

Or use the method mentioned on the previous page. First, select the photos you want to put in a new album, then create a new album and click the checkbox that says "Use selected items in new album."

To rename an album:

Double-click the album name to highlight it, then type a new name.

To delete photos from an album:

If you delete a photo from an *album,* it will *not* be deleted from the Library; the photo in the album *references* the original photo in the Library. **But** if you delete a photo from the *Library,* it *will* disappear from the Library and every album that referenced it.

1. Select one or more photos to delete.

2. Press the Delete key. **Or** Control-click on the photo selection, then choose "Delete From Album" in the shortcut menu.

To duplicate an album:

You may want to experiment with different arrangements of photos for a book project or a slideshow. You can duplicate an entire album, then rearrange photos, delete some photos and add others. It won't affect the original album or add to the size of your Library because albums just *reference* the original photos in the iPhoto Library.

1. Select an album in the sidebar, then from the Photos menu, choose "Duplicate" (or press Command D).

   Or Control-click an album, then choose "Duplicate" from the shortcut menu.

2. To rename a duplicate album, double-click the new album in the sidebar, then type a new name.

Create Smart Albums

Creating albums and manually dragging photos into them is an easy way to organize your photos, but it can be a lot easier. You can create a Smart Album that automatically finds photos matching certain criteria that you set. For instance, you might create a Smart Album named "Vacations" that looks for photos that have a five-star rating and a keyword of "vacation." iPhoto finds all five-star rated photos with a keyword of "vacation" and places them in the "Vacations" Smart Album.

To create a Smart Album:

1. Click the Add (**+**) button in the bottom-left corner of the window.

2. In the toolbar of the sheet that drops down, choose "Smart Album," then type a name for the new Smart Album.

This option is visible when more than one search condition is chosen from the pop-up menus.

*To find more photos, choose "match **any** of the following conditions" instead of "**all** conditions."*

3. Use the pop-up menus to set the criteria that photos must match to be automatically added to this Smart Album.

   To add more conditions, click the plus (**+**) button on the right side of the sheet. To remove a condition, click its minus (**-**) button.

4. Use the top pop-up menu to choose between "Match **any** of the following conditions" or "Match **all** of the following conditions."

5. Click OK. The new Smart Album appears in the Source list (left). Existing and future photos that meet the conditions you set are automatically added to the Smart Album.

To edit the settings of a Smart Album:

1. Select a Smart Album in the Source list.

2. From the File menu, choose "Edit Smart Album."

3. The Smart Album sheet drops down again (shown above). Make the changes you want, then click OK.

Organize with Folders

As your collection of photos and iPhoto projects (books, calendars, cards, and web galleries) grows larger, the importance of keeping everything nicely organized becomes more important. If you create lots of new albums to stay organized, you can easily end up with a very long, scrolling list of albums in the Source list. That's not really a bad thing, because you can also create Folders in the Source list to create groups of albums.

A folder can contain albums, Smart Albums, and other folders. Click the small disclosure triangle (right) to show or hide the items in a folder.

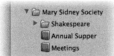

To add a new folder to the Source list:

1. From the File menu, choose "New Folder."
   Or Control-click in a blank space in the Source list, then from the shortcut menu, choose "New Folder."

2. A new folder appears in the Source list named "untitled folder." Select the folder, then type a custom name.

To reorganize albums and folders in the Source list, drag a folder to any other folder. Or drag an album to any folder.

You can also drag one or more photos from an album to any other album. The photos remain in the original album *in addition to* being placed in the new album. If you drag one or more photos to a *folder*, a new *untitled* album is created in the folder that contains the selected photos.

To delete a folder in the Source list, select it, then press Delete.

iPhoto's Toolbars

The appearance and functionality of iPhoto's toolbar changes slightly depending on which view mode you're in (Events or Photos). Also, some tools may or may not be present in your toolbar, depending on what items are selected in the View menu option, "Show in Toolbar" (right). These following examples show the toolbars with default settings; therefore, not every tool is visible. The unselected tools are covered later in this chapter.

In Events and Photos mode, items in toolbars are organized into three groups: (1) editing tools, (2) iPhoto projects, and (3) photo sharing options. The following explanations refer to the editing tools. The project and sharing tools are covered later in the chapter.

Editing Tools in Events Mode

Merge: Click to merge two or more selected Events into one Event. If you double-click an Event to show its individual photos, the Merge tool turns into a **Split** tool (left). To remove selected photos from the current Event and place in a new, untitled Event, click "Split."

New Event: Click to create a new Event. A new placeholder Event thumbnail appears at the bottom of the viewing area.

Edit: Click to open the selected Event in Edit mode. See page 24–31 to learn more about the editing tools in Edit mode.

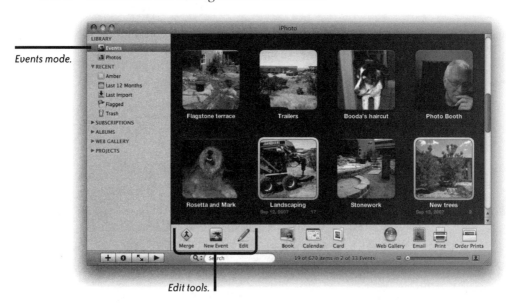

Events mode.

Edit tools.

Editing Tools in Photos Mode

When "Photos" is selected as the view mode in the sidebar's Library category, the toolbar changes, as shown above. The tools now include:

Edit: Click to open the selected photo in Edit mode. Learn more about Edit mode on pages 24–31.

Rotate: Click to rotate selected photo (or photos) 90°. To change the direction of rotation, press the Option key. To change the *default* direction of rotation, open iPhoto Preferences. In the "General" pane, choose clockwise or counter-clockwise (right).

Hide: Click to hide selected photos. See page 36 for details.

Flag: Click to mark selected photos as flagged. Flagged photos are marked with a small red flag (right). To see all flagged photos from all events, click the "Flagged" folder in the Source list (below).

Flagged photo.

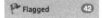

Create a new Event from flagged photos

To automatically create a new Event using flagged photos, from the Events menu, choose "Create Event From Flagged Photos."

Add flagged photos to a selected Event

To automatically add flagged photos to a selected event, from the Events menu, choose "Add Flagged Photos To Selected Event."

Editing Tools in Edit Mode

Select a photo in the viewing area that you want to edit, then click the Edit button in the toolbar. The viewing area displays the selected photo, along with a modified toolbar (circled, bottom). The editing tools in Edit view are the same ones that appear in Full Screen mode, although Full Screen mode also includes an Info button and a Compare button that makes it easy to compare two or more photos (see page 32).

Selected photo.

Select a photo, then click "Edit" to show the photo in Edit mode (below).

To resize thumbnails, drag the dimpled bar (circled) up or down.

To hide thumbnails, from the View menu choose "Thumbnails," then choose "Hide."

Editing tools.

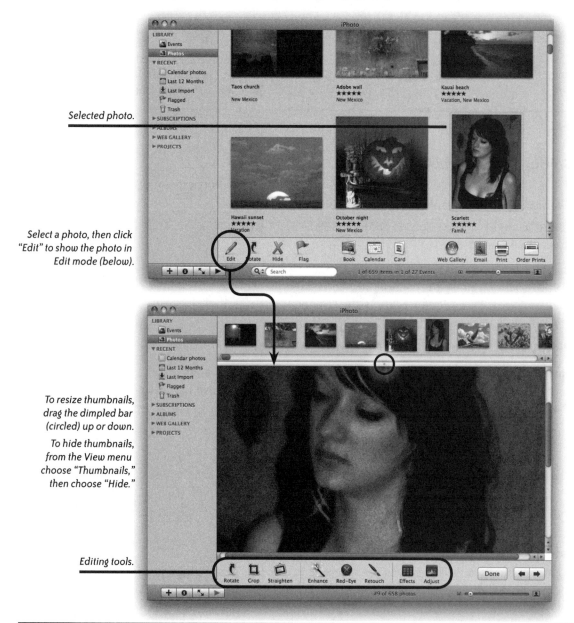

Use the following tools in the toolbar to edit an image in a variety of ways.

Rotate

Click the Rotate button to rotate selected photos 90°. The photo is rotated in the same direction that the arrow icon shows in the toolbar. To change the rotation direction, go to iPhoto Preferences. Select "General" in the Preferences toolbar, then choose a "Rotate" direction. **Or** press the Option key to temporarily change the direction of the Rotate button.

Rotate

Crop

Click the Crop button to show a highlighted cropping area shape. A black control bar that provides resizing options also appears. Drag the bar to reposition it anywhere on the screen. Drag a corner or side of the crop shape to change its size and proportions. If you want to change the image's pixel size or proportions, select a size option in the control bar pop-up menu (right). To constrain the crop shape to the proportion selected in the pop-up menu, click the "Constrain" checkbox in the control bar. When you're ready to crop, click the "Apply" button.

The Constrain pop-up menu contains common size and proportion options, plus a "Custom" option for creating a photo of any size.

Some of the size options permit you to also choose "Constrain as landscape" (a horizontal format) or "Constrain as portrait" (a vertical format).

The Crop control bar.

Straighten

Use the Staighten button when you want to straighten a horizon line or realign a vertical alignment, such as a tree, or the side of a building. Or perhaps you just want to create a dramatic effect with a tilted photo.

To straighten a photo:

1. Click the Straighten button. A grid and a control bar appear.

2. Drag the control bar slider that appears on the photo to the left or right. **Or** click the small Tilt icons on either side of the slider to make incremental angle changes of 0.1°.

   Press the Shift key to see a comparison of the photo's original orientation to the current setting.

   To reset the photo to its original angle (*before* you apply the Straighten setting, and while the Straighten grid is still visible), Control-click the photo, then choose "Reset Straighten."

3. To apply the Straighten setting to the photo, click the Close button (the circled-X). **Or** click the Straighten tool again.

   To reset the photo angle *after* you've applied a Straighten setting, Control-click the photo, then choose "Revert to Previous."

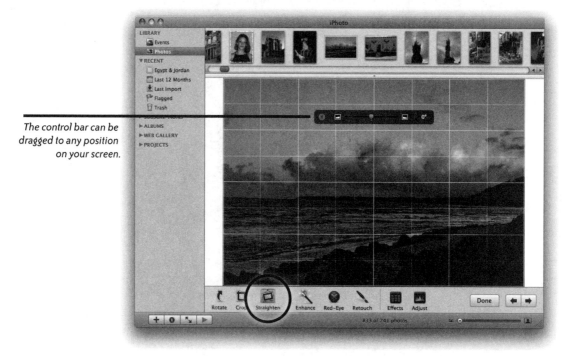

The control bar can be dragged to any position on your screen.

Enhance

Use the Enhance tool when you want to enhance colors automatically. iPhoto does its best to analyze a photo, then applies the changes such as color saturation, hue, contrast, and brightness.

Click the Enhance button once. iPhoto does its best to analyze the photo and makes changes to the photo.

To compare the enhanced version to the original photo, press the Shift key.

To undo the enhancement, from the Edit menu, choose "Undo Enhance Photo." **Or** from the Photos menu, choose "Revert to Previous."

Depending on the image, the Enhance tool might work great, or it might make changes you don't like at all. If you don't like the results, experiment with the settings found in the "Adjust" palette (page 31).

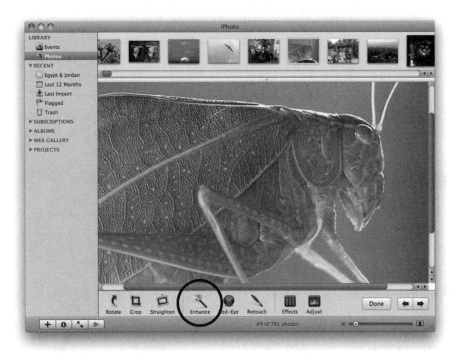

Red-Eye

The Red-Eye button removes the red reflection that flash photos often cause in the subject's eyes.

1. Click the Red-Eye button to show the Red-Eye control bar.

2. From the "Size" pop-up menu in the control bar, choose "Manual" or "Automatic" to size the Red-Eye brush.

   The "Automatic" setting works well with photos when the subject's eyes are small in the frame. Click on the red in the subject's eyes to remove it.

   If the photo is a closeup, choose "Manual" so you can manually enlarge the Red-Eye brush size to fit the red part of the Eye.

3. Drag the control bar slider to resize the Red-Eye brush. **Or** tap the Left and Right Bracket keys on the keyboard to resize the brush. Position the brush over the subject's eye, then click.

   To reset the photo to the original unmodified version, Control-click the photo, then choose "Reset Red-Eye."

4. To exit the Red-Eye tool and apply the changes, click the Close button (the circle-X). **Or** click the Red-Eye tool in the toolbar.

Before you apply the change, press the Shift key to show the unmodified photo. *After* you've applied the change, you can still revert to the original photo—Control-click the photo, then choose "Revert to Previous."

The Red-Eye brush, sized to fit the red area in the photo.

The brush has already been clicked on the other eye.

The Red-Eye control bar.

Retouch

The Retouch button does an amazing job of removing dust and scratches, or wrinkles and blemishes, from photos. iPhoto analyzes the pixels underneath the brush, then blurs and blends the color information.

1. Click the Retouch button. The Retouch control bar appears. Drag the bar to a position where it's not in the way of areas you want to retouch.

2. Drag the Retouch "Size" slider in the control bar to resize the retouch brush. **Or** tap the Left and Right Bracket keys on the keyboard to resize the brush. A small brush size is best for small detail, such as removing specs of dust, small blemishes, or even wrinkles. A larger brush makes areas look smoother.

3. Click or drag the brush in the area you want to retouch. In the example below, the Retouch brush is dragged across wrinkles.

   Press the Shift key to show the unmodified version of the photo. To reset the photo to the original version, Control-click the photo, then choose "Reset Retouch."

4. To apply the Retouch changes, click the Close button on the control bar (the circled-X). **Or** click the Retouch brush in the toolbar.

After changes have been applied, you can still revert to the original photo. Control-click the photo, then choose "Revert to Previous."

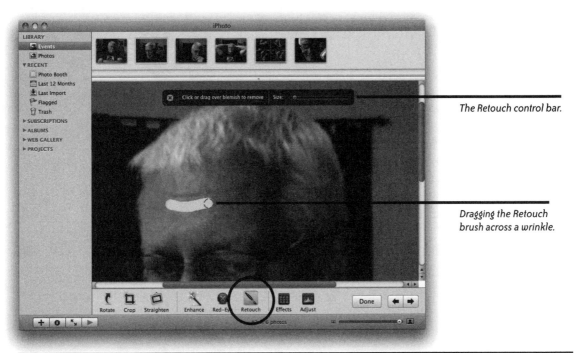

The Retouch control bar.

Dragging the Retouch brush across a wrinkle.

Effects

iPhoto includes eight Effects filters that you can apply to a photo.

1. Select a photo in the thumbnails pane to show it in the viewing area, then click the Effects button in the toolbar.

   The Effects panel opens and shows thumbnail previews of the selected photo with various effects applied.

2. Click one or more of the Effects thumbnails to apply the effect to the photo, visible in the iPhoto viewing area.

   When you click the thumbnail previews (except for "B & W" and "Sepia,") the number "1" appears in a dark bar at the bottom of the thumbnail, as seen in the top-right corner of the panel below.

   Click the thumbnail again (or click the small right-facing arrow), and the number in the bar changes to "2" to show how many times the effect has been applied. The filter is applied to the photo again, increasing the effect. You can repeat this procedure 1–24 times, depending on the effect you use.

   To undo the effects one at a time, click the left-facing arrow. **Or** Option-click anywhere on the thumbnail.

   To revert to the original photo, click the center thumbnail, labeled "Original." **Or,** in the viewing area, Control-click the photo, then choose "Revert to Previous."

To apply multiple effects to the same photo, click additional Effects thumbnail panes.

Your effects settings are applied to the photo when you click "Done" in the Edit toolbar, or when you choose another photo in Edit mode. The thumbnail photo shown in the thumbnails pane at the top of the iPhoto window keeps the appearance of the original, unmodified photo until the effect is applied.

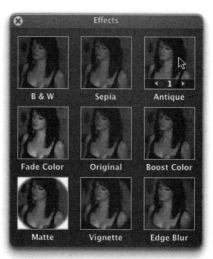

The Antique effect is selected (top-right corner). Click up to 9 more times to increase the effect. Option-click to decrease the effect.

Adjust

Use the Adjust palette to modify a photo's exposure, contrast, brightness, color, sharpness, and more. Select a photo, then click the Adjust button in the toolbar. The Adjust palette opens to show the following controls:

Histogram: The chart at the top of the palette is called a histogram. Drag the far-left slider to the right to make shadows darker. Drag the far-right slider to the left to make highlights lighter. Drag the center slider left to make mid-tones lighter, and drag right to make mid-tones darker.

Exposure: Adjust the overall exposure of a photo.

Contrast: Adjust the contrast of light and dark tones in a photo.

Highlights: Increase detail by darkening highlights.

Shadows: Increase detail by lightening shadows.

Saturation: Adjust color intensity.

Temperature: Adjust color temperature between cool and warm.

Tint: Adjust red and green tint.

Eyedropper tool: Let iPhoto automatically make color adjustments. Select the eyedropper, then click a white or gray area that is very close to the color it should be. iPhoto automatically adjusts the photo's colors.
This can produce strange results, so if you don't like the result, undo it (Command-Z).

Sharpness: Increase the sharpness of the photo. For best results, save this adjustment for last.

Reduce Noise: Smooth out the grainy quality of a photo.

Reset button: Click to reset sliders to default settings.

Copy button: Copy the current settings into memory.

Paste button: Apply the settings that have been copied into memory to the currently selected photo.

To compare the current settings to the original photo, press the Shift key. The photo in the viewing area reverts to the original, unmodified version.
Release the Shift key to show the photo with the current settings applied.

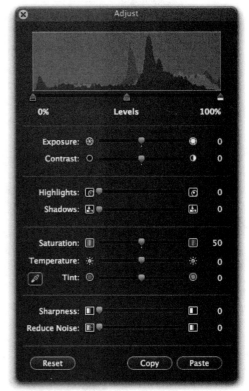

To move sliders in small, preset increments, click the tiny icons on either side of a slider.

The Full Screen Toolbar

With the exception of the Info and Compare buttons, the editing tools in Full Screen mode (pages 33–35) are the same as those in Edit mode (pages 24–31).

Info

The Info button

When viewing a photo in Full Screen mode, click the Info button to show an Information dialog (right) that contains information about the photo. If you haven't already assigned a title, a rating, or comments to a photo, you can do it here while in Full Screen mode.

Information	
title	Pueblo Church
date	11/14/2006
time	9:06:01 AM
rating	★★★★★
keyword	
kind	JPEG Image
size	1846 × 1319
	68 KB

Taos Pueblo church. Shoot into the sun. Use for poster.

Compare

The Compare button

With a single photo selected, click the Compare button. The viewing area shows the original selection on the left, and shows the *next* photo in the Event or album on the right. Click the Compare button again to revert to a display of only the original selection. To compare the selected photo to any other photo in the Event or album, click the Compare button, then use the Left or Right Arrow buttons (or use the Arrow keys on the keyboard) to cycle through photos. As you click the Arrows, the photo on the right changes, and the original selection stays visible on the left.

Left: *the original photo selection.*
Right: *the current selection.*

Use the Arrow buttons to change the current selection.

Full Screen Mode

The best environment for working with your photos is Full Screen mode. Photos are displayed as large as possible, and lots of editing tools are easily accessible. To enter Full Screen mode, click the Full Screen button in the bottom-left corner of the iPhoto window (shown on the right). **Or** from the View menu, choose "Full Screen." Or, Control-click an Event, then from the shortcut menu, choose "Edit using full screen."

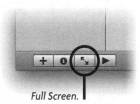

Full Screen.

The thumbnails pane at the top of the screen (below) shows all the photos in the currently selected Event (or Events). If no Event is selected, the entire Library is shown in the thumbnails pane. Slide the horizontal scroll bar below the thumbnails to scan quickly through large collections of photos. You can also use the small Back and Forward arrows on the right side of the horizontal scroll bar. Press and hold an arrow button to scroll quickly through the thumbnails, or click once to scroll through one thumbnail at a time.

To select a single photo and show it in the viewing area, click one of the thumbnails. As you select different thumbnails, they're displayed in the viewing area (shown below).

To select and show multiple photos, click one thumbnail, then Shift-click a second photo. Using the Shift key selects the two selected photos and any other photos that are between them. Full Screen mode can only show eight photos at a time in the viewing area. If your selection includes more than eight photos, iPhoto ignores them.

Thumbnails pane.

Navigation window.

Toolbar.

Full Screen mode.

*Full Screen mode with
eight thumbnails selected.
Selected photos are
indicated in the top
thumbnails pane by an
olive-colored background.*

To select multiple photos *without* selecting other photos that happen to be positioned between the clicked photos, Command-click the thumbnails you want. Only the photos you click are added to the selection.

To remove a photo from the viewing area when multiple photos are displayed, click the **circle-x** in the selected photo's top-left corner. The photo remains in the thumbnail collection, but not in the viewing area.

When you zoom in to see detail in a photo, a small Navigation window appears (below). The window shows the entire image, with a highlighted section that shows the current view. The highlighted area changes as you zoom in and out, using the zoom slider in the toolbar. To change the current view, drag the highlighted section around inside the Navigation window.

Navigation window.

Even while multiple photos are displayed in the viewing area, you can edit a selected photo. The Crop tool is active in the selected photo, below-left.

Also notice how much larger the thumbnails below are, compared to the example on the previous page. **To resize the thumbnails pane,** position your pointer over the bottom edge of the horizontal scroll bar until the pointer changes into a bi-directional arrow, as shown on the right. Press and drag the bar up or down to make the thumbnails pane larger or smaller.

Drag bar to resize thumbnails pane.

Selected thumbnails have an olive-colored background.

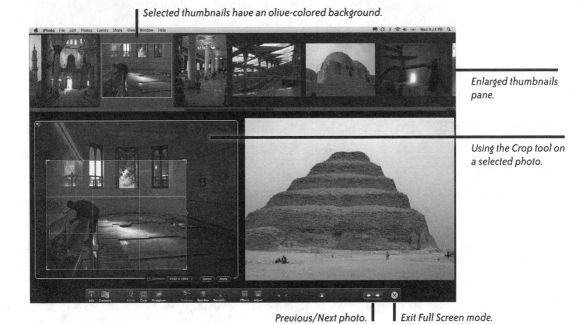

Enlarged thumbnails pane.

Using the Crop tool on a selected photo.

Previous/Next photo. Exit Full Screen mode.

To delete photos, select one or more thumbnails, then hit Delete on the keyboard. If you delete a photo in an *Event*, the original photo is placed in the Trash in the Source list, and is also removed from albums, books, calendars, or other projects it was in. If you delete a photo from an *album*, it's deleted from the album only, while the original photo remains in the iPhoto Library.

To restore a photo that has been deleted from the Library, click the Trash icon in the sidebar to show deleted photos. Select the photo you want, then from the Photos menu, choose "Restore to Photo Library." **Or** Control-click the photo you want to recover, then from the shortcut menu, choose "Restore to Photo Library."

To exit Full Screen mode, click the white circled-X in the toolbar. **Or** tap the Escape key on your keyboard.

Hide Photos

When you want to remove photos from view, but don't want to throw them away, you can hide them.

1. Select the photos you want to hide.

2. Click "Hide" in the toolbar. **Or,** from the Photos menu, choose "Hide Photo." **Or** Control-click on photo selection, then from the shortcut menu, choose "Hide Photo."

The presence of hidden photos in an Event is indicated by a text alert to the right of the Event title. In the example below, it says "Show 3 hidden photos." Click the alert text (circled) to show the hidden photos.

To show hidden photos in *all* Events instead of just the current Event, from the View menu, choose "Hidden Photos."

*When **Events mode** is selected in the Source list, the "hidden photos" alert text is located on the far right side of the bar above the viewing area.*

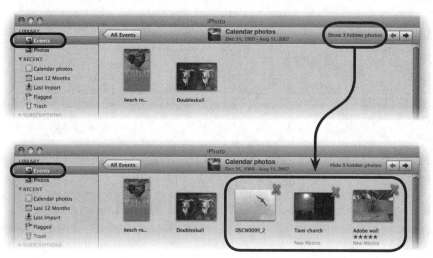

Hidden photos are marked with a **red X.** To hide the photos again, click the text alert again, which now says "*Hide* 3 hidden photos" (above).

To remove the "hidden" status from a photo, select it, then from the Photos menu, choose "Unhide Photo." **Or** Control-click on the photo, then choose "Unhide Photo." **Or** select it, then click "Hide" in the toolbar.

*When **Photos mode** is selected in the Source list, the "hidden photos" alert text floats to the right of the Event name.*

Create a Duplicate Photo

When you edit a photo, you alter its appearance in the Library *and* in all other albums or projects in which that photo appears. This may be exactly what you want, but maybe not. To avoid changing the photo's appearance in every occurrence, create a *duplicate* of the photo and edit the duplicate.

1. Select a photo in the Library, in an album, or in a project such as a Book, Calendar, Card, or Slideshow.

2. From the Photos menu, choose "Duplicate." **Or** Control-click on a photo, then choose "Duplicate," as shown below.

   If you duplicate a photo in an Event in the Library, the duplicate appears in that Event. If you select a photo from an album or project in the Source list, then duplicate it, a duplicate is placed in both the Library Event and the album or project.

3. iPhoto automatically renames the duplicate by adding "copy" to the title, but you can change the name: select the duplicate, click the "Info" button in the bottom-left corner, then enter a custom name in the "title" field of the Information pane.

*Control-click a photo to
show the shortcut menu.*

Edit Photos in a Separate Window

You can choose to edit a photo in its own, separate edit window rather than in the iPhoto window. This enables you to keep more than one photo open and editable at one time. If you're comparing photos or editing for color harmony between photos, working with several open windows can be helpful.

To open a photo in a separate window, Control-click on a photo, then choose "Edit in separate window." The separate window contains the same Edit tools found in Edit mode and in Full Screen mode.

To make selected photos automatically open in a separate window when you click the Edit button, in the General pane of iPhoto Preferences, set the "Edit photo" pop-up menu to "In separate window." With this Preference chosen, you can also Option-double-click a photo to open it in a separate window.

"Fit to window" resizes the photo as you resize the window.

Cycle through other photos in the selected album, Event, or project.

After you've made edits, click the red Close button in the top-left corner to close the window and apply your changes.

To make room on your screen, set the Size pop-up menu to "Fit in window," then drag the bottom-left corner of the window to resize it. As you drag, the photo resizes to fit the window. If you drag the window too small, some of the edit tools disappear from the toolbar. They are replaced with the double right-facing arrow, shown circled below. Click the double arrow to reveal a pop-up menu that contains the hidden tools.

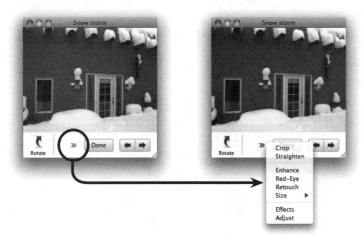

To revert to the original, unedited photo, Control-click on the photo and choose "Revert to Previous." **Or** from the Photos menu, choose "Revert to Previous." You can also revert to the original at any time later from the main iPhoto window. Select the photo, then from the Photos menu, choose "Revert to Original."

Show Photo Info

When you import photos, you also import all sorts of metadata (information) that's attached to digital photos. The model of your digital camera determines how much information is attached.

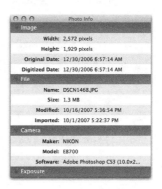

Select a photo, then from the Photos menu, choose "Show Photo Info." In the Photo Info window, click the small disclosure triangle next to a category to hide or show that information.

Keywords

Keywords can be extremely helpful when you search for photos—especially when the number of photos in your iPhoto Library gets into the thousands. Keywords can be as specific or generic as you want, and you can assign as many keywords to a photo as necessary to help you find it later.

The Keywords window

The Keywords window is where you create, edit, and manage keywords.

Open the Keywords window:

1. Select one or more photos.

2. From the View menu, choose "Show Keywords." The Keywords window (below-left) opens. It is divided into an upper "Quick Group" pane and a lower "Keywords" pane.

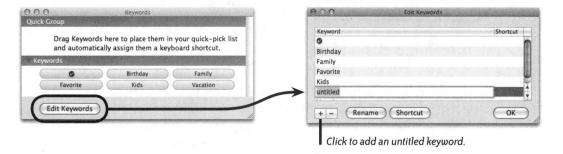

Click to add an untitled keyword.

Add, delete, and edit keywords:

1. From the View menu, choose "Show Keywords."

2. Click the "Edit Keywords" button (above-left).

3. **To add a keyword,** in the "Edit Keywords" window (above-right), click the Add (**+**) button. A new "untitled" keyword is added to the list. Type a word to replace "untitled."

   To delete a keyword from the list, select it, then click the Minus (**-**) button. **Or** hit the Delete key.

   To rename a keyword, select it, click the "Rename" button (above-right), then type a new keyword. **Or** double-click the keyword to select it, then type a new keyword.

   To create or change a keyword's shortcut, select it, click the "Shortcut" button (above-right), then type the letter you want to assign (left). **Or** double-click the shortcut field (in the "Shortcut" column), then type the letter you want to assign as the shortcut.

Quick-picks

iPhoto automatically assigns a keyboard shortcut to keywords you create or that you drag to the Quick Group pane. The shortcut appears in a black circle next to the keyword (right-top). The first letter of the keyword becomes the keyboard shortcut. If that letter is being used by another keyword, the second letter of the word is used.

A keyword and its keyboard shortcut.

To use a keyboard shortcut, click in the "add keywords" area beneath a photo (right), then type the shortcut for the desired keyword ("d," for "Dogs," for instance).

Assign keywords to selected photos

1. Select one or more photos.

2. If you know the shortcut for the keyword you want to assign, tap the shortcut key on your keyboard. If you don't know the shortcut, or if you want to use keywords that don't have shortcuts assigned, go to Step 3.

3. From the View menu, choose "Show Keywords." The Keywords window opens (right).

4. Click one or more keywords that you want to assign to the selected photos. To see the results in iPhoto's Viewing area, make sure keyword visibility is turned on. In the View menu, checkmark the "Keywords" item.

Drag keywords up to the Quick Group pane to automatically create a keyboard shortcut.

Remove keywords from selected photos

1. Select one or more photos that are tagged with a keyword you want to remove.

2. Open the Keywords window. Keywords that are assigned to the selected photo are highlighted in blue (right). Click the highlighted keyword that you want to remove. The keyword appears in red for a split second on top of the photo, then disappears in a puff of animated smoke.

   Or you can select the keyword where it appears under a photo in the Viewing area, then hit Delete.

Search for Photos

As your collection of photos gets larger, finding the photos you want can get increasingly difficult and time consuming. iPhoto's Search field enables you to conduct several different kinds of searches.

Search for All

Click this icon to open the Search pop-up menu.

By default, iPhoto's Search field is set to "All," indicated by a small magnifying glass icon (shown on the left). With this option selected, iPhoto searches for photos that contain your search word in a photo title, an Event title, an album title, as a keyword, or in a photo's comments.

1. To limit your search to a single album, select an album in the Source list. To search the entire Library, select "Events" or "Photos" in the Source list. This applies to all types of searches.

2. Type a word in the Search field that you might have used in a title, as a keyword, or in a photo comment. The search results (photos) appear in the main viewing area.

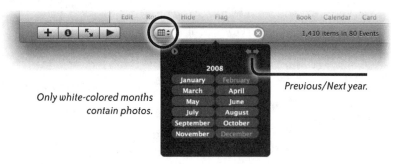

Search by Date

1. Click the magnifying glass icon to open the Search pop-up menu. Choose "Date" (shown above).

2. The Date pane opens (below). Click a month name that appears in white to see photos that were shot during that month. To add other months to the search, press the Command key, then click other months. Click the year ("2008" in this example) to search for all photos shot that year. To search the same month across multiple years, press the Option key as you select.

Only white-colored months contain photos.

Previous/Next year.

3. Click the toggle triangle in the upper-left corner to switch the view to a single month (below). Click a white day to show photos that were shot that day. To add additional days to the search, press the Command key, then click other dates. Double-click a week row to select the entire week. Click the month ("January" in this example) to search for all photos shot that month. To search the same week or day across multiple years, press the Option key as you select.

Click to toggle between Month and Year views.

Previous/Next month.

Click this Reset button to clear the search results and show all photos in the search target— one or more selected albums, Events, or the entire Library.

Only white-colored days contain photos.

Search by Keyword

1. Click the Search pop-up menu and choose "Keyword."

2. The Keywords pane opens (below). Select one or more keywords. Learn how to create keywords that appear in this window on page 40.

Search by Rating

1. Click the Search pop-up menu and choose "Rating."

2. Click a dot in the Search field to search for all photos that have been assigned the rating you choose (one to five stars).

iPhoto Preferences

To set basic characteristics that affect iPhoto's behavior and how you view your photos, go to the iPhoto application menu and choose "Preferences…."

General preferences

Click the **General** button to show the General preferences. Options provided in this pane include:

Sources:

Select **Show last (12) months album** to set how many months of recent photos are shown when this album is selected in the Source list (the sidebar). Choose between one and 18 months. To remove this album from the Source list completely, uncheck the checkbox.

Checkmark **Show item counts** to show how many photos are contained in each of the Source list albums, as shown in the example on the left.

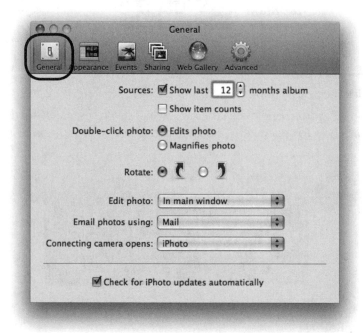

Double-click photo:

Choose what happens when you double-click a photo:

Choose **Edits photo** to make a double-click open the photo in Edit mode. Depending on your setting in the "Edit photo" pop-up menu (explained below), Edit mode will open the photo in iPhoto's main window, in a separate window, in full screen mode, or in some other application that you choose.

Choose **Magnifies photo** to make a double-click magnify the photo and fill the viewing area.

Rotate:

Choose a default direction to rotate photos. To rotate a photo in the opposite direction of the default setting, press the Option key when you click the Rotate button.

Edit photo:

From the pop-up menu, choose what happens when you double-click a photo to edit it, or when you click the Edit button in the toolbar. The options include opening the photo **In main window, In a separate window, Using full screen,** and **In application....**

If you choose "In application…," a Finder window opens so you can choose some other application—such as Adobe Photoshop—for editing photos.

Email photos using:

From the pop-up menu, choose the email application you want iPhoto to integrate with when sending photos. If you don't have America Online, Eudora, or Microsoft Entourage installed, the only option available is "Mail."

Connecting camera opens:

From the pop-up menu, choose the application to open when you connect a digital camera to your computer. The options are **iPhoto, Image Capture,** and **No application.**

Check for iPhoto updates automatically:

Checkmark this checkbox to keep iPhoto up to date. If you don't have a full-time Internet connection, this option will cause your dial-up modem to attempt a connection with Apple at unexpected (and sometimes inconvenient) times.

Appearance preferences

These preferences help determine the appearance of the iPhoto window.

Border:

Click the **Outline** checkbox to place a small black border around thumbnail images in the viewing area.

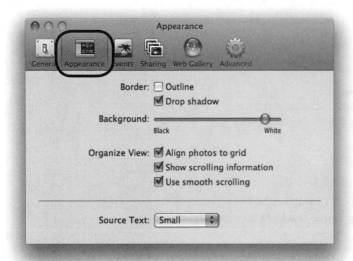

Select **Drop shadow** to add a drop shadow to thumbnail images.

Background:

Use the slider to change the background color of the viewing area. Choose black, white, or any shade between.

Organize View:

Checkmark **Align photos to grid** to arrange thumbnail images in columns and rows. When this option is not selected, thumbnail images are organized in rows only, which saves a little space and may allow more photos to show at one time in the viewing area.

Checkmark **Show scrolling information** to show the Scroll Guide when you scroll in Photos mode (below). The Scroll Guide's content changes to show the date and title of Events as you scroll through the photo library.

The Scroll Guide.

Use smooth scrolling makes scrolling smoother on slower systems.

Source Text:

Choose Large or Small text for the Source list items.

Events preferences

These preferences enable you to modify some of the Events behaviors in Events mode (when Events is selected in the Source list).

Double-click Event:

Choose what happens when you double-click an Event.

Choose **Shows Event photos** to show all photos of an Event in the viewing area when you double-click the Event thumbnail.

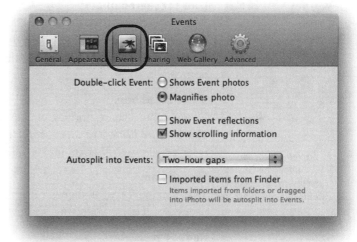

Magnifies photo lets you skim through photos as usual in the Event thumbnail—but now you can double-click on a specific thumbnail image as you skim, and have it magnify to fill the viewing area. This option also reveals a "Show Photos" button when your pointer hovers over an Event thumbnail. Move your pointer on top of the Show Photos button, and the Event thumbnail changes to show an index sheet of the photos in the Event (right). To show all of the Event photos in the viewing area, click the "Show Photos" button.

Show Event reflections adds a beautiful reflection effect underneath the Event thumbnails.

Show scrolling information shows the Scroll Guide—similar to the Scroll Guide shown on the previous page—when you scroll in Events mode. The Scroll Guide shows date information as you scroll through the photo library. If, however, you've set the Sort Events option in the View menu to "By Title," the Scroll Guide cycles through an alphabetical display (a–z) as you scroll through the photo library.

Autosplit into Events:

Choose how to split photos into Events when you import photos. iPhoto splits photo imports into Events, based on the date and time photos were taken. This pop-up menu specifies the time frame that constitutes an Event (right). For details, see page 4.

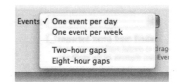

To autosplit **Imported items from Finder** into Events, checkmark this item. Deselect this item if you don't want photos imported from the Finder to be split into different Events, based on when they were taken.

Shared photos appear under the "Shares" category. In this example, Robin has enabled sharing for two albums.

Sharing preferences

These preferences let you set up how (or if) to share your photos with others on your local network.

Look for shared photos

When you checkmark this item, iPhoto looks for other computer users with iPhoto on the local network that have "Share my photos" selected. When another iPhoto user is found, his photo library appears in your Source list.

Share my photos

If you want to share photos, checkmark "Share my photos." Then choose **Share entire library** or **Share selected albums.** If you choose to share only selected albums, checkmark the albums in the album list you want to share.

Shared name:

Type a name for your shared photos. This is the name that appears in other users' Source list when they share your photos.

Require password:

You can password-protect your shared photos. Checkmark this item and type a password. Only those you've given the password to will be able to share your photos.

Status: On

This status message tells you photo sharing is on. If you uncheck "Share my photos," the status message changes to "Off."

Web Gallery preferences

Web Gallery is an online gallery of photos (and movies) that you can create if you have a .Mac account. When you publish a .Mac Web Gallery, it appears in the Source list under the category "Web Gallery" (as shown on the right). To learn about Web Gallery and how to publish albums to it, see pages 52–59.

The Web Gallery preference pane contains these items:

Check for new photos:

From this pop-up menu, choose how often iPhoto checks for new photos in *subscribed* Web Gallery albums. Choose hourly, daily, weekly, or manually.

Check Now

Click "Check Now" to check for new photos in subscribed Web Galleries.

You can publish many albums (and even movies) to your .Mac Web Gallery.

Continued...

Web Gallery Title:
Type a name for your Web Gallery. This is the name that appears on your Web Gallery home page. You can change the title whenever you want.

Albums you published as "album name:"
This list shows the albums or Events that have been published using your .Mac account name.

Stop Publishing
To stop publishing an album, select it, then click the "Stop Publishing" button. **Or** select a published album in the iPhoto Source list, then press Delete.

iDisk Storage
Web Gallery uses your .Mac iDisk storage space to store photos that you've uploaded from your computer. The iDisk Storage bar shows how much space is currently being used.

Buy More
If you need more storage space, you can buy it. Click the "Buy More" button to connect to your .Mac account and upgrade your storage capacity.

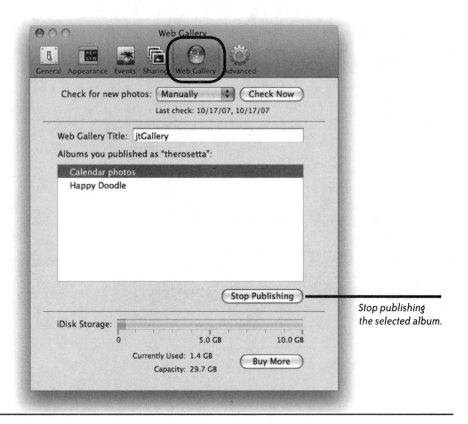

Stop publishing
the selected album.

Advanced preferences

These preferences relate to importing photos from your hard disk (not from a digital camera), and to using photos that are in RAW format, a non-compressed format that many digital cameras support (and popular with professional photographers).

Importing:

Checkmark **Copy items to the iPhoto Library** if you want iPhoto to duplicate the photos that you plan to import from your hard disk.

If you don't want to *copy* photos to iPhoto, uncheck this option. iPhoto will point to the original files instead of copying them. When you edit photos that haven't been copied to iPhoto, the edited versions are saved in the iPhoto Library, leaving the original untouched.

Checkmark **Embed ColorSync profile** to assign a color profile. iPhoto usually assigns a profile called "cameraRGB," which allows image colors to closely match Apple monitors.

If you don't checkmark the top item ("Copy items to the iPhoto Library"), ColorSync profiles are not embedded, and the photos located on your hard drive are imported in their current state.

If the photo files you import specify use of the Adobe RGB color profile, iPhoto assigns that profile.

RAW Photos:

Checkmark **Use RAW when using external editor** to have RAW photos open in an external editor such as Adobe Photoshop. The RAW file is sent to the external editor, not the JPEG or TIFF copy that iPhoto makes when it imports a RAW photo. This allows you to edit RAW photos outside of iPhoto.

Checkmark **Save edits as 16-bit TIFF files** to save edited RAW photos as TIFFs. Leave this item unchecked to save RAW photos in JPEG format.

.Mac Web Gallery

If you don't have a .Mac account, this feature alone will make you want one. You can publish your favorite photos in a beautiful online Web Gallery that's synced with a duplicate Web Gallery in iPhoto. The online Web Gallery is automatically updated when you make changes to the Web Gallery in iPhoto. Make the Web Gallery public or password-protected. Family and friends can view your albums online, or subscribe to them. You can enable others to download your photos, or to upload their own photos to your Web Gallery.

Publish a Web Gallery

First, make sure you have a .Mac account and an Internet connection. If you have more than one .Mac account, make sure the account you want to use is currently shown in the Account pane of .Mac System Preferences.

1. Select an Event, album, or a group of photos.

2. Click the Add (**+**) button in the bottom-left corner of the iPhoto window. In the toolbar at the top of the dialog that opens, click the Web Gallery button. The dialog expands to provide the settings shown below.

    Or click the Web Gallery button in iPhoto's toolbar. This same dialog appears, but without a toolbar at the top of the dialog.

    Or, from the Share menu, choose "Web Gallery."

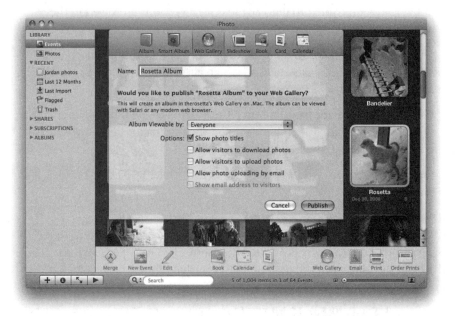

3. In the dialog shown on the previous page, type a name for the published album, then choose one of the following publishing options:

Album Viewable by:

From this pop-up menu (right), choose who can view your album. Select "Everyone" to make it a public site. Select "Only me" to create a private site that only you can view.

To password-protect the gallery,
select "Edit names and passwords." Another dialog slides down (right). Click the Add (**+**) button to add an account name and password that allows access to the album. Any name and password will do, as long as you follow the guidelines spelled out at the bottom of the dialog below. Click OK to return to the publishing options dialog shown on the previous page.

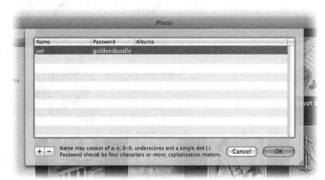

Options:
Checkmark the options you want (see the previous page). You can choose to show the photo titles from iPhoto, allow visitors to download photos, allow visitors to upload photos, or allow uploading by email. If you allow uploading, you can also choose to show your email address to visitors so they can use it to upload photos.

4. Click the "Publish" button (shown on the previous page). The album appears in the Source list, under the "Web Gallery" category. An upload icon (right, top) indicates uploading progress. When uploading is complete, the upload icon changes to a publish icon (right, bottom).

Uploading.

Published.

To interrupt an upload of photos: Click the Upload icon (the "Uploading" circle shown on the right). To resume the upload at a later time, click the Upload icon again.

To stop publishing a Web Gallery album: Select the album in the Source list, then press the Delete key. **Or** go to iPhoto Preferences. Open the Web Gallery pane, then select an album and click "Stop Publishing." When you stop publishing a .Mac Web Gallery album, your subscribers are notified the next time their computer tries to access the album for an update.

During the upload process, a black title bar shows the album name, and a progress bar shows the status of the upload. When the upload is complete, the Web Gallery web address is shown in the black title bar (below).

Click the web address to open Safari (or any modern browser) and view the album online (below). The buttons above the photos are explained on the next page. The toolbar below the photos lets viewers choose how to view the gallery, set the background color, and adjust the thumbnail size.

The Options bar. Click the "Hide Options" button on the right to hide/show these buttons.

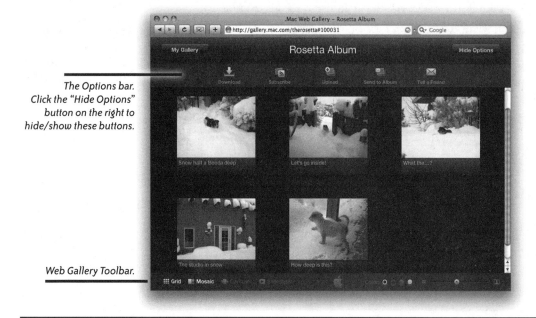

Web Gallery Toolbar.

Web Gallery's Online Option buttons

When a published Web Gallery album opens in your browser, an Options bar (above) appears at the top of the window, providing different ways to share photos. To hide the Options toolbar, click the "Hide Options" button in the top-right corner of the browser window (shown on the previous page).

If certain options are not available (dimmed), it's because the publisher of the Gallery did not checkmark those options in the Publish dialog (page 52) before the album was published. The Web Gallery Options include:

Download

Click "Download" to download *all* of the photos in a Web Gallery album to your computer. To download an *individual* photo, click the photo you want to download. The photo fills the window and includes a download button below the photo, along with other view controls. Click the "Download" button (circled, right).

Subscribe

Click "Subscribe" to subscribe to an RSS feed of the album. This opens an RSS web page of the album. To subscribe, bookmark the URL. When someone adds photos to the album, Safari notifies you by putting the number of new photos in parentheses next to the bookmark name (shown right).

*An RSS feed in Safari's
Bookmarks bar.*

Upload

Anyone can upload photos (or movies) to an online album *if* the publisher of the album checkmarked "Allow visitors to upload photos" in the Publish dialog (page 52). Click "Upload" in the Web Gallery Options bar to open an "Upload" dialog (right).

Enter your name, email, and a verification security code, then click the "Choose Files…" button to open a window from which you select the photos you want to upload.

Make sure files you upload have web-friendly names: no spaces or unusual characters (hyphens and underscores are OK). File names must include an appropriate suffix, such as .jpg.

If you *created* and *published* an album, it's easier just to drag photos to the album in the iPhoto window, then let iPhoto update Web Gallery.

Send to Album

To send photos to the album by email (or from a mobile phone), click "Send to Album." A dialog opens to show a Web Gallery email address. Click the email address to open an email message form, click the "Attach" button, then select a photo to send. You can send .jpg, .png, or .gif photo formats, or .mpg, .mov, .m4v, .mp4, or .3gp movie formats to a Web Gallery.

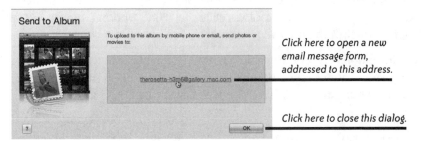

Click here to open a new email message form, addressed to this address.

Click here to close this dialog.

Tell a Friend

Click "Tell a Friend" to send the album's web address to someone (below). Enter your email address, your friend's email address, and a message, then type the image verification code shown in the blue field. The image verification is a security technique to prevent automated programs from creating an account that can access your information. Click "Send."

An automated email sends an invitation similar to the one shown below. The recipient can click the album image or the "View Album" button in the email message to view the album. The message also contains an email link that the recipient can use to send photos to this album.

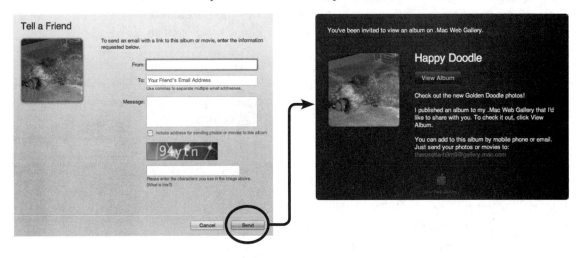

Rename a Web Gallery

By default, your Web Gallery is named "My Gallery," as shown below. To change its name, go to iPhoto Preferences, then click the "Web Gallery" icon. In the Web Gallery pane, type a name in the "Web Gallery Title" field. iPhoto automatically updates the online Web Gallery.

Web Gallery name.

Access a password-protected Web Gallery album

If an album is password-protected, it displays a generic thumbnail on the Web Gallery page and includes a small lock icon in the lower-right corner (circled, above). When a visitor clicks a locked album thumbnail, a dialog opens in the browser (right). If the correct account name and password (page 53) are entered, the visitor is given access to the album.

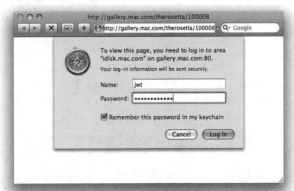

Check for new Web Gallery photos

Anytime you launch iPhoto, Web Gallery is updated automatically. To *manually* update Web Gallery subscriptions, click the publish icon located next to the album name in iPhoto's Source list. You can tell iPhoto how often to check for new photos in a subscribed Web Gallery. Go to iPhoto Preferences, then choose "Web Gallery" in the upper toolbar. From the "Check for new photos" pop-up menu, select a time frame (every hour, day, week, or manually).

Two Ways to Subscribe to a Web Gallery Album

There are different ways to subscribe to Web Gallery albums: as an **RSS Feed** or as a **Photo Feed.**

Subscribe as an RSS Feed

This technique allows you to view Web Gallery albums as an RSS Feed, the same way you might view the RSS feed of a news site or a popular blog.

1. When you receive an email announcement from a friend to visit a Web Gallery web address, click the URL in the email message to visit the site, then click the "Subscibe" button in the Options bar at the top of the Web Gallery window (see the bottom of page 54).

2. Another web page opens that shows an RSS version of the album, shown below-left. To economize space, in the right column, drag the "Article Length" slider all the way to the left. This reduces the page to just the captions, as shown below-right.

An RSS feed in Safari's Bookmarks bar.

3. To finish subscribing, and to have Safari notify you when new photos have been posted by the publisher of the album, drag the web address from the address field to Safari's Bookmarks bar. When new photos are available, the number of new photos appears next to the bookmarked album name, as shown on the left.

To show the photo at actual size, click it. If the browser window is not large enough to show the photo actual size, the photo enlarges as much as possible to fill the window, and the pointer turns into a magnifying glass. Click the photo again to enlarge the photo to actual size within the limited window dimensions. Use the scroll bars (or the keyboard's Arrow keys) to move the photo around inside the available window space.

To visit the album, click the RSS title.

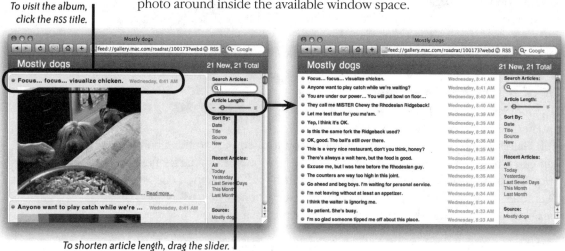

To shorten article length, drag the slider.

Subscribe as a Photo Feed

When you subscribe to a Web Gallery album as a Photo Feed, the album photos are automatically downloaded to your computer, and you can view the album without being online.

1. Visit a friend's Web Gallery page online, then copy the URL (the web address) that appears in the browser's Address field.

2. Open iPhoto, then from the File menu, choose "Subscribe to Photo Feed…" (shown on the right).

3. In the dialog sheet that slides down, paste the URL into the text field (shown below).

4. Click the "Subscribe" button.

   The Web Gallery album photos are copied to your computer. The album name appears in the Source list, in the "Subscriptions" category. Click the album name to view the album photos, even if you're not connected to the Internet.

Your Mac can automatically update the album when changes are made to the online Web Gallery album. In iPhoto Preferences, set how often iPhoto checks for new photos in subscribed albums (see page 49). You can also check for updates manually: click the Update icon that appears next to the subscribed album name in the Source list (shown to the right). **Or** open iPhoto Preferences, then click "Check Now."

Click here to check for updates.

To unsubscribe, select a subscribed album in the Source list, then press Delete. **Or** Control-click the album name, then choose "Delete Album."

Paste the web address of a Web Gallery page.

iPhoto Books

iPhoto provides tools to create several amazing projects—Slideshows, Books, Calendars, and Cards.

The Book project creates a professionally printed, softbound or hardbound book that you lay out from templates, using your own photos and captions. You can choose from many design themes, such as a catalog, picture book, story book, or portfolio. iPhoto Books are perfect for personal keepsakes, unique gifts, or professional presentations.

Create a Book

1. Select one or more albums or Events that contain photos you want to use in a Book. The first photo in the album is used for the cover of your Book (you can always rearrange the photos in a Book project).

2. Click the "Book" button in the toolbar (left) to start building your book. In the dialog that opens (below), choose a book type from the "Book Type" pop-up menu and a theme from the scrolling list of themes. Click the "Options + Prices" button to open an Apple web page that contains links to pricing information.

3. Click "Choose."

4. A new project album appears in the Source list, under the "Projects" category, and the main viewing area previews the book template.

5. Drag photos from the thumbnails bar at the top of the screen onto the photo placeholders in the book template. **Or** click the Autoflow button (circled below) to let iPhoto lay out the book automatically.

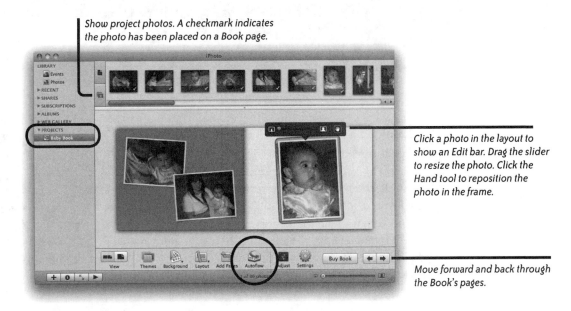

Show project photos. A checkmark indicates the photo has been placed on a Book page.

Click a photo in the layout to show an Edit bar. Drag the slider to resize the photo. Click the Hand tool to reposition the photo in the frame.

Move forward and back through the Book's pages.

Use the buttons in the bottom toolbar to modify the Book project:

View: Choose to show the Book as double-page spreads or single pages.

Themes: Change the design theme. When you click this button, the dialog shown on the previous page opens again.

Background: Click on a page, then choose a different background.

Layout: Choose different layouts for the selected page.

Add Pages: Click to add one or two new pages, depending on the "View" (double-page spread or single page).

Autoflow: Let iPhoto automatically place project photos in the Book.

Adjust: Open the Adjust palette to make changes to the selected photo. See page 31 for more information about the Adjust palette.

Settings: Change the default font settings. Also, choose whether or not to include an Apple logo, automatically enter photo information (such as titles), print double-sided pages, and show page numbers.   *Continued...*

To change the thumbnails pane from a view of *project photos* to a view
of *Book pages* (shown below), click the "page" icon or the "photos"
icon on the left side of the thumbnails.

*Click the top "pages" icon to show
page layouts as thumbnails.*

*To jump to any page,
click its thumbnail.*

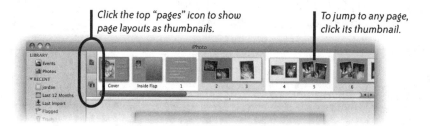

Add text to a page

If a page already has placeholder text on
it, select the text and type the text you
want. If the page doesn't have placeholder text, click the Layout button in
the bottom toolbar, then choose a layout
that contains a text placeholder. If you

don't like the layout choices, change themes. With the new theme applied,
click the Layout button to choose a layout with placeholder text.

Change font style, size, or color

To change the look of your text, select it, then press Command-T to open the
Fonts palette (below). Choose a font family, typeface (bold, etc.), and size.
Click the green button at the top of the palette to open the Colors palette
and choose a color. To add a drop shadow, click the Drop Shadow button,
then use the controls to the right to adjust the shadow opacity, blur, offset,
and angle. Click the Drop Shadow button again to remove a drop shadow.

Choose font color.

*Drop Shadow
button and
controls.*

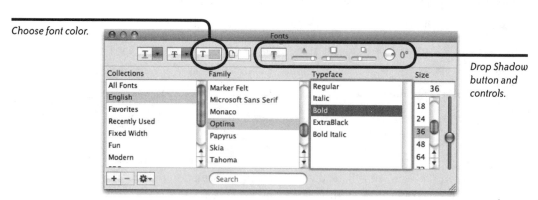

Book tips

▼ To display a book page in the Preview pane, find the page you want in the scrolling Page View Thumbnail pane, then single-click that page.

▼ To change the order of pages, drag double-page spreads in the thumbnail pane left or right.

▼ You can drag a photo thumbnail to any page in the Preview pane, even if a photo is already placed there. You can also drag photos into a blank area of a page to add a photo to existing photos.

▼ To resize the preview, drag the Size slider in the bottom-right corner.

▼ To remove a photo from a page, select it in either the Page View Thumbnail pane or the large Preview pane, then press Delete. Don't worry—the deleted photo is still available in the thumbnail pane. Click the Unplaced Photos button to see it and other unused photos.

▼ In the Preview pane, you can drag a photo from one side of a double-page spread to the other side to change the layout.

▼ You can add titles, comments, or captions to most photo pages, depending on the theme style and page layout you choose.

▼ To open a Book photo in Edit mode, double-click it in the Book page, or in the thumbnails bar.

Buy Book

After you're satisfied with the layout and design of the Book, you can buy copies of it using your Internet connection.

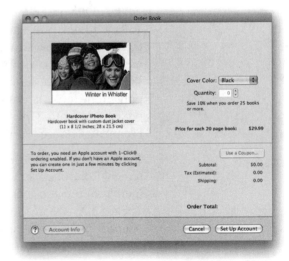

1. Click the "Buy Book" button in the toolbar.

2. An "Order Book" window opens (right). To order, you need an Apple account with 1-Click® ordering enabled. Click the "Set Up Account" button to sign in to your Apple account, or to set up a new account.

3. After you log in, just follow the instructions on the screen. Your Book is assembled, uploaded, and delivered to your address in about a week.

Low-resolution warning

A yellow triangle alert symbol on a photo is a warning that the photo resolution is too low to print in high quality. You should use the photo in a smaller size, or replace it with one that has a higher resolution.

Share Your iPhoto Book

There are several ways to share a Book other than having it professionally printed through an online service. You can print Book pages using your own printer, create an instant slideshow to view on your screen, or save the Book as a PDF. A PDF can be sent to others via email, burned to a disc, or uploaded to your .Mac iDisk for others to download.

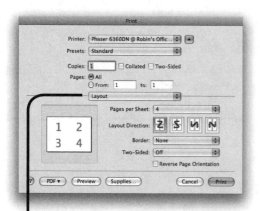

Choose "Layout" to show the options shown here.

Print a Book

Print your Book using your home printer. From the File menu, choose "Print…." In the Print dialog, choose the print settings you want.

In the Print dialog (left), change the pop-up menu in the middle of the dialog from 'iPhoto' to "Layout." Now you have more options for printing the Book. Notice that you can choose to print more than one "Pages per Sheet." In other words, you can reduce the size of Book pages so that two, four, six, nine, or 16 pages fit on a single sheet of paper. You can choose to print just one specific page ("All" pages), or a range of pages.

Save a Book as a PDF

To save a Book project as a PDF, Control-click in the iPhoto Preview area, then from the shortcut menu, choose "Save Book as PDF…." A PDF is saved on your Desktop. If you prefer, you can print from the PDF, instead of from the Book project in iPhoto. Open the PDF, then from the File menu, choose "Print…."

To show a PDF *preview* of the book on your screen, Control-click the Preview area of iPhoto, then from the shortcut menu, choose "Preview Book…." A PDF of the project is created and opened, providing a large, high-quality temporary preview. If you close the PDF, no PDF file remains. You can choose to save the PDF, however. Open the PDF, then from the File menu, choose "Save As…."

Another way to save the project as a PDF is to open the Print dialog (from the File menu, choose "Print…"), click the "PDF" button in the bottom-left corner (right), then choose one of the PDF options.

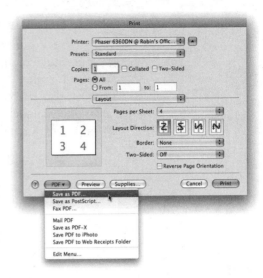

The "Mail PDF" option in the pop-up menu (right) creates exactly the same file as the "Save as PDF…" option and places it in an email message form. The resulting PDF may be too large to be suitable for email.

To create a *smaller* PDF that's more suitsable for email, don't choose the "Mail PDF" option. Instead, choose "Save as PDF." Open the new PDF in Preview. From Preview's File menu, choose "Save As…." In the Save As dialog (below), click the "Quartz Filter" pop-up menu, then choose "Reduce File Size." The resulting PDF should be much smaller, and more suitable for email.

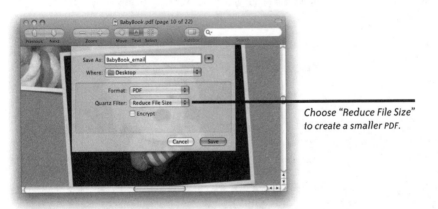

Choose "Reduce File Size" to create a smaller PDF.

Show a Book as a Slideshow

To show the Book pages as a Slideshow on your screen, click the Play Slideshow button (shown on the right) in the bottom-left corner of the iPhoto toolbar. In the Slideshow dialog that opens, make changes you want to the Slideshow Settings (transitions, slide durations, etc.), and choose Slideshow Music. When you click the "Play" button in the Slideshow dialog, the Book pages display as a full screen Slideshow. To exit the Slideshow, click anywhere on the screen. **Or** press the Escape key. **Or** press Command-period.

iPhoto Calendars

This is one of our favorite iPhoto projects. A customized Calendar makes a great keepsake or gift, and it can be a pretty cool souvenir for any group that you're a member of. This feature creates a professionally printed calendar that's easy to lay out with templates, using your own photos. Choose from many design themes, automatically add birthdates that are in your Address Book, add national holidays, and more.

Create a Calendar

1. Select one or more albums or Events that contain photos you want to use in a Calendar.

2. Click the "Calendar" button in the toolbar. In the dialog that opens (below), choose a design theme from the scrolling list of themes. Click the "Options + Prices" button to open an Apple web page that contains links to pricing information.

3. Click "Choose." A second dialog opens with options for you to choose (shown at the top of the next page).

4. From the "Start calendar on" pop-up menu (next page), choose the month and year to start the calendar. Choose the number of months to include (between 12 and 24). From the "Show national holidays" pop-up menu, choose a country (or choose "None"). The "Import iCal calendars" list shows the calendars in your iCal. Checkmark the ones whose events and To Do items you want to include. Checkmark "Show birthdays from Address Book" for those dates to appear in your Calendar project.

5. Click OK. Another dialog (not shown) opens that instructs you to drag photos manually from the left-side thumbnails bar or click the Autoflow button in the toolbar to let iPhoto lay out the calendar automatically. Click OK to open the project, then use one of the methods above (manual or Autoflow) to add photos to Calendar pages.

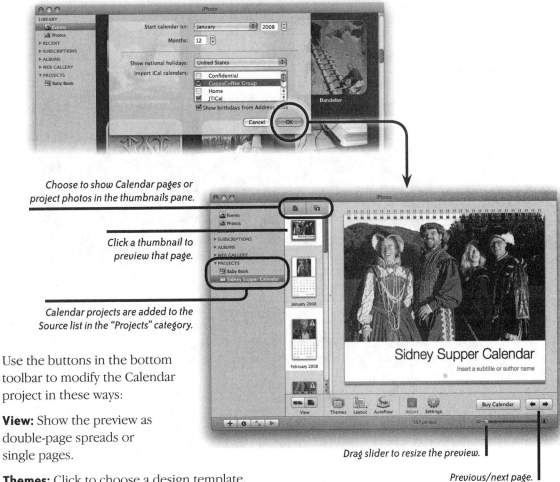

Choose to show Calendar pages or project photos in the thumbnails pane.

Click a thumbnail to preview that page.

Calendar projects are added to the Source list in the "Projects" category.

Drag slider to resize the preview.

Previous/next page.

Use the buttons in the bottom toolbar to modify the Calendar project in these ways:

View: Show the preview as double-page spreads or single pages.

Themes: Click to choose a design template.

Layout: Click to choose different layouts for the selected page.

Autoflow: Click to automatically place photos in the Book project.

Adjust: Click to open the Adjust palette (see page 31).

Settings: Click to open a Settings dialog. A "Calendar" button opens the dialog shown on the previous page. A "Styles" button opens the default font settings pane. To add an Apple logo, checkmark "Include Apple logo."

Edit Calendar photos

To resize a photo or to reposition it in the frame on the page, click it. A Resize control bar opens above the photo (shown below). Drag the slider to resize the photo. To reposition the image within the frame, click the Hand tool on the Resize control bar, then drag the image around inside the frame.

For more extensive editing, double-click the photo to open it in Edit mode. **Or** Control-click the photo, then choose "Edit Photo."

Click a photo to show the Resize bar.

Photos that have been placed on a page are indicated by a checkmark.

Add text to a page

If a page already has placeholder text on it, select the text, then type the text you want. If the page doesn't have placeholder text, click the Layout button in the bottom toolbar, then choose a layout that contains a text placeholder. If you don't like the layout choices, consider changing themes. Click the Themes button to choose a different theme. With a new theme applied, click the Layout button and choose a layout that includes placeholder text.

Change font style, size, or color

To change the look of the text, select it, then press Command-T to open the Fonts palette (**or,** from the Edit menu, choose "Font," then choose "Show Fonts"). From the "Fonts" palette that opens (shown on page 62), choose a font family, typeface, color, and size.

Calendar Tips

▾ To delete a photo from a Calendar page, select it in the Preview pane, then press Delete. **Or** Control-click the photo, then choose "Remove Photo."

▾ Checkmarked photos in the vertical thumbnails pane have already been placed on a Calendar page.

▾ Drag a photo from the thumbnail pane to any page in the Preview pane, even if a photo is already placed there. You can also drag photos into a blank area of a page to add them to existing photos.

▾ Drag photos from one placeholder to another on the same page to switch the photo positions.

▾ To make a copy of a photo so it can be used in multiple page locations, Option-drag it from the thumbnails pane to a Calendar page.

▾ To resize the preview, drag the Size slider in the bottom-right corner.

Buy Calendars online

After you're satisfied with the layout and design of the Calendar, you can order copies of it using your Internet connection.

1. Click the "Buy Calendar" button in the toolbar.

2. An "Order Calendar" dialog opens. To order, you need an Apple account with 1-Click® ordering enabled. Click the "Set Up Account" button to sign in to your Apple account, or to set up a new account.

3. After you log in, just follow the instructions on the screen. Your Calendar is assembled, uploaded, and delivered to your address in about a week.

Low-resolution warnings

A yellow triangle alert symbol on a photo (right) is a warning that the photo resolution is too low to print in high quality. You should use the photo in a smaller size, or replace it with one that's larger or has a higher resolution.

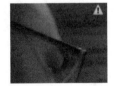

Other ways to share a Calendar

Another way to share a Calendar, other than uploading it to be printed by a commercial printer, is to save it as a PDF. The PDF can be given to others on a disc, sent via email, or printed.

You can also send a Calendar project straight to your own printer from iPhoto, or play it as a full screen Slideshow. (See pages 64–65.)

iPhoto Cards

Create customized cards for special occasions, upload them, and get professionally printed cards delivered to your door.

Create a Card

1. Select a photo, album, or Event.

2. Click the "Card" button in the toolbar (left). A dialog opens (below). From the pop-up menu, choose "Greeting Card" or "Postcard." Then choose a card design from the scrolling list of themes. You can choose to show "All" Card designs, or just certain categories, such as "Seasonal," shown selected below.

   Click the "Options + Prices" button to open an Apple web page that contains links to card information (sizes and prices).

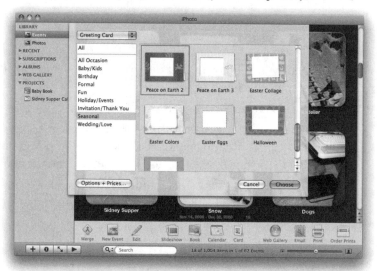

3. Click "Choose." Your Card project is added to the Source list on the left, and the Card design is displayed in the Preview area (next page).

   If you selected a single photo in Step 1, only that photo appears in the thumbnails pane. If you selected an album or Event, all photos in those items appear in the thumbnails pane.

4. Drag a photo from the thumbnails pane to the image area of the Card. Replace placeholder text with your own.

5. Click the "Buy Card" button.

   An "Order Card" dialog opens. Log in to your .Mac account (or set up a new account), provide the requested information, set a quantity, then click the "Buy Now" button.

Edit the Card

To resize a photo or to reposition it in the frame on the page, click it (see page 61). For more extensive editing, double-click the photo to open it in Edit mode. **Or** Control-click the photo, then choose "Edit Photo."

Use the following buttons in the toolbar to make other changes:

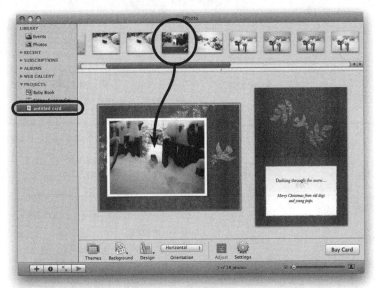

Themes

Change design themes.

Background

Change background color. Hold down the Option key when selecting a color to change only the selected side of the card.

Design

Choose different layouts.

Orientation

Pick "Horizontal" or "Vertical."

Adjust

Click to open the Adjust palette (see page 31).

Settings

Click to open a Settings dialog and change the default font settings. Checkmark "Include Apple logo on back of card" if you want to include a cool-looking, prestigious logo in your design.

Save as a PDF

You can save your project as a PDF to send to someone, or to preview a large, high-quality version of the Card. Control-click in the Preview area, then choose "Save as PDF…" or "Preview Card…." The former actually saves a PDF to your Desktop. The latter opens a PDF without saving it. If you decide to save it, from the File menu, choose "Save As…." **Or** from the File menu, choose "Print," then in the Print dialog, click the "PDF" button and choose "Save as PDF…."

Print Cards using your own printer

If you don't want to wait for an online printer to send you printed cards, you can print them yourself. Follow the same instructions for printing a Book or Calendar on pages 64–65.

Create a slideshow

Create a slideshow from any selection of photos. You can also set a slideshow to repeat and use it as a screen saver.

A quick slideshow

This method is quick and temporary. You can only show this slideshow on your computer. You can't save or export it, and when you close it, it's gone.

1. Select one or more Events, albums, or any selection of photos.
    Or create a new album just for the slideshow and drag photos into it from Events or other albums.

2. Click the triangular Play Slideshow button in the bottom-left corner of the iPhoto window (circled, left).

3. In the "Slideshow" window that opens, click the "Settings" button at the top of the window to set a transition style and speed, slide duration, and other slideshow settings (below-left).

4. Click the "Music" button at the top of the window to assign music to the slideshow (below-right). Select one or more albums, a song, or multiple songs. When you're satisfied with your settings, click the "Play" button.

To skip past the settings window and play the slideshow immediately, Option-click the Play Slideshow button in the bottom-left corner of the iPhoto window.

Transition preview.

Turn Slideshow music on or off.

If you choose a transition that is directional, set the direction here.

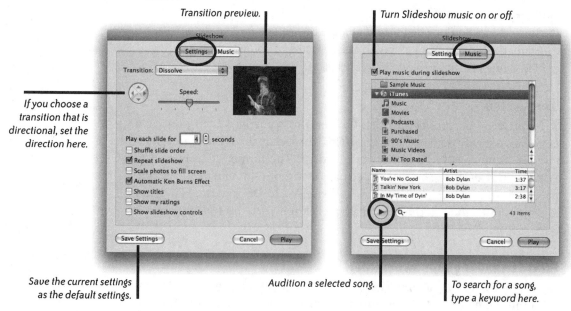

Save the current settings as the default settings.

Audition a selected song.

To search for a song, type a keyword here.

A more versatile slideshow

This method gives you more control of transitions, the availablility of an Adjust palette, and more options in the Settings window. It also creates a Slideshow project in the Source list that you can open at any time. You can export the slideshow as a movie, or send it to iDVD.

1. Select one or more Events, albums, or any selection of photos.
   Or create a new album for the slideshow and drag photos into it from Events or other albums.

2. Click the "Slideshow" icon in the toolbar (right) to open the Slideshow view, shown below. This view includes a scrolling thumbnail pane that contains all of the photos in the slideshow. iPhoto automatically creates a Slideshow album and places it in the Source list (circled below).

Slideshow

3. From the "Effect" pop-up menu in the toolbar, choose an effect if you want one.

4. From the "Transition" pop-up menu, choose a transition style. All photos in the slideshow use the designated default transition, unless another one is chosen here. The new transition you choose affects only the current photo.

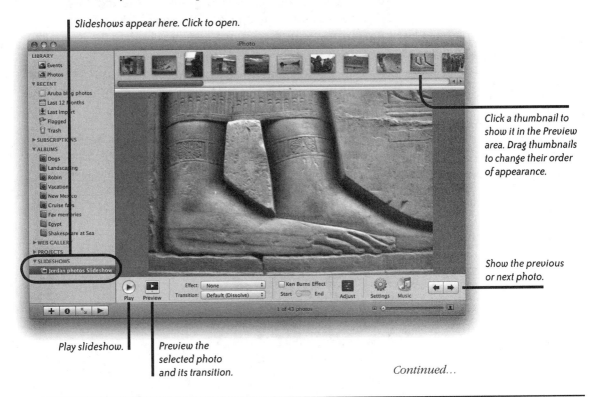

Slideshows appear here. Click to open.

Click a thumbnail to show it in the Preview area. Drag thumbnails to change their order of appearance.

Show the previous or next photo.

Play slideshow.

Preview the selected photo and its transition.

Continued...

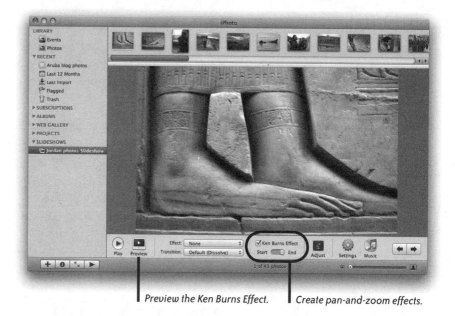

Preview the Ken Burns Effect. | Create pan-and-zoom effects.

5. Checkmark the "Ken Burns Effect" to create a pan-and-zoom effect that adds movement to still photos. To customize the effect:

   ▼ Move the toggle switch to the "Start" position. Size and position the photo as you want it to appear at the *start* of the effect. Use the Size slider, then press-and-drag the photo to the desired starting position.

   ▼ Move the toggle switch to the "End" position. Size and position the photo as you want it to appear at the *end* of the effect.

   ▼ Click the "Preview" button to preview the effect.

6. To make more adjustments to *individual* photos, click the "Adjust" button. The "Adjust This Slide" window (below) lets you change the photo duration, transition style, transition speed, or transition direction (if the selected transition style is directional).

7. Click the "Settings" button to choose default settings that affect the *entire* slideshow (below). These *global* settings will be overridden by any settings in the Adjust palette that you might make for individual photos, as shown on the previous page.

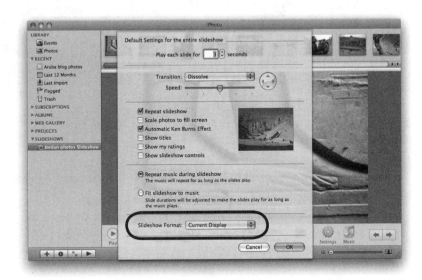

▼ Set a slide duration, a transition style, and a transition speed. If the selected transition is directional, click one of the quadrants of the direction button (right) to set the direction for the transition.

The small Preview window automatically previews your choices.

▼ Checkmark the options in the middle area that you want as defaults.

▼ Choose "Repeat music during slideshow" if you have lots of slides whose duration is probably longer than the selected music. **Or** choose "Fit slideshow to music" to automatically adjust slide durations to match the selected music's duration.

▼ From the "Slideshow Format" pop-up menu (circled, below), choose a format proportion that works best with how you plan to view the slideshow—using the current display screen proportions, standard TV proportions (4:3), or widescreen (16:9).

▼ Click OK to apply the settings.

Continued...

8. Click the "Music" button in the Slideshow toolbar to open the Music dialog (below). The top pane contains a folder of sample music and your entire iTunes library, including any custom albums that you created. Toggle open the iTunes folder to show its albums, then select an album to show its songs in the bottom pane. Select one or more songs to play during the slideshow.

   If you have other songs stored in a folder other than iTunes, you can add the folder by dragging it into this pane. iPhoto automatically creates a new folder named "Folders," with your folder of music inside, as shown below.

   Click OK to close the Music dialog.

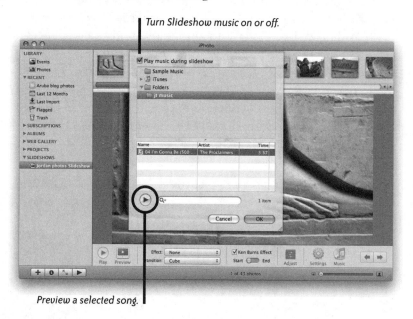

Turn Slideshow music on or off.

Preview a selected song.

9. Click the "Play" button in the Slideshow toolbar to play the Slideshow in full-screen mode.

10. To exit a Slideshow, click anywhere on the screen. **Or** press the Escape key on your keyboard. **Or** type Command Period (.).

Ways to Share Your Slideshow

Not everyone can go to your house and watch your Slideshow on your computer screen. There are several ways to share a Slideshow, other than buying airline tickets for your friends.

Export your Slideshow as a QuickTime movie

One way to share your slideshow is to save it as a QuickTime movie. You can burn the QuickTime movie to a disc, send via email (if it's a small, short movie), upload to an FTP site so others can download it, or place it on a web page (if you're familiar with web page design).

1. Select a Slideshow project in the Source list.
2. From the File menu, choose "Export...."
3. In the Export dialog that opens (below), choose a location to save the file, then from the "Movie Size" pop-up menu, choose a size (Small, Medium, or Large).
4. Click "Export."

Email a Slideshow

You can attach a QuickTime movie to an email, but QuickTime movies are huge. Even if you choose the small movie size in the window above, the file is usually too large to email. Make the Slideshow duration short (fewer photos) if you plan to email it. You can also select one or more photos in the Slideshow thumbnails pane, then from the Share menu, choose "email." The selected photos are automatically attached to a new message form in Mail.

iDVD

Send the Slideshow to iDVD

This is a great way to share a Slideshow. Send it straight to iDVD, then burn it to a disc.

1. Select a Slideshow project in the Source list.

2. From the Share menu, choose "Send to iDVD." iDVD opens, with your Slideshow already included in the iDVD project.

3. To edit the text that is automatically generated (the project title and menu link), click the text to select it, then type new text.

4. To change Themes, click one of the themes in the pane on the right. If the Theme you choose includes Drop Zones (empty areas designed to hold photos or video), from the Project menu, choose "Autofill Drop Zones…." Photos are automatically placed in the Drop Zones.

5. Click the Burn button (shown below).

Of course, you can make all sorts of other modifications to the iDVD project, but it really is this easy if you're in a hurry. You can add more content, such as movies or more slideshows. You can add additional files to the disc storage area (ROM), such as high resolution originals of photos, so others can download them to their own computers.

The iDVD chapter explains how to wow your friends, relatives, or clients with sophisticated DVD design, including motion menus.

Burn project to a disc.

Use a Slideshow to Preview and Edit Photos

A Slideshow is a good way to make an initial evaluation of imported photos. As the Slideshow displays the photos in full screen mode, you can use pop-up controls (shown below) to rotate left or right, assign a rating, and delete photos you don't want. A Slideshow usually advances to the next photo after a set number of seconds, but if you need more time to decide on a rating or to make some other decision, just click the Pause button. Click the left and right arrows to show previous or next photos.

Play/Pause button and Previous/Next arrows.　　*Rotate.*　　*Rate photo.*　　*Delete photo.*

The pop-up controls remain hidden until you move your mouse. To make the controls stay visible, click the "Settings" button in the Slideshow toolbar, then checkmark the "Show slideshow controls" box (right).

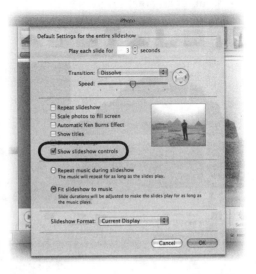

More Ways To Share Photos

iPhoto lets you share your photos in many ways other than the Slideshows, Books, Calendars, and Cards described on the previous pages. You can email photos, print photos, set a Desktop photo, order prints over the Internet, create a web site (iWeb), create a slideshow, create a .Mac Slides site, create an interactive DVD (iDVD), or burn photos to a disc (CD or DVD). If any of these icons (shown below) is not visible in the iPhoto toolbar, go to the View menu, choose "Show in Toolbar," then checkmark the tools you want shown in the toolbar.

Share Photos through Email

It's easy to select and email photos straight from iPhoto.

1. In the Viewing area, select one or more photos.

2. Click the "Email" icon in the toolbar (left).

3. In the "Mail Photo" window that opens, choose a photo size from the "Size" pop-up menu, then choose whether to include photo titles and comments.

4. Click the "Compose" button. An email message window opens containing your photo (below).

5. Enter an email address in the "To" field, then click the "Send" button. Your Mac connects to the Internet and sends the photo.

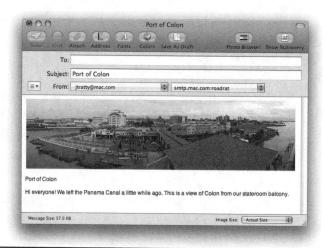

Print photos using a desktop printer

You can print photos using a printer that's connected to your home or office Mac, or one that's available on your local network.

1. Select a single photo, multiple photos, an album, or an event.

2. Click the "Print" icon in the toolbar.

3. In the left pane of the Print dialog sheet that opens, choose a style option. Each style displays your selected photos in a Preview pane on the right (shown below). Click the "Customize…" button if you want to resize, crop, or adjust the images. See page 83–85 to learn how you can customize your printed pages while in Printing mode.

When "Contact Sheet" style is selected, the Preview area shows the selected photos as contact sheets. The other styles display a single photo in the Preview area.

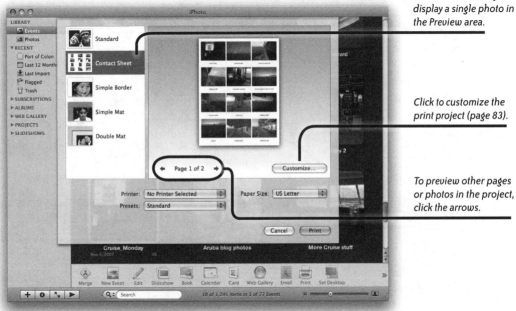

Click to customize the print project (page 83).

To preview other pages or photos in the project, click the arrows.

4. From the "Printer" pop-up menu, choose a printer. If a printer isn't available in the pop-up menu (as in the example above), click "Print" to open the "Print" dialog (shown on the following page). If your printer's name is already in this pop-up menu, skip to Step 8.

Continued…

5. From the "Printer" pop-up menu, choose "Add Printer…" (Figure 5).

6. A window opens showing all connected printers (Figure 6). Select a printer in the list, then click "Add." The selected printer is added to the list of items in the "Printer" pop-up menu (Figure 7).

7. From the "Printer" pop-up menu (Figure 7), select the printer you added in Step 6.

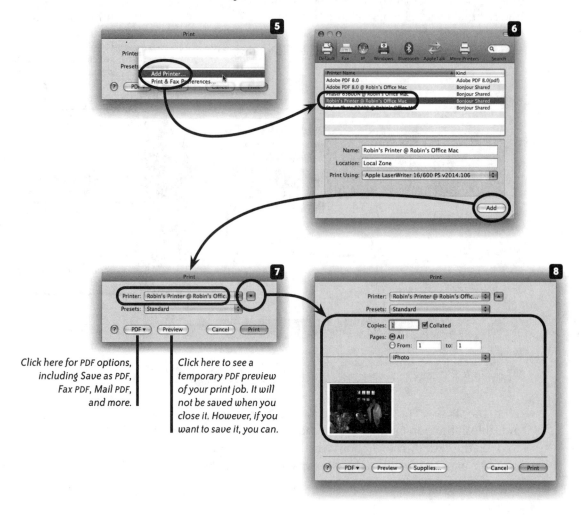

Click here for PDF options, including Save as PDF, Fax PDF, Mail PDF, and more.

Click here to see a temporary PDF preview of your print job. It will not be saved when you close it. However, if you want to save it, you can.

8. Set how many copies to print, or set a range of pages to print: click the blue disclosure button (circled, Figure 7). The dialog expands to show those options and more (see Figure 8).

9. After setting the options in Step 8, click "Print."

Customize your iPhoto print project

When you're ready to print your photos, as single prints or as contact sheets, you have the opportunity to customize your print project in many ways.

1. Select the photos (or events) you want to print, then click the "Print" icon in the toolbar.

2. Click the "Customize…" button in the Preview pane of the Print dialog that drops down (shown on page 81).

   The iPhoto window changes to a Customize window with a thumbnails pane at the top and a new toolbar at the bottom.

The thumbnails can be viewed as Pages (the pages of your print project), or as Photos (the photos you selected for your print project). To choose a thumbnail view, click the Page button or the Photos button on the left side of the thumbnails pane (circled below). Page thumbnails are always numbered, as shown below.

Click the icons in the bottom toolbar to change themes, set the background color, customize photo borders, choose layouts, make image adjustments, or change font settings of captioned layout templates. To add captions, click the "Layout" icon and choose a layout that contains placeholder text.

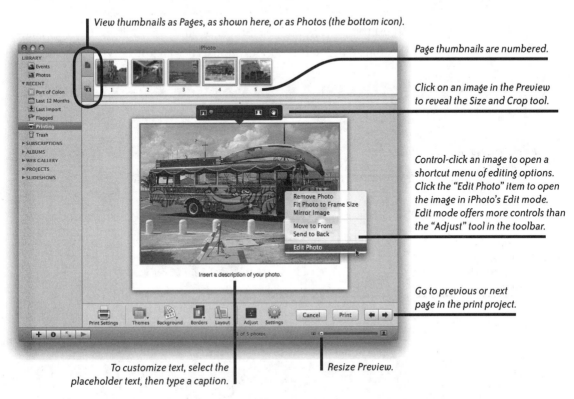

View thumbnails as Pages, as shown here, or as Photos (the bottom icon).

Page thumbnails are numbered.

Click on an image in the Preview to reveal the Size and Crop tool.

Control-click an image to open a shortcut menu of editing options. Click the "Edit Photo" item to open the image in iPhoto's Edit mode. Edit mode offers more controls than the "Adjust" tool in the toolbar.

Go to previous or next page in the print project.

To customize text, select the placeholder text, then type a caption.

Resize Preview.

More about customizing print projects

When you choose Standard, Simple Border, Simple Mat, or Double Mat styles to print, the "Customize" button opens the project view shown below. In this view you can do the following:

▼ Show the thumbnails pane as Pages or Photos (click the Page or Photos icon on the left side of the thumbnails pane).

▼ Drag photos (or pages) in the thumbnails pane to change their order.

▼ Switch the thumbnail pane to Photos view (click the Photos icon on the left side of the thumbnails pane), then drag a thumbnail to replace an existing photo on the page in the Preview area.

▼ Click the photo in the Preview area to reveal the Size and Crop tool. Control-click an individual photo in the Preview area, then from the shortcut menu that opens, choose one of the edit options (shown on the previous page).

▼ Change themes: click the "Themes" icon in the toolbar.

▼ Change background color: click "Background" in the toolbar.

▼ Choose a border: click the "Borders" icon in the toolbar.

▼ Change layout: click the "Layout" icon in the toolbar. To add captions to photos, choose a layout that includes placeholder text.

▼ Adjust the photo: click the "Adjust" icon in the toolbar.

▼ Customize text settings for captions: click "Settings" in the toolbar.

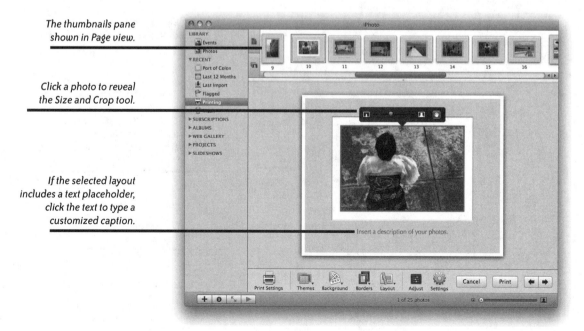

The thumbnails pane shown in Page view.

Click a photo to reveal the Size and Crop tool.

If the selected layout includes a text placeholder, click the text to type a customized caption.

More about customizing print projects that use the Contact Sheet style

When you choose the Contact Sheet style to print, the "Customize" button (shown on page 81) opens the project view shown below. In this view you can do the following:

- ▼ Show the thumbnails pane as Pages or Photos (click the Page or Photos icon on the left side of the thumbnails pane).

- ▼ Drag pages in the thumbnails pane to change their printing order.

- ▼ Switch the thumbnail pane to Photos view (click the Photos icon on the left side of the thumbnails pane), then drag a thumbnail to replace an existing photo on the contact sheet in the Preview area. If the contact sheet page isn't full, you can drag thumbnails to the page to fill in blank spaces.

- ▼ Edit individual photos in the contact sheet that's displayed in the Preview area: Click a photo to reveal the Size and Crop tool. Control-click an individual photo in the Preview area, then from the shortcut menu that opens, choose one of the edit options (shown on page 83).

- ▼ Drag existing photos that are placed on the contact sheet in the Preview area to reaarange them on the page.

- ▼ Drag the "Columns" slider in the toolbar to set the number of columns on a page.

- ▼ Use any of the other tools in the bottom toolbar to customize as you would when printing other projects.

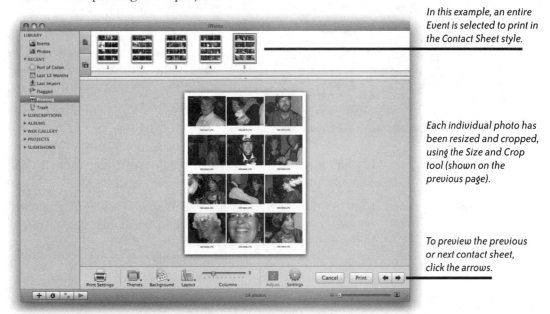

In this example, an entire Event is selected to print in the Contact Sheet style.

Each individual photo has been resized and cropped, using the Size and Crop tool (shown on the previous page).

To preview the previous or next contact sheet, click the arrows.

Order Traditional Prints of Your Photos

Order professional prints of any photo or collection of photos.

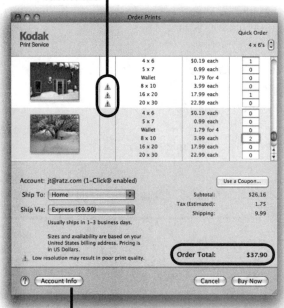

Order Prints

1. Make sure you're connected to the Internet.
2. Select an Event, an album, or any collection of photos in iPhoto.
3. Click the "Order Prints" button (left) in the Organize toolbar.
4. If the button in the lower-right says "Set Up Account" instead of "Buy Now," click it. You will be asked to create an Apple account and provide your name, address, and credit card information, as well as your shipping preferences.

   If you already have an account set up, the "Set Up Account" window that opens lets you sign in with your Apple ID and password.
5. Select the size and quantity you want of each photo in the "Order Prints" window.

This symbol alerts you that the photo's resolution is too low to print at the selected size.

Click here to access your account info, or to create an account.

In the top-right corner, you can "Quick Order" 4x6 prints. Click the top arrow button to order one 4x6 print of each photo in the list. Click again to change the order to two 4x6 prints of each photo. Every click adds to the order. To lower the quantity, click the bottom arrow button.

Type a number in the quantity fields to buy prints of various sizes, such as two 8x10s, or four wallet-sized prints.

As you enter a quantity for each photo, the total cost amount is instantly calculated at the bottom of the window. To remove the order for a photo, type "0" (zero) in the quantity field next to it.

Photos in the list that have resolutions too low for certain sizes will display a low resolution warning (a yellow triangle) next to the sizes that will not print in high quality.

6. Click the "Buy Now" button. Depending on the shipping option you choose in the "Ship Via" pop-up menu, you could receive your prints in the mail in just a few days.

Send photos to iWeb

If you have a .Mac account, you can quickly create and publish a photo web page. Below is a very quick look at how to create and publish a Photo Page using iWeb.

1. Make sure you have a .Mac account and that you're connected to the Internet.

2. Select an Event, an album, or any collection of photos in iPhoto.

3. Click the "iWeb" button in the iPhoto toolbar (above-right). From the iWeb pop-up menu, choose "Photo Page" (right). **Or** from the Share menu, choose "Send to iWeb," then choose "Photo Page."

4. iWeb opens. In the Theme dialog sheet that opens, choose a design template. iWeb automatically places your photos on the page.

5. Click the existing text on the page, then type your own custom text. Drag photos to change their position on the page.

6. Click the top item in the sidebar (the red globe icon) and type a custom name for the site.

7. Click the web page icon in the sidebar (the red book icon) and type a custom name for the web page.

8. Click the "Publish" button in the bottom-left corner.

    Your iWeb site is uploaded to your .Mac iDisk and published on the Internet. A dialog opens that announces "Your site has been published" and displays your site's web address. Click the "Visit Site Now" button to open your browser and go to the site.

Click text to customize it.

.Mac Slides

Publish a Slideshow as a screen saver with .Mac Slides

If you have a .Mac account, the .Mac Slides feature lets you publish a Slideshow to your .Mac iDisk. When friends subscribe to the Slideshow, it is made available in the Screen Saver System Preferences on their computers.

Create a .Mac slideshow

1. Make sure you're connected to the Internet, then select an Event, an album, or any collection of photos in iPhoto.
2. Click the ".Mac Slides" button in the toolbar.
    Or go to the Share menu, then choose ".Mac Slides."
3. A dialog opens (below-left). Click the "Publish" button to upload the selected photos to your .Mac iDisk (below-right).
4. After uploading your photo selection, another dialog opens (bottom-right) with instructions about how to set the .Mac slideshow as your screen saver. Click OK. **Or** click the "Announce Slideshow" button to send an email announcement to friends. An automatically generated email opens in Mail that contains instructions about how to subscribe to your .Mac Slideshow. Address the email, then send.

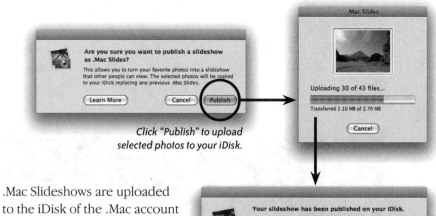

Click "Publish" to upload selected photos to your iDisk.

.Mac Slideshows are uploaded to the iDisk of the .Mac account that's set up in the .Mac pane of your System Preferences. When you publish a .Mac slideshow, it replaces any other slideshow you may have previously published to that .Mac account name.

Subscribe to a .Mac slideshow

Anyone using Mac OS X version 10.2 or later with a fast Internet connection can subscribe to your published .Mac Slideshow and use it as a screen saver. Here's how:

1. Open System Preferences, select "Desktop & Screen Saver," then click the "Screen Saver" tab (circled, below-left).

2. In the "Screen Savers" list on the left side of the window, choose ".Mac and RSS" (circled, below-left).

3. Click the "Options" button beneath the Preview pane. In the dialog sheet that opens (below-right), click the Add Subscription button (+). From the pop-up menu (inset, below-right), choose "Add .Mac subscription." Type the .Mac member name of the person whose slideshow you want to subscribe to.

4. In the same dialog, checkmark the display options you want. Click OK to close the dialog.

5. Back in the Screen Saver pane (below-left), click one of the "Display Style" buttons beneath the Preview pane, then click the "Test" button to see a preview of how the display style looks with the photos.

6. Move the "Start screen saver" slider to set the duration of inactivity to allow before the screen saver automatically activates.

7. To set a Hot Corner for the screen saver, click the "Hot Corners..." button. Choose the corner of the screen that will automatically launch Screen Saver when your pointer is placed there.

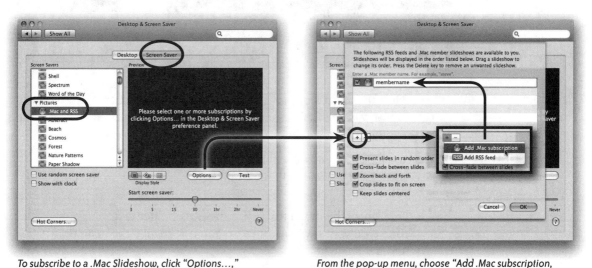

To subscribe to a .Mac Slideshow, click "Options...," then click the Add Subscription button (right).

From the pop-up menu, choose "Add .Mac subscription, then enter a .Mac member name.

Send Photos to iDVD

On page 78 we explained how to send a Slideshow created in iPhoto to iDVD. You can also send any collection of photos from iPhoto straight to iDVD and let iDVD create the slideshow.

1. Select a collection of photos, or one or more albums or Events.

2. Click the "iDVD" button in the iPhoto toolbar.
   Or from the Share menu, choose "Send to iDVD."

3. iDVD opens (below), complete with a main menu and your selected photos already organized into a slideshow, shown as a link in the menu. The link is named the same as the album or Event you selected in iPhoto.

If you click the Burn icon now, you'll create a functional DVD. But you can make lots of other modifications. The following is a brief overview—see the iDVD chapter for detailed information.

1. To change themes, click the "Themes" button in the lower-right corner, then select a theme from the Themes pane on the right side of the window.

2. Customize the menu text. Click the placeholder text, then type your own custom text. You can change the main title and the link text.

3. Rearrange the order of photos in the slideshow. Double-click the slideshow link in the main menu to show thumbnails of the project photos (below). Drag a thumbnail to change its position.
   To delete a photo, select it, then press the Delete key.
   To return to the main menu view, click the "Return" button located in the Slideshow toolbar.

4. To add titles or comments to photos, click the "Settings" button. A dialog sheet drops down with those and other options.

5. Each theme includes theme music, but you can use any music you you have on your computer. Click the "Media" button in the lower-right corner, then click the "Audio" tab at the top of the Media pane. Drag a song in the list to the audio well (left of the volume slider).

6. From the pop-up menus on the left side of the Slideshow toolbar (below), choose a slide duration and a transition style.

7. Most themes include Drop Zones—image placeholders into which you can insert photos or movies. Click the "Edit Drop Zones" button to show empty Drop Zone wells below the main window. Drag photos from the Photos Media pane into the Drop Zone wells. Click the "Edit Drop Zones" button again to return to the Main menu.

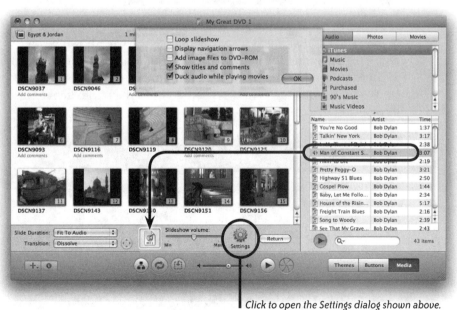

To set slideshow music, drag a song to the Audio well.

Click to open the Settings dialog shown above.

Burn Selected Photos to a Disc

Use iPhoto to burn a disc of photos that you plan to use with iPhoto. When you insert a CD or DVD of photos that was created by iPhoto, you can drag photos from the disc to iPhoto. But when someone without iPhoto tries to drag photos from the disc to a folder on his computer, the operation fails.

To burn photos to a disc:

*To burn a disc that you can share with someone without iPhoto, do this: in iPhoto, **export** the photos to a folder. **Or** drag a collection of photos from iPhoto to a folder anywhere on your computer. Then burn the folder to a disc using the disc burning feature of Mac OS X.*

1. Select a collection of photos (one or more albums, photos, or Events).

2. Click the Burn button in the toolbar.
   Or from the Share menu, choose "Burn Disc."

3. A dialog sheet drops down (shown below) and requests that you insert a blank disc. Click OK and insert a CD or DVD.

4. In the Burn bar that opens above the iPhoto toolbar (shown below), type a name for the disc in the "Name" field. Notice the Burn bar also includes text and a disc icon that indicates how much disc space will be used. If the disc is too full, deselect some of the photo items. Or, if you inserted a CD, try using a DVD instead.

The green color on the disc shows how much disc space the selected photos take up.

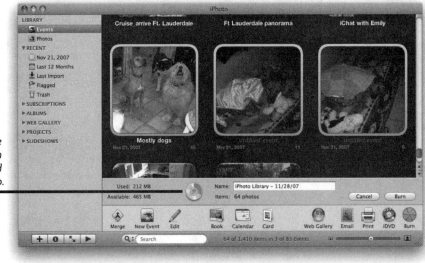

5. In the "Burn Disc" window that opens (shown below), click the "Burn" button. **Or** to access more options, click the blue disclosure triangle button (circled below).

The window expands to show the Burn Disc options (below).

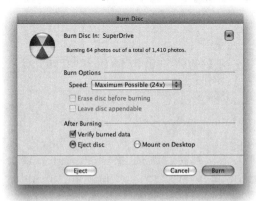

6. Click the "Burn" button. When the burning is finished, the disc either ejects or opens on your Desktop, depending on the options you selected above.

Set a Photo as Your Desktop Picture

Select one of your photos to use as a Desktop picture. It's a fun, easy way to customize the appearance of your Mac.

1. Select **one** photo in any album or Event.

2. Click the "Set Desktop" icon in the toolbar.
   Or from the Share menu, choose "Set Desktop."

   The photo instantly appears as your Desktop picture. To change how the photo fits the screen, open System Preferences, then choose "Desktop & Screen Saver." From the pop-up menu (shown on the right), choose one of the options for how the photo fits the screen.

Export Photos in Various Formats

It's hard to imagine, but there are still more ways to share photos using iPhoto. You can export photos as various file formats, as a web page, or as a QuickTime slideshow.

Export copies of photos in a variety of file formats

You might want to export photos to a different project folder or to another computer, or convert photos to another file format. This does *not* remove the photos from the iPhoto Library. The converted or exported photos will be *copies* of the originals; any changes you make to those copies will not affect the originals.

To export or convert photos:

1. Select one or more photos, albums, or Events, or any mixed collection of photos in iPhoto.

2. From the File menu, choose "Export...."

3. In the "Export Photos" window (below), click the "File Export" tab.

4. From the "Kind" pop-up menu, select a file format for the exported photos: The "Original" option saves photos in whatever format they were created in. "Current" uses the current format, and the other options include "JPG," TIF," and "PNG."

   If you're not familiar with file formats, **JPG** is a safe choice that anyone can use. Most digital cameras create photos in this format, and it's the most common format for photos destined for web pages.

   The **TIF** format is often used for images that will be placed in a page layout program and printed by a high-quality commercial printer.

   The **PNG** format is used primarily in web site design when multiple levels of transparency are required by the site's design.

   If you choose JPEG, select a quality setting in the "JPEG Quality" pop-up menu. **Or** you can enter specific dimensions in pixels.

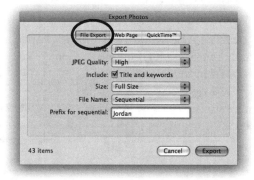

5. Click the "Include" checkbox to include photo titles and keywords.

6. From the "Size" pop-up menu, choose one of the pre-set options. **Or** choose "Custom" to set a maximum width, height, or dimension (below-right).

7. From the "File Name" pop-up menu, choose one of the file naming options: "Use title" (use a title you created in iPhoto); "Use filename" (use the original file name, usually something like DSCN3869.jpg); "Sequential" (name the photos with sequential numbers); or "Use album" (use the iPhoto album name plus sequential numbers). If you choose "Sequential" as the file naming option, type a descriptive prefix in the "Prefix for sequential" field. This helps to identify the photos later (bottom example).

8. Click "Export." In the "Export Photos" window that opens, choose where to save the exported photos, then click OK.

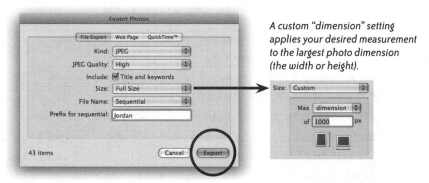

A custom "dimension" setting applies your desired measurement to the largest photo dimension (the width or height).

These photos exported with a File Name setting of "Sequential" and a Prefix of "Jordan."

Export your photos as a web site

The "Web Page" option of the "Export Photos" window is different from using iWeb to create a web site. This technique creates a plain, simple web site and saves it only on your computer—it does not publish the site on the Internet. You can upload this site yourself to a server of your choice, or you may want to burn the site to a CD to share with others.

To export your photos as a web site:

1. Select a collection of photos. We recommend you create a new album that contains the photos you want to use. The order of the photos in the album determines the order of photos on the web page you create.

2. From the File menu, choose "Export…."

3. In the "Export Photos" window that opens, click the "Web Page" tab.

4. In the Web Page pane, make the following choices:

   Title: Enter a page title that will appear on the Home page (the first page of the web site).

   Columns and Rows: Choose how many columns and rows of thumbnail photos appear on the Home page.

   Template: From the pop-up menu, choose "Framed" or "Plain."

   Background: To choose a background color, click the color swatch, then choose a color from the "Colors" palette.

   Text Color: To choose a text color, click the color swatch, then choose a color from the "Colors" palette.

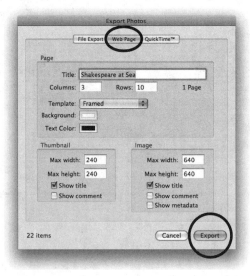

Thumbnail: Set the maximum width and height for thumbnails. To display titles or comments with thumbnails, checkmark "Show title" and "Show comment."

Image: Set the maximum width and height for photos that the thumbnails link to. To display photo titles or comments with thumbnails, checkmark "Show title" and "Show comment." Checkmark "Show metadata" to show info such as date, shutter speed, etc.

5. Click "Export" (circled on the previous page).

6. In the Finder sheet that drops down, create a new folder in a location of your choice (click the "New Folder" button).

    If you plan to upload the site to a web host, name the folder without using spaces between the words. Instead, use dashes or underscores between words, such as **Shakespeare_at_Sea**. Otherwise, your web site will have an address that looks something like this: **www.website. com/Shakespeare%20at%20Sea** (web addresses don't allow spaces).

7. Click OK.

To see your new web page (which is really a web *site*, not an individual web *page*), open the new folder you just made. Double-click the file named **index. html.** The site opens in your default web browser, *but it's not online!* You're actually just opening files on your own hard disk. The Web Page export feature just builds the site for you—it's your responsibility to upload it to a web host if you want to publish it online.

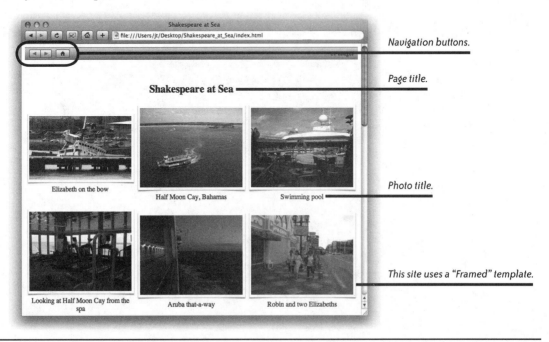

Navigation buttons.

Page title.

Photo title.

This site uses a "Framed" template.

Export photos as a QuickTime slideshow

You can export photos as a QuickTime slideshow that plays in the QuickTime player or in a program that supports QuickTime, such as a web browser. The QuickTime slideshow can be put on a CD and sent to friends, posted on a web page, inserted into a PDF, or placed in another software aplication that recognizes QuickTime, such as Keynote, Apple's presentation software.

To export as a QuickTime slideshow:

1. Select an album, a group of photos within an album, an Event, or any collection of photos. The best technique is to create a new album that contains the photos you want to use so you can arrange the photos in the order you want them to appear in the movie.

2. From the Share menu, choose "Export…."

3. In the "Export Photos" dailog (below), click the "QuickTime" tab.

4. In the QuickTime pane, make the following choices:

   Images: Set the maximum width and height for the slideshow images; 640 by 480 pixels is a standard measurement that works well. In the "Display image for" box, set how many seconds each image will stay on the screen.

5. **Background:** Choose a background color or a background image.

6. **Music:** Checkmark "Add currently selected music to movie." The slideshow will play the song previously chosen in the slideshow settings window.

7. Click "Export."

8. In the Finder sheet that drops down, name the file and choose the location where you want to save it (shown below). Click OK.

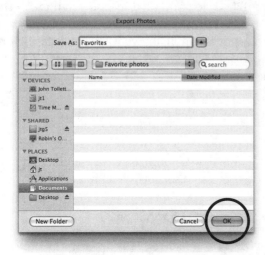

To open your QuickTime slideshow, locate the QuickTime movie file on your hard disk, then double-click it to open it in the QuickTime Player (shown below).

To play the QuickTime slideshow, click the Play button in the QuickTime Player's toolbar (below).

An exported slideshow, shown in QuickTime Player.

The Play button.

Adjust the Date and Time of Photos

Do you ever wish you could change the date or time of one or more of your photos? No? Me neither, but iPhoto lets you do it in case you think of some reason to. Seriously, there is one reason that might be useful—changing the date or time of an Event (or photos within an Event) will change the order in which they appear in the Viewing area if you've chosen to sort Events or photos "By Date" in the View menu.

1. Select one or more photos or Events.
2. From the Photos menu, choose "Adjust Date and Time...."
3. In the dialog sheet that drops down (shown below), click on an element in the "Adjusted" time field (month, date, year, hour, minutes, seconds, AM or PM), then click the small Up or Down arrows to adjust the settings.
4. To save your settings, click the "Adjust" button.

Batch Change Information of Multiple Photos

If you ever need multiple photos to have the same title, date, or description, you can change them all at once.

1. Select multiple photos or Events.
2. From the Photos menu, choose "Batch Change...."
3. In the dialog sheet that opens, use the pop-up menus to modify the title, date, or description of the selected photos.

iMovie '08

Your first home movie experiences were probably similar to ours—you shot some video tape, connected the camera to the TV, watched it once, then never looked at it again. In fact, we just stopped carrying our video camera with us on trips because it was big and heavy and we knew that we would never get around to looking at the footage again when we returned home.

Why did this happen? Because it's *boring* to watch unedited movies! We see beautifully edited movies every day—at movie theaters, on TV, and on the Internet. We've become too sophisticated as viewers to enjoy sitting through unedited home movies that for the most part look like —hmm, what's a good term to use here—home movies.

That's where iMovie comes in. Get rid of the boring and repititous shots. Toss the scenes that have bad lighting. Make video adjustments and color enhancements to a scene. Add titles and a music soundtrack. Place professional transitions between scenes. iMovie makes all of this incredibly fun and easy.

When you connect a digital video camera to your computer and launch iMovie, you're ready to create home movies that you'll watch again and again.

iMovie makes it easy to share your movies with others in a variety of ways. Create full-quality movies or smaller movies that you can email or upload to a .Mac Web Gallery, or to YouTube.

Digital video (DV) requires a lot of disk space for storage. When we imported a two-minute clip of HD (High Definition) video into iMovie '08, the imported file was 500 MB (Megabytes). We created a two-minute iMovie project from the imported HD clips, and that project file added over 100 MB to our hard disk. Even SD (Standard Definition) video requires quite a bit of storage space. When we imported two minutes of SD video, the import was 32 MB. The two-minute iMovie project we created from that import added 18 MB to our disk. If you're serious about making movies, or if you just can't control your excitement after making your first movie, buy a large, external FireWire hard disk to store your movie projects.

Once you've seen what a difference editing can have on audience reactions, you'll be inspired to make lots of movies. And you'll finally get your money's worth out of that video camera.

iMovie '08 Overview

The iMovie '08 window is completely redesigned from earlier versions of iMovie, and it's very different from other movie editing programs. But it's easy to learn and fun to use, even if some of the more advanced features from earlier versions are missing, such as special effects filters and variable volume control for audio tracks.

When you open iMovie '08 for the first time, an empty iMovie window opens. The window is empty because no content (video clips, music, and photos) has been imported yet. It will be easier to understand iMovie '08 if we look at the window populated with video footage, as shown below.

Project Library.   Project browser.   Viewer.

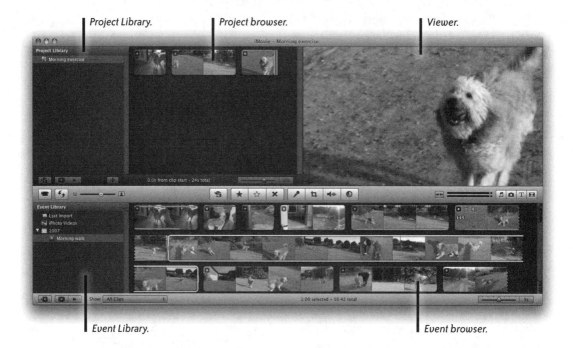

Event Library.   Event browser.

The Event Library

When you import video into iMovie, the video clips are placed in the Event Library—the lower section of the window. The Event Library is actually made of two elements—the Events list (on the left), and the Event browser (on the right). The thumbnails in the Event browser represent imported video.

When you import video, the Events list shows each separate import as an Event item in the list. Events are automatically categorized by the year the video was shot. If you have multiple Events (imports) in the list, select one of the Events to show its thumbnails in the Event browser on the right.

▼ To hide—or show—the Events list, click the Hide/Show button in the bottom-left corner of the list (shown on the right).

Hide/show the Events list.

▼ Events are named at the time you import video. To change an Event name, double-click the name, then type a new one.

▼ To combine two Events into one, drag one Event on top of another in the list. A dialog opens so you can name the combined Event.

The Events list contains two default items other than Events you've imported: **Last Import** and **iPhoto Videos.** Click "Last Import" to see thumbnails of your most recent import. Click "iPhoto Videos" to show any videos you may have in iPhoto, such as video you might have recorded using your digital still camera; video you recorded using your Mac's Photo Booth application and an iSight camera; or any other video you might have stored in iPhoto.

The video clips in the Events browser are used to create Projects (movies). Before you create a Project, you can make some basic editing decisions in the Event browser that will save time later. For instance, you can click-drag on a clip in the Event browser to make a selection of video frames, then mark them as a Favorite or as Rejected. Later, when you're ready to create a movie, clips you drag into the Project browser will already be trimmed to include just the best footage.

To make a selection in a video clip, click-press where you want to start the selection, then drag to the point you want the selection to end, as shown below. The yellow border indicates the selected portion of video. With this selection active, click the Favorite button (the Star button in the middle toolbar, shown on the right) to mark it as footage you want to use in a project. iMovie designates the Favorite footage with a green bar at the top of the clip. Later, when you're ready to drag this Favorite to the Project browser, just click on the green bar to select and highlight the Favorite footage (shown below).

Favorite button.

Notice also in the example below, a section of the video contains a horizontal red bar across the top of the clip. This is a selection that has been marked as Rejected, using the **X** button in the middle toolbar (shown on the right).

Reject button.

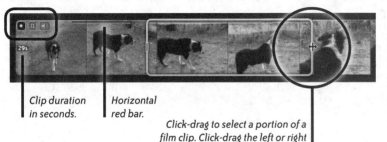

Clip duration in seconds.

Horizontal red bar.

Click-drag to select a portion of a film clip. Click-drag the left or right handle to adjust the selection.

When you move your pointer over a clip in the Event browser, three small icons appear in the top-left corner.
Click the first icon to open the Video Adjustments palette.
Click the second icon to crop, rotate, or apply a Ken Burns effect to the clip.
Click the third icon to open the Audio Adjustments palette.
When an icon is black, an adjustment of that type has been applied to the clip.

The Project Library

The Project Library consists of two elements also—the Projects list (in the upper-left corner), and the Project browser (to the right of the Projects list). The Projects list remains empty until you create a new project.

To create a new Project:

1. Click the New Project button (**+**) in the bottom-right corner of the Projects list. **Or** drag a clip from the Event browser to the Project browser. In the dialog that opens (shown below), type a project name and choose an aspect ratio from the pop-up menu.

    The aspect ratio determines the proportions of the movie.
    Standard (4:3) is a standard TV screen proportion. Many camcorders use this aspect ratio.
    iPhone (3:2) uses proportions that fit an iPhone screen.
    Widescreen (16:9) is for video shot in widescreen format.

2. Click "Create." The new Project is added to the Projects list on the left. When you add other Projects, select the one in this list that you want to work with.

To build a movie, drag clips from the Event browser (in the lower-right section of the window) to the Project browser (in the upper section of the window). Once you've dragged the footage you want to use into the Project browser, you can drag the clips to rearrange their order, and make other editing adjustments explained later in this chapter.

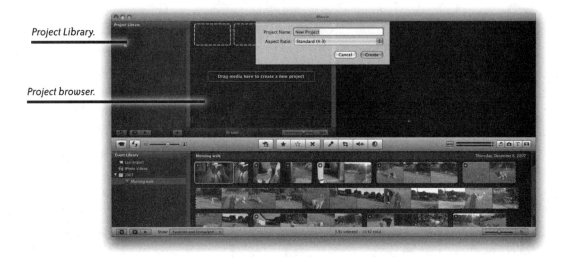

Project Library.

Project browser.

The Viewer

The Viewer—in the top-right section of the window—provides a preview of your movie. To set the Preview size, from the Window menu, choose "Viewer," then choose Small, Medium, or Large. To maximize the size of the entire iMovie window on your screen, from the Window menu, choose "Zoom." **Or** click the green Resize button in the top-left corner of the title bar.

Ways to preview video:

▼ To play an entire Project in the Viewer from its beginning, click the name of a Project in the Projects list, then click the Play button in the Projects toolbar (shown on the right).

▼ To play an entire Project in full screen mode, click the full screen Play button (right) located in the Projects toolbar. To exit full screen mode, press the Escape key.

▼ To play a single clip in the Project browser, click a clip to select it, then press the Spacebar. Press again to stop playback.

▼ To play all of the clips in the Event browser (the original, imported source video) in full screen mode, click the Play button located in the Events toobar (right). Press Escape to exit full screen mode.

▼ To play all clips from the Event browser in the Viewer, click the Play button (right) located in the Events toolbar.

▼ To skim quickly through video clips in the Viewer, move your pointer across video clips in the Project browser or the Event browser.

If you import video that was shot in the Standard (4:3) aspect ratio, but create a Project that uses the Widescreen (16:9) aspect ratio, iMovie enlarges and crops 4:3 footage to make it fit the 16:9 screen proportion (shown below). This image enlargement can make the video look a little soft or fuzzy.

A Standard 4:3 aspect ratio video clip, selected from the Event browser and shown in the Viewer.

The same clip, selected in the Project browser of a Widescreen 16:9 Project.

The iMovie '08 toolbars

The iMovie interface includes a middle toolbar and a bottom toolbar. The following is a brief description of each tool.

The Project's current duration.

Hide/show the Project list.

Adjust the number of seconds per thumbnail in the Project browser.

Voiceover, Crop, Adjust Audio, Adjust Color.

Hide/show browsers for Music, Photos, Titles, and Transitions.

Play full screen.

Play in the Viewer.

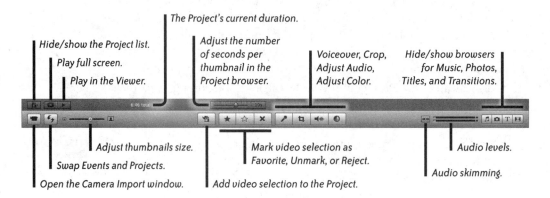

Adjust thumbnails size.

Mark video selection as Favorite, Unmark, or Reject.

Audio levels.

Swap Events and Projects.

Audio skimming.

Open the Camera Import window.

Add video selection to the Project.

The **middle toolbar** (shown above) contains the following tools:

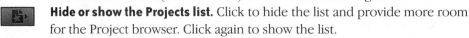

Hide or show the Projects list. Click to hide the list and provide more room for the Project browser. Click again to show the list.

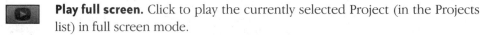

Play full screen. Click to play the currently selected Project (in the Projects list) in full screen mode.

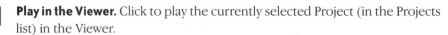

Play in the Viewer. Click to play the currently selected Project (in the Projects list) in the Viewer.

Adjust number of seconds per thumbnail. Drag the slider to adjust how many seconds of video are represented by each Project browser thumbnail. When you set the slider all the way to the left to 1/2s (one-half second) each thumbnail contains a half second of video. This setting makes it easy to skim through video in slow motion and select a specific frame for editing. Drag the slider to the right to pack more seconds of video into each thumbnail. Drag the slider to "All" (all the way to the right) to set a single thumbnail as the representative of all video in a clip, regardless of the length of the clip.

Open the Camera Import window. Click to open the Import window and import video from a digital camcorder.

Swap Events and Projects. Click to make the Events Library and the Project Library swap places. This can provide extra room for Project editing since the lower section of the window doesn't include the Viewer. Plus it's great fun to watch the two elements animate and swoop into position.

Adjust thumbnails size. Drag the slider to adjust the size of the thumbnails in the Project browser.

Add selection to the Project. Select a range of video frames in the Event browser (the original, imported clips), then click this button to automatically place the selection into the Project browser.

Favorite, Unmark, and Reject. Select a clip (or a portion of a clip) in the Event browser, then click the Favorite (black star) or Reject button (**x**) to mark the selection as a Favorite or as Rejected. To unmark a clip, select it, then click the Unmark button (white star).

Voiceover, Crop, Adjust Audio, and Adjust Color. The tools in this set of buttons let you record a voiceover track, crop video or photos, add a Ken Burns pan-and-zoom effect, adjust audio volume levels, and adjust color settings (Exposure, Brightness, Contrast, Saturation, Levels and White Point).

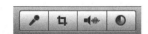

Audio skimming. Click to turn audio skimming on or off. When audio skimming is turned on, you can hear audio as you move your pointer across a video clip. This can help you locate a certain spot in a clip where you want to trim the clip or add an audio file, such as a sound effect or music track.

Audio levels. The Audio levels meter indicates the volume level of an audio track. As you play or skim a Project, if the volume indicators reach far enough to the right to turn red, it means the audio might be distorted in your movie. To avoid audio distortion, adjust the volume of audio tracks that show this visual warning.

Hide/show Music browser, Photos browser, Titles browser, or Transitions browser. Click to open one of these browsers, then drag an item (an audio file, photo, title, or transition) to the Project browser to add it to a movie.

Click one of the browser buttons to open its browser in the bottom-right corner of the iMovie window.

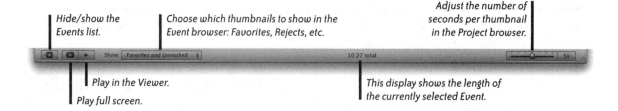

Hide/show the Events list.

Choose which thumbnails to show in the Event browser: Favorites, Rejects, etc.

Adjust the number of seconds per thumbnail in the Project browser.

Play in the Viewer.

Play full screen.

This display shows the length of the currently selected Event.

iMovie's **bottom toolbar** (shown above) contains the following tools:

Hide or show the Events list. Click to hide the Events list and provide more room for the Event browser on the right. Click again to show the list. In the example below, the Events list is hidden, providing more space for the clips in the Event browser (the lower section of the window).

Play selected Events full screen. Click to play the currently selected Event in full screen mode.

Play in the Viewer. Click to play the currently selected Event (in the Events list) in the Viewer.

The "Show" pop-up menu. From this pop-up menu (right, and circled below), choose which clips to show in the Event browser. Choose "Favorites Only" to show only selections that have been marked with a green bar. Choose "Favorites and Unmarked" to show clips that have been marked green as Favorites and also unmarked clips. Choose "All Clips" to show Favorites, Rejects, and Umarked footage. Choose "Rejects Only" to show only footage that you've marked as rejected.

Adjust the number of seconds per thumbnail. Drag the slider to adjust how many seconds of video are represented by each thumbnail in the Event browser. When you set the slider all the way to the left (to 1/2s—one-half second) each half-second of video is represented by a thumbnail. To see the individual frames that make up the half-second of video (aprroximately 15 frames), skim your pointer over the thumbnail. As you move this slider to the right, *fewer* thumbnails are shown, taking up less room in the browser. When *more* thumbnails are showing, it's easier to skim through video clips in slow motion and select a specific frame for editing. Drag the slider to the right to pack more seconds of video in each thumbnail. Drag the slider to "All" (all the way to the right) to set a single thumbnail as the representative of all video in a clip, regardless of the length of the clip.

Import Video from a Camcorder

The first thing you must do to make a movie is to import video content (or photos) into iMovie. The most common way to do that is to import video from your digital video camcorder.

Most camcorders are either tape-based—they record to DV tapes—or they're tapeless and they record to a DVD, HDD (hard disk drive), or Flash Memory. Tape-based cameras connect to your computer with a FireWire cable, and video is *converted* to a digital format during the import process. Tapeless cameras use a USB cable to connect and they *record* in a digital format—which allows you to preview or import clips in any order. There's no rewinding or fast-forwarding required to find a specific scene. Just select a clip's thumbnail, then preview or import it. Very cool.

A tapeless camera is sometimes referred to as a random-access device because it allows you to select and import video clips in a random, nonlinear way.

Import video from a tapeless camcorder

1. Set the video camera to Play mode, then connect the camera to the computer with the camera's USB cable. The Import window opens automatically (below) when the camera is detected, and the camera appears on your Desktop as a mounted device, as shown on the left.

   Depending on the camera you use, you may have to use the camera's built-in menu system to enable the USB connection. If your tapeless camcorder records to an 8 cm DVD, your Mac might mistakenly open the DVD Player. If so, close the DVD Player.

Transport controls. Click the Play button to show a preview of the selected thumbnail.

Choose "Automatic" to import all clips. Choose "Manual" to import only selected clips (clips that you checkmark).

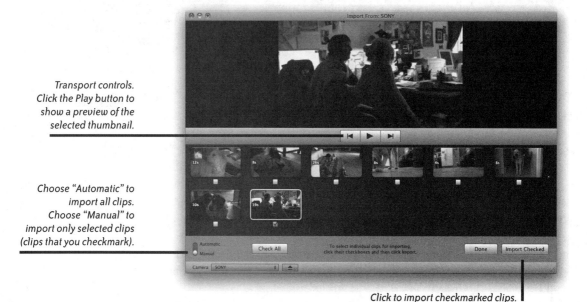

Click to import checkmarked clips.

The bottom section of the Import window (shown on the previous page) shows a collection of thumbnails that represent all of the video clips in the camera. To preview a clip, select it, then click the Play button located beneath the Preview.

2. Set the toggle switch in the bottom-left corner to "Automatic" to import all clips, then click "Import."

If you don't want to import all existing clips, set the toggle switch to "Manual." Click the checkboxes under the clips you want to import, then click "Import Checked."

3. In the dialog that opens (right), set these options: From the "Save to" pop-up menu, choose a location where you want to save the imported video. You can choose any location on your computer or any connected FireWire hard disk, as long as it has enough storage space available. An hour of standard definition video requires about 13 GB of disk space. An hour of HD video needs about 40 GB of space.

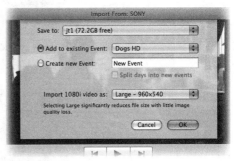

Choose "Add to existing Event" or "Create new Event." To automatically create a new Event for each day of recorded video, checkmark "Split days into new Events."

If you're importing true HD (1920 x 1080 interlaced high definition video), select "Large" or "Full size" from the "Import 1080i video as" pop-up menu. To save hard disk space, choose "Large" unless you plan to export the video to Final Cut Pro, or you plan to use the video for broadcasting.

4. Click "OK" to close the dialog and start the import. When the import is complete, iMovie alerts you (below).

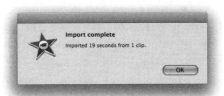

After you import video from a tapeless camera, unmount the device as you would any other external hard disk. Click the Eject icon next to the camera's disk icon in the sidebar of a Finder window. **Or** drag the camera's disk icon from the Desktop to the Trash. **Or** Control-click on the icon that's on the Desktop, then from the shortcut menu, choose "Eject."

Import video from a tape-based camcorder

1. Set the camera to Play mode. Your camera may call it VTR mode or something else. Make sure it's *not* in Record mode. Connect the camera to the computer. The Import window (shown below) opens automatically.

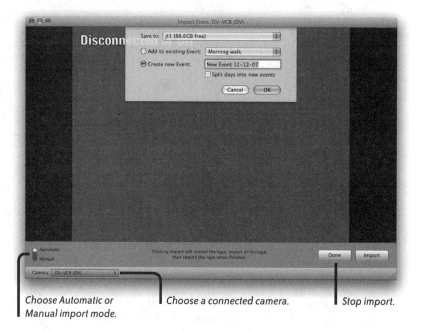

Choose Automatic or Manual import mode.   Choose a connected camera.   Stop import.

2. Set the Automatic/Manual switch:

   To import all footage from the tape, set the switch to "Automatic," then click "Import."

   To import specific footage, set the switch to "Manual." Click the Play button to preview the video. Click "Import" to start importing video. Click the "Stop" button when you want to stop importing. The tape preview continues to play until it reaches the end, or until you click the Stop button in the transport controls (the black square).

   If you know there are just a few scenes you want to import from the tape, use the transport controls in the window (Rewind, Forward, Stop, Play) to find a location where you want to start importing video. Click the Stop button (the black square), then click "Import." This method keeps you from loading up your hard disk with footage you don't need.

3. From the "Save To" pop-up menu (below), choose a location to store the imported video. You can choose any location on your computer or any connected FireWire hard disk, as long as it has enough storage space available. An hour of standard definition video requires about 13 GB of disk space. An hour of HD video needs about 40 GB of space.

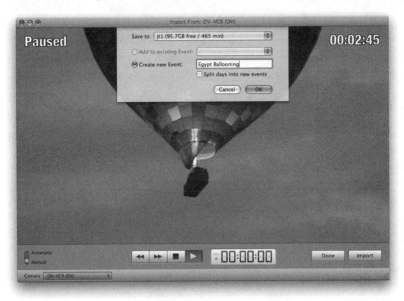

4. Choose "Add to existing Event" or "Create new Event."
To automatically create a new Event for each day of recorded video, checkmark "Split days into new Events."

5. Click "OK" to close the dialog.

6. **If the import mode is set to "Automatic,"** click "Import." iMovie imports all video on the tape. To stop importing, click "Stop."

   When the import mode is set to "Manual," you can import specific scenes on the fly (as the tape plays in the Import window), or you can carefully locate scenes, then import them.
   To import specific scenes on the fly, click the Play button in the transport controls. When the preview reaches a point where you want to import video, click the "Import" button. Click the "Stop" button to stop importing video.
   To locate a specific scene for import, use the transport controls (Play, Rewind, Forward, Stop) to find the beginning of a scene you want to import, then click "Import."

Rewinding and fast-forwarding a camera to find specific scenes can be a slow process. If you plan to import most of the scenes on a tape, it saves time to import the entire tape, then later delete the scenes you don't want.

Other Ways to Import Video

There are several other ways to import video into iMovie '08. You can import from an earlier version of iMovie, from a connected video camera, from iPhoto, or from the Finder.

Import projects from iMovie HD

iMovie HD is an earlier version of iMovie, also known as iMovie '06. You can import entire projects from iMovie HD, but some edits will not be included. Custom transitions will be replaced with cross-dissolves. Titles, effects, and music tracks in the original project will not be included in the import. Audio that you may have silenced in video clips will be present again.

If you don't mind re-editing the movie after you import it, this type of import may be OK with you. But if you don't want the extra work, and just want the project imported as you originally edited it, use the import method described on the next page: "Import from the Finder" (import a QuickTime movie that you exported from iMovie HD).

To import a project from iMovie HD:

1. From the File menu, choose "Import iMovie HD Project...."

2. In the Finder dialog that opens, locate an iMovie HD project on your computer, then choose the location where you want to save it.

   If you happen to be importing true *1080i video* (1920 x 1080 inter-laced video), choose an import size from the "Import 1080i video as:" pop-up menu— "Large – 960x540" or "Full – 1920x1080." Select Large to reduce the file size significantly with little quality loss.

3. Click "Import."

All the files from the iMovie HD project are copied to iMovie '08 and new thumbnails are generated. All of this processing can take more than just a few minutes, depending on the length of the imported project.

A new Event and a new Project are created in the iMovie '08 window, named the same as the iMovie HD project. In iMovie '08, the new Event shown in the Event browser contains *all of the source video* from the iMovie HD project. The new Project shown in the Project browser includes *only the trimmed clips* used in the edited version of the iMovie HD project.

Import from the Finder

If you have QuickTime movies from any source stored anywhere on your computer, you can import them into iMovie '08 from the Finder. You may want to import a masterpiece that you created in iMovie's previous version (iMovie HD), but don't want to lose all the custom editing, effects, music, or titles. You can export the movie as a "Full Quality" QuickTime file, then import the QuickTime file into iMovie '08.

To import a movie from the Finder:

1. From the File menu, choose "Import Movies."

2. In the Finder dialog that opens (below), locate a QuickTime file. From the "Save to" pop-up menu, choose a location to save it.

3. Choose to "Add to existing Event" or "Create new Event." To add the movie to an existing Event, choose one from the pop-up menu. To create a new Event, type an Event name in the text field.

4. Choose to "Copy files" (the movie will be copied to iMovie '08 and the original movie stays in its current location), or "Move files" (the movie is moved to iMovie '08 and the original movie is deleted. Choose "Move files" to preserve hard disk space.

5. Click "Import."

The QuickTime movie appears as a single clip in both the Event browser and the Project browser, with all original editing, effects, titles, transitions, etc. in place.

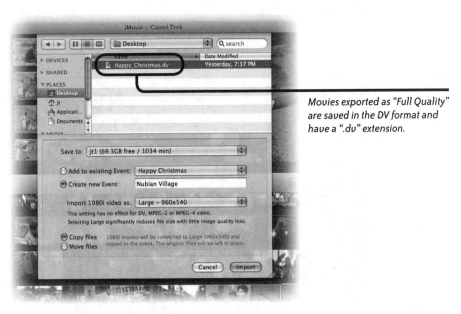

Movies exported as "Full Quality" are saved in the DV format and have a ".dv" extension.

Import live video from iSight or a FireWire camera

If your computer has a built-in iSight camera, a connected external iSight camera, or almost any connected FireWire-enabled video camera, you can capture live video into iMovie.

To import live video:

1. From the File menu, choose "Import from Camera."

2. Select a connected camera from the "Camera" pop-up menu in the bottom-left corner of the window (shown below). If you use an external video camera, make sure the camera is in Record mode.

3. Click "Import." In the dialog that opens (below), use the "Save to" pop-up menu to choose a location to save the file. To add the captured video to an existing Event, click "Add to existing Event," then choose an Event from the pop-up menu. **Or** click "Create new Event," then type an Event name in the text field.

4. Click OK to close the dialog, then click "Import." iMovie records until you click "Stop." Click "Done" to close the Import window. If you created a new Event, the video appears in the Events list. If you added the video to an existing Event, it appears in that Event.

Import videos from iPhoto

Some digital cameras that shoot still photos can also shoot short video clips, and iPhoto can import them from the camera. Photo Booth, another app on your Mac, can also make movies using an iSight camera and place them into iPhoto. If you have videos stored in iPhoto, you can drag them into an iMovie project.

To import video from iPhoto:

1. In the Event Library, select "iPhoto Videos." Any videos you have stored in iPhoto appear in the Events browser.

2. In the Projects list, click a Project to which you want to add an iPhoto video. **Or** create a new Project (click the Add (+) button beneath the Project list.

3. Select an iPhoto video (Command-click to select the entire clip) in the Event browser, then drag it to the Project browser (below).
   To select just a portion of an iPhoto video clip, click-drag anywhere in the clip to select the frames you want, then drag the selection to the Project browser.

   As you drag a selection to various positions in the Project browser, a vertical green bar indicates where the clip will be placed if you let go.

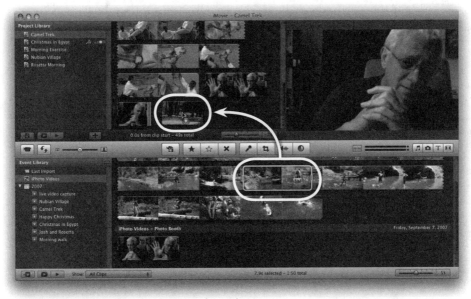

With "iPhoto Videos" selected in the Event Library, drag a video selection from the Event browser to the Project browser.

Working with Events

iMovie Events are *imports of video or photos*, grouped by date. The imported video (or other content) is called the source video.

The Events list and Events browser

Click a single Event in the Events list to show its content of video clips in the Event browser, located to the right of the Event Library pane. You can also select a year, a month, or multiple Events to show the content of all selected Events at once in the Event browser.

Skimming

Skimming is a fast and easy way to preview the footage in a video clip. When you move your pointer over a clip in the Event browser, the individual frames of the video underneath the pointer are shown in both the thumbnail and in the large Preview window.

This slider adjusts the number of frames per thumbnail. The number on the right tells the number of seconds of video per thumbnail (not the number of frames).

To change the speed of skimming, adjust the "Frames per Thumbnail" slider. Drag the slider left to show fewer frames per thumbnail. When the slider is moved all the way to the left, each thumbnail contains 1/2-second of video (about 15 frames). As you move the slider to the right, each thumbnail contains more seconds of video, thus more frames. When the slider is moved all the way to the right and set to "All," a single thumbnail contains all of the video in a clip, no matter how long the clip is.

When you move your pointer over a clip, its duration is shown at the starting edge.

In this example the Frames per Thumbnail slider is set to 10s (ten seconds of video per thumbnail). Since the clip duration is 21 seconds, it takes 3 thumbnails to represent the entire clip.

This is the same clip with the Frames per Thumbnail slider set to 30s (thirty seconds of video per thumbnail). Since the clip duration is 21 seconds, it takes only one thumbnail to represent the entire clip.

Reorganize the Event Library

As you import video to create Events, you might realize that some video really belongs in another Event, or that some Events should be merged into each other. iMovie lets you reorganize the Events in the Event Library in a number of different ways.

To merge two Events:

1. In the Events list, drag one Event on top of another.

2. In the dialog that opens (below), type a name for the merged Event, then click OK.

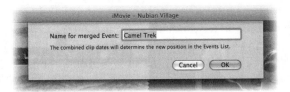

To split an Event into two separate Events:

1. Click on the Event in the list that you want to split.

2. In the Event browser, click on a thumbnail that begins the footage you want to split away.

3. From the File menu, choose "Split Event Before Selected Clip."
   Or Control-click on a clip, then choose "Split Event Before Clip."
   The split video appears as a new Event in the Events list.
   Double-click its default name to rename it.

To move one or more clips from one Event to another:

1. Click on an Event in the Events list to show its content in the Event browser.

2. Click on a clip in the Event browser to select it, then drag the clip from the Event browser to another Event in the Events list.

   To move multiple clips, press the Command key, click additional clips, then drag the clips to another Event in the Events list.

To delete an Event:

1. Select an Event in the Events list that you want to delete.

2. From the File menu, choose "Move Event to Trash."
   To remove the Event (and retrieve disk space) *permanently*, empty the Trash in the Dock.

Trimming clips in the Event browser

The video clips in the Event browser are referred to as the source video. These are the original clips that you imported. The source video usually contains footage that you don't want to use in the movie project. So, before you drag a clip to the Project browser, you should skim the clip thumbnails to preview the footage, then trim the clip so just the best footage is dragged to the Project browser and used in a movie project.

To trim a clip in the Event browser:

1. Click-drag on a clip to select a range of video you want to use. As you drag, a yellow border highlights your selection. If you decide to alter your selection, move your pointer over the left or right side of the selection border. The pointer turns into a bi-directional arrow icon (shown below). Drag either handle of the yellow border left or right to change the selection. As you drag, the number of seconds of video contained in the selection appears in yellow on the right side.

Drag the selection's handles to adjust the duration of the selection.

As you drag to create a selection, this number updates to show the duration of the selection.

2. If you want to leave the duration of the selection as it is, but change the range of video frames that are selected, you can make what's know as a **slip edit.** Move your pointer over the top or bottom border of the selection until you see a white hand icon with left and right arrows in it (shown below). Press on the top or bottom border with this slip edit icon, then drag left or right to move the selection border forward or back in the clip.

As you drag the selection border left or right, video frames that are selected change, but the duration of the selection stays as is.

When you move your pointer over a clip, the clip duration shows here.

3. Move your pointer anywhere within the selection. The pointer changes to a plain white hand (below). Drag the selection to the Project browser where you create movie projects.

Adjust the appearance of the Events Library

iMovie's View menu provides specific options that affect the appearance of the Events list and the Event browser.

Choose which clips are shown in the Event browser:

▼ Choose **Favorites Only** to show just clip selections you've marked as Favorites.

▼ Choose **Favorites and Unmarked** to show Favorites and clips that have not been marked at all.

▼ Choose **All Clips** to show clips you've marked as Favorites or Rejects, and also clips that are Unmarked (not designated as a Favorite or as a Reject).

▼ Choose **Rejected Only** to show clips you've marked as Rejects, and that you've deleted. When you're ready to delete Rejected clips from the project, choose this view (Rejected Only), then click "Move Rejected to Trash" (at the top of the Rejected Clips window). To permanently delete the rejected files and retrieve disk storage space, empty the Trash in the Dock.

Choose how Events are shown in the Events list:

▼ **Events By Volume** shows Events and the volume (hard disk) they're stored on. All connected hard disks are shown, even if they don't have Events stored on them (right-top). A "View by Volume" icon (a disk icon) appears in the top-right corner of the Event Library.

▼ **Events By Month** shows Events by the month, as a sub-category of the year (right-bottom).

▼ **Most Recent Events at Top** puts Events in descending order.

▼ **Separate Days in Events** categorizes video clips in an Event by date in the Event browser. Gray bars that contain video creation dates act as separators (circled below).

Events By Volume.

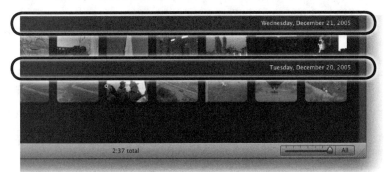

In the Events browser, separate video clips by the days they were shot.

Events By Month.

Create a Movie Project

Once you've imported video and have at least one Event in the Event Library, you're ready to edit a movie. The overview presented in the previous pages gives you a basic idea of how simple it is to import video, to preview video clips by skimming, and to trim clips so the best footage is selected for your project. Even though some of the following steps were mentioned earlier in the iMovie overview, they're repeated here to present them in the logical sequence of creating and editing a movie project.

Preview clips and mark as Favorites or Rejects

1. **Select an Event** in the Events list so its content is shown in the Event browser.

2. **Skim the clips** in the browser to preview the video and get an idea of what your clips look like.

Mark clip as a Favorite.

3. **Mark the best video clips as Favorites.** (Marking clips is not absolutely necessary, but it can help make the editing process easier). Drag across the thumbnails in the Event browser to select the frames you want to use. A yellow border surrounds your selection. With the selection active, click the Favorites button (the black star). A horizontal green bar appears at the top of the thumbnail, marking the selected frames of video as Favorites.

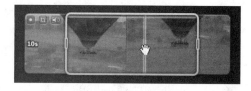

Mark clip as Rejected.

4. **Mark unwanted clips as Rejected.** Drag to select a range of video you don't want to use, then click the Reject Selection button (the **X**). A horizontal red bar appears in the top of the thumbnail, marking the selected frames as Rejects.

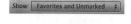

5. From the "Show:" pop-up menu (left), **choose which clips show in the Event browser**— "Favorites," "Favorites and Unmarked," "All Clips," or "Rejects Only." When you choose "Favorites" or "Favorites and Unmarked," the video marked as "Rejected" disappears from view. If you haven't marked any clips, choose "Favorites and Unmarked" or "All Clips."

Unmark a marked clip.

You can umark clips if you change your mind. Click the green or red bar at the top of a marked clip to select the marked frames of video, then click the Unmarked button (the white star).

Create a Project and add video clips

1. **Drag your Favorites to the Project browser.** Click on the green bar that runs across the top of the thumbnails you marked as Favorites. A yellow selection border automatically highlights the frames marked as Favorites. Place your pointer inside the yellow selection border so the pointer changes to a white hand (below-left). Drag the selection to the Project browser. Video that has been dragged to the Project browser is marked with an orange horizontal bar (below-right).

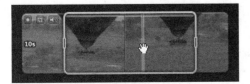

If you didn't mark any footage as Favorites, that's OK. Just drag across thumbnails in the Event browser to select the footage you want to use, then drag the selections to the Project browser.

If the Project list is empty, drag a video clip from the Event browser to the Project browser to automatically create a new Project. In the dialog that opens (right), name the Project and choose an aspect ratio to use—Standard (4:3), iPhone (3:2), or Widescreen (16:9).

You can also create a new Project by clicking the New Project button (+) located in the Project toolbar (right).

If the Project list already contains a Project you want to use, select it in the list, then drag video clips from the Event browser to the Project browser.

Another way to add clips to the Project browser: Select a clip or any range of video frames in the Event browser, then click the "Add Selection to Project" button (shown on the right). The selection is automatically added to the Project browser.

2. **Rearrange clips in the Project browser.** Drag clips in the Project browser to put them in any order you want. It's helpful to set the "Frames per Thumbnail" slider to "All," and set the thumbnails Size slider to the smallest setting, so more of the Project shows at once.

3. **Trim clips in the Trim Clip pane.** Control-click on a clip, then choose "Trim…." In the Trim Clip pane that replaces the Project browser, click and drag to select the portion of the video you want to use, then click "Done." At any time you can return and recover trimmed video.

Add Music

Adding music to a movie can make the difference between a boring movie and an interesting one. You can add music to just certain clips or as a background track for the entire movie. iMovie provides a library of sound effects that you can add, or you can add voiceover narration to your movie.

1. Click the Music and Sound Effects button in the middle toolbar (circled below). The Music and Sound Effects browser opens in the bottom-right corner of the window. This browser provides access to all the music in your iTunes Library, the iMovie '08 Sound Effects, the iLife Sound Effects, and music you created with GarageBand.

The Project browser.

The Music and Sound Effects browser.

Click the Play button to preview the selected audio file.

2. Click one of the category names in the top section to show its content of audio files in the lower part of the browser. To preview an audio file, double-click it. **Or** select a file, then click the Play button.

3. Choose an audio file and drag it to the Project browser.
   To create a background music track, drag the file to the dark gray background of the Project browser. A green background color surrounds the thumbnails that fall within the duration of the music file. If the music file is longer than the duration of video clips in the Project, the music is trimmed to fade out at the end of the last video clip (shown below).

This icon indicates that the background music file is trimmed and fades out here.

To add an audio file to a video track, drag the audio file from the Music and Sound Effects browser to the Project browser and drop it on top of the video clip you want it attached to.

A green audio marker (below) shows the location of the audio file in relation to the video. To remove it, select it and press Delete.

▼ To change the placement of an audio file, move your pointer over the green marker until it changes to a hand icon (below), then drag the marker to another position. The red vertical line shows the exact frame in the thumbnail where the audio file begins. This video frame is also visible in the Viewer.

▼ To trim the beginning or end of an audio file, move your pointer over the left or right edge of the green marker until it changes to a bi-directional arrow (below). Then drag the left or right edge of the marker to trim the file.

▼ Add multiple audio files to a Project. Drag audio files from the Music and Sound Effects browser to clips in the Project browser, as shown below. Drag the green audio markers to fine tune the placement.

A 19-second song, a 3-second sound effect, and a 2-second sound effect have been added to this video.

▼ To delete an audio track, select it, then press Delete.

Adjust the volume of music tracks

The Adjust Audio button.

1. Click the green audio clip in the background of the Project browser, then click the Adjust Audio button in the middle toolbar (shown on the left).

2. In the Audio Adjustments window that opens (below), drag the Volume slider left or right. To silence the video clip's audio completely, move the slider all the way left to 0%. When you've made the adjustments you want, click "Done."

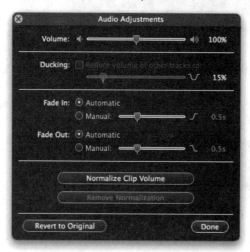

To change "Fade In" and "Fade Out" durations of a music track, adjust the Fade sliders. The default fade duration is .5 seconds. For a faster fade effect, drag the slider to the left. For a slower fade effect (up to two seconds), drag the slider to the right.

To remove all audio adjustments, click "Revert to Original."

When you're satisfied with your audio adjustments, click "Done."

Apply Ducking to an audio track

When multiple audio tracks are playing at the same time, you can select the track you want to be dominant and automatically lower the volume of other tracks while the dominant track plays. This technique is called Ducking.

1. Select an audio track that you've placed in the Project browser, then click the Adjust Audio button.

2. In the Audio Adjustments window (above), checkmark "Ducking."

3. Drag the slider to adjust how low to set the volume of other tracks while the selected track plays. Ducking automatically fades other tracks out and back in.

Add Voiceover

Narrative voiceovers are a great way to add interest to some movies. You can use your Mac's built-in microphone, or connect an external mic.

1. **Click the Voiceover button** (right) to open the Voiceover window shown below. Make the following settings:

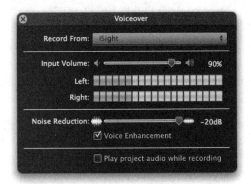

- ▾ Choose a mic to use in the "Record from" pop-up menu.
- ▾ Set the "Input Volume" slider. Speak into the mic and adjust the volume slider to as loud as possible without causing the level meters (the green bars) to go into the red zone on the far right. Red zone audio may be distorted during playback.
- ▾ Set the "Noise Reduction" slider all the way to the right to eliminate as much background noise as possible. Move the slider back to the right a little if you want some background noise.
- ▾ Checkmark "Voice Enhancement" for a smoother sound.
- ▾ Checkmark "Play project audio while recording" to hear the audio in the video clips as you record your voice.

2. **To start recording,** click on a thumbnail in the Project browser where you want to start recording a voiceover. Selecting a thumbnail starts a countdown in the Viewer so you can get ready to record.

3. **To stop recording,** click the spacebar. Your voiceover recording appears as a purple marker under the video thumbnails (below).

The Voiceover marker shows the audio duration (28 seconds).

Adjust Movie Color

You may be surprised—even amazed—by how much better many video clips look after using the color adjustment tools provided in iMovie '08. We're talking huge diff, not just slightly better.

The Adjust Video button.

1. Select a thumbnail clip in the Project browser or the Event browser that you want to adjust. If you adjust a clip in the Project browser, the original source clip in the Event browser is not affected.

2. Click the Adjust Video button (left) to open the Video Adjustment window (below). **Or** click the small Video Adjustment icon in the top-left corner of a thumbnail that appears when you move your pointer over a thumbnail in the Project browser or Event browser.

A vertical red line with a red dot in the middle appears in the thumbnail (left). Drag the red dot to a frame you want to reference as you adjust the color in the video. This frame appears in the Viewer.

Drag the red dot to select a target frame for color adustments.

3. Click the "Auto" button and let iMovie take its best shot at what adjustments need to be made. If you don't like the results, click "Revert to Original." But this setting often works great.

Experiment with the manual color adjustments: drag the various sliders in the window to make color changes. In the "Levels" graph, drag the sliders toward the middle to adjust the intensity of shadows (the left slider) and highlights (the right slider).

4. Click "Done" when you've finished making color adjustments.

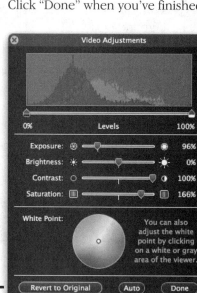

To recover the original version of a clip, before adjustments were made, click "Revert to Original."

A foggy, smoggy video shot in Egypt.

The same clip, after clicking "Auto."

Add Titles to Your Movie

Titles can add interest and information to your movie. You can use them for more than just the start and end of a movie. Try using titles throughout a movie to convey information or just for entertainment.

1. Click the Titles button (circled, right) to open the Titles browser (right). The Titles browser contains a collection of title styles.

2. Drag a title style from the Titles browser to a thumbnail in the Project browser. You can apply the title to the beginning, the end, or to the entire clip; as you drag the title across a thumbnail, a blue color highlights the center, left side, or right side of the thumbnail. Drag and drop the title to the position you want when you see that part of the clip highlighted in blue.

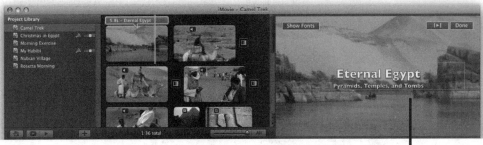

Select placeholder text and type custom titles.

3. In the Viewer, placeholder text for the Title style is shown. Select the placeholder text and type your own custom title (above-right).

   In the Project browser (above-left), the title is shown above the thumbnail as a blue marker that contains the title duration and text. To change the title duration, drag either edge of the blue title marker.

4. To customize the title appearance, click "Show Fonts" in the Viewer. In the Fonts window that opens, choose a font, size, color, etc.

   If the title style includes a background color, click the background color, then choose a new color from the Colors palette that opens.

5. To change the frame position of the title, drag the blue title marker to a new location in the Project browser. To change the title duration, drag one or both edges of the blue title marker. Titles can be stretched across as many clips as you want.

Add Photos to a Movie

Adding still photos to a movie can add a lot of interest, especially when you use the Ken Burns Effect—a pan-and-zoom technique that creates motion from static images. You can add still photos to existing video Projects, or you can create a new Project that contains only still photos.

1. Select a Project in the Projects list. **Or** create a new Project.

2. Click the Photos browser button (left, and circled below). The Photos browser opens in the bottom-right corner of the window (shown below). The pop-up menu at the top of the Photos browser gives access to your iPhoto Library, including Events, Albums, and .Mac Web Galleries. It also provides access to photos you may have created in Photo Booth with an iSight camera.

3. Select a photo you want to use in a Project. To see a larger preview of the photo, double-click it. It enlarges to fill the Photos browser pane. Click the enlarged preview again to return the browser to the normal thumbnails view. To select multiple photos, Command-click additional thumbnails.

4. Drag the selection of thumbnails from the Photos browser to the Project browser.

Once the photos are in the Project browser, you can add music, Ken Burns Effects, titles, or transitions. To change the duraton of a photo in the Project, select it, then from the File menu, choose "Set Duration...."

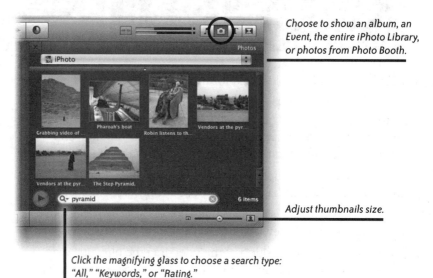

The Photos browser.

Choose to show an album, an Event, the entire iPhoto Library, or photos from Photo Booth.

Adjust thumbnails size.

Click the magnifying glass to choose a search type:
"All," "Keywords," or "Rating."
Choose "All" to search Keywords, Titles, and Comments.

Crop and Rotate Images

The Crop tool can be used on both still photos and video clips.

To crop a video clip:

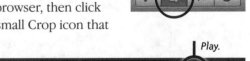

1. Select a clip in the Event browser or the Project browser, then click the Crop tool (shown on the right). **Or** click the small Crop icon that appears in the top-left corner of a clip.

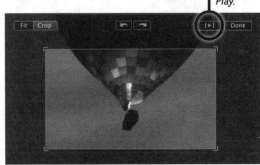

Play.

2. In the Viewer (right), click "Crop." Drag the corners of the green rectangle to resize the crop area. Drag inside the crop area to reposition the rectangle.

3. Click "Done."

   ▼ To undo the crop and make the video fit the window, click "Fit."

   ▼ To rotate the video left or right, click the one of the curved arrows.

   ▼ To play the clip, click the Play button.

To crop a still photo clip:

1. Select a photo clip in the Project browser, then click the Crop tool. **Or** click the Crop icon that appears in the top-left corner of a clip.

2. In the Viewer (right):

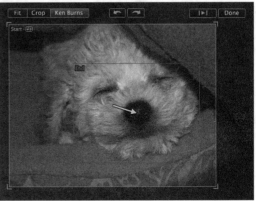

   ▼ Click "Fit" to make the photo fit the frame.

   ▼ Click "Crop" to resize and reposition the photo cropping.

   ▼ Click "Ken Burns" to apply a pan-and-zoom motion effect. A green rectangle determines the Start size and position of the photo. A red rectangle determines the End size and position. Click the red or green border to select and adjust that crop area.

   ▼ Click the red word, "End," to darken the cropped area of the photo and preview the ending crop.

   ▼ To swap the Start and End settings, click the double curved arrows next to the green word, "Start."

   ▼ Click the Play button to preview the entire clip.

   ▼ To remove the Ken Burns Effect, click "Fit" or "Crop."

3. Click "Done."

Add Transitions

A **transition** is a visual effect that creates a bridge from one scene to the next. iMovie '08 includes 12 different transitions.

Manually add a transition effect between two clips

1. Click the Transitions button (left) to open the Transitions browser in the bottom-right corner of the window (shown below). Move your pointer over a thumbnail in the browser to see a sample preview of the transition.

2. Drag a transition thumbnail to the Project browser and drop it between two clips. A Transition icon indicates that a transition is placed between the clips (circled below).

3. To adjust the duration of a transition, select the Transition icon, then from the Edit menu, choose "Set Duration...." In the dialog that opens (right), enter a duration, then choose if you want the duration change to apply to all transitions or just the selected transition. Click OK.

Transition icon.

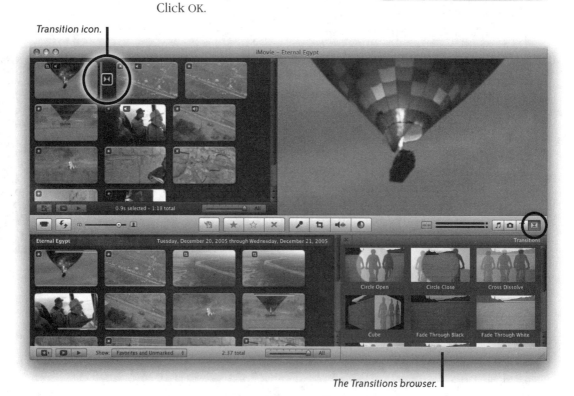

The Transitions browser.

Automatically add transitions between all clips

When you want transitions placed between all (or most) scenes, you can add them automatically.

1. Control-click in the Project browser. From the shortcut menu, choose "Project Properties…" to open the dialog shown on the right.

2. Checkmark "Add automatically."

3. From the "Transitions" pop-up menu, choose a transition style.

4. Adjust the "Transition Duration" slider to set the duration of the transition.

5. Click OK.

Another dialog opens (lower-right) that asks what you want to do to the ends of the clips in the project. A transition blends the end frames of one clip with the beginning frames of the next clip. If a transition has a one-second duration, it affects the last second of the first clip, and the first second of the next clip.

▼ "Overlap ends and shorten clip."
The overlapping video is used for the transition.

▼ "Extend ends and keep duration the same (where possible)." iMovie attempts to keep as much of the clip intact as possible by checking to see if any additional trimmed footage is available.

Remove automatically placed transitions

1. Control-click in the Project browser. From the shortcut menu, choose "Project Properties…" to open the dialog shown at the top of the page.

2. Uncheck "Add transitions" and click OK.

3. In the next dialog that opens (right), choose what you want to do with the existing transitions in the project.

▼ "Remove transitions and extend clip ends."
This recovers the frames used in the transitions.

▼ "Remove transitions and keep clip duration the same."
Shortened clips remain shortened.

▼ "Leave transitions in current locations."
This option seems to be the same as "Cancel."

4. Click OK.

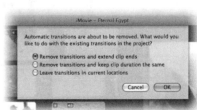

Advanced Audio Editing Techniques

Now that you know the basics of making a movie in iMovie '08, you're ready to learn some advanced techniques that can make movie editing more versatile and fun.

Extract audio from a clip

As you edit your movie, you might find that you want to use the audio track from a clip, but not the video. Or you might want to start a scene with a clip, using both its audio and video, then switch to different video while the same audio track continues to play. To make this kind of edit, you need to extract the audio from its video clip.

1. Select a clip (or a portion of a clip) in the Event browser or in the Project browser whose audio you want to extract. This clip is the source clip.

2. Hold down the Command and Shift keys as you drag the source clip and drop it on top of another clip (the target clip) in the Project browser. The extracted audio appears as a green audio marker below the target clip (below).

3. To adjust the audio of the target clip so the extracted audio can be heard over the target clip's original audio: Click the Adjust Audio button to open the Audio Adjustments window, then drag the "Volume" slider left to lower the target clip's volume.
   Or select the green extracted audio bar, then checkmark the "Ducking" option in the Adjust Audio window, then use the Ducking volume slider to adjust how low to set the ducked audio volume. The volume of any other audio will automatically decrease when audio from the extracted track is present.

The extracted audio.

In the example above, a boat video clip in the Event browser was selected, then its audio extracted by holding down the Command and Shift keys while dragging the clip to the same boat video clip in the Project browser. Now the boat clip audio is still matched with the boat video in the Project browser, but it's an external audio file that can be extended into the next clip. Ducking is set for the extracted audio, so the audio is easy to hear over the next clip.

Normalize audio in video clips

Sometimes video clips in a Project have a wide range of volumes. To make them all have the same volume, you *Normalize* the clip volumes.

1. Select a clip in the Project browser, then open the Audio Adjustments window (right).

2. Click "Normalize Clip Volume." Repeat for every clip you want to Normalize.

   To remove Normalization, select a clip, then click "Remove Normalization" in the Audio Adjustments window.

"Normalized" clips are tagged with this icon.

Copy audio or video adjustments and paste into other video clips

After you've made adjustments to a clip—audio, video, or cropping adjustments—you can copy and paste those adjustments to other clips.

1. Select a clip in the Event browser or the Project browser that includes adjustments you want to duplicate in another clip.

2. Copy the adjustments. From the Edit menu, choose "Copy." **Or** type Command C.

3. Select a clip in the Project browser into which you want to paste some or all of the copied adjustments.

4. From the Edit menu, choose "Paste Adjustments," then choose one of the following options:

   ▼ Choose "All" to paste video, audio, and cropping adjustments from the source clip.

   ▼ Choose "Video" to paste only video adjustments from the source clip.

   ▼ Choose "Audio" to paste only audio adjustments from the source clip.

   ▼ Choose "Crop" to paste only cropping adjustments from the source clip.

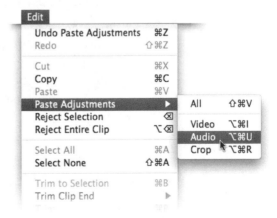

Trim audio clips

You can place multiple audio tracks in a movie Project, including music, sound effects, and voiceovers. When you want to use just a fraction of an audio track, you can **trim** the track to any length.

1. Select a music track that you've dragged to a video thumbnail in the Project browser, as shown below.

2. To shorten the track's ending, drag its right edge to the left.

3. To shorten the track from its beginning or end, open it in the Trim Clip view—from the Edit menu, choose "Trim…."

4. The track opens in the Trim Clip view, shown below. Drag the yellow handles left or right to select a portion of the track. The selected portion of the track is highlighted in purple. To preview your selection, click the Play button.

Trim Clip view also enables you to make a **slip edit.** Make a slip edit when you want the selected duration to stay set, but want to select another portion of the audio track. Press within the selection, then drag the highlighted selection left or right to make a new selection without changing the duration of the selection.

5. Click "Done."

Trim background audio tracks

You can place multiple background music tracks in a movie. iMovie lets you trim audio tracks to make them as short as you want.

1. From the Music and Sound Effects browser, drag a song to the background of the Project browser. Background audio files are shown as dark green shapes behind the video thumbnails (below).

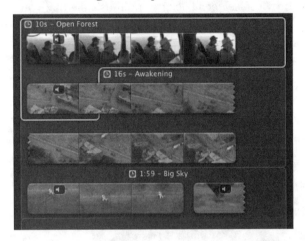

In this example, the Project browser contains three background music tracks. iMovie automatically cross-fades the end of one track with the beginning of the next track.

2. To change the duration of a background music file, click the Trim icon (the small clock shown above) to open the Trim Music window.

3. The Trim Music window (below) shows the entire music file, and highlights the part of the file that's currently being used (shown below). To adjust which part and how much of the music is used in the movie, drag either yellow handle left or right. The distance between the two yellow handles sets the duration of the clip.

   To keep the clip duration the same while selecting a different section of the music, drag the entire highlighted selection left or right. This technique is called a **slip edit.**

4. To preview the selection, click the Play button in the top-right corner.

5. Click "Done" to place your changes in the Project browser.

Pin a background audio track to a video clip

When you add a music track to the movie background, you can move it to start on any frame of any video clip, then pin it to that starting point. The music track will always start at that point in the video clip, even if you rearrange video clips in the project or trim the beginning of the music track.

1. In the Project browser, select a background music file that you placed in a movie.

2. Move your pointer over the top-left corner of the green-colored music region until it changes to a white hand icon (below).

3. Drag to the right until the playhead (the red vertical line) is over the exact frame where you want the music track to start playing. The current frame shows in both the browser thumbnail and in the Viewer.

   A pin icon appears (left) in the top-left corner of the music region to indicate the track is locked to a specific frame of video.

Arrange music tracks

You can rearrange the order of background music tracks in a Project.

1. From the Edit menu, choose "Arrange Music Tracks...."

2. In the dialog that opens (left), drag music tracks up or down in the bottom list to rearrange them.

   Any item in the top list is pinned to a video frame and cannot be moved, unless you unpin it. Select a pinned music track, then click the "Un-Pin Track" button. The track moves to the "Floating Music Tracks" list at the bottom of the dialog.

3. Click OK.

Advanced Video Editing Techniques

The following techniques provide more flexibility in your movie editing.

Show Advanced Tools

iMovie includes an Advanced Tools feature that enables a **dual mode toolbar** (Standard and Advanced modes) **keyword controls,** and advanced color adjustments in the Adjust Video tool.

To enable the Advanced Tools:

1. From the iMovie menu, choose "Preferences…."
2. Checkmark "Show Advanced Tools" at the bottom of the iMovie Preferences window.

With Advanced Tools enabled, the middle toolbar adds an Arrow button (high-lighted below) and a Keyword button (the key icon). Click the white arrow button to switch to Normal mode for editing (see the following page).

Marking tools.

Move Selection to Project.   *Adjust Video tool.*

If Advanced Tools are enabled, when you select a thumbnail in the Event browser, the Move tool and the Marking tool buttons in the toolbar change their appearance (above) to show a plus sign (+). This indicates that you can select one of these buttons, then select video in the Event browser, auto-matically applying that button's adjustment.

When you mark video frames as Favorites or Rejects, a horizontal color bar indicates the marked frames (right). To select previously marked frames while Advanced Tools are enabled, choose the white Arrow tool, then click the horizontal greenbar (Favorites) or the horizontal red bar (Rejected frames). A yellow selection highlights the marked frames.

Advanced Tools also provide additional color adjustments in the Adjust Video tool. Select a video clip, then click the Adjust Video button. The Video Adjustments window contains three additional sliders for Red Gain, Green Gain, and Blue Gain color adjustments.

Using the dual mode toolbar

When "Show Advanced Tools" is checkmarked in Preferences, the toolbar is in **dual mode.** Use both **Standard mode** and **Advanced mode** for *marking* clips and *moving* your video selections to the Project browser, then decide which mode you like best.

Standard mode: In Standard mode, you select a video clip first, then select a tool from the toolbar to mark the clip (as a Favorite, Reject, or Unmarked). To place video in a Project, select a range of video in the Event browser first, then click one of the tools in the toolbar to mark it as a Favorite, as Unmarked, or as Rejected. Then drag the selection to the Project browser. Or click the "Move Selection to Project" button. This is the same procedure you would use if "Show Advanced Tools" were not enabled in iMovie Preferences.

Advanced mode: In Advanced mode, you select a tool first, then select video that you want the tool to affect. This is a fast and efficient way to mark Favorites and Rejects, and to move selected video frames from the Event browser to the Project browser.

1. Select one of these Advanced tool buttons in the toolbar:
   Move Selection to Project, Favorite, Unmark, or Reject.

2. Skim over the video thumbnails in the Event browser to preview your footage. An icon associated wth the active tool button appears next to the pointer (shown below).

When the "Reject" tool is selected in the toolbar, this red X icon appears next to the pointer in the Event browser.

3. When the pointer is over the frame where you want to start your selection, press-drag to select a range of video frames (above). The video selection is automatically and instantly marked with the active button's mark—Favorite, Unmarked, or Rejected.

   If "Move Selection to Project" is the active button in the toolbar when you make a video selection in the Event browser (as shown below), the selection is instantly moved to the Project browser.

When the "Move Selection to Project" tool is selected in the toolbar, this icon appears next to the pointer in the Event browser.

Split an existing clip

To insert new video right in the middle of an existing clip, you can *split* the existing clip.

1. In the Project browser, drag to choose the portion of an existing clip that you want to split away from the rest of the clip (below-left).

2. From the Edit menu, choose "Split Clip." iMovie splits the clip into two separate clips (below-right).

3. Drag and drop another video clip between the split clips.

   To rejoin split clips, make sure the two clips are next to each other, as shown below-right, then from the Edit menu, choose "Join Clip."

Create a sepia tone effect

Create unlimited variations of sepia tone effects in a clip.

1. In iMovie Preferences, checkmark "Show Advanced Tools."

2. Select a clip in the Event browser or the Project browser.

3. Click the Adjust Video button to open the Video Adjustments window. The Playhead in the clip thumbnail appears as a red vertical line with a red dot in the center. Drag the red dot to the frame you want to use as a preview in the Viewer as you create a sepia tone effect. A Color icon appears next to the pointer (right) while the Video Adjustments window is open.

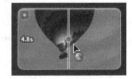

4. In the Video Adjustments window (right), drag the "Saturation" slider all the way left (0%). Then experiment with adjustments of one or more of the Gain sliders (Red, Green, and Blue).

5. When you're satisfied with the adjustments, click "Done."

6. Click "Revert to Original" at any time to undo your adjustments.

Color adjustments are visible in the Viewer, but not in thumbnails.

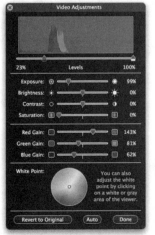

Color adjustments are shown in the Viewer.

Quickly add short clips to the Project browser

To make a fast-paced music video (or any kind of movie), set up iMovie so that a single click of a thumbnail in the Event browser selects a preset duration of video, then automatically adds the selection to a Project.

1. Select the Edit tool (shown on the left), also known as the "Move Selection to Project" tool.

2. Click a video clip in the Event browser. iMovie selects four seconds of video, starting at the point where you clicked, then automatically places the selection in the current Project.

   By default, clicking a clip in the Event browser automatically selects four seconds of video. To change the amount of video that's automatically selected with a click, from the iMovie menu, choose Preferences. Then choose "Clicking in Events browser selects" (circled below). Adjust the slider to a duration between one and ten seconds.

   Notice also that "Show Advanced Tools" needs to be selected for this technique to work. Otherwise, clicking will select the amount of video you've set with the slider, but the selection will not automatically be placed in the Project browser.

Click here to enable a single click in the Events browser to select an entire clip.

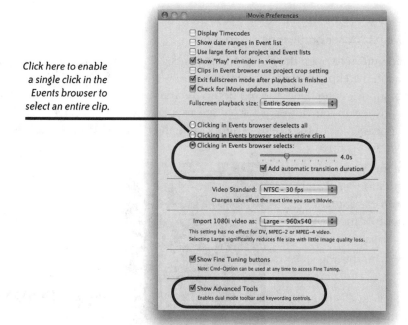

If the "Clicking in Events" preference is set to select a certain number of seconds of video, you can override this setting and select an entire clip when you click it by pressing the Command key when you click on a clip.

Remove part of a clip in the Project browser

Drag across a clip to select any portion of it, then press Delete. The original source clip in the Event browser is not affected.

Fine tune the beginning or end frame of a clip

1. Go to iMovie Preferences, then select "Show Fine Tuning buttons."
2. Move your pointer over a clip in the Project browser to show the Fine Tuning buttons in the bottom-left and bottom-right corners.

Fine Tuning button.

3. Click the Fine Tuning button in the bottom-left corner to change the starting frame. Click the button in the bottom-right corner to change the ending frame. An orange handle appears (above-right) when you click one of the Fine Tuning buttons.
4. Drag the handle left or right to *extend* or *trim* the video clip. Release the mouse to set the new start or end frame. You can add or remove up to one second of video. If you try to extend the beginning or end of a clip when the original source clip doesn't contain any extra, unused video, the orange handle turns red and can't be dragged out beyond the clip's edge.

Alternate access to the Fine Tuning feature

1. If the "Show Fine Tuning buttons" option is not checkmarked in iMovie Preferences, access the Fine Tuning feature by pressing Command-Option as you move your pointer over a clip in the Project browser. As the pointer nears a clip's edge, an orange handle appears.
2. Keep pressing the Command-Option keys until you press the orange handle to drag it.

   The white numbers that appear next to a handle as you drag it show how many frames are being added or removed (the top number), and the adjusted clip duration in seconds (the bottom number).

Trim the start or end of a clip one frame at a time

This shortcut tip is similar to opening a clip in the "Trim Clip" pane, then dragging the left and right selection handles inward towards the middle to trim frames from the beginning or end of the clip, except that you have the precision of trimming one frame at a time.

To trim frames from the beginning of a video clip, one frame at a time:

1. Move the pointer over the left edge of a clip in the Project browser so that the vertical red line (the Playhead) is near the left edge of the clip (below).

2. Press the Option key as you tap the Right Arrow on your keyboard. In effect, this drags the left selection handle to the right, one frame at a time. To add frames back in, Option-tap the Left Arrow.

   The current frame is shown in the Viewer.

To trim frames from the end of a video clip, one frame at a time:

1. Move the pointer over the right edge of a clip in the Project browser so that the Playhead is near the right edge of the clip (below).

2. Press the Option key as you tap the Left Arrow on your keyboard. This drags the right selection handle to the left, one frame at a time. To add frames back in, Option-tap the Right Arrow.

   The Viewer shows the current frame.

Delete a selection

To delete a specific selection of video in the Event browser or the Project browser, make a selection, then tap the Delete key.

Delete an entire clip

To delete an entire clip, click it, then press Option-Delete. Even if the click made just a partial selection of the clip, the entire clip is deleted.

Add a Still Frame to your Project

Capture a single frame of video and use it like a photo. It's a great way to end a movie, with the last frame of the last scene frozen on the screen as credits roll past, or as the screen fades to black. Or you might want to create a slide show effect using still frames from video clips. Switching from video to still images with a Ken Burns effect in the middle of a movie can have a strong emotional impact and add visual interest to your Project.

1. Position your pointer over a frame of video in the Event browser or the Project browser.

2. Control-click the frame, then from the shortcut menu choose "Add Still Frame to Project."

   To add or edit a Ken Burns motion effect, or to crop the image, click the Crop tool in the middle toolbar. To remove cropping or a Ken Burns effect, click the "Fit" button in the Crop window. See page 131 for more about cropping and the Ken Burns effect.

3. Still frames are automatically placed at the end of the project. Drag the still frame to any location you want in the Project.

4. By default, new stilll frames have a duration of four seconds. You can change the duration, from a minimum of 0.3 seconds to a maximum of 60 seconds.

   To change the duration of a still frame, do one of the following:

   ▼ Click the Trim button (the clock icon) at the bottom of the clip. A dialog opens for you to enter a duration.

   ▼ Drag in the still photo clip to select the amount of duration you want to delete, then from the Edit menu, choose "Delete Selection."
   Or make a selection of frames, then press the Delete key.
   Or Control-click on a selection of frames, then choose "Delete Selection."

   ▼ Control-click on a still frame, then choose "Set Duration."

   ▼ Select a still frame clip, then from the Edit menu, choose "Set Duration."

If you need a still frame duration of more than 60 seconds for a title or movie credits, make copies of the still frame and place them next to each other in the Project browser. Select and copy the existing still frame (Command C), position the playhead at the end of the existing still frame, then paste (Command V). Repeat the copy and paste procedure as many times as necessary to stretch the still frame duration to the desired length.

Tagging and Filtering with Keywords

Keywords are not just for photos. Now you can apply keywords to entire video clips, or to just a selected range of frames within a clip. Then you can filter the Event browser to show just the keyword-marked clips you want to see. For large projects, it's a nice way to unclutter the limited workspace provided by the Event Library.

Use Auto-Apply to tag video with keywords

1. Make sure iMovie's Advanced Tools are enabled: from the iMovie menu, choose "Preferences...," then select "Show Advanced Tools" (see page 139).

2. Click the Keyword button in the toolbar (left) to open the Keywords palette (below). Default keywords are listed in the palette. To create your own keywords, click in the "New Keyword" text field, type a new keyword, then click "Add" (**or** press Return).

   To edit a keyword, double-click it, then type your changes.

   To remove a keyword from the list, select it, then click "Remove."

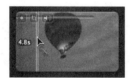

3. Click the "Auto-Apply" tab at the top of the palette, then checkmark the keywords you want to apply to video selections.

4. In the Event browser, move the pointer over a clip. A key icon appears next to the pointer (left-top). Click and drag to select an entire clip or just a portion of a clip.

   As you drag, the selected portion of video turns blue (left-bottom). When you release the mouse, the keyword-marked portion of video is marked with a horizontal blue bar along the top edge of the clip.

Use the Inspector pane to tag video with keywords

You can also use the Inspector pane to apply keywords and show which keywords have been applied to a video clip.

1. Click the Inspector tab at the top of the Keywords palette to show the Inspector pane (below).

2. Click and drag in a thumbnail (in the Event browser or Project browser) to select a portion or all of a clip.

3. In the Inspector pane, checkmark the keywords that you want to apply to the selected footage. Uncheck a keyword in the list to remove it from the video selection.

Create a new keyword using the Inspector pane

1. Select a range of video that you want to tag with a keyword.

2. Type a new keyword in the "Keyword" text field.

3. Click "Add to Clip." The new keyword is added to the selected video frames *and* to the list in the Keywords palette.

Use the Inspector pane to remove keywords from video clips

1. Select a thumbnail in the Event browser or Project browser that's tagged with one or more keywords. Keywords applied to the selected clip are checkmarked in the Inspector list, and they also appear near the bottom of the palette (below).

2. In the Inspector list, uncheck the keywords that you want removed from the selected video.

3. To remove all keywords applied to the video selection, click the "Remove All" button.

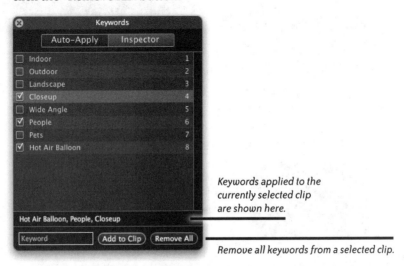

Keywords applied to the currently selected clip are shown here.

Remove all keywords from a selected clip.

Show a clip's keywords in the browser

1. From the View menu, choose "Playhead Info."

2. In the Event browser or Project browser, skim over thumbnails with your pointer. iMovie displays the clip's creation date and time, keywords, and clip duration (below).

Use shortcuts to apply keywords

To the right of the first nine keywords in the Keywords palette is a keyboard shortcut number that iMovie has automatically assigned.

- ▼ To apply a keyword quickly, select a video clip, then type the shortcut number of the keyword you want to apply.

- ▼ To change a keyword's shortcut number, drag the keyword in the list to another numbered row. The keyword's shortcut becomes that row's number.

Remove a keyword from part of a tagged video clip

When a selection of video has been tagged with a keyword, a horizontal blue bar shows the range of frames that are tagged. To untag a portion of the clip, click and drag to select the frames you want untagged, then uncheck the keyword's checkbox in the Keywords palette.

A keyword has been removed from the selected frames.

The blue bar indicates frames that are still tagged with a keyword.

Filter the Event browser using keywords

Tag video clips with descriptive keywords, then select one or more of those keywords to filter the clips in the Event browser. Filtering makes it easy to find keyword-tagged clips in the Event browser of a large project.

1. In the Event Library, choose an Event from the list that you want to filter in the Event browser.

2. Click the "Show or hide the Keyword Filtering pane" button in the bottom toolbar (right, and below). The Keyword Filtering pane appears left of the Event browser and contains a list of all keywords.

Show or hide the Keyword Filtering pane.

3. Checkmark keywords in the Keyword Filtering pane you want to use to filter the selected Event.

4. At the bottom of the Keyword Filtering pane, click the "Any" button to show clips tagged with *any* of the selected keywords. Click the "All" button to show clips tagged with *all* of the selected keywords.

5. At the bottom of the Keyword Filtering pane, click the "Include" button to *show* clips tagged with selected keywords. Click the "Exclude" button to *hide* clips tagged with selected keywords.

6. To turn Keyword filtering off, uncheck "Filter by Keyword" in the top part of the Keyword Filtering pane.

7. To hide the Keyword Filtering pane, click the Show/hide Keyword Filtering pane button.

In the example below, Keyword Filtering limits the Event browser to showing only clips tagged with the keyword "Hot Air Balloon." The blue bars indicate clips that are tagged with the selected keyword. The green bars indicate video that has been marked as "Favorites." The horizontal orange bars indicate video clips that have already been placed in the current Project.

The Keyword Filtering pane.

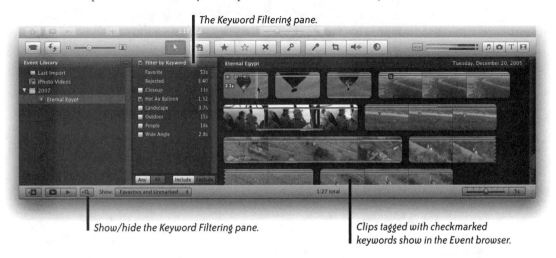

Show/hide the Keyword Filtering pane.

Clips tagged with checkmarked keywords show in the Event browser.

Sharing Your Movies

iMovie '08 provides a variety of ways to share a movie: Create a final movie file that plays on an iPod, an iPhone, or an AppleTV; uublish your movie on your .Mac Web Gallery or on YouTube; copy it to iTunes; share a movie using the Media Browser to make it available in iDVD and iWeb; export a movie in different formats, then copy it to media that you can send to others, such as a CD or DVD.

Share with iTunes

Send the selected movie Project to iTunes to make it accessible for viewing on your computer, or to sync it to an iPod or iPhone.

1. In the Project list, select a Project to send to iTunes.

2. From the Share menu (shown on the left), choose "iTunes...."

3. In the iTunes dialog that opens (below), choose one or more sizes for your movie (Tiny, Mobile, Medium, or Large).

   The blue dots in the chart indicate the sizes that are suitable for play-back on the various devices shown in the chart.

   Or click one of the device icons at the top of the chart columns to automatically choose the correct size for playback on that device.

4. Click "Publish." A dialog sheet appears that shows the progress of the "Preparing project" process.

   After iMovie has rendered the movie to the selected sizes, iTunes opens with your movie placed in the "Movies" album.

   To play your movie, double-click it in iTunes.

Share with the Media Browser

To make your movie accessible from within iDVD or iWeb, from the Share menu, choose "Media Browser...."

1. In the Project list, select a Project to send to iDVD's Media Browser.

2. From the Share menu, choose "Media Browser...."

3. In the dialog that opens (below), choose one or more sizes for your movie.

4. Click "Publish." A dialog sheet appears that shows the progress of the "Preparing project" process.

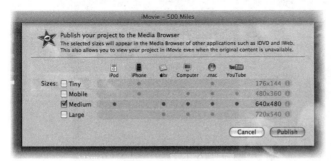

After iMovie has rendered the movie to the selected size, nothing noticeable happens. However, the movie is now available in the Media Browser of both iDVD (DVD authoring software) and iWeb (web site authoring software).

Share your movie on YouTube

Upload your movie to YouTube, the world's most popular video web site.

1. In the Project list, select a Project to send to YouTube.

2. From the Share menu, choose "YouTube...."

3. In the dialog that opens, enter your YouTube account information and information about your movie (right), then click "Next" and follow the instructions on the screen.
   If you don't have a YouTube account, click "Add..." to get one.

iMovie does the rest. YouTube limits movies to 10 minutes and 100 MB.

Projects that are published to .Mac Web Gallery or YouTube have a Publish icon placed to the right of the Project name in the Project browser. Next to the Publish icon, a Size icon indicates the sizes that have been published (Tiny, Mobile, Medium, or Large).

Share movies on your .Mac Web Gallery

If you have a .Mac account, you can publish your movies to your .Mac Web Gallery. Movies are uploaded to your iDisk (your .Mac account storage space on Apple's servers).

1. In the Project list, select a movie Project to share.

2. From the Share menu, choose ".Mac Web Gallery...."

3. In the dialog that opens, enter a title and description for your movie (shown below).

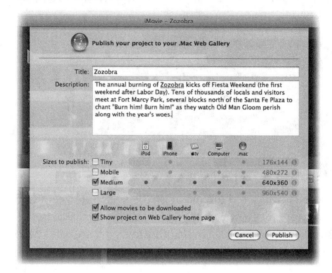

4. Choose a size to publish.

5. Checkmark "Allow movies to be downloaded" if you want others to be able to copy the movie from the web site to their computers. Checkmark "Show project on Web Gallery home page" to put the movie's thumbnail link on your .Mac Web Gallery home page.

6. Click "Publish." After iMovie finishes uploading your movie to the Web Gallery, a dialog opens (below) to show the movie's URL (web address) and to provide buttons to send email ("Tell a Friend"), visit the movie web page ("View"), or return to your Desktop ("OK").

Movies and photos published to your .Mac Web Gallery are published to the .Mac account that is enabled in the .Mac pane of System Preferences.

Export a QuickTime movie

To create a copy of your movie that you can save anywhere on your computer, and access it without having to go through iTunes or the Media Browser in iLife applications (such as iDVD or iWeb), use the "Export Movie" command. The QuickTime movie that's created is accessible through the Finder.

1. In the Project list, select a movie Project to share.

2. From the Share menu, choose "Export Movie...."

3. In the dialog that opens (below), type a name for the movie file and choose a location where you want to save it.

4. Choose one of the size options:
   Tiny: 176 x 144 pixels.
   Mobile: 480 x 272 pixels.
   Medium: Varies from 640 x 480 pixels (standard aspect ratio) to 640 x 360 pixels (widescreen).
   Large: 960 x 540 pixels (widescreen).
   If a large size is unavailable (dimmed), the original movie's resolution is not high enough to render in that size.

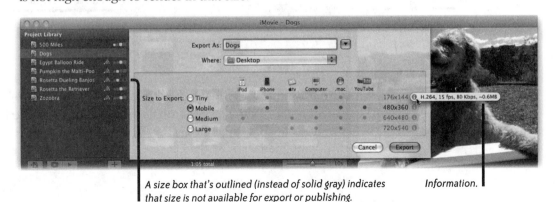

A size box that's outlined (instead of solid gray) indicates that size is not available for export or publishing.

Information.

The blue dots below each device icon indicate which movie sizes are recommended for that device. Hover the pointer over the Information icons ("i") to reveal a text pop-up (above-right) of additional information about the various size options. The items in the dialog are:

H.264: The video compression used in the exported movie.

fps: The frame rate of the movie (frames per second).

Mbps (or Kbps): The maximum rate the movie can stream over the Internet in Megabits per second (or kilobits per second).

MB: The movie file size in megabytes.

5. Click "Export."

Export using QuickTime

The export option of "Export using QuickTime…" is similar to the "Export Movie…" option—it creates a movie file and exports it to the Finder, but provides many more format options to choose from (all of which are compatible with QuickTime). This sharing option is for experts who want to customize their export settings.

1. In the Project list, select a movie Project to share.
2. From the Share menu, choose "Export using QuickTime…."
3. In the dialog that opens (below), type a name for the exported file. iMovie automatically adds a file format extension to the name (.mov, for example), based on the file format you choose in the "Export" pop-up menu. From the "Where" pop-up menu, choose a location where you want to save the exported movie.

Choose a file format for the exported file.

Choose custom settings for the selected export format.

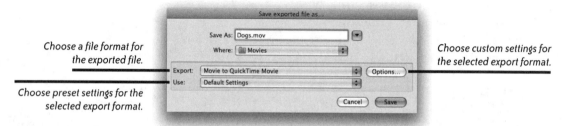

Choose preset settings for the selected export format.

4. From the "Export" pop-up menu (below-left), choose a file format.

    The content of the "Options…" button and the "Use" pop-up menu (below-right) change, depending on the file format chosen in the "Export" pop-up menu. To use default settings for export formats (recommended for most exports), leave the "Use" pop-up menu set to "Default."

5. After choosing the settings you want, click "Save."

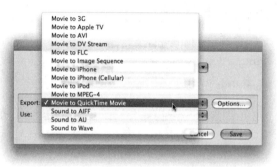

File format choices in the "Export" pop-up menu.

Preset settings in the "Use" pop-up menu.

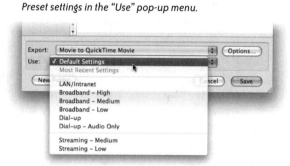

The "Export" pop-up menu in the "Save exported file as…" window provides the following file formats to choose from (all are compatible with QuickTime):

Movie to 3G: A video format for GSM-based mobile phones. GSM is a popular standard for mobile phones.

Movie to Apple TV: Uses the MPEG-4 video format, optimized for playback through an Apple TV device on a widescreen TV.

MOVIE TO AVI: A Microsoft video format.

Movie to DV Stream: Digital Video format. High quality. Compatible with many video editing applications.

Movie to FLC: An animation format used by AutoDesk Animator Pro.

Movie to Image Sequence: Export a movie as individual still images. Options let you choose the number of images created (8–30 frames per second), the file format, and more.

Use this export option to quickly *capture many still frames* from a movie, or to create a *time-lapse movie.* See pages 156–157 for details.

Movie to iPhone: Export a movie file optimized for playback on Apple iPhone's full-size screen.

Movie to iPhone (Cellular): Export a smaller movie, optimized for playback on smaller mobile phone screens.

Movie to iPod: Export a movie optimized for playback on a full-screen iPod.

Movie to MPEG-4: Export a movie using the MPEG-4 format, the same format used for "Movie to iPod," "Movie to iPhone," and "Movie to Apple TV." This selection, however, provides "Options" that can be custom set.

Movie to QuickTime Movie: Exports a movie in QuickTime format, providing many preset and custom settings.

Sound to AIFF: Exports only the audio track. AIFF is an Apple audio format.

Sound to AU: Exports only the audio track. AU is an Apple format used by applications such as GarageBand, Soundtrack Pro, Logic Express, Logic Pro, Final Cut Pro and most third-party audio software applications developed for Mac OS X.

Sound to Wave: Exports only the audio track. Wave is a Microsoft audio format, but is compatible with Mac.

Export Final Cut XML: A format compatible with Final Cut Pro and Final Cut Express software (professional-level video editing).

Export movie to Image Sequence

There are a couple of reasons why you might want to export a movie (or a portion of a movie) as an Image Sequence (many individual still images): (1) You may need one or more frames of video captured from a scene, and want to browse carefully through dozens (or hundreds) of frames to pick the perfect one. (2) You might want to create a time-lapse effect, such as slow-motion or fast-motion.

Create an Image Sequence

1. Create a new Project in the Project Library, then drag video clips you want to capture as still images into the new Project.
   Depending on your frames per second setting (Step 3), and your Project's duration, iMovie could create thousands of still images. So try to keep either the frame rate or Project duration low.

2. From the Share menu, choose "Export using QuickTime...."
   In the "Save exported file as…" window (below-left),
   set the "Export" pop-up menu to "Movie to Image Sequence."

   Create a New Folder for the exported image sequence so you can access it easily. If you don't see the "New Folder" button, click the blue disclosure triangle button (circled below-left).

3. Click the "Options…" button (circled below-left) to open the "Export Image Sequence Settings" dialog (below-right).
   From the "Format" pop-up menu, choose a file format for the Image Sequence, then set a frames per second frame rate.

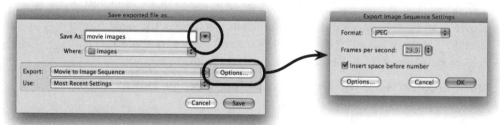

4. Click the "Options…" button (circled above-right) to show options for the format selected in the "Format" pop-up menu.

5. Click OK to return to the "Save exported file as…" window (above-left), then click "Save."

The exported Image Sequence is placed in the designated location.

To preview an Image Sequence:

You can preview an Image Sequence in Preview or QuickTime.

In **Preview,** from the File menu, choose "Open...." Choose the folder that contains the Image Sequence, then click "Open."

In **QuickTime,** from the File menu, choose "Open Image Sequence...." Choose the folder that contains the Image Sequence, then click "Open." For details, see "Create a time-lapse movie" below.

Create a time-lapse movie

1. Open QuickTime, then from the File menu, choose "Open Image Sequence...."

2. In the window that opens, select a folder that contains an image sequence, then click the "Open" button to show all the image files in the image sequence.

3. Select any file in the image sequence folder (to enable the "Open" button again), then click "Open" (circled below-left).

4. In the "Image Sequence Settings" dialog that appears (below-right), select a frame rate, then click OK.

   To create a fast-motion effect (dramatic, billowing cloud formations, for example), select a high frame rate, such as 60 frames per second. For a slow-motion effect, select a low frames per second rate.

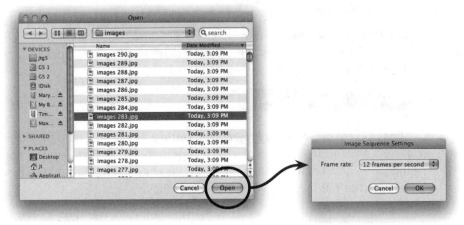

QuickTime processes the data and opens your movie in a QuickTime Player window. Save the movie (or export it) to your Desktop (or to any location on your computer) so you can play it or use it in an iMovie Project, iTunes, or any QuickTime-compatible application, such as iWeb, iDVD, iPhoto, or Mail.

iMovie Preferences

Experiment with different settings in the Preferences window to determine what works best for you. Click the items you want to enable.

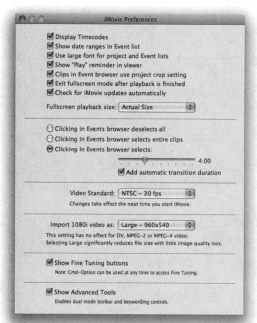

Display Timecodes: Show time durations in the format of *minutes:seconds:frames* (1:20:05, for example, as shown below). Uncheck this option to show durations as *minutes:seconds* (no *frame* count).

Show date ranges in Event list: Add dates beneath Event names that span the time period in which the video was created (below).

Use large font for project and Event lists: Enlarge the font in the Event Library and Project Library. The size change is not significant, but it could help if your eyes aren't perfect.

Show "Play" reminder in viewer: When you pause your pointer over a clip, a pop-up message appears in the Viewer that says "Press the space bar or double-click to Play" (shown below).

Clips in Event browser use Project crop setting: The aspect ratio of your Project and the aspect ratio of source clips in the Event browser may not be the same. Checkmark this option so the Viewer previews Event clips in the same aspect ratio setting as the Project settings.

To set a Project's aspect ratio, from the File menu, choose "Project Properties…," then from the "Aspect Ratio" pop-up menu, choose 4:3 (Standard), 3:2 (iPhone), or 16:9 (Widescreen). In the "Initial Video Placement" pop-up menu, choose "Fit in Frame."

If the source clips in the Event browser use different aspect ratios, choose "Crop" from the "Initial Video Placement" pop-up menu. iMovie crops clips when necessary to keep the shape and size of clips consistent in the Viewer.

Exit full screen mode after playback is finished: Checkmark this if you always want to exit full screen mode after playback is finished. For presentations, it can be nice to uncheck this, leaving the movie and its timeline on the screen and accessible.

Check for iMovie updates automatically: When this item is checkmarked, iMovie checks online for software updates every time you open it. If you have a broadband connection, this is a non-intrusive feature. If you have a dial-up connection, uncheck this feature to avoid unpleasant interruptions.

Fullscreen playback size: From the pop-up menu, choose what "fullscreen" really means (Entire Screen, Double Size, Actual Size, or Half Size). If you have a large screen, true full screen playback of small formats looks bad. Set the size to Actual or Double to fill the entire screen with black while the movie size you selected floats in the middle of the screen.

Clicking in Events: Choose the behavior for a single click in the Events browser—deselects all clips, selects an entire clip, or selects a preset number of seconds of video. If you choose the behavior option of selecting a preset amount of video, drag the duration slider to select how many seconds of video will be automatically selected by a single click in the Event browser (choose between one and ten seconds, in half-second increments).

Add automatic transition duration: A transition between two clips uses frames from the end of one clip and the beginning of another, which shortens the duration of each clip. Checkmark this Preference item to make iMovie add enough extra frames to the preset amount of video selection to enable the clip selection to retain the preset amount of duration after a transition is added to one or both ends of the clip.

Video Standard: Choose the video standard you want to use. NTSC is the standard for North America, Japan, and various other countries. PAL is the standard for most of Europe, Asia, Australia, the Middle East, and various other countries. NTSC video is recorded at 29.97 frame per second. PAL video is recorded at 25 frame per second.

The NTSC standard of 29.97 frames per second is often called 30 fps.

Import 1080i video as: Choose "Large – 960x540" or "Full – 1920x1080." This option applies only if you're importing high definition 1080i video (1080 vertical scan lines, interlaced). Unless you plan to export the video to Final Cut Pro, or use the video for broadcasting, you should choose "Large" to dramatically reduce file size.

Show Fine Tuning buttons: The Fine Tuning buttons let you easily adjust the beginning and end points of clips. See page 143.

Show Advanced Tools: Adds extra functionality and tools to the toolbar. See page 139.

iMovie Tips

The following items are some iMovie tips that we find most useful.

Reposition the text in a Title

When you choose a Title style, you might not be completely satisfied with the placement of the text. Some minor adjustments can be made to some of the Title styles.

The movie clip shown below uses the Title style of "Lower Third." To raise the text to the top of the frame, click to the right of the title text, then press Option-Return to add a blank line below the existing text (which raises the title one line). Keep pressing Option-Return until the text is as high as you want. In this example, the subtitle text was unnecessary and deleted.

The original Title template.

To raise the Title, place the cursor at the end of the line and press Option-Return.

The final Title placement.

Learn keyboard shortcuts for fast editing

As you edit a movie, knowing just the most basic keyboard shortcuts can really speed up your work. If you forget a shortcut, hover the pointer over a tool until the shortcut tip appears.

To mark video as Favorites or Rejects:

Make a selection in the Event browser, then tap "F" to mark as "Favorite."
Tap "R" to mark selected video as "Rejected."
Tap "U" to unmark video that is marked as a "Favorite" or "Reject."

To access tools in the toolbar:

For the Selection Arrow, press the Escape or Return key.
For the Voiceover tool, type "O."
For the Crop, Rotate, and Ken Burns tool, type "C."
For the "Adjust Audio" tool, type "A."
For the "Adjust Video" tool, type "V."

To show or hide the Music and Sound Effects browser, press Command 1.
To show or hide the Photos browser, press Command 2.
To show or hide the Titles browser, press Command 3.
To show or hide the Transitions browser, press Command 4.

Trim to selection: a shortcut

You can trim Project clips in the Trim Clip pane (page 123), but it's easier and faster to use a shortcut.

Drag inside a clip to select the range of frames you want to keep, then from the Edit menu, choose "Trim to Selection."

Or Control-click on the clip, then choose "Trim to Selection."

Or just press the keyboard shortcut, Command-B.

Select a range of video, then press Command-B.

Duplicate transitions

If you've already placed a transition between two clips, you can copy that transition and its settings and paste it into another position in the Project.

1. Click a transition in a Project to select it, then from the Edit menu, choose "Copy" (or use the keyboard shortcut Command-C).

2. Place your pointer between two clips, then paste the transition into that position—from the Edit menu, choose "Paste."
    Or press Command-V to paste.

    You can also Option-drag a transition to create a copy of the original transition and drop it between two clips. As you drag across the clips, a vertical green bar appears to show where the transition can be placed (shown below).

Option-drag a transition to a new position. The green Add icon (+) indicates a copy of the transition is being added at the green bar.

Duplicate titles

You can Option-drag an existing title on top of another clip to create a copy of the title. This might be helpful if you've made a lot of modifications to a title style (font, font size, font color) that you want to use as a caption style for other clips. Rather than re-style multiple titles, copy the original, drag and drop it on a clip, then edit its text.

Option-drag an existing title on another clip to make a copy. The blue region indicates the frames affected by the title.

To play the title over the entire clip, drag it to the center of the clip. When the entire clip turns blue, release.

Unpublish a movie Project

If you've published a movie Project to your .Mac Web Gallery, to the Media Browser, or to YouTube, you can unpublish it through the Share menu.

1. Select the movie you want to unpublish.

2. From the Share menu, choose one of the "Remove" options:
   Remove from iTunes…
   Remove from Media Browser…
   Remove from .Mac…
   Remove from YouTube…

   Publishing options that have not been used for the selected movie are dimmed in the menu, leaving only published venues to choose.

3. In the dialog that opens (below), checkmark the movie size you want to remove. In this example, two sizes were published to the Media Browser. Sizes that weren't published are dimmed.

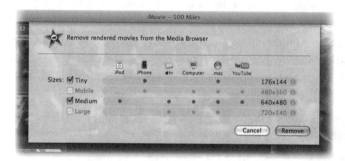

Navigate a movie in full screen mode

 When you click the Play Full Screen button (left), the movie starts a full screen playback from its beginning.

To make the preview *fill* the screen, press F1 or F4.

To show a *full-size* preview (right), press F2.

To show a *small* preview, press F3.

Move your mouse to make a timeline appear below the movie preview.

Double-click anywhere in the timeline to start the playback at that point.

The Space Saver feature

Reclaim storage space on your computer by having iMovie move unused video, and clips marked as rejected, to the Trash.

1. In the Event Library, select the Event, or the year, you want to rid of unused video (right).

2. From the File menu, choose "Space Saver...."

3. In the dialog that opens (right), checkmark one or more of the criteria to use to determine if a video clip is moved to the Trash: "Not added to any project," "Not marked as Favorite," and "Not marked with a keyword."

   If you've added clips to a Project that are not marked as Favorites, or have not been marked with a keyword, then only checkmark the "Not added to any project" item.

4. Click "Reject and Review." All clips in the selected Event that meet the chosen criteria are marked as Rejected (a horizontal red line marks the clip). The Event browser view changes to "Rejected Only" so you can review the video that's been marked and is ready to move to the Trash.

   If you see video clips that you don't want to remove, select them, then click the Unmark button in the toolbar (right).

    *The Unmark button.*

5. Click "Move Rejected to Trash" in the top-right corner of the Event browser. The rejected clips are moved to the Trash in the Dock. To delete the files permanently from the Trash and reclaim hard disk space, empty the Trash.

If there's a possibilty that you might want access to all of your original imported source clips later, do not use this Space Saver feature.

Move Rejected to Trash.

The Event browser view changes to "Rejected Only" and shows only rejected clips.

The Publish bar

When you select a movie in the Project Library that has been published to YouTube or to your .Mac Web Gallery, a Publish bar appears at the top of the Project browser (below). The bar identifies where the movie is published, and provides a link to "Tell a friend" (an email form opens), and a link to "Visit" the published movie.

Published to YouTube.   Published to .Mac Web Gallery.

Print an Event or a Project or save as a PDF

For some projects, it might be useful to have a printed copy, or a PDF, of the Event or Project thumbnails.

1. Click in the Event browser or the Project browser. The one you choose is the one whose thumbnails are used to create a PDF.

2. From the File menu, choose "Print Event…," or "Print Project…," depending on which browser you chose in Step 1.

3. In the dialog that opens, choose "PDF," "Preview," or "Print."

Choose "Preview" so you'll know if you need to go back to iMovie and make adjustments to the thumbnail sizes and frames per thumbnail setting.

Print the Event or Project thumbnails, or save as PDF to send to others.

iMovie Alerts

At some point you might see a yellow triangular Alert icon at the beginning clip in the Project browser. Hover your pointer over the icon and a text alert appears that says, "This clip's media files are not currently available." This just means the source video—the original imported clips—can't be found in the Event Library, or shown in the Event browser.

 **iDVD**

iDVD doesn't help you *edit* a movie—it *assembles* movies that have already been edited into a beautiful presentation with built-in navigation controls that you can burn to a DVD and play in a computer or TV's DVD player. iDVD projects can contain multiple movies and slideshows, just like commercial DVDs.

iDVD can create slideshows from still photos. You can even add a movie to a slideshow. Because iDVD is closely integrated with other iLife applications, it's easy to access iMovie, iPhoto, or iTunes from within iDVD to add various types of content to a project.

The same disc that you create for your movies and slideshows can also deliver other types of content to anyone's computer: PDF files, high-resolution photos, archived files, web sites, and almost any other type of digital file you want to include on the disc. Since DVDs are not platform-specific, they work on any Mac or PC that has a DVD drive.

Creating a DVD interface and navigation system and burning a disc might sound complicated, but it's really as simple as this:

1. Select a theme for your menus.
2. Drag media files to the menu.
3. Customize some of the design elements (such as renaming links, or changing the appearance of buttons).
4. Burn a disc.

FYI: In the world of DVD design and authoring, the term "menu" refers to the DVD interface in which users click on links to play specific movies, movie scenes, slideshows, or to show submenus that provide links to more content.

When you open iDVD, choose one of the project types in the start window.

iDVD Requirements and Specifications

If your Mac has a SuperDrive (a drive that reads and writes DVDs), you can use the iDVD software to create and burn professional-looking DVDs that will play on almost any current DVD player or on any computer that can play DVDs.

Supported disc formats

You need blank discs on which to burn your project. iDVD prefers a type of "general media" disc called **DVD-R** (pronounced *DVD dash R*). iDVD is also compatible with these disc media formats:

DVD+R (*DVD plus R*) is a similar, but competing format.

DVD-RW (*DVD dash RW*), **DVD+RW** (*DVD plus RW*), which are rewritable media. And **DVD+RW DL** *(Double Layer),* which holds twice as much content as a single-layer disc.

Disk and project limitations

A single-layer disc can store approximately 4.2 gigabytes of content (about 60 minutes of video, including video used in motion menus).

A double-layer disc can store 7.7 gigabytes (about 120 minutes of video).

iDVD projects have a maximum of 99 tracks (99 movies and slideshows in any combination) and 99 menus.

Menus can have a maximum of 12 buttons (depending on the theme) that link to content or other menus.

The video used in motion menus and motion buttons can total a maximum of 15 minutes per project.

A project can have a maximum of 30 motion menus.

You can have a maximum of 99 chapter markers in a movie.

An iDVD project can contain a maximum of 9,801 photos (or fewer, depending on their size). Every group of 99 images in a slideshow takes up one of the 99 allowable tracks in the project.

Open the Project Info window to see how much disc space is being used by the various elements of the project. From the Project menu, choose "Project Info...." See page 178 to learn more about the Project Info window.

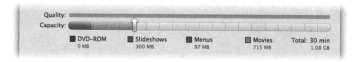

Quality:				
Capacity:				
■ DVD-ROM	■ Slideshows	■ Menus	■ Movies	Total: 30 min
0 MB	300 MB	97 MB	715 MB	1.08 GB

Make a OneStep DVD

If you need to create a simple DVD from unedited video, or if you want to just create a backup copy of video footage, iDVD's **OneStep DVD** feature can capture video from your video camera and automatically create a DVD disc that's set to *autoplay*. When you insert the OneStep DVD in a DVD player (or a computer with a DVD drive), it automatically starts playing—no menu system is present, or necessary. When playing the disc you can pause, rewind, or fast forward the video as you can with any DVD. If your video camera is a newer model that records in the high definition HDV format, you can't use the OneStep feature. If your video camera records to tape, and has a FireWire connection, you probably can use the OneStep feature.

iDVD automatically captures video until the tape ends, **or** until after 10 seconds of no video, **or** until you click "Stop" (circled, below). When you click the "Stop" button a dialog appears so you can choose to cancel the entire process or stop only the capture of *additional* video and continue the OneStep DVD process with the video that's already been captured.

1. Connect your video camera to your Mac.

2. Turn the camera on and set it to Play mode (some cameras call this mode VCR or VTR mode).

3. Open iDVD, then click the "OneStep DVD" button in the start window, shown on the next page. **Or** if IDVD is already open, from the File menu, choose "OneStep DVD." A dialog prompts you to insert a recordable DVD media (a blank disc) into the computer's SuperDrive.

4. After you insert a blank DVD, a sheet appears (right) that shows the progress of each step of creating the OneStep DVD.

5. When the last stage ("Burn") is complete, the disc ejects and a dialog instructs you to "insert another disc now" if you want to create another DVD.

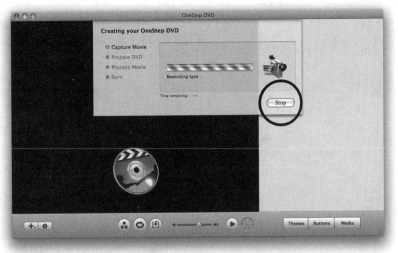

Make a Magic iDVD

The Magic iDVD feature lets you automatically and quickly create a professional-quality DVD. All you have to do is select a theme and some content. iDVD does the rest, including the creation of menus that enable you to navigate the contents of the disc (your movies and slideshows). You'll need to have content available on your computer

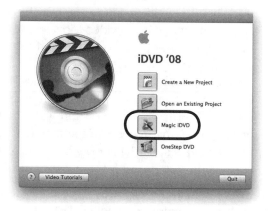

(movies and photos), or on an external hard disk that's connected to your computer, so iDVD can access it.

1. Open iDVD. In the start window that opens (above), click the "Magic iDVD" button.

2. In the "Magic iDVD" window that opens (below):

    ▼ **Name the DVD** in the "DVD Title" field.

    ▼ **Choose a Theme.** Click one of the theme thumbnails in the top row. Click the Themes pop-up menu to see more themes.

    ▼ **Add a movie to your DVD.** Click the "Movies" tab at the top of the Media pane, then drag a movie from the Media pane (on the right side of the window) to a drop well (the blank thumbnail placeholders) in the "Drop Movies Here" row.

▼ **Preview a selected movie before you place it:** click the Preview button in the bottom-left corner of the Media pane. Click again to stop the preview.

▼ **Create a slideshow.** Click the "Photos" in the Media browser, then drag an entire photo album or Event to a Photo drop well. Each drop well represents a slideshow.

▼ **Add music to a slideshow.** Click the "Audio" tab at the top of the Media pane, then drag a song from the Media pane and drop it on top of a slideshow thumbnail. Slideshows that include audio have an audio icon on their thumbnails.

To preview a selected song, click the Preview button in the bottom-left corner of the Media pane.

3. Preview your DVD to test the links and make sure it works as expected. Click the "Preview" button in the bottom-left corner of the window. Use the virtual remote control that appears next to the preview to test the menu buttons that link to the project's content.

To change themes, click "Exit" on the remote, click another theme thumbnail in the Magic iDVD window, then click Preview again to test the new menus.

Click "Exit" on the remote to return to the Magic iDVD window.

4. **Burn the project to a disc.** Insert a blank iDVD disc into the Super-Drive, then click the "Burn" icon in the bottom-right corner. A dialog sheet opens to show the progress of the burn process.

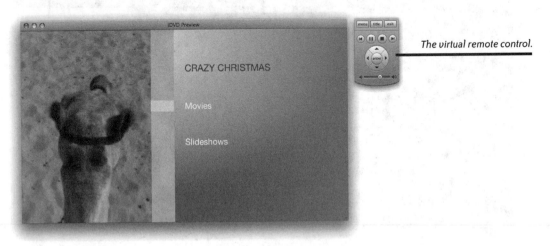

The virtual remote control.

Create a New iDVD Project

DVDs use *menus* to provide navigation to the content in a project. iDVD provides professionally designed **menu themes** for you to choose from. Many of the themes contain motion and are called *motion menus*.

1. Open iDVD. In the start window, click "Create a New Project."

2. In the dialog that opens, name your project and choose a location where you want to save it. Also choose an "Aspect Ratio" for the project. This refers to the width-to-height proportion of the project. Choose "Standard" or "Widescreen."

   Click "Create" to open the iDVD window shown below.

3. Replace the default menu title (circled below) with a custom name. This can be done at any time. The text change will also appear in the background animation.

4. Click the "Themes" button in the bottom-right corner, then choose a theme from the list of thumbnails in the Themes pane. To see more themes, click the Themes pop-up window at the top of the pane.

   Click the small disclosure triangle next to a theme to show its submenu variations.

   To preview the motion built into a theme, click the Start/Stop Motion button at the bottom of the window.

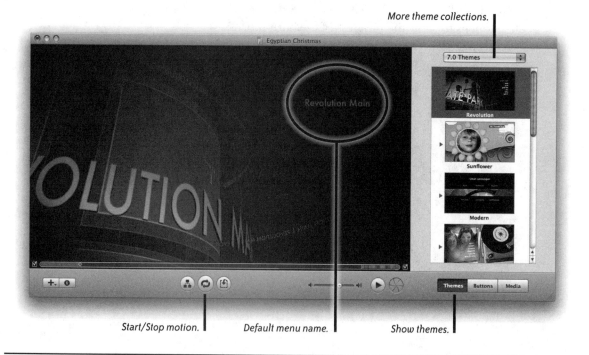

More theme collections.

Start/Stop motion.   Default menu name.   Show themes.

5. Add content to the theme's Drop Zones. A Drop Zone is a place-holder in the menu that can hold a movie, a photo, or a slideshow.

   Click the "Media" button in the bottom-right corner of the window to show the Media Browser (below), then click either the "Photos" tab or the "Movies" tab.

   Drag a photo, an album of photos, or a movie to a Drop Zone area in the menu. The Drop Zone highlights with a yellow and black and black striped border when you hover content over it (below).

   Or click the "Edit Drop Zones" button at the bottom of the window to show Drop Zone drop wells in the lower section of the Preview pane (below). Drag and drop content from the Media browser to the drop wells. To replace the *background* of the menu theme, drag content from the Media Browser to the "Menu" drop well in the lower section of the preview pane.

To remove content from a drop zone, click the Edit Drop Zones button in the toolbar, select a drop well thumbnail, then hit Delete.

6. Customize the theme music. Click the "Audio" tab at the top of the Medial Browser, then drag a song to the preview pane.

7. Add a movie to the project. Drag a movie from the media browser to the menu. A button named the same as the movie is automatically created. To change the name, click the button, then type a new name.

8. Preview your project. Click the Play button beneath the Preview pane. Use the virtual remote to test the project. Click "Exit" on the remote to return to the iDVD window.

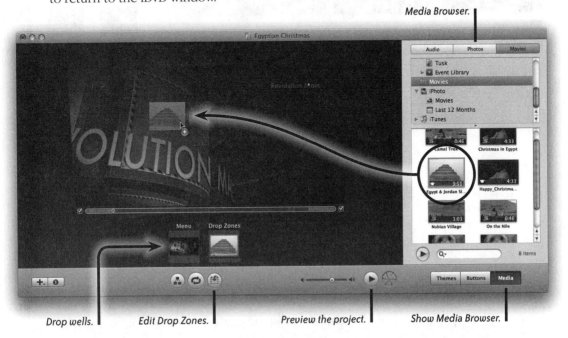

Media Browser.

Drop wells.   *Edit Drop Zones.*   *Preview the project.*   *Show Media Browser.*

iDVD Slideshows

In addition to movies, you can add slideshows that you create within your DVD project. Drag albums, events, or any selection of photos from the Photos pane of the Media Browser to the menu. Then make adjustments to the slide durations, order of appearance, transitions, and the music track.

1. Click the "Media" button in the bottom-right corner of the iDVD window, then click the "Photos" tab at the top of the Media Browser.

2. In the Media Browser, select an album or an Event from the iPhoto library, or make a multiple selection of photos by holding down the Command key as you click on photos to select them.

3. Drag your selection to the menu in the Preview pane. A button is automatically created, linked to the slideshow. Click the button to rename it.

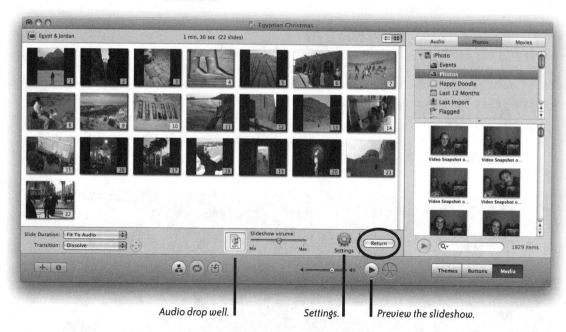

Audio drop well.   Settings.   Preview the slideshow.

4. Double-click the new button to open the Slideshow editor (above). The editor shows thumbnails of all photos included in the Slideshow.

   ▼ To reposition a photo, drag it to another location.

   ▼ To remove a photo, select it, then press Delete.

   ▼ To set a duration for the photos in a slideshow, use the "Slide Duration" pop-up menu located in the editor's toolbar. Choose "Manual" to enable the DVD viewer to control the slideshow. If the slideshow includes a music track, the manual setting is not available.

- ▼ To add another photo, drag one from the Media Browser, or from any location on your computer, to the Slideshow editor.

- ▼ To set a transition style for the slideshow, use the "Transitions" pop-up menu located in the editor's toolbar.

- ▼ To add music to the slideshow, click the Audio tab at the top of the Media Browser. Select a song from the Media Browser and drag it to the background of the Slideshow editor. **Or** drag it to the audio drop well in the editor's toolbar. Adjust the audio track volume with the "Slideshow volume" slider in the toolbar. The "Slide Duration" pop-up menu is automatically set to "Fit to Audio" when an audio track is added.

5. Click the "Settings" icon in the Slideshow editor's toolbar. A dialog opens (right) with additional options for the Slideshow.

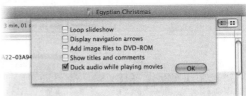

- ▼ "Loop slideshow" makes the slideshow loop (repeat endlessly).

- ▼ "Display navigation arrows" displays Previous and Next navigation arrows in the Slideshow.

- ▼ "Add image files to DVD-ROM" copies the original, high-quality photos to the DVD-ROM area of the disc, for others to access.

- ▼ "Show titles and comments" provides editable title and comment fields in the editor (shown below). The titles and comments appear with the photos when the Slideshow plays.

- ▼ Select "Duck audio while playing movies" if you added a movie to the Slideshow. The Slideshow's audio track volume is automatically lowered when it conflicts with the movie's soundtrack.

6. To preview a Slideshow, click the Play button in the iDVD toolbar.

7. To return to the DVD menu, click the "Return" button, circled on the opposite page.

Change views of the Slideshow editor.

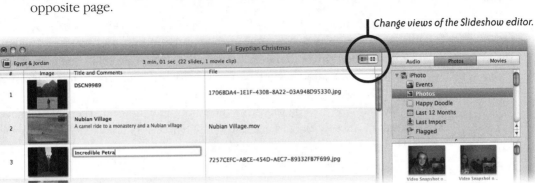

Create Chapter Markers for Movies

Chapter markers make it easy for the viewer to jump to specific scenes in a movie. When you place a movie in iDVD that includes chapter markers, iDVD creates a submenu for the movie that includes two buttons: one that links to the entire movie ("Play Movie"), and one ("Scene Selection") that links to another submenu with buttons that link to scenes in the movie that have been marked with chapter markers. If you place a movie in your project that doesn't already contain chapter markers, you can create them within iDVD.

1. Click once on a button in a project menu that links to a movie.

2. From the Advanced menu, choose "Create Chapter Markers for Movie."

3. In the dialog that opens (below), set how often, in minutes, you want chapter markers placed in the movie. Click OK.

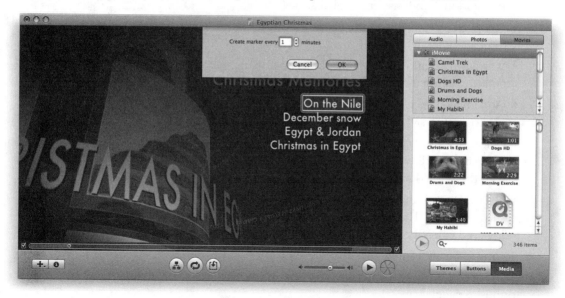

After you set chapter markers for a movie, you can hide them later by deleting the Scene Selection button in the submenu that iDVD creates. But the chapter markers are still there, and working. When you click the Next Chapter button on a remote control, the movie jumps to the chapter that was created. Even if you delete the movie from the project and place it again, the chapter markers are still there. To get rid of the chapter markers, you'll have to create a new project, since the chapter markers are created within the project, not the movie.

4. Now when you double-click that movie button, or when a viewer selects that button while viewing the finished DVD, a new submenu opens that contains buttons for "Play Movie" and "Scene Selection" (below, top). Click the "Scene Selection" button to open another submenu that contains video buttons for each scene (below, bottom).

To create chapter markers for multiple movies at the same time, press the Shift key as you select movie buttons, then go to the Advanced menu and choose "Create Chapter Markers for Movie."

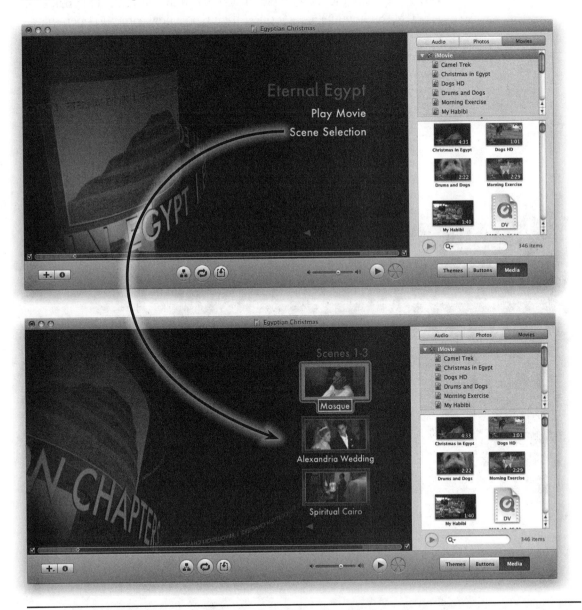

Add a Submenu

A project might possibly include more movies and slideshows than you can fit into one menu (the maximum number of buttons in a menu is 12). Or you might want to organize your content into several categories, each with its own menu (as shown below). The solution is to create submenus.

1. Click the Add (+) button in the bottom-left corner of the window.

2. From the pop-up menu, choose "Add Submenu." A new button is placed in the menu (below). To change the button default name ("My Submenu"), click it once, then type a new name. To open this new submenu and add content (movies, slideshows, or links to other submenus), double-click the button.

   You can also add content to a submenu by dragging an item from the media browser and dropping it on top of the submenu button.

3. The Add pop-up menu also lets you create *buttons* that link to a movie or slideshow. This is an alternative to the technique of dragging content straight to the menu background from the media browser (or from any location on your computer), which automatically creates a new button in the menu.

The Motion Playhead

An iDVD menu that includes motion displays a Motion Playhead bar at the bottom of the Preview pane. Motion menus often include a separate Intro (animation that brings in the main menu and its motion), and an Outro (animation that creates a transition to content or to the next menu when you click a button). The Motion Playhead represents the entire menu animation. The extreme left and right sides of the bar that are highlighted with vertical white stripes represent the Intro and Outro sections of the animation. To disable either one, uncheck the small checkbox on either side of the Motion Playhead bar.

To preview the menu animation, click the Start/Stop Motion button (shown below). **Or** press on the playhead in the Motion Playhead (the diamond shape) and drag it left or right. Even if you plan to keep the Intro and Outro as part of the project, you might find it helpful to uncheck these two items while you build and test your project, just so you won't have to wait for those effects to play when you click a link.

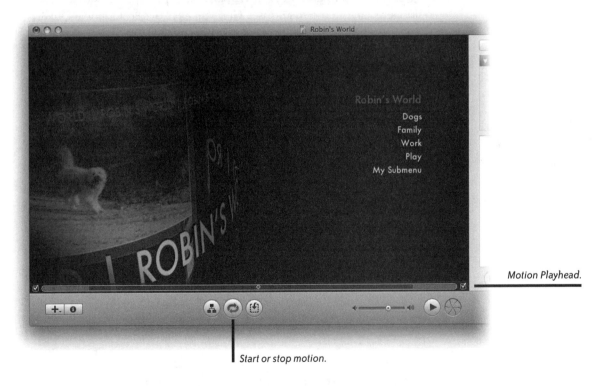

Motion Playhead.

Start or stop motion.

The Project Info Window

The Project Info window provides important information and settings for your DVD projects. Go to the Project menu, then choose "Project Info."

- ▼ **Disc Name:** Type a name for your project disc. If the disc already has a name, you can change it here at any time.

- ▼ **Video Mode:** Different parts of the world use different TV and video standards. The two most common standards are NTSC and PAL. Most of North America uses NTSC, while most of Europe uses PAL. If you want to send a DVD to someone in Europe, switch this setting to PAL so your disc will play on a PAL DVD player.

- ▼ **Encoding:** This setting affects the quality and size of the final project, and also how fast the encoding can be processed. Encoding always involves a compromise between speed, quality, and size. Choose "Best Performance" for the fastest encoding. Your files encode in the background while you work on your project. This setting is best for projects that are under one hour of duration. For projects that are longer than one hour, choose "High Quality" or "Professional Quality" (this setting takes longest to encode).

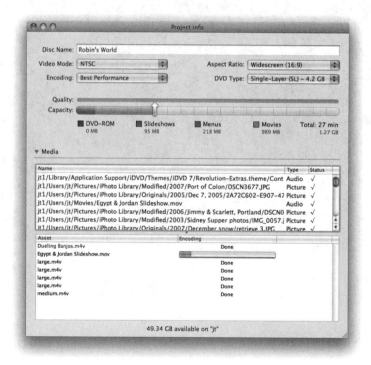

- ▾ **Aspect Ratio:** This refers to the width and height proportions of the project. If your video was shot in widescreen format, choose "Wide-screen (16:9)." Even if your video was shot in the Standard Aspect Ratio (4:3), you can choose widescreen, but the top and bottom of the video will be cropped to the widescreen 16:9 aspect ratio. Like-wise, if your video was shot in widescreen format, but you choose the Standard aspect ratio of 4:3, the left and right sides of the video will be cropped to fit Standard proportions.

- ▾ **DVD Type:** Choose to burn a Single-Layer or Double-Layer DVD. Single-Layer discs are compatible with a larger variety of DVD players.

- ▾ **Quality and Capacity:** The Capacity bar shows how much space is required by different elements of the project—slideshows, movies, menus and DVD-ROM (the space on a disc used to store and deliver digital files to others, *not* for the purpose of being part of the DVD interface). The far right side of the bar shows how much content will be burned to a disc, in minutes and bytes (megabytes or gigabytes). The Capacity arrow points to a quality prediction color. Green means the quality will look good at the current encoding setting. If the arrow points to yellow or red colors in the Quality bar, change the encoding setting to "Professional Quality."

Modify Menus

The iDVD themes are well designed and you can use them just as they are, but you also have quite a few options for customizing the text, buttons, and background of existing themes.

Edit the font and size of text buttons

1. Click the text in a button.

2. Use the pop-up menus that appear beneath the button (below) to change the font selection or the font size.

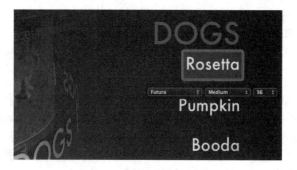

Use the built-in alignment guides

If you've set button positioning to "Free positioning" (see page 183), you can drag buttons anywhere in the menu. When certain alignments are present—such as flush right, centered, or flush left—yellow guides appear to indicate the alignment. In the example below, the yellow guide shows that the elements are aligned flush right. The arrows on the yellow line indicate equal vertical spacing between items.

Replace text buttons with photo or movie buttons

1. Select a button in a menu in the Preview pane.

2. Click the "Buttons" button under the media browser. From the pop-up menu at the top of the Buttons pane, choose one of the graphic button styles (Frames, Artistic, Rectangle, or Rounded). The button pane shows collections of buttons based on your choice in the pop-up menu.

3. Select a button style. The button in the menu changes to the new style, and displays an image from the linked slideshow or movie. To reposition the button in the menu, drag it. To preview the button playing a slideshow or movie, click the Start/Stop Motion button in the toolbar.

Edit photo and movie buttons

Click a movie button. Drag the slider that appears (above) to the point in the movie where you want the button animation to start playing. If you prefer a still image in the button, check the "Still Image" box. For a button that links to a Slideshow, drag the slider to show the photo you want to use as the button image. These controls can also be found in the Inspector window (see the next page).

The Inspector window

The Inspector window provides settings for buttons, menus, and text. To open the Inspector window (right), go to the View menu and choose "Show Inspector." Or click the "i" icon in the bottom-left corner of the iDVD window (left).

The Button Info pane

With the Inspector window open, click on a *button* in a menu to show the Button Info pane (right).

Font controls: From the pop-up menus, choose a font style and size for buttons, and set a button alignment (left, center, or right).

Shadow: Turn the text drop-shadow effect on or off, and choose a drop-shadow color.

Movie: Drag the slider to set the point in a movie where the button's movie starts to play.

Still Image: Check this box to use a still image from the movie (set with the "Movie" slider) for the selected button's image.

Size: Enlarge or reduce the size of the selected button.

Custom thumbnail: Usually, the image in a button is from the content that's linked to that button. To set some other photo, movie, or graphic as the button's image, drag an image or movie from the media browser (or from any location on your computer) to this drop well.

Label: From the pop-up menu, choose where to place a button's label (the button's title or caption).

Transition: From the pop-up menu, choose the type of transition that plays when the selected button is clicked. If the transition type you choose is directional (such as "Flip"), use the lower pop-up menu to set a direction (such as "Right to Left").

The Menu Info pane

With the Inspector window open, click on a *menu's background* to show the Menu Info pane (right).

Background: Uncheck the "Intro" or "Outro" boxes to disable those animations off. Checkmark the boxes to enable the animations.

Loop Duration: Drag this slider to adjust the duration of the main motion menu (the middle thumbnail at the top of the pane).

Audio: To replace the menu's existing audio track, drag a song from the media browser (or from any location on your computer) and drop it on this drop well. **Or** drag a song from the media browser straight to the background of a menu.

To remove audio from the menu, drag the audio file icon in this drop well to the Desktop. It disappears in a poof of smoke.

Menu Volume: Drag the slider to adjust the volume of the menu's audio.

Snap to grid: This option snaps items to an invisible grid when you drag items to rearrange them in a menu.

Free positioning: This option lets you drag and position items anywhere in the menu, without snapping to a grid.

Show drop zones and related graphics: If you don't want to use the drop zones feature, you can disable it here. This is an easy way to personalize a theme: uncheck this item, then drag your own photo or movie to the menu background.

The Text Info pane

With the Inspector window open, click on *text* in a menu—not a button's label—to show the Text Info pane (right).

These settings are the same as the ones at the top of the Button Info pane, shown on the previous page.

Add Text to a Menu

It's usually adequate that a menu has a title, and that the menu buttons include labels (captions). But some projects might benefit from extra text in the menu to provide comments, a description of the content, or for any other creative use you can think of.

1. From the Project menu, choose "Add Text." Default text appears on the menu that says "Click to edit."

2. Click the text to select it, then type the text you want to use.

3. Open the Inspector window (go to the View menu and choose "Show Inspector") to customize the text font and style (page 183).

Text added to the menu.

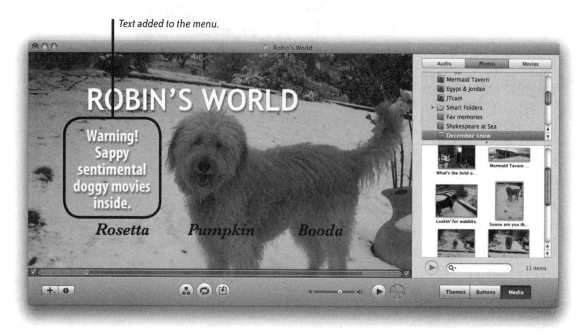

Save a Customized Menu as a Favorite

If you spend a lot of time customizing a menu, you can save it to use again for other projects.

1. From the File menu, choose "Save Theme as Favorite...."

2. In the dialog that opens, type a name for this theme Favorite. Check the box, "Shared for all users," to make this favorite accessible to other users who have accounts on this computer.
To *replace* an existing favorite, name the current favorite the same as the favorite you want to replace. Click the "Replace existing" box.

3. Click OK.

To use a favorite, click the "Themes" button, then from the pop-up menu at the top of the themes pane, choose "Favorites." The new favorite appears in the Favorites list. Click the favorite to apply it to the current project.

Delete a favorite

To **delete a favorite** that you've created, you must go to the Favorites folder where Favorites are stored and manually drag it to the Trash.

1. Quit iDVD.

2. Find the Favorites folder where the favorite is located.

If you selected "Shared for all users" in the dialog sheet shown above, the favorite is saved in a "Favorites" folder located within the Users folder in your *startup disk folder.* Open the Users folder on the startup disk. Next, open the Shared folder. Then open the iDVD folder. Finally, open the Favorites folder. Favorites you've saved are located there. The folder path looks like this: YourStartupDisk/Users/Shared/iDVD/Favorites.

If you did not select either of the checkboxes, **or** if you selected the "Replace existing" checkbox, the Favorite is saved in your *Home folder.* The folder path looks like this: YourHomeFolder/Library/Application Support/iDVD/Favorites.

3. Drag the Favorite from the Favorites folder to the Trash.

Robin's World.favorite

This is what a Favorite file looks like in the Favorites folder.

The DVD Map

To show a DVD Map of your project, click the DVD Map button in the toolbar (shown circled on the left).

The DVD Map shows a graphic representation of your project. Menus, submenus, movies, and slideshows appear as icons in a graph with navigation lines that show the connections between items. This is a great way to see the overall organization and structure of your project.

You can modify your project within the Map pane. Drag movies or photo albums from the media browser to a menu thumbnail (it has a *folder* icon in the top-left corner). To add photos to a slideshow, drag photos from the media browser to a Slideshow thumbnail (it has a *slide* icon in the top-left corner). You can even rearrange content here—drag a movie or Slideshow thumbnail on top of another menu thumbnail. To create a *submenu* full of content, drag a menu thumbnail to another menu thumbnail. To delete a menu or content, select its thumbnail, then hit Delete.

To hide a menu's content, click the disclosure triangle located on the right edge of the thumbnail.

The DVD Map pane is where you can add an **autoplay** movie or slideshow. An autoplay movie automatically plays when a DVD is inserted in a player, then moves automatically to the main menu (unless you've set the autoplay to loop). This is similar to the FBI warning screen you've seen on other DVDs.

To loop a movie or slideshow, select its thumbnail, then go to the Advanced menu and choose "Loop movie" or "Loop slideshow."

To create an autoplay movie, drag a movie, slideshow, or graphic from the media browser, or from anywhere on your computer, onto the Project thumbnail (the first item in the Map View diagram).

To remove an autoplay movie, drag it out of the Project thumbnail.

Project thumbnail.

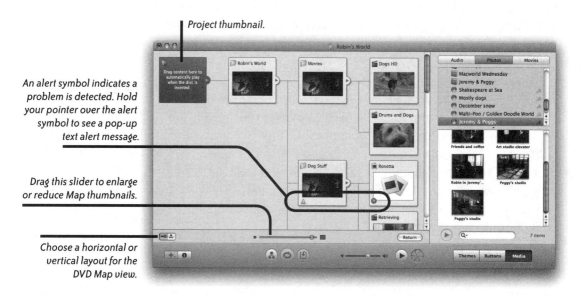

An alert symbol indicates a problem is detected. Hold your pointer over the alert symbol to see a pop-up text alert message.

Drag this slider to enlarge or reduce Map thumbnails.

Choose a horizontal or vertical layout for the DVD Map view.

Burn Your Project to a DVD

When you're satisfied with your menus and you've added all the movies, slideshows, and DVD-ROM content, it's time to render, encode, and *multiplex* all those files into the official DVD format and burn them onto a DVD. Happily, all of those complex operations happen with a click of the "Burn" button.

Multiplexing, also known as "muxing," refers to the process of assembling DVD assets into an official format that DVD players can use.

1. Make sure your Energy Saver preferences are *not* set to make your computer go to sleep. This could interrupt the burning process.

   Your hard disk should have as least twice as much free space available as the project takes up.

   Open the "Project Info" window to check the project size— from the Project menu, choose "Project Info…." **Or** click the Info button (the "i") in the bottom-left corner of the window.

   Turn on motion: click the "Start/Stop Motion" button in the toolbar.

2. Click the "Burn" button in the toolbar. A dialog opens and instructs you to insert a recordable DVD disc.

3. iDVD starts rendering, encoding, *multiplexing*, and burning all the files and menus that are part of the DVD project. A dialog keeps track of the progress (below).

The final DVD that you burn will be named the same as your iDVD project.

To change the project name (and thus the disc name), go to the Project menu and choose "Project Info…." Type a new name in the "Disc Name" field. Any spaces you type will be replaced with an underscore. You can use numbers, upper and lowercase characters from A to Z, and the underscore.

The Burn button.

iDVD Preferences

The iDVD preferences window provides many important settings for DVD projects. Go to the iDVD menu and choose "Preferences…."

General preferences

Menus:

- ▼ **Show drop zone labels:** Check this to show the drop zones in menus.
- ▼ **Show Apple logo watermark:** Places the Apple logo in menu designs.
- ▼ **Fade volume out at end of menu loop:** This makes the transition back to the beginning of the loop more pleasing to most people.

When changing themes:

- ▼ **Use theme default values:** When you change themes, even if you've made menu design changes (such as button font sizes), the new theme uses its own default settings for text, audio, and any other elements that may be customizable.
- ▼ **Retain changes to theme defaults:** When you change themes, keep the changes you've already made in the original theme.
- ▼ **Always ask:** When you change themes, a dialog asks if you want to use default values or retain changes.

Check for iDVD updates automatically

Check this option to make iDVD automatically connect to the Internet each time you open it, and check for software updates.

Reset Warnings button

Click the "Reset Warnings" button if you've turned off certain alert messages when they appeared, but would like to see them again.

Projects preferences

If you change these settings while working on a project, the current project will not be affected. Changes to these settings will apply to new projects.

Video Mode:

Choose "NTSC" if your DVD will be played on a consumer DVD player in North America or Japan. A few other non-European countries also use the NTSC format. Most European and other countries use the PAL format.

Encoding:

- ▼ **Best Performance:** Choose this setting for the fastest encoding. Your files encode in the background while you work on your project. This setting is best for projects that are under one hour of duration. iDVD will evaluate how much video you have and produce the best quality possible for the number of minutes in the project.

- ▼ **High Quality:** Choose this for projects that are longer than one hour.

- ▼ **Professional Quality:** This choice provides the best quality, but takes longest to encode.

DVD Type:

- ▼ **Single-Layer or Double-Layer:** Choose the DVD type that your project will fit on. To check the size of your project, go to the Project menu, then choose "Project Info...."

Slideshow preferences

▾ **Always add original slideshow photos to DVD-ROM contents:** iDVD converts photos for a DVD slideshow to a low resolution—72 ppi (pixels per inch). To make iDVD copy the *original,* high-resolution photos to a folder on the DVD disc, choose this option. Anyone who has the disc can drag the high-resolution photos from the disc to his computer—an ideal way to deliver high-resolution photos to someone. The DVD slideshow provides the preview, and the hi-resolution originals are included on the disc for anyone who needs them. This works well for professional photographers who want to deliver photos to a client, or for friends who want to share photos.

Uncheck this option if you want to conserve space on the DVD, or if the user doesn't need access to the original, high-resolution images. You can also set this option in the Settings dialog of the Slideshow editor (see pages 172–173).

▾ **Always scale slides to TV Safe Area:** Check this option to ensure that photos won't be cropped when viewed on a television. To see the Safe Area in iDVD menus, from the Advanced menu, choose "Show TV Safe Area."

▾ **Fade volume out at end of slideshow:** Check this option to prevent the slideshow music track from ending too abruptly.

▾ **Show titles and comments:** If you've added titles or comments, choose this option to include them in the slideshow. This option is also in the Settings dialog of the Slideshow editor (see page 173).

Movies preferences

In this preferences pane, you choose whether or not iDVD will create chapter submenus and where iDVD should look for movie files.

When importing movies:

▼ **Create chapter submenus:** If this option is chosen, when you drag an iMovie with chapter markers to an iDVD menu, iDVD creates a submenu with two menu buttons: one named "Play Movie" and one named "Scene Selection."

The "Scene Selection" button links to another submenu that contains buttons linking to each chapter marker (scene) in the movie. If there are more than 12 chapter markers in the movie, iDVD creates another submenu containing buttons that link to the remaining chapter markers. iDVD is limited to 2 buttons per menu.

▼ **Do not create chapter submenus:** Choose this option to ignore a movie's chapter markers. When you place a movie with chapter markers, a button is created that links to the movie, but not to scenes.

▼ **Look for my movies in these folders:** iDVD automatically looks for movies in the Movies folder located in your Home folder. If you store movies in some other folder on your computer, or in a folder on an external hard disk, you can add those other locations for iDVD to search. The folders you add here will appear in iDVD's media browser, so you can easily find and place movies in a project.

Click the "Add…" button, then select any folder on any drive. Your selection will appear in the list (above). To remove a location from this list, select it, then click "Remove."

Advanced Preferences

Use the Advanced pane to create and manage a list of designated folders for storing themes. Also in this pane, you can change the default location for capturing OneStep DVD video footage, and set a default DVD burning speed.

Archive Your Project

Archiving a project bundles all of the project assets together, making it easy and convenient to store complete projects or move them to another computer. You may need to move a project to a computer that has a SuperDrive so you can burn a disc, or take it to someone else's Mac so he can work on the project. When you *archive* your project, it's saved as an iDVD project (.dvdproj) that can be opened with iDVD.

To archive an iDVD project:

1. From the File menu, choose "Archive Project."

2. In the Archive Project dialog sheet that opens (below), type a name for the archive and choose a location to save the archived file. iDVD automatically adds "Archived" to the file name.

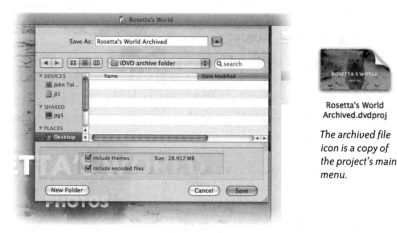

Rosetta's World Archived.dvdproj

The archived file icon is a copy of the project's main menu.

3. If you've used customized themes, check the "Include themes" box to archive the themes with the project. You can uncheck this check-box if you've used standard iDVD themes.

4. Check the "Include encoded files" box to avoid having to re-encode project files after they're moved to another location. If you're more interested in a faster archiving speed and economizing hard disk space, uncheck this option.

5. Click the "Save" button.

Save Your Project as a Disc Image

How is this process different from the "Archive Project" on the opposite page? When you *archive* a project, it remains in the iDVD format so you can open and revise it at any time. When you save as disc image, the iDVD files are converted to the special DVD-specification format. These files cannot be opened and edited without special software—they can only be *played* (by a desktop or computer DVD player).

The "Save As Disc Image" command does everything to create a final DVD *except* burn the files to a disc. The disc image that's created contains DVD files that can be burned to a DVD disc. A disc image file is an easy way to copy your entire project, completely encoded, to another computer—ready to burn to a DVD. To burn a DVD from the disc image, double-click the disc image to open it, then burn the two folders inside (see the example on the right) to a DVD disc. If you want to create a copy of your project that *can* be edited, you should *archive* the project as described on the previous page.

To save a project as a disc image:

1. Open a project. From the File menu, choose "Save As Disc Image…."

2. In the "Save Disc Image As…" window that opens, type a name in the "Save As" field and select a location to save the file.

3. A dialog sheet keeps track of the DVD creation progress.

4. When the disc image has been created, a dialog opens and shows a "Disc image created" message. Click OK.

Use the **DVD Player** application (right) to play a DVD project that's saved as a disc image. Open DVD Player (it's in the Applications folder). A blank DVD viewer window opens. Double-click the disc image you created to open it. The project starts playing in the DVD Player window.

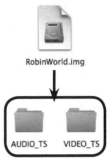

This is a DVD project saved as a disc image file.

RobinWorld.img

Double-click the disc image file (top) to see the contents—two folders.

The "AUDIO_TS" folder is empty, but required by DVD specifications.

The "VIDEO_TS" folder contains all of the specially encoded project files.

DVD Player.app

Save as VIDEO_TS Folder

"Save as VIDEO_TS folder…" is another option you'll find in the File menu. Two folders are created: VIDEO_TS and AUDIO_TS. There's nothing in the audio folder, but it's required by DVD specifications. These are the same DVD files and folders that are created when you save as a disc image, as described above, without being packaged into a single disc image file.

To play a VIDEO_TS folder, open DVD Player. From the File menu, choose "Open VIDEO_TS Folder…." In the Finder dialog that opens, locate the VIDEO_TS folder you want to play, then click the "Choose" button.

To create a working DVD, burn the two folders that are created (AUDIO_TS and VIDEO_TS) to a DVD disc.

Extra Tips

Many of the iDVD features and items in menus don't need explanations, but here are a few tips that might be helpful.

The Motion command

Choosing "Motion" from the View menu is the same as clicking the "Start/ Stop Motion" button in the iDVD toolbar. To work efficiently, turn motion *off* while you build a project. Turn Motion *on* to preview a project or burn a disc.

Hide the Motion Playhead

This command in the View menu hides the Motion Playhead bar at the bottom of the Preview pane. If the Motion Playhead is distracting to you, select this option, which hides it in the Preview pane. To show the Motion Playhead, select this item again, which places a checkmark next to it.

Show TV Safe Area

Choose this item in the View menu to show red guide lines that indicate a "TV Safe area" (shown below). Some TVs may distort or clip the outer edges of DVD menus and movies. When you customize menus, make sure important elements such as text and buttons fall within the TV Safe area.

Show Standard Crop Area

Standard Crop Area.

TV Safe Area.

Choose this item in the View menu to show the cropping area of a standard TV screen (4:3 proportion). The red guide lines (below) show how much of the project will show on a standard TV.

New Menu from Selection

This option is in the Project menu. As your project becomes more complex, you may want to reorganize the menus. You can use existing buttons in a menu to automatically create submenus.

1. Select one or more buttons that you want to move to a submenu (below-left). Hold down the Shift key to select multiple buttons.

2. From the Project menu, choose "New Menu from Selection."

3. The buttons are removed from their original location, replaced by a new "My Submenu" button (below-right) that links to the new submenu. Click "My Submenu" to edit the button name.

   The new submenu that's created contains the original buttons, still linked to their content.

Apply Theme to Project

From the Advanced menu, choose this option to apply a selected theme to every menu in a project.

Apply Theme to Submenus

From the Advanced menu, choose this option to apply a selected theme to a specific menu *and all of its submenus.*

1. Open a menu whose theme you want to change, and at the same time change all of the menu's *submenus.*

2. In the Theme pane, choose a theme. From the Advanced menu, choose "Apply Theme to Submenus." The theme is applied to the selected menu and all of its submenus.

Delete Encoded Assets

Choose this command in the Advanced menu to reclaim disk space taken up by the encoded DVD files that iDVD made to create and burn a DVD disc. If you do this, the next time you want to burn a DVD of this project, iDVD has to encode the files again, slowing the process quite a bit.

Create DVD-ROM Content

In addition to menus, movies, and slideshows, DVDs can store and deliver any files from your computer, making them accessible for anyone with a DVD drive. This data storage feature is called DVD-ROM (DVD–Read Only Memory). A small business may want to include PDFs, forms, documents, maps, or other data on a disc. Or when you create a DVD slideshow, you may want to include the original, high-resolution photos on the disc for someone to use in a brochure or family album. Remember that files you add to the DVD-ROM section of a disc add to the total space used for the rest of the project. Be sure to check the Project Info window (see page 178) to ensure that everything will fit on a disc.

To put DVD-ROM content in your DVD project:

1. From the Advanced menu, choose "Edit DVD-ROM Contents…."

2. In the "DVD–ROM Contents" window that appears, click "Add Files…." Browse and select the files you want, then click the "Open" button.

   Or drag files from the Finder into the "DVD-ROM Contents" window.

Create new folders to help organize files, change the order of folders and files, and delete items from the DVD-ROM section of the disc.

▼ **To create a new folder,** click the "New Folder" button at the bottom of the window. Double-click the new folder to rename it.

▼ **To reorganize** the DVD-ROM contents, drag the folders up or down in the list, or drag files and folders in or out of other folders.

▼ **To delete** an item from the DVD-ROM contents, select the item, then press the Delete key.

To access the DVD-ROM content that's on a DVD disc:

1. Insert the disc into a DVD drive, then double-click the DVD disc icon.

2. In the window that opens, double-click the folder, "DVD-ROM Contents." The folder may also have the same name as your project.

3. Drag any of the files in the DVD-ROM folder from the disc to any location on the local computer.

Section Two

The coolest Mac apps for productivity

We spend a lot of time on our Macs—probably more than the average Mac user—and the apps in this section are the ones that make us most productive and keep us organized.

You may think iTunes is really more for fun and enjoyment than work, but its integration with iPhoto, iMovie, and iDVD make it a valuable partner of the creativity apps in Section One.

Mail is more than an email program—it's now an information center where you can organize email, To Do items, Notes, and RSS feeds from your favorite news sites; Address Book keeps all your contact information organized; iChat and Bonjour revolutionize the way you communicate with friends and associates; Safari keeps you informed and in touch with the world; iCal is much more than just a calendar; Dashboard widgets provide all sorts of information for you; Photo Booth is just good, wacky fun; and Time Machine makes automatic backups of everything you do so you never again lose an important file.

iTunes

iTunes is your one-stop digital media hub. With iTunes you can import music, organize it, play it, and share it with others. You can also use iTunes to watch movies, music videos, and TV shows. If you own an Apple device such as an iPhone, iPod, or Apple TV, you can use iTunes to download critical software updates to your device and sync it with your Mac.

Create your own playlists that contain the songs and videos you want, in the order you want. Then burn a CD of your favorite collections to take with you. Create Smart Playlists that automatically organize songs and videos into collections based on conditions that you set. If you want to play songs randomly, use iTunes' "Party Shuffle" feature to shuffle songs around in a playlist.

The online iTunes Store provides a place to preview and purchase music, music videos, movies, and TV shows. Thirty-second previews of more than a million songs are available, including thousands of exclusive prerelease tracks and many rare, out-of-date albums. You can also search for and download podcasts—free audio and video shows produced by amateurs and professionals alike.

iTunes is closely integrated with the other iLife applications—iPhoto, iMovie, iDVD, iWeb, and GarageBand—making it easy to add music to slideshows, movies, DVDs, websites, podcasts, and to your own music arrangements.

The iTunes Interface

A quick overview of the iTunes interface is shown here and on the next page. Most of the controls you need are located directly on the iTunes interface. Almost every control is explained in detail elsewhere in this chapter.

In the example below, the **Music** library is selected in the **Source list** (the section on the left side of the window), and the Music library's contents are shown in the Detail window (the large pane to the right of the Source list). When you select an item in the Source list, its contents appear in the Detail window on the right.

Source list.
To eject a CD or to unmount a device, click the Eject symbol to the right of the item.

Show or hide the mini-graphic equalizer.

Status display.

View. Display items in the Detail window with List, Album, or Cover Flow views.

Search field.

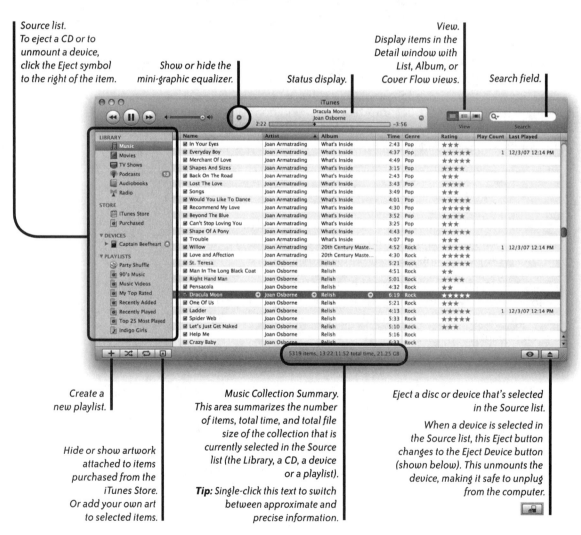

Create a new playlist.

Hide or show artwork attached to items purchased from the iTunes Store. Or add your own art to selected items.

Music Collection Summary. This area summarizes the number of items, total time, and total file size of the collection that is currently selected in the Source list (the Library, a CD, a device or a playlist).

Tip: *Single-click this text to switch between approximate and precise information.*

Eject a disc or device that's selected in the Source list.

When a device is selected in the Source list, this Eject button changes to the Eject Device button (shown below). This unmounts the device, making it safe to unplug from the computer.

In the example below, a **playlist** is selected in the Source list. For each item in the Source list, you can customize the Detail window view to show the columns of information you want. See "View Options" on page 229.

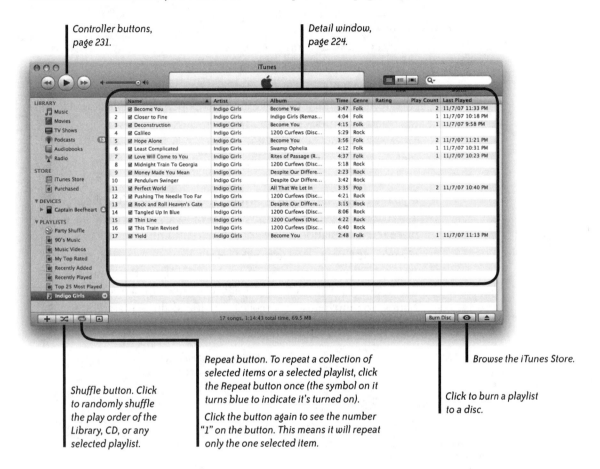

Controller buttons, page 231.

Detail window, page 224.

Shuffle button. Click to randomly shuffle the play order of the Library, CD, or any selected playlist.

Repeat button. To repeat a collection of selected items or a selected playlist, click the Repeat button once (the symbol on it turns blue to indicate it's turned on).

Click the button again to see the number "1" on the button. This means it will repeat only the one selected item.

Browse the iTunes Store.

Click to burn a playlist to a disc.

Play CDs

You can play any music CD in your Mac. Make sure your sound is on and turned up.

To play a music CD:

1. Insert a CD into the computer CD drive.

2. Open iTunes, if it isn't already open:
   - ▼ If the iTunes icon is in your Dock, click once on it.
   - ▼ If there is not an icon in the Dock, open the Applications folder, find the iTunes icon, then double-click it.

3. The CD icon appears in the Source list, as shown below. Click the CD icon to see its song list and other information in the Detail window.

   If you're connected to the Internet, iTunes will automatically go to a CD database web site, retrieve the song titles and other data, and place the information in the appropriate columns.

   If you're NOT connected to the Internet when you insert a CD, song titles will appear as track numbers. You can select the generic track names and type in real song names: click once on a title in the "Name" column, pause, then click the title again to highlight it. Type a new name for the song.

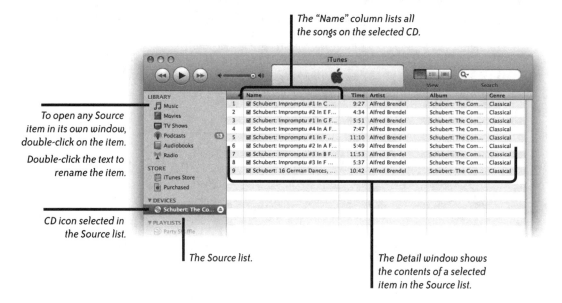

The "Name" column lists all the songs on the selected CD.

To open any Source item in its own window, double-click on the item.

Double-click the text to rename the item.

CD icon selected in the Source list.

The Source list.

The Detail window shows the contents of a selected item in the Source list.

To see the actual song titles, if they have not appeared:

1. Connect to the Internet (if you're not already connected).
2. From the Advanced menu, choose "Get CD Track Names."

If you want iTunes to do this automatically every time you put in a CD, set the behavior in iTunes preferences (see page 251).

To choose the songs on the CD you want to play:

When you insert a CD, all of the songs have checkmarks next to them. If the box is checked, the song will play. To customize the list, check only the songs you want to hear. iTunes skips over songs that do not have a checkmark.

1. Click on the CD icon in the Source list.
2. Click on a song in the "Name" column to select it.
3. Click the Play button (the middle controller button),
   or double-click a title in the "Name" column.

To check or uncheck
all songs at once,
Command-click on
any checkbox.

Play or
Pause.

Click on the lower line to
toggle between band name
and album name information.

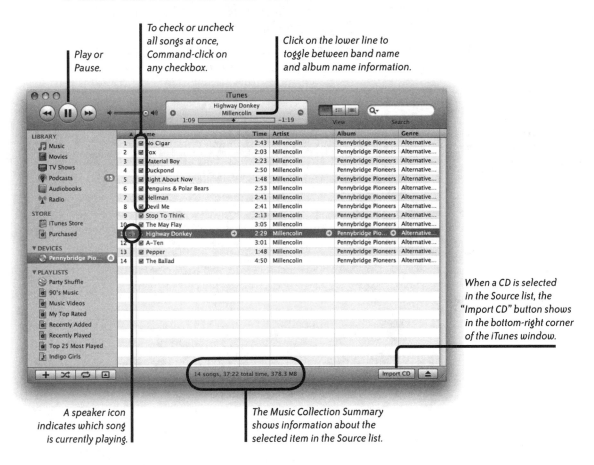

When a CD is selected
in the Source list, the
"Import CD" button shows
in the bottom-right corner
of the iTunes window.

A speaker icon
indicates which song
is currently playing.

The Music Collection Summary
shows information about the
selected item in the Source list.

Import CDs

File formats: The MPEG-4 AAC format compresses song files to a smaller size than the MP3 format without a noticeable quality difference. We encoded a 3-minute, 20-second song into both formats: the MP3 file encoded to 3.8 megabytes, the MPEG-4 file to 3.1 megabytes, a significant storage savings when you have a large library.

If you have a highly refined ear for music, set the iTunes "Importing" preferences to encode songs in "Apple Lossless" format. This format encodes CD-quality music at half the size of the original CD format.

Tip: Each song takes up at least 3 to 5 megabytes (depending on the file format specified in iTunes Preferences) of hard disk space, so make sure you have plenty of disk space available before you go crazy importing music files!

When you import music files from a CD, iTunes encodes it as an MPEG-4 AAC file and places it in the Music Library. Once a song is in the Library list, you can add it to a customized playlist, as explained on the following page. Simply playing songs from a CD does not add them to the Music Library.

To add songs to the Library:

1. Insert a music CD into the computer CD drive.

2. In the Detail window, click each song's checkbox that you want to add to the Library.

3. Click the "Import CD" button in the bottom-right corner of the window.

You may already have music files somewhere on your computer that you want to add to the iTunes Library. There are two ways to do this:

▼ **Either** go to the File menu and choose "Add to Library…," then find and select your music files.

▼ **Or** drag a file from any location on your hard disk to the Music library icon in the iTunes Source list, as shown below.

Drag a music file from anywhere on the computer to the "Library" in the Source list. The highlighted Library box indicates the song will be copied to the iTunes Library.

This shows how much hard disk space is being used to store the selected music files in the Library.

Create Your Own Playlists

A **playlist** is your customized collection of audio and video files. You can create as many playlists as you like, and you can rearrange the items in your playlists by dragging selections up or down. You create playlists so you can play custom collections of songs and videos on your computer, download them to a device, or burn them onto CDs.

When you create a new playlist, iTunes assumes you'll want to change its name so it highlights the text for you. Just type to replace the existing text.

Create a new playlist and add songs to it

1. Type Command N, **or** click the "New Playlist" button (the **+**) in the bottom-left corner of the iTunes window. A playlist icon appears in the Source list with the default name "untitled playlist."

2. Change the name of the new playlist to something descriptive by typing over the highlighted default name.

   You can change a playlist name at any time: Click once on the title to highlight it, click a second time to make the text editable, then type a new name in the highlighted field.

To add selections to the playlist from a CD:

1. Insert a CD whose songs you want to add to a custom playlist.

2. Click the CD icon in the Source list to open its song list.

3. Drag desired selections from the "Name" column and drop them on your new playlist in the Source list, as shown below.

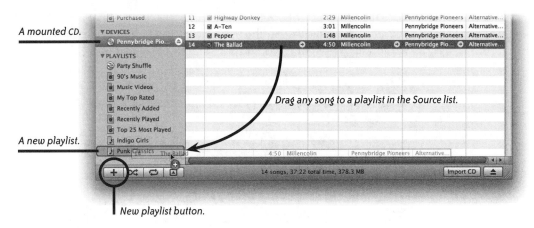

A mounted CD.

Drag any song to a playlist in the Source list.

A new playlist.

New playlist button.

When you drag a song directly from a CD to a playlist, the song is automatically encoded (imported) to the AAC format, or whatever format you last chose in the Importing preferences pane. The song is placed in the iTunes Library and added to the playlist.

This icon to the left of a song name means encoding is in progress.

To add an item from the Library to a playlist:

Note: When you drag a song file from the Library to a playlist collection, as explained on these pages, the song remains in the Library. *You're not actually moving the digital file*—you're creating an *alias* that tells iTunes which songs are attached to different collections. You can put the same song in as many playlist collections as you want without bloating your computer with extra copies of large music files.

1. In the Source list, click "Music" to display your entire Library.

2. Drag a selection to a playlist in the Source list.

There's **another method for creating a new playlist** that's even easier:

1. In the Source list, click "Music" to display your entire Library.

2. Select all the songs you want from the "Name" column (see how to make *multiple selections* below).

   Note: The **checkmarks** *do not* indicate that a file is selected. The checkmarks indicate two things: songs that will *play* when you click the "Play" button, or songs on a CD that will be *imported* when you click the "Import CD" button.

3. From the File menu, select "New Playlist From Selection." iTunes automatically creates the playlist and adds the selected songs to it.

You can drag **multiple selections** all at once to a playlist:

▼ To make a *contiguous* selection of songs (songs that are next to each other in the list), Shift-click the song names. **Or** single-click on one song, then Shift-click on another song; all songs between the two clicks will be selected.

▼ To make a *non-contiguous* selection of songs (songs that are *not* next to each other in the list), click a song, then Command-click additional song names you want to add to the selection.

This example shows a non-contiguous selection of songs.

Smart Playlists

Smart Playlists are collections of songs and videos that are generated automatically when imported items meet certain conditions that you define. iTunes provides several Smart Playlists (indicated by the gear symbols) in the Source list: '90s Music, Music Videos, My Top Rated, Recently Added, Recently Played, and Top 25 Most Played. You can create new Smart Playlists that meet other conditions, such as your favorite African songs, punk music, or certain artists.

Smart Playlists display a gear symbol.

To create a new Smart Playlist:

1. From the File menu, choose "New Smart Playlist…." **Or** Option-click the "New Playlist" button—the "plus" symbol on the button changes to a "gear" symbol (Smart Playlist) when you press the Option key.

2. In the Smart Playlist window that appears (shown below), use the menus and text fields to set conditions for the new Smart Playlist.

3. Click OK.

Press the Option key to change the "Playlist" button to a "Smart Playlist" button.

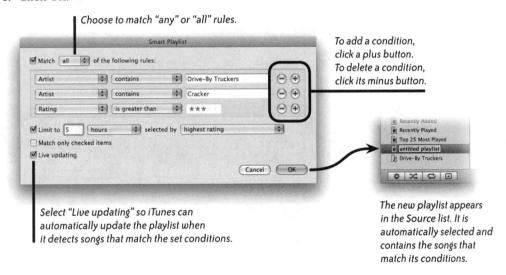

Choose to match "any" or "all" rules.

To add a condition, click a plus button. To delete a condition, click its minus button.

Select "Live updating" so iTunes can automatically update the playlist when it detects songs that match the set conditions.

The new playlist appears in the Source list. It is automatically selected and contains the songs that match its conditions.

A new Smart Playlist appears in the Source list (shown above-right). Any items in your Library that meet the conditions you set are now listed in the "Name" column of the Detail window. Rename the playlist something descriptive.

Burn an Audio CD

Making your own audio CDs with iTunes is easy. Just create a playlist with your favorite music, click the "Burn Disc" button, and insert a blank CD. iTunes will take care of the rest.

Audio CDs created with iTunes can be played in any regular CD player. To burn your music files onto DVDs or MP3 CDs, set the disc format to DVD or MP3 in the Burning pane of the Advanced pane of iTunes preferences (see page 252).

Not all blank audio CDs can store the same amount of music. Some CDs can hold 74 minutes of music, and others can hold 80 minutes or more. Before you burn a disc, check the capacity of your CDs and adjust your playlist accordingly.

To burn a CD:

1. Select a playlist in the Source list.
2. Check any songs you want recorded on the new CD. Uncheck songs you don't want to burn to the CD.
3. Click the "Burn Disc" button.
4. The Status display instructs you to insert a blank CD.
5. When finished, a new CD icon representing your newly created music CD appears on your Desktop.

Uncheck songs you don't want to burn to a CD.

After you click "Burn Disc," the Status display instructs you to insert a blank CD.

Check the total time of your playlist to make sure all of the songs will fit onto your audio CD.

Click the Burn Disk button to burn your playlist to CD.

Play the Radio

Click "Radio" to open the **Radio Tuner**. You can tune into the **Internet radio stations** that are built into iTunes (or whose addresses you have entered). These stations play a wide variety of music, news, and talkshow programs.

To play the radio in iTunes:

1. Click "Radio" in the Source list to see the radio options in the "Stream" column (the same column that is labeled "Name" when the selected Source is a CD, an album, or your Library).

2. Click the disclosure triangle of a radio category to see the various choices of streaming Internet connections.

3. Double-click a stream to begin playing it. iTunes will open the designated URL (web address) and start playing the content.

Choose which columns to display in the Radio Tuner window: From the View menu, choose "View Options..."

iTunes uses technology that allows content to start steaming immediately. It continues to download data as the file plays. If you do not have a full-time Internet connection, connect to the Internet before you double-click a radio selection.

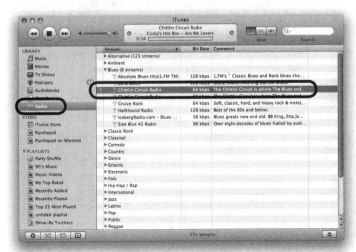

Some radio stations are available in several bit rates (kilobits per second) which affect the quality of the streams. Streams with higher bit rates sound better, but tend to break up over slow connections.

To enter another radio address:

If you know the web address of a streaming radio station that's not in the iTunes Radio Tuner, you can manually enter it.

1. From the Advanced menu at the top of your screen, choose "Open Stream...."

2. In the text field of the "Open Stream" window, enter the web address. The address must be a complete URL (it must include "http://").

The iTunes Store

If you have a slow Internet connection, see page 248 to learn how to improve the quality of the iTunes Music Store song previews.

The iTunes Store is an interactive multimedia store where you can preview and purchase millions of songs, music videos, TV shows, movies, and audiobooks. If you're not interested in buying anything, you can browse thousands of free items available for download, such as independently produced podcasts and taped college and university lectures in iTunes U. You can even rent movies to watch on your computer, iPhone, iPod, or Apple TV.

Click this button to log in, log out, or see your iTunes Store account information.

The Home button takes you back to the iTunes Store home page.
Use the left and right arrow buttons to show previous and next pages.

Type an album, artist, or item name into this box to search the iTunes Store.

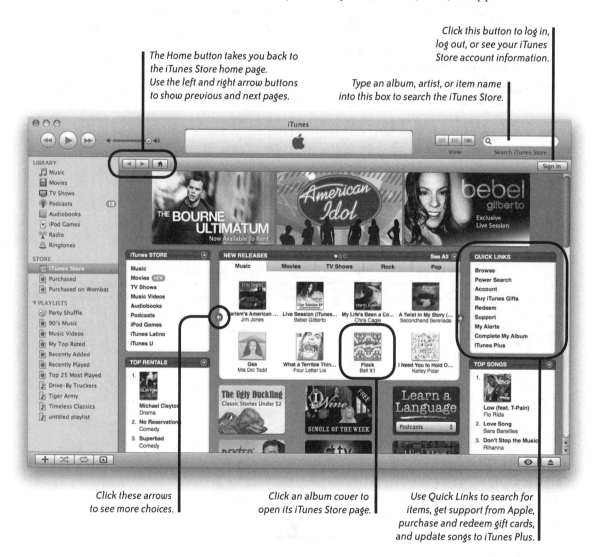

Click these arrows to see more choices.

Click an album cover to open its iTunes Store page.

Use Quick Links to search for items, get support from Apple, purchase and redeem gift cards, and update songs to iTunes Plus.

When you purchase songs or videos from the iTunes Store, they start downloading to your computer immediately. Apple will charge your credit card for the item and email you a receipt.

The iTunes Store also has a number of community features that make it easy to share, rate, and discover music. Create an iMix to share your playlist with the world. Rate songs and albums to tell others what you think about them. Scan the "Just for You" section on the iTunes Store home page to discover new music.

iTunes also uses your Apple Account information to keep track of the machines authorized to play your music. See page 274 for more information.

Click the text buttons that are stacked to the right of the Home button to jump directly to previously visited pages.

Once you've logged into the iTunes Store, your account name will be displayed here. Click to see your account information.

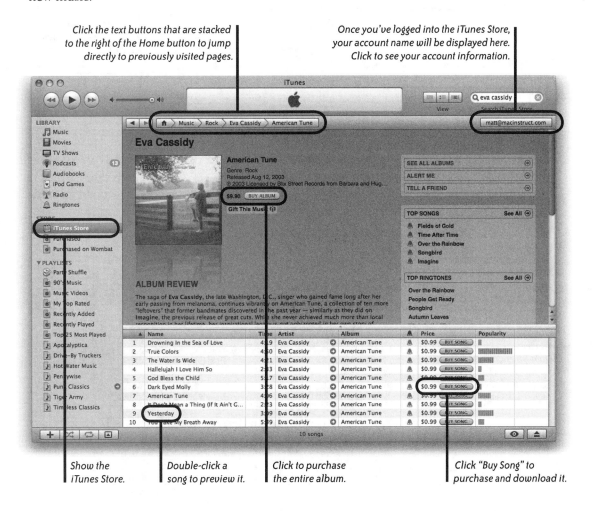

Show the iTunes Store.

Double-click a song to preview it.

Click to purchase the entire album.

Click "Buy Song" to purchase and download it.

Preview and purchase multimedia content

The first time you try to buy items from the iTunes Store, you'll be asked to sign in to your existing Apple account or create a new account. After you finish this quick and simple procedure, you can buy songs, albums, TV shows, movies, audiobooks, and more with a single click of the "Buy" button.

If you don't already have an account, click here to create a new one.

Enter your Apple ID and Password, then click "Sign in" to log in to iTunes.

Select the AOL option to log in to iTunes with an AOL account.

The iTunes Store provides a thirty-second preview of nearly every song, video, movie, TV show, and audiobook. Select an item, then double-click it to play the preview. To purchase an item and download it to your computer, click the "Buy" button.

Every item you purchase from the iTunes Store will be listed in the Purchased playlist.

Rent or buy a movie.

Click this button to watch the movie trailer.

Download free content

Previewing and purchasing content isn't the only thing you can do at the iTunes Store. You can also download thousands of free podcasts, songs, videos, and TV shows.

Podcasts are especially interesting. Anyone can create these short audio and video programs and then upload them to the iTunes Store. You'll find everything from professional TV shows to amateur home videos in the podcast section of the iTunes Store (shown below). There are thousands of podcasts freely available to download! You can also *subscribe* to podcasts, which ensures that new episodes of your favorite podcasts will be downloaded to your computer.

If you have a hankering to learn something (for free), check out the Podcasts and iTunes U sections of the iTunes Store. iTunes U has tens of thousands of audio and video files from colleges and universities around the world.

Downloaded podcasts are stored in the Podcasts Library.

Click "Subscribe" to automatically download new episodes of this podcast as they become available.

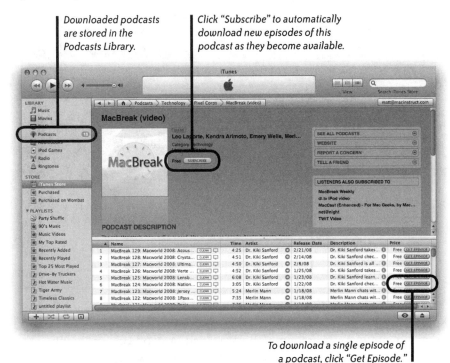

To download a single episode of a podcast, click "Get Episode."

Apple offers a new "Single of the Week" in the iTunes Store every week. They also offer a slew of free songs, videos, and TV shows in the "Free on iTunes" section. Look for it on the iTunes Store home page.

Another free iTunes Store feature is iTunes U. Originally developed for colleges and universities around the world, this section now features free audiobooks and musical performances by college ensembles, as well as audio and video recordings of lectures, presentations, and seminars. These invaluable educational recordings are made available at no cost to the general public.

Rent movies

If you'd like to watch a movie but you don't want to purchase one, you're in luck. You can use the iTunes Store to rent and watch movies on your computer, iPhone, iPod, or Apple TV. There are hundreds of movies available–everything from the newest releases to the black-and-white classics.

Apple puts some limitations on movie rentals. You have 30 days to start watching your movie after you download it. You can transfer the movie between your computer, iPhone, iPod, and Apple TV, but only one device at a time can hold the movie. Once you start watching your movie, you have 24 hours to finish it and watch it again as many times as you want.

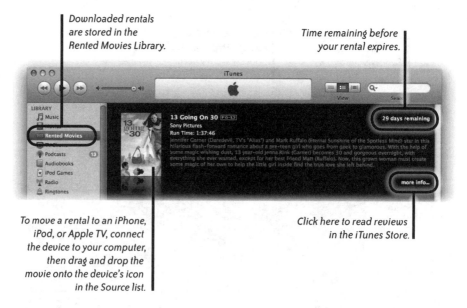

Downloaded rentals are stored in the Rented Movies Library.

Time remaining before your rental expires.

To move a rental to an iPhone, iPod, or Apple TV, connect the device to your computer, then drag and drop the movie onto the device's icon in the Source list.

Click here to read reviews in the iTunes Store.

Movies are large files that can take a while to download. Depending on the speed of your Internet connection, movies could take anywhere from a couple minutes to several hours to download. A good rule of thumb is to start the download a couple hours before you plan to watch your rental.

If you transfer movies to your iPhone, iPod, or Apple TV, they're removed from your computer.

Create and publish your own iMix playlist

Do you have a favorite mix of songs available from the iTunes Store that you'd like to share? If so, you can put them in a playlist and publish them as an **iMix.** iMix is an iTunes Store feature that publishes song mixes submitted by iTunes users. You must use music available from the iTunes Store. The published iMix plays a thirty-second preview of each song in the mix. It's fun and useful for sending song discoveries and recommendations to friends.

To view iMix collections submitted by others, select "iMix" on the iTunes Store music page.

1. Create a playlist that contains only music available from the iTunes Store. When you select any playlist in the Source list, an iMix publish button (a white arrow in a circle) appears to the right of the playlist name (shown circled below).

2. Click the iMix button to publish the playlist as an iMix. In the window that opens, click "Create iMix." In the next window that opens, click "Create" (shown below).

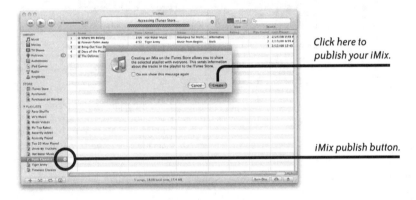

Click here to publish your iMix.

iMix publish button.

3. Sign in with your Apple ID and password.

4. On the page that opens (shown below), type a title and description.

5. Click the "Publish" button.

Tip: When you publish a playlist as an iMix, the iMix publish button stays visible. To modify your iMix collection at any time, click the iMix button again.

Publish your iMix.

Use Search, Power Search, or Browse to find specific songs

To **search,** type a complete or partial artist, album, or item name in the Search field, then hit Return on the keyboard. The search results appear in the bottom section of the iTunes window, as shown below.

Select the "Browse" or "Power Search" options from the Quick Links section on the iTunes Store home page.

Type an album, artist, or item name.

The top section of the search shows albums, books, and videos that match the search term. The bottom section shows songs that match.

To **Power Search,** choose "Power Search…" from the Search pop-up menu. In the Power Search pane, shown below, enter as much information as possible, then click the "Search" button.

iTunes automatically attempts to complete your search phrase while you're typing. To select an artist, click on a name in the list.

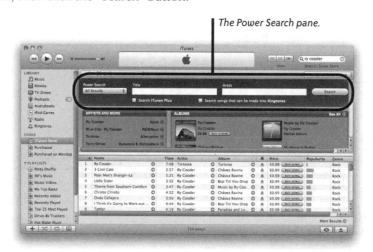

The Power Search pane.

Use the **Browse** button to search for audiobooks, movies, music, music videos, podcasts, and TV shows. Click the "Browse" button to show the Browser pane, circled below. Different columns will be available for different types of media. If you're searching for music, select a genre from the "Genre" column, select an item from the "Subgenre" column, choose an artist from the "Artist" column, then choose an album from the "Album" column. After you make your selections, the matching results show in the bottom section of the window.

Tip: To leave the Browser, click the "Browse" button again. You can also click the Back button (the left-facing arrow) or the Home button.

The Browser pane.

The Browse results for Taj Mahal's "Señor Blues."

The "Browse" button.

Get support from the iTunes Store

If you're having problems purchasing items or accessing the items you purchased from the iTunes Store, you may need to submit a support request to Apple. Fortunately, the iTunes Store has an excellent support team waiting to respond to your issue. Click the "Support" link in the Quick Links section of the iTunes Store home page to get started.

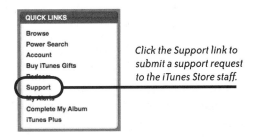

Click the Support link to submit a support request to the iTunes Store staff.

Tip: If you can't find the songs and videos you purchased anywhere on your Mac, try checking the iTunes Store for your purchases. Select "Check for Purchases" from the Store menu. iTunes will download your purchased items if it hasn't already.

To purchase these items, select "Buy iTunes Gifts" from the Quick Links section on the iTunes Store home page.

Giving iTunes Gifts

You've seen how easy it is to click the "Buy" button and download music through your Apple Account. But what if you'd like to buy music for someone else and let him download it to his own computer? The iTunes Store provides several easy and convenient ways to do this.

Allowance: Set up an allowance when you want to let your kids buy a preset amount of music without a credit card. You can set a monthly amount between $10 and $200.

1. Click the "Buy iTunes Gifts" link on the iTunes Store home page, and then click the "Allowances" link.

2. In the setup window that opens, fill in the required information (the recipient needs an Apple Account), then click "Continue."

3. A window opens asking you to confirm your purchase. Check the information, then click the "Buy" button.

To cancel an allowance at any time, click your "Account" button in the iTunes Music Store window.

Set up an iTunes Allowance

An iTunes Allowance provides a simple way for family members and friends to buy music without giving them your credit card. Monthly allowances can be purchased in amounts from $10.00 to $200.00. Recipients must have an Apple account for use in the US store, which you can easily set up below. Allowances may be canceled at any time by visiting your Account Info page.

Your Name:	Matthew
Recipient's Name:	
Monthly Allowance:	$20.00 ⎯ from $10.00 to $200.00
First Installment:	◉ Don't send now, wait until the first of next month ○ Send now, and on the first of next month
Recipient's Apple ID:	○ Create an Apple Account for recipient ◉ Use recipient's existing Apple Account
Apple ID:	
Verify Apple ID:	
Personal Message:	

iTunes sends a message to the recipient.

Cancel   Continue

Gift certificates: Because gift certificates can be emailed and printed, they're a great idea for last-minute gifts that otherwise don't have a chance of getting there on time.

1. Click the "Buy iTunes Gifts" link on the iTunes Store home page, then choose a delivery method: "Email" or "Printable."

2. In the form that opens, fill in the required information. Use the "Amount" pop-up menu to select an amount from $10 to $200. Click "Continue."

3. Enter your Apple Account ID and password, then click "Continue."

4. In the "Confirm Your Purchase" window, click the "Buy" button.

Gift cards: Here's another solution for a gift or for someone who doesn't have a credit card—purchase gift cards. To redeem an iTunes Gift Card, the recipient clicks on the "Redeem" link on the iTunes Store home page, then follows the instructions. You can also redeem gift cards on the iPhone and iPod Touch.

iTunes Prepaid Cards.

Gift music: You can purchase music and videos for others using the "Gift This Music" option. Just click the "Gift This Music" button on any page in the iTunes Store. iTunes will help you select the songs and send your gift.

Click this button on any page in the iTunes Store to send songs or videos as a gift.

You can also create a playlist on your computer and then send the entire playlist as a gift.

1. Create a playlist, and then fill it with songs and videos.
2. Click the Gift button to send the music to others. In the window that opens, click the "Give Playlist" button.

3. Enter the recipient's information, click the "Continue" button, and then click the "Buy Gift" button.

Shopping cart: Use a shopping cart if you want to store song selections and buy them later, or if you want to review the music that your children have chosen before it's purchased. To set up a Shopping Cart:

$0.99 **BUY SONG**

When you enable an iTunes Shopping Cart, the "Buy Song" button in the Music Store changes to "Add Song."

1. From the iTunes menu, choose "Preferences…."
2. Click the "Store" button to open the Store preferences pane.
3. Select "Buy using a Shopping Cart." Music is added to your cart when you click an "Add" button. To purchase and download a *single song* in the shopping cart, click its "Buy Song" button. To purchase and download *all songs* in the shopping cart, click "Buy Now" at the bottom of the window.

    To remove songs from the shopping cart, select "Shopping Cart" in the Source pane. Select a song in the Shopping Cart and click the tiny Delete button that appears to the right of the "Buy Song" button.

A new "Shopping Cart" icon appears in the Source pane, as shown above.

Manage and Play Videos in iTunes

iTunes can manage much more than music. It can also manage movies, TV shows, music videos, and homemade videos you've created in applications like iMovie and Final Cut Express. Use iTunes to watch your videos and synchronize them with your iPhone, iPod, or Apple TV.

Download videos from the iTunes Store

When you purchase video content from the iTunes Store, iTunes stores it in the appropriate library. Double-click the video file to play it. The video plays in the bottom-left pane of the iTunes window (unless you set a different preference, explained on the next page). Click once on the video and it opens in a separate window, as shown at the top of the next page.

The video icon denotes music videos in the Music library.

You can configure iTunes to play videos in the artwork window.

iTunes categorizes your videos and stores them in different libraries. Music videos are stored in the Music library, TV shows are stored in the TV Shows library, video podcasts are stored in the Podcasts library, and movies and homemade videos are stored in the Movies library.

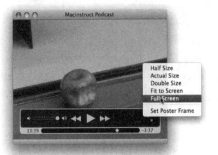

When you open a video in a separate window, you have access to the Play controls so you can place the playhead anywhere in the movie.

Control-click on the video's window to open a contextual menu from which you can change the movie size.

Import your own QuickTime videos

If you have QuickTime movies that you exported from iMovie or that were imported into iPhoto from your digital camera, store them in iTunes and play them whenever you want, without having to search your hard disk for them. You can drag a QuickTime file from any location on your computer to the iTunes window to put it in the Movies library.

Tip: If you burn a disc of a playlist that contains video, the videos are burned to the disc as audio files only.

Set a default for video playback

When you select a video in the song list and click the Play button (or when you double-click a song to play it), it might play "in the main window" (the small video pane in the bottom-left corner of the window, as shown on the previous page), "in a separate window" (as shown above), or in "full screen" mode.

To set a default for how a video plays, open the iTunes preferences, then click the "Playback' button in the toolbar. Select the "Play movies and TV shows" option. From the pop-up menu, choose the way you want iTunes to initially show a video. Repeat this process for the "Play music videos" option then click OK.

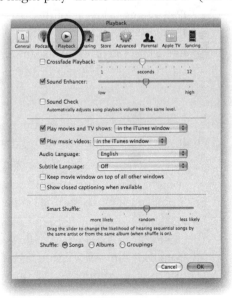

The Source List

This is where you select the media collection that you want to display in the Detail window. Sources are grouped into five categories: Library, Store, Devices, Shared, and Playlists. These items help you navigate all of the multimedia content you have stored in iTunes.

Library

The sources in this category contain your entire collection of iTunes media.

To delete a playlist in the Source pane, select it, then press the Delete key on your keyboard.

- ▼ **Music** is your entire collection of iTunes music. Click "Music" in the Source list to view all the songs in iTunes.

- ▼ **Movies** keeps track of the videos you've added from your computer, as well as the movies you've purchased from the iTunes Store.

- ▼ **Rented Movies** collects movies you've rented from the iTunes Store. See page 214 for details.

- ▼ **TV Shows** keeps track of the television shows you've purchased from the iTunes Store.

- ▼ **Podcasts** collects podcasts. Podcasts that you've subscribed to through the iTunes Store are automatically downloaded and stored here. The number of new podcasts will appear next to "Podcasts." See page 213 for details.

- ▼ **Audiobooks** keeps track of the audiobooks on your Mac.

- ▼ **iPod Games** stores all of the games you've purchased for your iPod from the iTunes Store.

- ▼ **Radio** lets you listen to streaming Internet radio stations. Learn how on page 209.

Store

The items in this category allow you to interact with the iTunes Store and the content you've purchased from the iTunes Store.

- ▼ **iTunes Store** is where you preview, purchase, rent, and download content. Click "iTunes Store" to connect directly to the online iTunes Store. Learn more starting on page 210.

- ▼ **Purchased** keeps track of the content you've purchased from the iTunes Store. If you have a device capable of purchasing content from the iTunes Store, you'll also see a "Purchased on…" playlist that displays the content you've purchased on that device.

Devices

This category lists Apple devices connected to your computer and CDs inserted into your CD drive.

- ▼ **CD** displays the tracks on the CD in your computer's CD drive. If your Mac is connected to the Internet, this item will automatically display the actual album and track names.

- ▼ **Devices** allows you to interact with your other Apple devices. After you connect your iPod, iPhone, or Apple TV to your Mac, select this item to upload media content to your device, configure synchronization options, and download software updates. A click on the disclosure triangle reveals all of the playlists on your device.

Shared

If you've set iTunes to "Look for shared libraries," and if it finds a Shared playlist on your local network, a new icon appears in the Shared category— a stack of documents with a music note on top. Click this icon to reveal all the playlists in that Library. Learn how to access shared Libraries on pages 234 and 247.

Playlists

This category lists all of the playlists you've created in iTunes.

- ▼ **Party Shuffle** is an automated playlist that selects a designated number of songs and plays them for you, constantly refreshing the playlist with selections based on your Party Shuffle settings. See page 232 for details.

- ▼ **Smart Playlists** have a gear symbol on their icons. Some of these automated playlists were created by Apple for you. You can also create your own automated playlists to collect music that meets your preset conditions. See page 207.

- ▼ **Playlists** have an icon with a note symbol on them. Learn more about ordinary playlists on pages 205.

The Detail Window

The **Detail window** displays various columns of song information. The visible columns in the Detail window vary depending on which source you select in the Source pane and which options you choose in the View Options window (see page 229).

Press Command J to open "View Options" and choose which columns show here in the Detail window.

Select and play songs

To play any song in the "Name" column, double-click its title. When that selection has finished, iTunes plays the next song in the list *that has a checkmark next to it.*

When you insert a CD, by default *all* the song titles have a checkmark next to them, which means they will all play in order when you click the "Play" button. The checkmark also determines which songs will be encoded and placed in iTunes when you click the "Import CD" button (page 204).

- ▾ **To select (check) all songs at once,** Command-click on any *empty* checkbox.

- ▾ **To deselect (uncheck) all the songs at once,** Command-click on any checkbox that has a *check* in it.

- ▾ **To select a group of contiguous songs** (songs that are adjacent to each other in the song list), click on one song, then Shift-click another song. All titles between the two clicks will be automatically added to your selection.

- ▾ **To select a group of non-contiguous songs** (songs that are not adjacent to each other in the song list), Command-click on the songs you want to select.

Resize or rearrange columns

If song titles are cut off by the narrow width of the "Name" column or if one of the columns is too narrow or too wide, you can **resize the column.** Place your cursor over the thin gray dividing line that separates two columns. The cursor becomes a bi-directional arrow. Press-and-drag the line to the left or right as far as necessary to resize the column to your liking.

Drag the divider line left or right to resize columns.

To rearrange the columns, press on a column's title bar. When you start to drag, the arrow turns into a grabber hand as shown below. Drag the column left or right to a new position.

Above, you can see the grabber hand as it drags the "Time" column from its original position to the position between the "Artist" and the "Album" columns.

Organize the column information

The Detail window is always **organized** by the **selected** column. In the example above, the information is organized alphabetically by artist name—you can see that the "Artist" column heading is highlighted.

Click the small triangle to the right of a *selected* column name to **reverse the order** in which the information is displayed. For instance, if you select the column head, "Rating," and then click its triangle, the songs will be listed in order of how you rated them; click the triangle again to reverse the order of the ratings.

View the iTunes Libraries

When your Libraries contain a large collection of items by many different artists, you can choose to browse a Library's contents using several different view modes.

▼ To change the **View,** use the View buttons in the iTunes toolbar. You can select the List view (left button), the Album view (center button), or the Cover Flow view (right button). You can also change view modes from View menu.

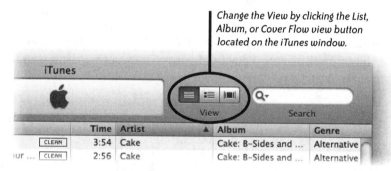

Change the View by clicking the List, Album, or Cover Flow view button located on the iTunes window.

List View

The List view displays all of your songs and videos in a long list that can be organized by the selected column. This is the default View setting in iTunes.

Click the List button to change into the List view.

Album View

The Album view groups your songs and videos according to album. iTunes will display cover art next to all of your albums, if cover art is available. Like the List view, the Album can be organized by the selected column.

Click the Album button to switch to Album view.

These songs are all from the same album, listed in their correct album order.

Cover Flow View

Tired of scrolling through lists of songs? Use the Cover Flow view and turn iTunes into a virtual jukebox. Flip through your album artwork and play your selection by pressing the Return key. You can even display Cover Flow full screen and use your Apple Remote to control it.

If iTunes is not displaying album artwork for your music, you might need to download the artwork from iTunes. See page 108 for more information.

Click the Cover Flow button to change into the Cover Flow view.

Click this button to show Cover Flow in full screen.

To focus a search, click the tiny triangle and choose a category that you want to search.

Search the iTunes Libraries

The **Search** field enables you to quickly find songs from an iTunes Library, an iTunes playlist, or a mounted CD.

To search:

▼ In the Search field (circled below), type a word or phrase that's part of the item name, artist name, album name, or composer name.

You don't need to hit Return—a list will appear instantly in the Detail window that includes only songs that contain your search terms. As you type each letter, the list updates to show the matching results.

For instance, in this example we search for a song by Joan Armatrading called "Merchant of Love." As we type the word, "merchant," into the Search field, the results list instantly shows dozens of songs that have "m" in either the song title, artist name, or album name. After we continue to type letters, the list changes to show the only songs that contain "merch." If we continue to type the entire song name, the results list is reduced to only the song that contains that title.

Type a search term in the Search field.

Search results.

View Options

Set the Detail window to show just the information you want. Select a source in the Source list, then from the Edit menu choose "View Options...." The top item in the "View Options" window is the name and icon of the selected source. As shown below, the options in this window change depending on the item you select in the Source list. Check the columns you want to show in the Detail window, then click OK.

Most items in the Source list have the same view options available as those for the Library, shown below-left. "Radio" and mounted CDs have fewer view options, as shown below. Some items such as "Movies" and "iTunes Store" have no view options available.

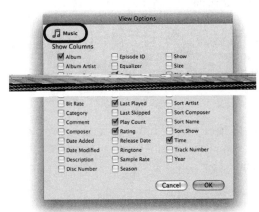

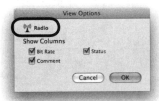

The items you choose here determine which columns are visible in the Detail window when you view the songs in the Music Library.

Select "Radio" in the Source list, then choose which of these columns you want to show in the Detail window.

These are the View Options when a CD is selected in the Source pane. Select the "Disc Number" option if you want to identify multiple CDs that are part of a set.

When a CD from a set of three is mounted, its disc number shows in the Detail window as "1 of 3," "2 of 3," or "3 of 3."

When a single CD is mounted, its disc number shows in the Detail window as "1 of 1."

Close, Minimize, and Zoom Buttons

As with every window in Mac OS X, you see the **three colored buttons** in the upper-left corner of the window, but they act a little differently in iTunes.

▼ Click the **red button** (the left button) to hide the iTunes window, even while music is playing. It won't affect the music.

To show the player again, from the Window menu choose "iTunes."

Or use the keyboard shortcut Option-Command 1 (one) to show and hide the window while iTunes is active.

▼ Click the center **yellow button** to minimize the player and send it to the Dock. The selected song continues to play.

To bring the player back to the Desktop, single-click it in the Dock.

▼ Click the **green button** (the Zoom button, on the right) to reduce the size of the player window to its smallest possible size, as shown below. Click the green button again to return to full size.

Controller Buttons

The **controller buttons** act just like the controls on most CD players:

- ▼ **To select the Next song,** click the Forward button (double arrows pointing to the right).
- ▼ **To Fast Forward** the current selection, press-and-hold the Forward button.
- ▼ **To select the Previous song,** click the Back button (double arrows pointing to the left).
- ▼ **To Rapid Rewind** the current selection, press-and-hold the Back button.
- ▼ The middle button toggles between **Play** and **Pause** when a song file on your computer (or on a CD) is playing.

  The same button toggles between **Play** and **Stop** when the Radio Tuner is active.

Back   Forward

The middle button switches between Play and Pause when a song is playing.

It switches between Play and Stop when the Internet Radio is playing.

Video Controller Buttons

The **video controller buttons** appear when you are playing video content in iTunes. The buttons are similar to the controller buttons that appear in the main iTunes window.

- ▼ **To select the Next movie chapter,** click the Forward button (double arrows pointing to the right).
- ▼ **To Fast Forward** through the video, press-and-hold the Forward button.
- ▼ **To select the Previous movie chapter,** click the Back button (double arrows pointing to the left).
- ▼ **To Rapid Rewind** through the video, press-and-hold the Back button.
- ▼ The middle button toggles between **Play** and **Pause**.
- ▼ **To select a chapter in a movie**, click the Chapter button (the book icon).
- ▼ **To enter full-screen mode**, single-click the Screen Mode button (the diagonal arrows icon on the right side).

Party Shuffle

The Party Shuffle automatically creates a **dynamic playlist** based on your set-tings (shown below). It constantly updates, adding a new song whenever the current song ends. You can add songs manually, delete songs, or rearrange the order of songs at any time. Songs that you add manually stay in the list.

To create a Party Shuffle playlist:

1. Select "Party Shuffle" in the Source list. If it's not there, go to iTunes Preferences, click the "General" button, then check (or uncheck) "Party Shuffle."

Party Shuffle's automatic playlist.

Party Shuffle options.

To manually "re-shuffle" the Party Shuffle playlist, click the "Refresh" button.

2. Party Shuffle instantly shows a playlist based on the option settings found at the bottom of the window, circled above.

3. Use the "Source" pop-up menu to select the Music Library or any playlist as a source from which Party Shuffle can choose songs. Party Shuffle will see only songs that are checked. Unchecked songs in the selected source will be ignored.

4. Click "Play higher rated songs more often" if you've *rated* your songs, as described on page 241.

5. Use the "Display" pop-up menus to set how many *recently played songs* and *upcoming songs* you want added to the list (up to 100).

Quick Links

Quick Link buttons (an arrow inside a circle) can be seen in the "Name" column, the "Artist" column, and the "Album" column. They are literally quick links to pages in the iTunes Store. Quick Links for the same item that are in different columns may go to different Store pages, depending on the column the Quick Link is in. If you click on a Quick Link in the "Name" column, iTunes will search for that particular song or video in the iTunes Store.

All songs, albums, and videos have a Quick Link button, but it only works if the item is actually available in the iTunes Store.

When you click a playlist in the Source list, a Quick Link button appears next to it. These buttons in the Source list are links to publish the playlist as an iMix (read about iMix on page 215). If you try to publish a playlist that contains some songs that are not available at the iTunes Store, iMix will ignore those songs and publish only the ones available there.

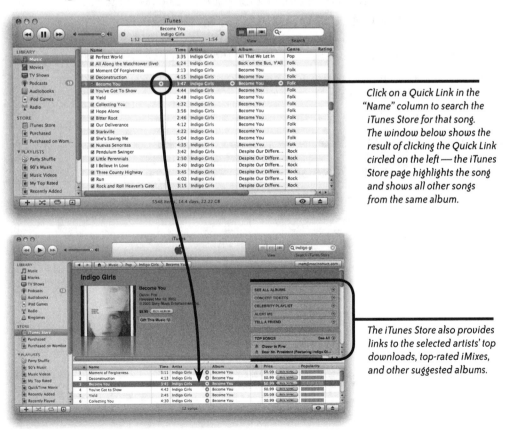

Click on a Quick Link in the "Name" column to search the iTunes Store for that song. The window below shows the result of clicking the Quick Link circled on the left — the iTunes Store page highlights the song and shows all other songs from the same album.

The iTunes Store also provides links to the selected artists' top downloads, top-rated iMixes, and other suggested albums.

Share Music Over a Local Network

If you have two or more computers on a local network, users can **share their music collections** without copying any songs from one computer to another. iTunes can *stream* music files over a local area network (LAN) to a computer that has set iTunes Preferences to look for shared music.

Set one (or more) of your computers to share its iTunes Libraries or selected playlists:

iTunes automatically finds shared music on the local network and puts it in the Source pane, as shown here. Click one of the shared playlists to display its songs, or click the shared Library icon ("Michael Rey's Library" in this example) to see the contents of all the shared playlists.

1. From the iTunes menu, select "Preferences…," then click the "Sharing" button.

2. Select "Look for shared libraries" to make iTunes place an icon in the Source list for any shared playlists it finds on the local network.

3. Select "Share my library on my local network" to make your iTunes music collection available on the local network to other computers that have been set to look for shared music (as in Step 2).

   If you select "Share my library on my local network," you must choose whether to "Share entire library" or "Share selected playlists." If you choose the latter, select the playlists you want to share.

4. To restrict access to your music, select "Require password" and type a password in the text field.

5. Click OK.

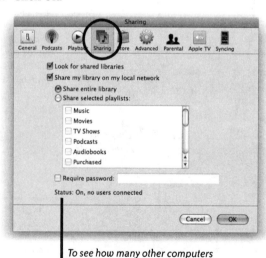

To see how many other computers are connected to your shared playlists, check this "Status" line.

Print CD Jewel Case Inserts, Song Listings, or Album Listings

Being able to burn a CD of your own customized playlists is really cool. Then you have to clumsily scrawl some kind of description on it with a felt tip pen so you'll know what's on it. Oh, wait—that was last century. Now you just select a design and let iTunes **print a beautiful CD case insert** that includes album art and a list of songs. You can also print song lists and album lists.

To print a CD jewel case insert, song listing, or album listing:

1. Select a playlist in the Source list.

2. From the File menu, choose "Print…."

3. In the dialog box, choose one of the "Print" options: "CD jewel case insert," "Song listing," or "Album listing."

4. From the "Theme" pop-up menu, choose a layout style.

5. Click the "Print…" button to send to a printer.

Tip: The choices in the "Theme" pop-up menu change depending on the "Print" option you choose. CD jewel case themes are provided in both color and black and white.

A thumbnail preview of your theme selection.

A description of the selected theme.

Themes are available for each of the Print options available.

Song Information and Options

Get information about songs and videos, add lyrics and comments, adjust the volume control, and make other adjustments in the **Information** window.

To open the Song Information window:

1. Select one song or video, or multiple songs and videos.

2. Type Command I to open the Information window.

If you select more than one song, you'll get a different dialog box from the one shown below. See the bottom of page 238.

If you make a single song selection, the Information window contains seven tabs: Summary, Info, Video, Sorting, Options, Lyrics, and Artwork.

Summary

The **Summary** pane gives information about the *selected* item. To get information about other songs in the selected playlist without leaving this window, click the "Previous" or "Next" button (circled below-left).

Info

The **Info** pane provides additional information, as you can see, above-right. There is also a "Comments" field in which you can add your own comments, such as "Used as theme for Ben's graduation movie."

Mark items as a **compilation** (circled, above-right) to group them together.

When you mark a *song* as part of a compilation, a new folder is created in the iTunes Music folder named "Compilations," and the song is placed in a sub-folder named for the album the song came from.

When you mark a *CD* as a compilation CD, a new folder named for the CD is placed in the Compilations folder. This causes any song you import from the CD to be marked as "Part of a compilation."

Compilations can be copied to an iPod, shared with others by copying them to another computer, or burned onto a CD.

Video

If you select a video, the **Video** pane, shown below-left, lets you enter information about the video, including the video type and episode number.

Use the **Video Kind** pop-up menu to set the video type for the selected video. This information helps iTunes determine where the video should be stored. Movies are stored in the Movies library and Music Videos are stored in the Music library. This menu is only available if you added the video to iTunes manually. Movies and videos purchased from the iTunes Store already include this information, and it cannot be changed.

If you selected a TV show, you can enter information in the "Show," "Season Number," "Episode ID," and "Episode Number" fields. This information helps iTunes organize your "TV Shows" library.

Sorting

Override the default sorting options for any song, video, or album by entering information in the **Sorting** pane (above-right). The boxes in the left column contain information about the item (the same information displayed in the **Info** pane). By default, iTunes will sort the song using this information. Enter information in the boxes in the right column to override the default sort information without modifying the existing song information.

Options

The **Options** pane allows you to set the **Volume Adjustment** for individual songs. This is cool when you're a serious rocker, and cranking up the other volume controls just isn't loud enough.

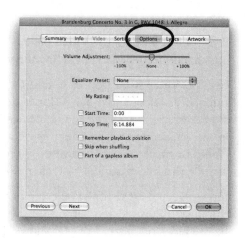

Use the **Equalizer Preset** pop-up menu to select one of the preset equalizer settings for the selected song. You can also set this in the main iTunes window if you've configured "View Options" to show the Equalizer column (as explained on page 229).

Set **My Rating** for the selected song between one and five stars. This setting can also be set in the iTunes main window if you've configured "View Options" to show the Rating column.

Set a **Start/Stop Time** for a song. In the event you want to **play or import just a section** of a long song, enter the "Start Time" and

"Stop Time" in a minutes:seconds format (00:00). To determine which time settings you need, first play the whole song. Watch the "Status" display at the top of the iTunes window, and write down the beginning and ending "Elapsed Time" of your desired music segment.

If you selected more than one song, the "Multiple Song Information" window, shown on the right, combines all the previous information and options into one window. The "Volume Adjustment" affects all selected tracks.

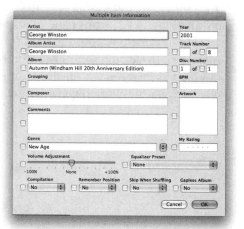

Lyrics

You can paste song lyrics into the **Lyrics** pane and then display them on your Mac and your other Apple devices, such as an iPod or iPhone. This is a great way to memorize your favorite songs.

Finding lyrics and manually adding them to every song is rather cumbersome. Fortunately, there are several free tools that automate the process, such as the "Sing that iTune!" widget (http://www.apple.com/downloads/dashboard/music/singthatitune.html).

Doug's AppleScripts for iTunes (http://dougscripts.com/itunes/) is a great resource for automating iTunes. There are over 400 AppleScripts available for iTunes, including scripts that automatically find lyrics and add them to your iTunes songs.

Artwork

The **Artwork** pane displays the artwork associated with the selected item. Songs and videos you buy from the iTunes Store automatically include the artwork, and it appears in this window. This artwork also appears in the Artwork pane of the main iTunes window (far right). Click the Artwork button, circled in the example, to show or hide the song artwork. To see a full-size version of the artwork in its own window, single-click the artwork.

When you manually import songs and videos into iTunes, those items won't have any artwork. You can search the iTunes Store for artwork. From the Advanced menu, choose "Get Album Artwork." iTunes will contact the iTunes Store and download any artwork it can find.

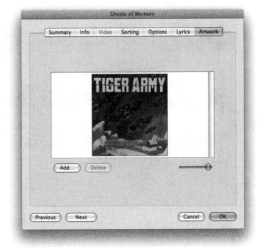

Click the Artwork button to hide or show this pane.

Status Display

When iTunes is playing a song or video, the **Status display** (at the top of the iTunes window) shows three lines of information: item name, artist identification, track time, and an audio track bar.

The **item name** (the top line) in the Status display always shows the name of the song or video playing.

The **artist identification** is shown in the middle line. This line automatically scrolls through the artist and collection name. Click on it to cycle through these two bits of information.

The **audio track bar** on the bottom line indicates the current location of playback in relation to the entire song. **To move to any point in a song or video,** drag the playhead (the small black diamond) left or right. **Or** just click anywhere along the length of the audio track bar to position the playhead.

When iTunes is playing the **Radio Tuner,** the Status display is similar.

The top line shows the name of the station. The middle line shows the name of the song playing or the URL (Internet address) of the radio station. The bottom line is a **blank audio track** bar. You can't drag ahead or back in Radio streaming files.

No matter what you're listening to, you can turn the Status display into a **mini graphic equalizer:** Click the small triangle button on the left side of the window. This feature doesn't offer control of any kind, but it's fun. Click the button again to return to the normal display of status information.

iTunes also includes a controllable equalizer (see page 260).

The SnapBack button

The curved arrow on the right side of the Status display is a **SnapBack** button. The SnapBack button returns you to the song that's currently playing. For example, you play a song from a CD, then you switch to the Library, and then to the iTunes Store, and then to a shared playlist. You may not remember where the song that's playing is coming from, but when you click the Snap-Back button, iTunes instantly shows the CD's contents and highlights the song that's playing.

Rate Your Songs

You can **rate songs** on a scale of one to five **stars.** The rating can be used to sort songs or create playlists, or as a criterion in creating Smart Playlists.

To rate your songs:

1. If the "Rating" column isn't showing in the iTunes window, Control-click on one of the column heads, then choose "Rating" from the pop-up menu that appears. **Or** from the View menu, choose "View Options…," then click the "Rating" checkbox.

2. Click on a song you want to rate. Notice that five dots appear in the "Rating" column.

3. Click on the first dot to add a single star. Click on dots further to the right to add more stars to your rating. You can also drag across the dots to add stars.

To sort the current songs by your rating, click the "Rating" column heading. The order of songs will be rearranged with the highest-rated songs at the top of the list. **To reverse** the order of the list, click the small toggle triangle on the right side of the column heading.

Tip: If you're looking for a different way to rate your songs, look no further than "Moody." This free application helps you rate songs according to the mood they put you in. Download it at ***http:// www.crayonroom.com/ moody.php.***

You can also set a song's rating in the information window. Select a song, then press Command I, or from the File menu, choose "Get Info." Click the "Options" button, then set "Rating" between one and five stars.

Export Playlists as Plain Text, Unicode, or XML Files

Export playlists as text files if you want to archive the Library information, or if you want to import the information into another program, such as a database application.

Export as XML if you want to use the playlist in iTunes on another computer. When you import the XML file into iTunes on another computer, iTunes looks in its Library for the songs and videos listed in the imported playlist. Songs and videos that are not in the Library will not show up in the "Name" column.

Export as Unicode if you're using a double-byte alphabet such as Japanese or Chinese.

This procedure creates a file that includes information for every column in iTunes, even if some columns are not visible in your iTunes window.

1. Select a playlist. From the File menu, choose "Export…"
2. In the "Save" window that opens, name the file. Set the "Format" pop-up menu to "Plain Text," "Unicode Text," or "XML," then choose a location where you want to save it.

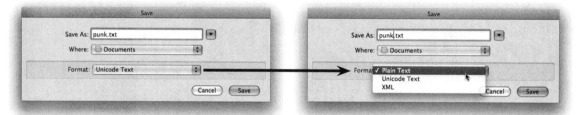

To create a text file (.txt) of song information that includes *only* the columns you have chosen to be visible (from the View menu, choose "View Options…"):

1. Select one or more songs or videos that appear in the "Name" column.
2. From the Edit menu, choose "Copy." **Or** Control-click on the song selection, then choose "Copy" from the pop-up contextual menu.
3. Open *another* application such as TextEdit, then from the Edit menu, choose "Paste." **Or** press Command V (for paste).

iTunes Preferences

The **iTunes** preferences allow you to adjust a number of settings. From the iTunes menu, choose "Preferences…."

General preferences

Click the **General** button to see the General preferences.

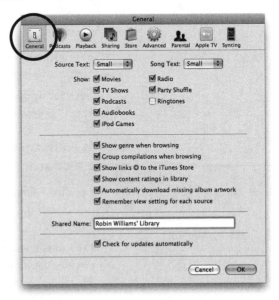

- ▼ **Source Text** and **Song Text:** Choose to use "Small" or "Large" text in the Source list and in the Detail window. The actual size difference between "Large" and "Small" is not dramatic.

- ▼ **Show:** Select items to show them in the Source list.

- ▼ **Show genre when browsing:** This option can be helpful when using the Browse feature (pages 217) to search through a large collection of music files. It adds a "Genre" column to the "Artist" and "Album" columns that become visible when you click the "Browse" button.

- ▼ **Group compilations when browsing:** This creates an item in the "Artist" column of the Browser named "Compilations." A compilation is a collection of songs that you choose to group together.

  To make any song part of a compilation, select the song, then press Command-I to open the Song Information window. Click the "Info" button, then click "Part of a compilation." In the Browser, the song will appear in "Compilations" under its album name (see page 236).

- ▼ **Show links to Music Store:** This makes the Quick Link buttons visible in iTunes' Source list and Detail window. Quick Links are shortcuts to the iTunes Store.

- ▼ **Show content ratings in library:** This allows you to see whether content you've purchased from the iTunes Store is "Clean" or "Explicit."

▾ **Automatically download missing album artwork:** This option allows you to configure iTunes to automatically download artwork for albums that are missing their album artwork. Albums that you import from a CD do not have album artwork automatically associated with them. Enable this option to automate the downloading of cover art.

▾ **Remember view setting for each source:** This option allows you to preserve the view options you set for each source in the iTunes Source list.

▾ **Shared Name:** Enter a name to identify your shared music collection when it appears in another user's iTunes Source list.

▾ **Check for updates automatically:** This option checks Apple's web site to see if software updates are available for iTunes.

Podcasts preferences

Click the **Podcasts** button to see the Podcasts preferences.

▾ **Check for new episodes:** This option checks Apple's web site for new episodes of the podcasts to which you are subscribed. You can set iTunes to check every hour, every day, every week, or not at all.

▾ **When new episodes are available:** Set iTunes to download all episodes, only the most recent episode, or to do nothing.

▾ **Keep:** This tells iTunes which podcast episodes to keep. You can choose to keep all episodes, some episodes, or no episodes at all. iTunes deletes podcasts that it removes from your Podcast library.

Playback preferences

Click the **Playback** button to change how your music plays.

▼ Check the **Crossfade playback** checkbox to fade music smoothly between songs without a long gap of silence. This effect is one of our favorites. The slider adjusts the amount of time it takes to fade out of one song and to fade in to the next song. Move the slider all the way to the right for the smoothest transition with the least amount of silence between songs.

▼ Check the **Sound Enhancer** box to add depth and liven the quality of the music. The slider increases or decreases the effect, which is subtle but noticeable.

▼ Check the **Sound Check** box to make all songs play at the same volume level.

▼ Check the **Play movies and TV shows** box to set how iTunes displays this content. You can tell iTunes to play movies and TV shows in the artwork viewer, the iTunes window, a separate window, in full screen mode, or in full screen mode with visuals.

Full screen (with visuals) is great for playing mixed playlists of songs and videos. Videos will play full screen, and the visualizer will appear when songs start playing. It's perfect for parties!

When you burn a CD, these effects do not carry over to the CD.

▼ Check the **Play music videos** box to set how iTunes displays music videos. You can tell iTunes to play them in the artwork viewer, the iTunes window, a separate window, in full screen mode, or in full screen mode with visuals.

▼ **Audio language** and **Subtitle language** lets you enable subtitles and listen to videos in a different language, if that option is available in the video.

▼ Check **Keep movie window on top of all other windows** to keep your movies front and center. This is especially useful if you run applications that like to alert you throughout the day.

▼ Check **Show closed captioning when available** to turn on closed captioning.

▼ **Use error correction when reading Audio CDs** if you're having problems with CD audio quality. Error correction slows the importing process, but may be helpful.

▼ Use the **Smart Shuffle** slider to increase or decrease the likelihood of hearing back-to-back songs by the same artist when the shuffle option is turned on in iTunes. Leave the slider in the middle to keep the songs completely random.

▼ Set the **Shuffle** option to "Songs," "Albums," or "Groupings" to shuffle individual songs, whole albums, or entire groupings.

Sharing preferences

The Sharing pane is where you enable iTunes to share music with others on a local network. Instead of copying music from another computer on your network, you can have it *stream* to you. Songs from one computer can *play* on another computer, but the song stays in its original location.

- ▼ **Look for shared libraries:** Check this box and your computer will look for other Macs on the local network that have music sharing enabled.

- ▼ **Share my library on my local network:** Select this option to make your iTunes Libraries or individual playlists available to others on the network. With this option selected, choose to **Share entire library** or **Share selected playlists.**

  If you choose to share *selected playlists,* put a checkmark next to one or more of your playlists that are shown in the window pane.

- ▼ **Require password:** If you want to limit access to your shared music collection, select this option. Type a password in the text field, then give the password to certain people. When someone tries to access the playlist by clicking the shared playlist icon in his Source list, he'll be asked for the password.

- ▼ **Status:** This line of text reports how many users on the local network are connected to your shared playlist.

Store preferences

The **Store** preferences pane lets you choose how you want to interact with the iTunes Store, along with several other options.

- ▾ **Buy and download using 1-Click:** If you have an Apple Account, when you click a song's "Buy" button in the Music Store, the song is purchased and downloaded immediately. Very easy and convenient.

- ▾ **Buy using a Shopping Cart:** This selection puts a "Shopping Cart" icon in the Source list, under the "Music Store" icon. All "Buy Now" buttons in the Music Store change to "Add" buttons. When you click a song's "Add" button, the song is added to the shopping cart until you're ready to buy. Then you can click "Buy Song" to purchase a single song in the shopping cart, or click "Buy Now" to purchase all items in the shopping cart.

  A shopping cart is useful for collecting songs you want to consider buying or for reviewing songs that your children have selected.

- ▾ **Automatically download prepurchased content:** If you check this box, iTunes will automatically download any pre-purchased content when it becomes available.

- ▾ **Automatically create playlists when buying song collections:** If you check this box, iTunes will automatically create a new playlist when you purchase an iMix collection.

- ▾ **Load complete preview before playing:** If a slow Internet connection causes the streaming previews in the Music Store to stutter and stop, click this box to ensure a full-quality song preview. iTunes will download the complete preview stream before playing it.

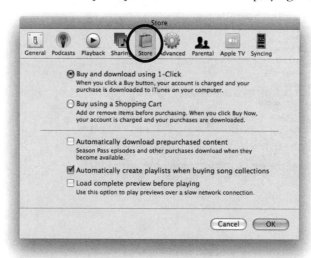

Advanced preferences

The **Advanced** preferences pane consists of three panes—General, Importing, and Burning. The **General** pane allows you to designate a location for storing your music files, as well as set options for remote speakers and Internet playback.

▾ **iTunes Music folder location:** Music files created by iTunes are automatically stored on your startup hard disk. Specifically, they are stored in a folder called "iTunes Music," which is in a folder called "iTunes," which is in your "Music" folder. This folder contains all of the music files you've encoded. You can change this default location to any location you choose: Click the "Change..." button and select another folder or hard disk.

Every individual user account has an "iTunes" folder inside the home "Music" folder.

▾ **Keep iTunes Music folder organized:** This places song files into album and artist folders (in the iTunes Music folder), and names the files based on the disc number, track number, and song title.

▾ **Copy file to iTunes Music folder when adding to library:** Puts a copy of a song in the iTunes Music folder if you import songs from other locations on your computer. The original song remains in its original location. This is similar to the "Consolidate Library" command in the Advanced menu, which makes sure every song in your Library is stored in the iTunes Music folder.

▾ **Use iTunes for Internet music playback:** This option sets iTunes as your default multimedia audio player when you download an audio file or click an audio file link on the web.

▾ **Streaming Buffer Size:** Refers to the Radio Tuner and the iTunes Store preview songs. The buffer size determines how much streaming data is cached (temporarily stored) on your hard disk when you listen to an Internet radio stream or play a preview. The buffer is like padding that compensates for connection problems that can affect the quality of a direct stream. If your connection to the Internet is slow, change this setting from "Medium" to "Large." A large buffer gives iTunes more downloaded streaming data to use for compensation as it deals with slow or faulty connections. If your connection to the Internet is high-quality, you can change this setting from "Medium" to "Small." A small buffer can free up space on your hard disk. A small buffer size also enables a streaming file to start playing sooner.

▼ Select **Look for remote speakers connected with AirTunes** if you have an AirPort Express connected to remote speakers. *AirPort Express* is a small device you plug into the wall, then connect to powered speakers. *AirTunes* is the technology that lets iTunes stream music wirelessly to the remote speakers through the AirPort Express.

▼ Select **Disable iTunes volume control for remote speakers** if you want to control the volume of remote speakers from the remote speakers, instead of using the iTunes volume control on your computer. This can be very useful when the remote speakers are in a different room.

▼ Select **Allow iTunes control from remote speakers** if you want to control iTunes from remote speakers, or a device such as the Apple TV.

▼ When you click the green Zoom button in the top-left corner of the iTunes window, the window minimizes to a small, space-saving Mini Player. Select **Keep Mini Player on top of all other windows** to always keep the Mini Player visible and on top of other windows.

▼ **Visualizer Size:** Set visualizer to appear within the iTunes window in one of three sizes: "Small," "Medium," or "Large."

▼ Select **Display visualizer full screen** if you want the visualizer to fill your entire screen.

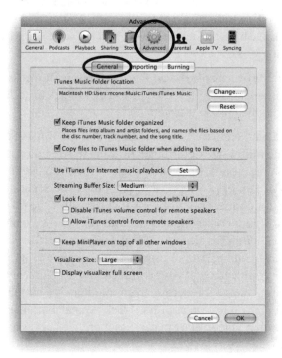

The **Importing** pane allows you to set encoding preferences.

▼ **On CD Insert** lets you configure the action iTunes will take when you insert a music CD into your Mac. iTunes can automatically play the CD, import the CD, or ask you if you want to import the CD.

▼ **Import Using** lets you choose which encoder will be used to import music files: AAC Encoder, AIFF Encoder, Apple Lossless Encoder, MP3 Encoder, or WAV Encoder (these file formats are described on page 255). The default setting of AAC is ideal for listening to and sorting music on your computer, because it combines maximum compression (smaller file sizes) and good sound quality.

▼ **Setting** is a quality setting. Higher quality settings result in better sounding audio files, but the resulting files can take up more space on your hard disk.

▼ You can listen to a song as it's being ripped (encoded) by checking the **Play songs while importing or converting** option. Encoding is very fast. The encoding of a song finishes well before the music has finished playing.

▼ **Automatically retrieve CD track names from Internet** enables iTunes to connect to the Internet whenever you insert a CD so it can retrieve song titles and other information from CDDB, an Internet database of CD albums.

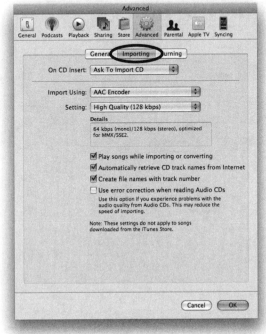

If you choose to uncheck this option, you can still manually retrieve CD titles whenever you like: Connect to the Internet, then from the "Advanced" menu, choose "Get CD Track Names."

▼ Check **Create file names with track number** to force imported songs to be stored in your Music folder in the same order they appear on the CD.

▼ Check **Use error correction when reading Audio CDs** if you're having problems with CD audio quality. Error correction slows the importing process, but may be helpful in eliminating clicks and other audio imperfections.

The **Burning** pane allows you to set preferences for burning discs.

- ▼ **Preferred Speed:** Set the speed at which your CD burner will burn CDs. The default setting of "Maximum Possible" lets iTunes adjust to the speed of your hardware. If you have problems, try setting "Preferred Speed" to a low number.

- ▼ **Disc Format:** Choose a disc format for burning CDs.

  Audio CD uses the standard CD-DA format common to all commercial CD players. You can store approximately 75 minutes of music on a CD using this format.

  Gap Between Songs lets you set the amount of silence you want between songs.

  Use Sound Check creates a consistent volume for all songs.

  Include CD Text adds artist and track information to audio CDs. This information can be displayed on some special consumer CD players.

  MP3 CD format can store over 12 hours of music, but can only be played on computers and some special consumer CD players. If you want to archive MP3 music files on CDs for backup, choose "MP3 CD" for the most efficient storage solution.

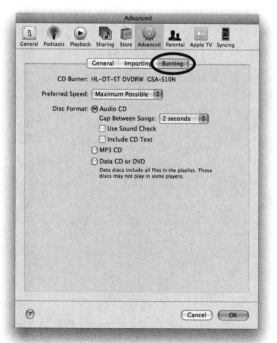

Data CD or DVD formatted discs include all files in a playlist, but may not work in many players. Use this option to make a backup of your music.

CD-RW (CD-ReWritable) discs will play in your computer, but most stereos and commercial CD players don't recognize them.

CD-R (CD-Recordable) discs can play on computers and most CD players.

DVD data discs hold five times as many songs as CDs, but they aren't playable on most consumer DVD players.

Discs must be blank to record music on them. You can erase a CD-RW disc and then use it to burn a music CD. CD-R and DVD discs cannot be erased, and they cannot be used if they already have files on them.

Parental Control preferences

The **Parental Control** preferences pane is where you can disable certain iTunes features. Restrict access to movies and TV shows, and turn off sources that younger members of the family don't need to access. Set up a new User account on your Mac for a child, then set these parental controls in that account.

▼ **Sources:** Select the sources you want to disable. The disabled items will not appear in the Source list.

▼ **Ratings for:** Select your country to customize your preferences for your locations.

▼ **iTunes Stores:** If you are making the iTunes Store available to your children, you can control the content they can access by restricting movies, TV shows, and explicit content.

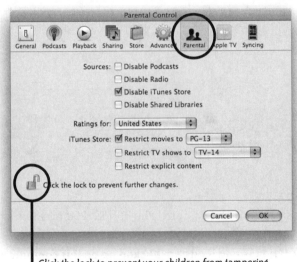

Click the lock to prevent your children from tampering with the Parental Control preferences.

Your settings will be visible after you click OK. However, to prevent your children from tampering with the Parental Control preferences, you should click the **Lock**. This will require anyone attempting to modify the Parental Control preferences to type an administrator password.

Apple TV preferences

The **Apple TV** preferences pane allows you to control how Apple TVs access your Mac.

- ▼ **Look for Apple TVs:** Select this option if you'd like your Mac to automatically find Apple TVs in your household.

- ▼ **The following Apple TVs are allowed to connect to iTunes:** Displays the Apple TV units that you have allowed to connect to your Mac in the past.

- ▼ **Remove Apple TV:** To remove an Apple TV from your list, select it in the list, then click this button. In the future, the Apple TV will not be automatically allowed to connect to your Mac.

Syncing preferences

iTunes creates and maintains a backup for every iPod and iPhone you sync with your Mac.

A new backup is created when iTunes detects that the data on the iPhone or iPod has changed since the last backup.

Backups store data that is not included in the sync process, such as iTunes content, contacts, calendar events, bookmarks, and photos.

The **Syncing** preferences pane displays any iPhone and iPod backups stored on your Mac. It also controls how iPhones and iPods sync with iTunes.

- ▼ **The following iPhones and iPods are backed up on this computer:** Displays the current iPhone and iPod backups that have been stored on your computer. See page 270 for information about restoring your iPod from a backup.

- ▼ **Remove Backup:** Select a backup from the list, then click this button to remove it permanently from your Mac.

- ▼ **Disable automatic syncing for all iPhones and iPods:** Select this option if you do not want iTunes to automatically sync information with your iPod or iPhone.

Music File Formats

iTunes works with five **audio file formats:** AAC, AIFF, Apple Lossless, MP3, and WAV. Using the Import feature, iTunes can encode files from a CD to any of the five file formats. It can also automatically encode multiple file formats when burning a CD. Each file format is suited for a specific purpose.

- ▼ **AAC** (Advanced Audio Coding) format compresses files even smaller than MP3 without a noticeable loss of quality. When iTunes imports a song from a CD to your computer, by default it encodes the CD-DA formatted song to an AAC format. MP3s and AACs are ideal for storing music on your computer, requiring 80 to 90 percent less disk space than other formats.

- ▼ **AIFF** (Audio Interchange File Format) is sometimes referred to as Apple Interchange File Format. It is a music format used by the Macintosh operating system. Web designers sometimes use snippets in the AIFF format for sound files that can play in web pages on a Macintosh computer. The file size of the Beatles song "I Want to Hold Your Hand" is 24.3 MB as an AIFF file, compared to 2.7 MB as an MP3 file.

- ▼ **Apple Lossless** encodes CD-DA files (CD music files) into a size that's half the size of the original file, without any loss of quality. This format creates files that are larger than the MP3 and AAC formats, but if you have a discriminating ear for music, the Apple Lossless format provides the best quality possible.

- ▼ **MP3** (MPEG-3) is a highly efficient compression system that reduces music files up to 90 percent, but maintains a very high quality. Highly compressed, MP3s are ideal for downloading from the Internet or for storing on your computer.

- ▼ **WAV** (Windows waveform format) is a music file format used by the Microsoft Windows operating system. Web designers use snippets in the WAV format for sound files that can play in web pages on a Windows computer. The file size of the Beatles song "I Want to Hold Your Hand" is 24.3 MB as a WAV file, compared to 2.7 MB as an MP3 file.

iTunes Visualizer

The **iTunes Visualizer** is mesmerizing. Just double-click a song, choose one of the four visualizer settings available, and press Command T. Colors and patterns undulate and morph to the beat of the music.

There are four different visualizer settings available: iTunes Visualizer, Lathe, Jelly, and Stix. Each visualizer setting provides a distinctly unique light show. iTunes will use the iTunes Visualizer setting by default, but you can select a different setting from the View menu. Try all of the settings until you find one you like.

Customize the iTunes Visualizer by choosing one of the four different visualizer settings available.

You can show the Visualizer effects in the iTunes window or in **Full Screen** mode. To start the Visualizer, select "Turn on Visualizer" from the View menu (**or** press Command T).

To show the Visualizer in full-screen mode, turn on the visualizer, then select "Full Screen" from the View menu (**or** press Command F).

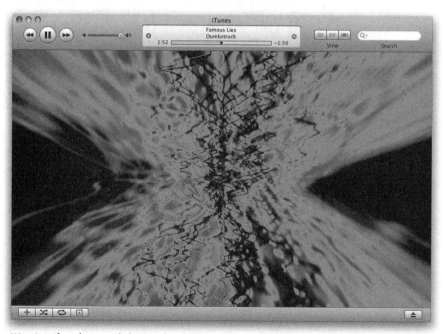

Warning: *If you have work that needs to be done, **do not** turn off all the lights, put headphones on, play great music, and click the Visualizer button. Most importantly, **do not** start pressing the R key in beat with the music. That kind of irresponsible behavior put this entire chapter in jeopardy.*

Visualizer configurations

The **iTunes Visualizer** setting can be even more fun if you know how to control it. (These configurations do not apply to the Lathe, Jelly, or Stix settings.) The Visual Effects Generator uses three different **configurations** to create visuals. You can see these listed in the top-right corner of the window if you press the C key while visual effects are playing (shown below). The three configurations listed change randomly and morph into one another as music plays. You can change any of these configurations while music is playing.

Press C to show the effect names in the top-right corner of the window.

The first configuration in the list affects the **foreground** of the Visualizer, the primary lines and shapes that modulate and interact with the beat of the music more obviously than the other graphics on the screen. Cycle through all the built-in effects for this configuration by alternately pressing the Q and W keys (Q for the previous selection and W for next selection).

Press Q or W to change the primary lines and shapes.

The second configuration in the list affects the **background** graphics, the shapes and patterns that stream from the primary shapes in the top configuration. Cycle through all the built-in effects for this configuration by alternately pressing the A and S keys (A for the previous selection and S for the next selection).

Press A or S to change the secondary shapes and patterns.

The third configuration in the list affects the **color scheme** applied to the visuals. Cycle through all the built-in effects for this configuration by using the Z and X keys (Z for the previous selection and X for the next selection).

Press Z or X to change the color scheme.

To manually and randomly change configurations at any time, press the R key. Press the R key in beat with the music to become the conductor of an amazing musical light show.

Press R to change everything randomly.

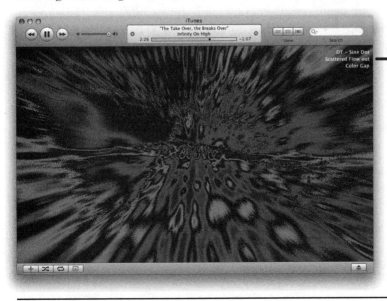

Press the C key to show the current foreground, background, and color scheme display settings.

Visualizer modes

To cycle through three Visualizer modes while using the iTunes Visualizer setting, press the M key repeatedly:

▼ **To play the random visual effects** generated by iTunes, press the M key several times until "Random slideshow mode" appears in the top-left corner of the window.

▼ **To force iTunes to play the current configuration** until instructed otherwise, press the M key several times until "Freezing current config" appears in the top-left corner of the window.

▼ **To play only the configurations that have been saved as presets** under the numeric keys, as described below, press the M key repeatedly until "User config slideshow mode" appears in the top-left corner of the window.

Save a favorite configuration

When you change an individual configuration while using the iTunes Visualizer setting (by using the keys mentioned on the previous page), the new effect fades slowly in as the configuration description in the upper-right corner fades out. If you fall in love with an effect, you can save that particular configuration as a preset that you can activate at any time.

To save a favorite configuration as a preset:

1. Press the M key to cycle through the three different options: "Random slideshow mode," "User config slideshow mode," and "Freezing current config."

2. When you get to the "User config slideshow mode," stop pressing the M key. This mode plays configurations you have saved as presets.

3. Wait until you see a visual effect you like, or create a custom effect using the keys described on the previous page. Hold down the Shift key and tap one of the numeric keys (0 through 9) while the desired effect is playing. You can save up to ten different preset effects.

   Note: To get rid of an old preset, just save a new one over it. Use the steps above and assign the same numeric key.

   To play your preset, tap the numeric key that you assigned to your preset configuration. Try tapping different numeric preset keys to the beat of the music for fantastic visual effects.

Visualizer Help

A separate **Help** file of keyboard shortcuts is available in the Visualizer. While the iTunes Visualizer is turned on, press the **?** key (or the H key) to show a list of keyboard shortcuts. The "Basic Visualizer Help" list appears on the left side of the window.

Press the **?** key again (or the H key) to toggle to another list of keyboard shortcuts, "Visualizer Config Help" (shown below).

iTunes Equalizer

iTunes provides an **Equalizer** that enables you to make dramatic adjustments to the sound output of your music files. Make adjustments manually or select from over 20 presets. You can even save custom settings as a preset and add it to the preset pop-up menu, as explained below.

An equalizer represents the various frequencies of the sound spectrum, or more specifically, the spectrum of human hearing. The spectrum is expressed as a measurement known as *hertz* (hz).

The iTunes Equalizer represents the frequencies of the spectrum with vertical sliders, also known as **faders.** The faders are used to increase or decrease the volume of each frequency, expressed as *decibels* (dB).

The lowest frequencies (bass): 32, 64, and 125 hz faders.

The mid-range frequencies: 250 and 500 hz faders.

The highest frequencies (treble): 1K through 16K (kilohertz) faders.

To show the Equalizer, choose "Show Equalizer" from the View menu. Check the **On** box to activate the Equalizer.

Choose a preset from the pop-up **menu** to automatically adjust the faders.

The **Preamp** slider on the left side of the Equalizer is a secondary volume adjustment. If a music file was originally recorded too quietly or loudly, adjust the volume here. Or if you're looking for maximum room-booming sound, slide the "Preamp" knob up to the top.

To save your custom settings as a preset:

1. Adjust the faders to your satisfaction.

2. From the pop-up menu (where it says "Rock" in the example above), choose "Make Preset...."

3. In the "Make Preset" dialog box, enter a name for your preset, then click OK.

   Your custom preset now appears in the pop-up menu.

You can **rename equalizer presets** in the pop-up menu, or **delete** presets you don't use.

To edit the preset list:

1. From the pop-up menu in the Equalizer window, choose "Edit List…."

2. In the "Edit Presets" window (shown on the right), click on a preset to select it, then click the "Rename…" button or the "Delete" button.

To apply Equalizer settings to a song, use one of the following methods.

▼ Select a song, then choose "Show Equalizer" from the View menu. Select a preset from the Equalizer pop-up menu, or use the faders to create a custom setting.

▼ **Or** add an Equalizer column to the iTunes Detail window: From the View menu, choose "View Options…." Check the "Equalizer" box, then click OK. An "Equalizer" column appears in the Details window, from which you can choose a preset for each song in the list (below-right).

▼ **Or** Control-click on a column heading, then choose "Equalizer" from the pop-up menu that appears (shown below-left). This adds the "Equalizer" column to the window (below-right), from which you can select a preset for a song.

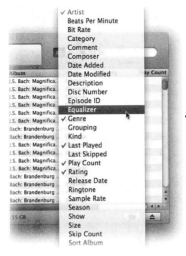

Control-click on a column heading to open a contextual menu, then select "Equalizer" to add an Equalizer column to the iTunes window.

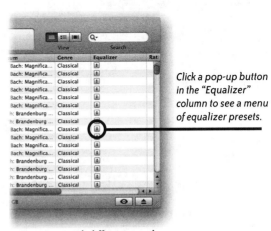

Click a pop-up button in the "Equalizer" column to see a menu of equalizer presets.

Experiment with different sound settings by choosing various presets in the Equalizer column.

Connect an iPhone, iPod, or Apple TV

The **iPhone, iPod,** and **Apple TV** are digital devices designed to work with iTunes. For information about current models/prices, visit **www.apple.com.**

In addition to storing hundreds of hours of songs and videos, your Apple device can also hold podcasts, TV shows, photos, Address Book contacts, iCal events, email messages, and bookmarks. You'll use iTunes to transfer all of this information from your computer to your iPhone, iPod, or Apple TV.

When you connect an Apple device to your computer, iTunes will automatically switch to the device interface (shown below). All of the controls you need to control your iPhone, iPod, or Apple TV are located in this interface. A quick overview of this interface is shown here.

Use the tabs to navigate the device interface. Each tab contains settings that control how your device interacts with your computer.

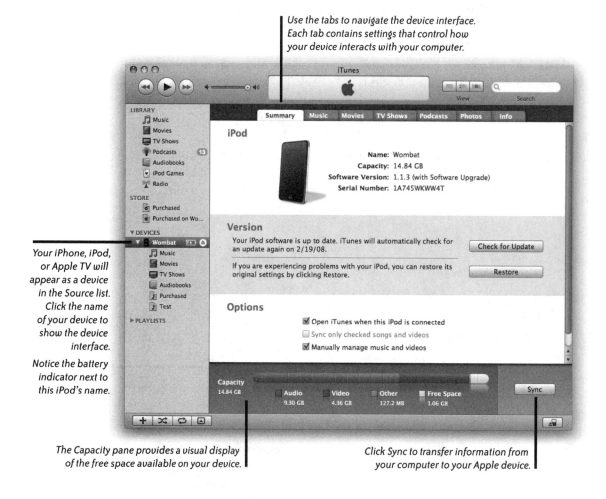

Your iPhone, iPod, or Apple TV will appear as a device in the Source list. Click the name of your device to show the device interface.

Notice the battery indicator next to this iPod's name.

The Capacity pane provides a visual display of the free space available on your device.

Click Sync to transfer information from your computer to your Apple device.

Transfer content to an iPhone, iPod, or Apple TV

iTunes provides a number of different options for transferring music, videos, and other content to your device. Generally speaking, there are three different approaches to managing content on your device:

- ▼ **Automatically sync music, movies, and TV shows:** iTunes will automatically copy all of the music, movies, and TV shows on your computer to your iPhone, iPod, or Apple TV.

- ▼ **Automatically sync selected content only:** iTunes will automatically copy selected content onto your iPhone, iPod, or Apple TV. This is a good option if your iTunes Library is larger than your device's storage capacity.

- ▼ **Manually manage music and videos:** If you select this option, you must manually copy content to your device. This is a good way to add music to your device from other authorized computers without completely replacing all music on the iPod with the current computer's iTunes collection. You must select this option if you want to see individual device playlists in the Source list, or if you want to select and play songs from the device through the computer.

Be sure to eject your iPhone or iPod before you unplug it from your computer. Click the eject button in the bottom right corner of the iTunes window, or click the eject symbol next to the iPhone or iPod in the Source list.

Automatically sync music, movies, and TV shows

1. Connect an iPhone or iPod to your Mac using a USB connection. If you're using an Apple TV, make sure it's turned on and wirelessly connected to your Mac.

2. Open iTunes if it's not already open. The device appears in the iTunes Source list.

3. Select the device.

4. Make sure **Manually manage music and videos** is deselected.

5. Click **Apply.**

Tip: Make sure the device you're automatically syncing has enough storage space to hold all of your Mac's music and videos. Select the device, then compare its capacity (shown below) with the size of your iTunes Library.

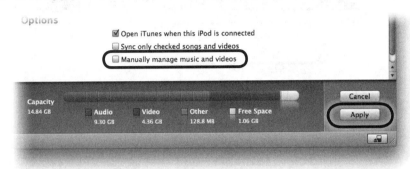

Automatically sync selected content with your device

iTunes allows you to sync music, movies, and TV shows with your iPhone, iPod, or Apple TV. But it also allows you to transfer other valuable information from your computer, such as Address Book contacts, iCal events, Safari bookmarks, and photos from your iPhoto library.

1. Connect an iPhone or iPod to your computer using a USB connection. If you're using an Apple TV, make sure it's turned on and wirelessly connected to your computer.

2. Open iTunes if it's not already open. The device appears in the iTunes Source list.

3. Select the device.

4. Make sure **Manually manage music and videos** is selected.

5. Select a content tab in the device interface (below).

6. Make sure the Sync checkbox is selected. For most content types, iTunes lets you choose to sync all of the content or only selected items.

7. Click Apply in the bottom right corner of the iTunes window.

Manually manage music and videos

1. Connect an iPhone or iPod to your computer using a USB connection. If you're using an Apple TV, make sure it's turned on and wirelessly connected to your computer.

2. Open iTunes if it's not already open. The device appears in the iTunes Source list.

3. Select the device.

4. Make sure **Manually manage music and videos** is selected (shown on previous page).

5. To transfer music to your device, drag songs and videos from your iTunes Libraries and drop them onto the device's icon.

If your device is selected in the Source list, you can click
this button to create a new playlist directly on the iPod,
then drag any song you want into the playlist.

Remember that you must manually transfer all of the content to your iPhone, iPod, or Apple TV when you select the **Manually manage music and videos** options. You can automatically sync only some content to your iPod, such as a playlist or list of podcasts, by setting iTunes to transfer this content. See page 263.

Use an iPod as an external hard disk

In addition to playing music and videos, most iPods can store and transport computer files. Not all iPods can be used as external hard disks.

1. Connect an iPod to your Mac using a USB connection.

2. Open iTunes if it's not already open. The iPod appears in the iTunes Source list.

3. Select the iPod.

4. Select **Enable disk use.**

5. Click **Apply**.

Your iPod is now available as an external hard disk in the Finder. To copy files or folders to your iPod, drag them from your computer to the iPod window (you will not be able to see your music files).

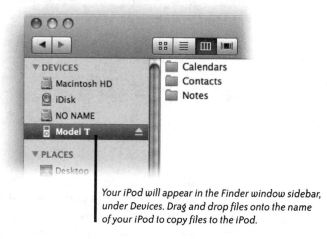

Your iPod will appear in the Finder window sidebar, under Devices. Drag and drop files onto the name of your iPod to copy files to the iPod.

Sync Contacts, Calendars, and more to your iPhone or iPod

Use iTunes to synchronize your iCal and Address Book information to an iPhone or iPod. Some devices can also store your Safari bookmarks, your Mail account settings, and your Yahoo! Address Book contacts. After syncing, you can access your important information while on the go.

1. Connect an iPhone or iPod to your Mac using a USB connection.
2. Open iTunes if it's not already open. The device appears in the iTunes Source list.
3. Select the iPhone or iPod.
4. Select the **Info** tab.

*iTunes may not automatically sync your device when you plug it into your computer. To manually sync your iPhone, iPod, or Apple TV, select the device in iTunes, then click the **Sync** button in the bottom-right corner of the iTunes window.*

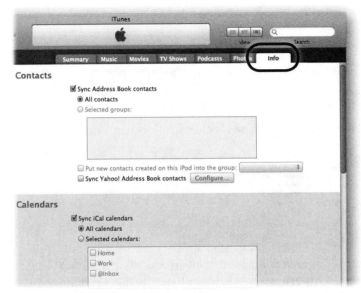

5. Check the **Sync Address Book contacts** and **Sync iCal calendars** boxes. You can choose to sync all calendars and contacts, or only selected contact groups and calendars.
6. If you own an iPhone or iPod capable of synchronizing your bookmarks or email account settings, you can also enable those features.
7. Click **Apply**.

Create Ringtones for an iPhone

Ringtones cost $0.99 from the iTunes Store, even if you already own the song.

You can use iTunes to create custom ringtones for your iPhone. Select a ringtone-compatible song from your Library, then use iTunes to create a 30-second ringtone complete with fades and loops.

1. Open iTunes if it's not already open.

2. Select "Preferences" from the iTunes menu, then click "General."

3. Make sure the **Ringtones** checkbox is selected.

4. Select "View Options" from the View menu.

5. Make sure the **Ringtone** checkbox is selected.

6. Find a ringtone-compatible song in your iTunes Library. Songs that can be converted into ringtones have a bell in the "Ringtone" column.

Songs that can be changed into ringtones will have a bell symbol in the "Ringtone" column.

7. After you've found a song you want to change into a ringtone, click the bell symbol next to the song. The iTunes Ringtone interface will open (shown opposite page).

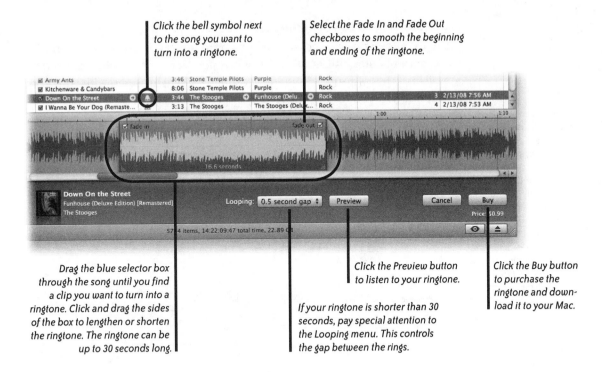

Click the bell symbol next to the song you want to turn into a ringtone.

Select the Fade In and Fade Out checkboxes to smooth the beginning and ending of the ringtone.

Drag the blue selector box through the song until you find a clip you want to turn into a ringtone. Click and drag the sides of the box to lengthen or shorten the ringtone. The ringtone can be up to 30 seconds long.

Click the Preview button to listen to your ringtone.

If your ringtone is shorter than 30 seconds, pay special attention to the Looping menu. This controls the gap between the rings.

Click the Buy button to purchase the ringtone and download it to your Mac.

8. Create the ringtone using the iTunes Ringtone interface (shown above). Your ringtone can be up to 30 seconds long and as short as three seconds.

9. When you're satisfied with the ringtone you've created, click the **Buy** button. iTunes will connect to the iTunes Store to create the ringtone, then it will appear in the Ringtones Library.

Note: Make sure the ringtone is the way you want before you purchase it! Ringtones can't be modified after you purchase them.

iTunes will automatically place the ringtone on your iPhone the next time you connect it to your computer and synchronize it with iTunes.

Your ringtones are stored in the Ringtones Library, which can be found in the Source list.

Update or restore your iPhone, iPod, or Apple TV

iTunes automatically checks Apple's website for iPhone, iPod, and Apple TV software updates and notifies you when new versions of software become available. iTunes also backs up devices that are synchronized with your computer, so you can restore them to their previous state.

Tip: Apple usually makes older versions of iPhone, iPod, and Apple TV system software available for download on its website. To install an older version of system software onto your device, download it from Apple's website, then hold down the Option key and click the *Restore* button. You'll be prompted to select the file.

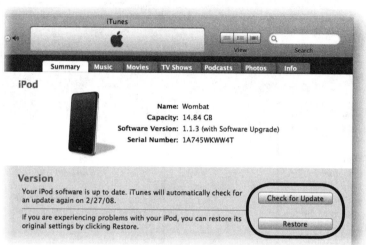

Click the **Check for Update** button to manually check for new software and update your device. Click the **Restore** button to return your device to a previous version of its system software.

Transfer iTunes Wi-Fi Music Store purchases to your computer

You can access the iTunes Wi-Fi Music Store from the iPhone and some iPods. This portable version of the iTunes Music Store allows you to purchase music and download it directly to your device, while on the go.

Purchases made with your iPhone or iPod should automatically transfer to your computer the next time you sync the device. You can also manually transfer purchases made with your iPhone or iPod.

From the File menu, select "Transfer Purchases from…." iTunes will download all of the music purchased from the iTunes Wi-Fi Music Store onto your computer.

Back up the iTunes Libraries

The music, videos, and audiobooks in your iTunes Libraries represent a significant investment in time and money. Protect that investment by periodically backing up your collection to CD or DVD. In the unlikely event of a hardware failure, you will be able to restore your entire iTunes collection.

To back up your iTunes Libraries:

1. Open iTunes, if it isn't already open.

2. From the File menu, select "Back Up to Disc."

3. Select one of the backup options available. You can back up the entire iTunes library and all of your playlists, only your iTunes Store purchases, or only the items that have changed since your last backup (if you've performed a backup before).

To restore your iTunes Libraries from a backup, insert the first backup disc and then click "Restore."

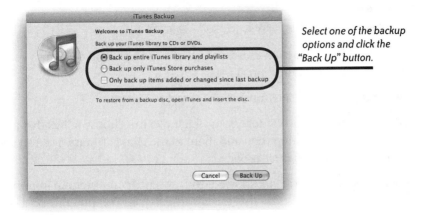

Select one of the backup options and click the "Back Up" button.

4. Click the "Back Up" button.

5. The iTunes Status display will ask you to insert a blank disc. You can insert a blank CD-R, CD-RW, DVD-R, or DVD-RW.

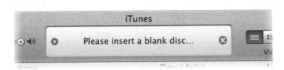

6. iTunes will start the back up. The process could take a while, but be sure to keep an eye on your computer. Depending on the size of your Libraries, iTunes might ask you to insert additional discs.

If your computer has a SuperDrive, you can back up your iTunes Libraries with CDs or DVDs. Which type of disc should you use? CDs are cheaper than DVDs, but they can't store as much information, which means you'll probably have to use more of them.

Menu Commands

Most of the commands in the iTunes menu bar are covered elsewhere in this chapter, but there are a few commands that exist only in one of the menu bar items.

You can activate most commands by clicking a button or with a keyboard shortcut, which is usually easier than using the menu bar. For instance, we never go to the File menu and choose "New Playlist"—we just click the plus sign beneath the Source pane. The menu bar is the best place to look for commands when you can't remember where or how to do something.

The following pages list the commands in each menu (except for the most self-explanatory ones) and give brief descriptions of each one.

File menu

New Playlist creates a new playlist. See page 205.

New Playlist from Selection creates a new playlist based on the songs you have selected (highlighted) in iTunes.

New Smart Playlist creates a new Smart Playlist. See page 207.

Add to Library opens a window from which you can choose songs that are stored on your computer, then add them to the iTunes Library. You can add an entire folder of songs all at once.

Import playlists that you've exported from another computer. An imported playlist will only show songs that are already on your computer or on a connected drive.

Export so you can have the same playlist on another computer. Select a playlist, then choose this command to make a copy. Copy the exported playlist to another computer, then go to the other computer and from the File menu, choose "Import...." Choose "XML" from the "Format" menu. Exported playlists do not export the actual songs, just a list of the songs.

Export Library saves a copy of all your playlists in XML format. Use the copy as a backup, or copy it to another computer to be imported.

Back Up to Disc lets you create a backup of your iTunes Libraries. See page 271.

Get Info provides information for a selected song.

Rating lets you choose 1–5 stars in a submenu.

Edit Smart Playlist lets you change the conditions of a Smart Playlist.

Show in Finder opens the folder in the iTunes Music folder that contains the song file you selected in iTunes.

Show Current Song shows the current song (the one that's playing) in the iTunes window.

Burn Playlist to Disc burns a CD of the selected playlist. This is the same as clicking the "Burn Disc" button.

Create an iMix lets you publish a collection of music on the iTunes Store for others to enjoy.

Sync iPod syncs content on your computer to a connected iPod.

Transfer Purchases from iPod transfers music purchased with your iPhone or iPod to your computer.

Page Setup opens a pre-printing dialog box in which you can choose settings, a printer, paper size, page orientation, and scale.

Print gives you access to templates for printing CD jewel case inserts, song lists, and album lists.

Controls menu

Shuffle shuffles songs in a playlist or the Library.

Repeat Off turns off the repeat feature. After a song plays, iTunes moves to the next song in the playlist that has a checkmark next to it.

Repeat All turns on the feature that repeats songs or playlists. When "Repeat All" is selected, the symbol on the Repeat button is blue.

Repeat One limits the repeat to just the song that's selected. When "Repeat One" is selected, the symbol on the Repeat button is blue and includes a small "1" symbol.

Mute turns the sound off. When "Mute" is selected, the little sound waves coming out of the speaker symbols that appear on either side of the volume slider disappear.

View menu

Show Browser turns on the iTunes browser.

Show Artwork opens the artwork viewer in the iTunes window. See pages 220 and 239.

Show MiniStore turns on a mini-iTunes Store that is always available in the iTunes Detail window.

Show Equalizer displays the iTunes equalizer. See page 260.

Turn On Visualizer starts the visual effects show in the iTunes window. When Visualizer is on, the command changes to "Turn Visualizer Off."

Visualizer lets you change the visualizer effects. See page 256.

Half Size, Actual Size, Double Size, Fit to Screen, Full Screen are options for choosing how videos and movies will be displayed on your screen.

Full Screen displays visual effects full-screen, hiding the iTunes window.

Show Duplicates identifies duplicate items in your iTunes Libraries.

View Options lets you set which columns appear in the iTunes Detail window. See page 229.

Store menu

Create Ringtone lets you turn the selected song into a ringtone, if that option is available for the song you have selected. See page 268.

Check for Purchases connects to the iTunes Store and checks to see if there is music you have purchased but haven't yet downloaded to your computer.

Authorize Computer lets you sign in to the iTunes Store and authorize your computer to play your purchased music.

Deauthorize Computer disables the computer from buying music from the Music Store or from playing purchased music. To buy music from the iTunes Music Store, you must authorize the computer you order from. You can deauthorize a computer to prevent others from using your Apple Account to buy music.

Also, iTunes permits up to five computers to play purchased songs. If you want to use a particular computer to play purchased songs, but you've already authorized five computers, you can deauthorize one of them. Remember to deauthorize your computer before you sell it or give it away.

Advanced menu

Open Stream lets you enter the URL (web address) for an Internet radio station or other webcast. Type the URL in the "URL" text field.

Subscribe to Podcast lets you enter the URL (web address) for an Internet podcast. Type the URL in the "URL" text field.

Convert Selection to ___ enables you to select a song and convert it to the file format shown in the menu command (AAC, in the example on the right). The file format is determined by what you chose for "Import Using" in Importing preferences. See page 251.

Consolidate Library makes a copy of all songs that are stored in other places on your computer and puts them in the iTunes Music folder.

Get Album Artwork connects to the iTunes Store database and downloads missing album artwork for your music, if the artwork is available.

Get CD Track Names connects to a CD database and enters the track names of a mounted CD into the iTunes window.

Submit CD Track Names lets you submit song information for a CD if the information is not available on the CD database that iTunes uses. Select a CD, then type Command I (Get Info). Enter the CD's artist, album, and genre information. Select each song on the CD, open Get Info, then enter the song name information. Finally, select the CD again, then from the Advanced menu, choose "Submit CD Track Names."

Join CD Tracks imports two adjacent CD tracks as one.

Favorite Keyboard Shortcuts

These are the **iTunes keyboard shortcuts** that you'll have the most fun with:

Command Option 1	toggles between Show Player and Hide Player
Command T	toggles Visuals on and off
Command F	toggles Visualizer full-screen mode on and off
Command DownArrow	turns the volume down
Command UpArrow	turns the volume up
LeftArrow	first tap selects the beginning of the current song; second tap selects the previous song
RightArrow	selects the next song
Option Command DownArrow	mutes the sound
Spacebar	toggles between Pause and Play

Other keyboard shortcuts:

Command N	creates a new playlist
Shift Command N	creates a new playlist from the *highlighted* songs (*not* the songs that are checked)
Command A	selects all songs in the current song list
Shift Command A	deselects all songs in the current song list
Command R	shows current song file in the Finder
Command E	ejects a CD
Command M	minimizes Player window to the Dock
Command ?	launches iTunes Help
Command Q	quits iTunes

Visualizer shortcuts:

R	changes Visualizer to a new random set of visual effects
M	cycles through Visualizer modes
N	toggles between Normal and High Contrast colors
D	resets Visualizer to the default settings
I	displays song information
F	toggles Frame Rate Display on and off
B	displays the Apple logo briefly when Visuals are turned on

Mail

5

You probably already know that you use Mail to write, send, and receive email messages. And that it has many useful built-in tools for organizing, formatting, searching, and filtering messages.

But now Mail has added new features that make it even more versatile, making it the central location on your Mac for gathering and organizing information.

Collect your thoughts. Quickly create **Notes** and access them from Mail (see page 302).

Create **To Do items** from selected content in email messages. To Do items are automatically added to iCal (page 296).

Subscribe to **RSS** feeds and have news articles delivered to your Inbox (see page 304).

In Mail, your cursor becomes a **Data Detector.** Hover your cursor over certain data in an email message, such as a contact name, an address, or a date or time, and a pop-up menu appears that lets you open the contact name in Address Book, open a street address as a Google map, or enter the date or time into iCal as an Event (see page 299).

Create beautiful email messages from professionally designed templates, called **Stationery.** Most templates include photo drop zones that you can drag and drop photos into (see page 286).

When you compose a new message, you can now utilize a new **Photo Browser** button in the toolbar that provides access to iPhoto so you can effortlessly find and attach photos to messages (see page 283 and 287).

With Mail's **improved text formatting** you can automatically create bulleted and numbered lists in Notes or email messages (see page 302).

Use Mail's new **Archive** command to keep all your important mailboxes safe and recoverable (see page 312).

Creating a new email account in Mail is easier than ever. Just enter an email address and password, then let Mail configure all other settings for you (see page 278).

Add Email Accounts to Mail

It's easy to add an email account to Mail if you didn't do it when you first installed Leopard or turned on your new Mac.

1. In Mail, go to the File menu and choose "Add Account…."

2. A window, shown below, opens. Enter your name, email address, and password. If you checkmark "Automatically set up account" (below-left), you can click "Create" and you're done. Mac will fill in everything else and set up your account.

   To create an account manually, *uncheck* the automatic setup box. The "Create" button turns into a "Continue" button (below-right). Click "Continue" to manually enter the account settings.

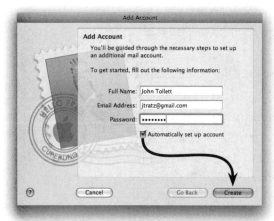 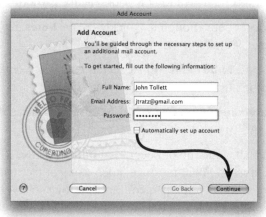

Checkmark the auto setup box to automatically create an email account that appears as an Inbox in Mail's sidebar.

Or uncheck the auto setup box to manually enter settings and create an email account.

3. The next window (shown on the following page) asks for details about your account, including "Account Type." If you don't know what kind of account it is, call your Internet Service Provider and ask. Generally speaking, this is how to choose the type of account:

   Choose POP if you have an email account with your ISP, or if you have a domain name that you paid for and you opted for an email account with it (regardless of whether there are actually web pages for that domain name). This is the most common type of email account.

   Choose IMAP if your account is the kind that you can use on any computer and always access your mail. This is usually provided with a paid service such as a .Mac account, or an email account provided by a large workplace with a system administrator. An IMAP account enables you to keep a sychronized copy of all your mail and mailboxes on a remote server that can be accessed from any computer.

POP (Post Office Protocol) is a common set of Internet rules and standards for delivering incoming mail.

Choose Exchange if your company uses the Microsoft Exchange server and the administrator has configured it for IMAP access. See your system administrator for details.

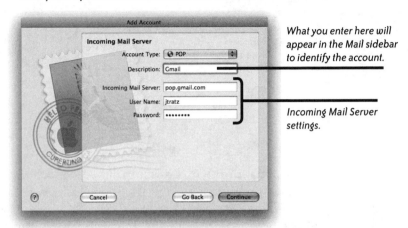

What you enter here will appear in the Mail sidebar to identify the account.

Incoming Mail Server settings.

Each account type has slightly different information to enter.

If you choose a POP account, Mail wants to know the **Incoming Mail Server** (above). It's usually something like *pop.domain.com* or *mail.domain.com.* The word "domain" of course, is replaced with the domain name of your email. For example, if your email address is *joe@dogfood.com,* it's a good guess that the Incoming Mail Server could be pop.dogfood.com. If you're not sure, check your email host's web site or call and ask for the "incoming mail server" address.

If you use a **webmail** service, such as .Mac, Hotmail, GMail, AOL, Yahoo, etc., you have to know the settings information for those services (but make sure you try the automatic setup procedure first, described on the previous page). Because this information changes all the time, check this great web site: **www.EmailAddressManager.com.** Go to "Email Tips" and find the addresses for incoming and outgoing mail servers and port number information for your service.

4. The **User Name** for a POP account might be different from your email name, or it might be your entire email address (this is most often the case), or it might be something different altogether. If your email address doesn't work, ask your provider.

5. Enter the password assigned by your provider or set up by you when you signed up for the email account.

6. Click "Continue" to open the Outgoing Mail Server settings (shown on the next page).

Continued…

Outgoing Mail Server settings.

7. The **Outgoing Mail Server,** or **SMTP,** sends mail out. A .Mac account will automatically be set up with a .Mac SMTP (*smtp.mac.com*). If you pay Comcast for an Internet connection, your SMTP address is *smtp.comcast.net*. Your most reliable outgoing mail server is usually going to be the company that you pay to connect you to the Internet.

Some providers, like Qwest here in the West, have a broadband option that does not allow you to have an outgoing mail server. You are forced to go to Microsoft's web page to check and send your mail. If that's your situation and you don't like it, call them and upgrade your service so you can have an SMTP address. Or change providers.

In the **Description** field, enter a descriptive name that you can identify when you see it in a menu.

Unless your provider insists, you usually don't have to enter a user name and password for authentication, so for now you can leave those fields blank.

8. Click "Continue." In the Account Summary window that opens (below), click "Create." The new account appears as a new Inbox in Mail's sidebar.

To add another account or edit an existing account:

At any time you can add another account or edit an existing one in
Mail preferences.

1. Go to the Mail menu and choose
   "Preferences…."

2. Click the "Accounts" icon in the toolbar.

3. **To add a new account,** click the **+** sign
   at the bottom of the Accounts column.
   Fill in the information on the right.

   To edit an existing account, click the
   account name in the Accounts column,
   then make edits on the right side.

4. When finished, close the Preferences
   window (or click another icon in the
   toolbar). A dialog appears to ask if you
   want to save your changes.

The Mail Icon in the Dock

When new email is received, the Mail icon in the **Dock** displays a little red tag
telling how many messages are unread (right).

Click on this Mail icon to bring the Mail window to the front. You can close
the Mail window and leave the Mail application open, so you'll know when
new messages arrive. The glowing blue light under the Mail icon in the Dock
means the application is actually open, even though you don't see its window.
This, of course, is true for all icons in the Dock.

Press (don't click) on the Mail icon in
the Dock to show a pop-up menu that
can serve as a convenient shortcut for
certain commands. The menu provides
easy access to the commands, "Get
New Mail," "Compose New Message,"
and "Compose New Note" (right).

Read and Send Email

The default in Mail is to automatically check your mail every five minutes. This, of course, assumes you use a full-time broadband connection. If you use a dial-up connection, go to the Mail preferences (from the Mail menu), click the "General" tab, and change the setting to "Manually."

As shown on the previous page, when you have messages in Mail that are unread, the Mail icon in the Dock shows the number of unread messages in a red tag.

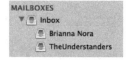

To read mail that has arrived:

1. If you have more than one account, your "Inbox" will have a disclosure triangle next to it. Click on the triangle to see the individual accounts (shown left and below).

2. In the sidebar, select the account you want to see. Email messages are displayed in the message pane on the right side of the window. Unread messages have a **blue orb** next to them.

3. **To read a message,** click it in the list that appears in the upper section of the window. The message will be displayed in the lower section of the window. **Or** double-click on a message in the list and it will open into a new window.

See page 285 for a tip about viewing messages without accidentally opening junk mail.

Click "New Message" to open a new message form.

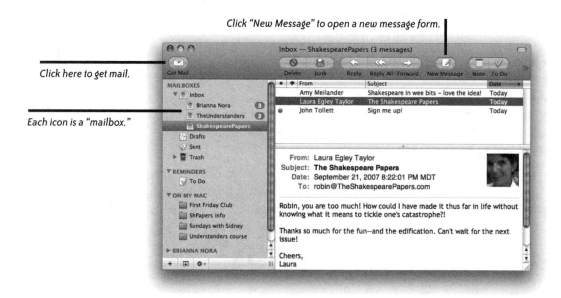

Click here to get mail.

Each icon is a "mailbox."

To send an email message:

1. Click the "New Message" button in the toolbar, or press Command N.

2. Enter an email address in the "To" field.

   If you have the email address in Address Book or if you've sent a message to this person before, as soon as you start typing, the rest of the email address appears. If there's more than one match with those beginning letters, a list of possibilities pops up. Select the addressee you want, then hit Return to place that address in the field.

   If the "Address" button is in the toolbar, click it to open the Address Book pane, a limited version of your Address Book. Double-click on a contact's name to add it to the "To" field.

   If the "Address" button is not in the toolbar, you can add it. Learn how to customize the toolbar on page 319.

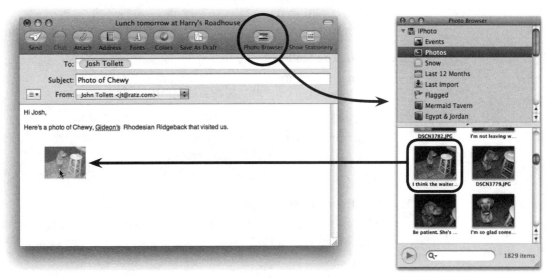

Drag photos from the Photo Browser to the body of an email message.

3. Enter a subject in the "Subject" field. Do not type something that might sound like junk mail, such as "Hi" or "About last night."

4. Type a message. Mail automatically checks your spelling and highlights suspect words with a red dotted underline (above).

5. To send a file as an attachment, drag it into the message window.

6. To add a photo, click the "Photo Browser" button in the toolbar, then drag photos from the Photo Browser window into the message pane.

7. Click the "Send" button in the toolbar. **Or** click the "Save As Draft" button to save it for later completion. To open the draft later, click the "Drafts" icon in the sidebar, then double-click the draft in the message list. Finish composing the email, then click "Send."

Customize the Message Window

You can customize message headers, the message toolbar, and add or delete various columns of information in the message list area.

To add or delete columns of information in the message list:

1. Make sure the Mail window is open.

2. From the View menu, choose "Columns," then from the flyout list (right) select a column name (checkmark it) that you want to add to the message list pane. To remove a column from the message list pane, select its name in this flyout list (remove its checkmark).

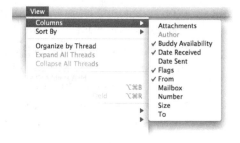

To customize the toolbar:

1. From the View menu, choose "Customize Toolbar...."
   Or Control-click on the toolbar, then choose "Customize Toolbar...."

2. Drag items into the toolbar from the Customize pane.

   To rearrange items in the toolbar, press the Command key as you drag items to different positions.

   Learn more about customizing Mail's toolbar on page 319.

To customize message headers:

1. Open a new message (click the "New" button in the Mail toolbar).

2. Click the menu button (shown circled, below-left), then choose "Customize..." to open the dialog shown below-right.

3. Check the boxes of the items you want to add to your message headers. Click OK when you're done.

Do Not Display Junk Mail!

Some junk mail sends an invisible message back to its sender as soon as you open it, telling the despicable junk mailer that this is a working email address. To prevent opening junk mail, hide the message pane.

Press the gray divider bar that separates the message list from the message viewing pane. Drag the bar all the way to the bottom of the window, leaving only the message list showing.

Now when you click on a message to delete it, it doesn't automatically open in that pane. **When you want to read a message,** double-click on it and it will open in a separate window.

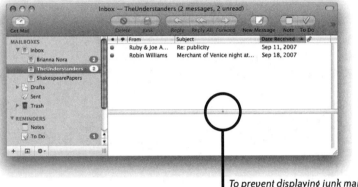

To prevent displaying junk mail before you throw it away, drag this bar all the way to the bottom.

Delete Junk Mail without Ever Seeing It!

Mail has a **junk mail filter** that can delete your spam automatically. While in "training," it puts spam in a special brown "Junk" mailbox in the sidebar where you can check to make sure messages really are junk before you delete them. Once you're confident it's doing a good job, use the rules described on page 331 to delete junk mail immediately.

To turn on Junk Mail filtering, go to the Preferences pane (in the Mail menu), click the "Junk Mail" icon, then check the box to "Enable junk mail filtering" (below). Carefully read the choices in the pane and choose your options. See page 328 for more information about the Junk Mail filter.

Use Stationery to Send Fancy Mail

It's actually called "HTML" mail, not "fancy" mail. HTML just means it has HTML code written into the message for you that creates the layout, the space for photos, the fonts, etc. You don't have to write one single piece of code. All you do is choose a stationery template, type your message, and drag your own photos on top of placeholder photos.

To create an email with stationery:

1. Open a new email message (press Command N).
   Or click the "New Message" button in Mail's toolbar.

2. Click the "Show Stationery" button on the right side of the message toolbar (shown on the left).

3. A collection of stationery templates appears, shown below. Click a template category on the left to show its design options on the right. To apply a template, click its thumbnail. To change templates, click another thumbnail.

When you click this button, it changes to "Hide Stationery," circled in the toolbar below.

When you select a photo in a template, a slider lets you resize the photo in the photo drop zone.

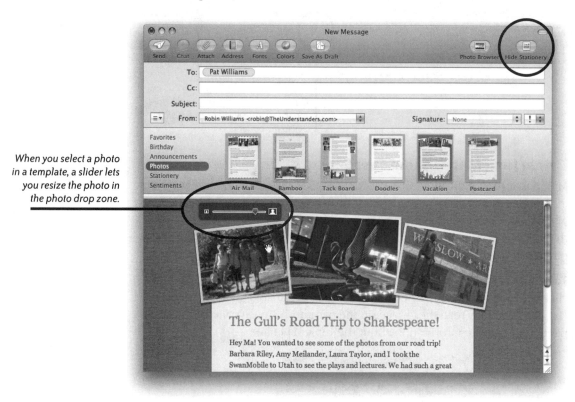

4. **To replace the placeholder text** in a template, click the text. All the text in that section is automatically selected. Whatever you type replaces the placeholder text, but retains the font styling.

5. **To add photos,** you can do several things:

   Click the "Photo Browser" button in the toolbar. This opens the Photo Browser and displays all the photos you have in iPhoto, Aperture, or Photo Booth. Just drag an image from the Photo Browser and drop it directly on top of the placeholder image you want to replace.

   Or drag an image from anywhere on your Mac and drop it on top of a placeholder image.

   Or open iPhoto and drag an image directly from iPhoto onto a placeholder image.

6. **To resize photos,** double-click on a photo and a little slider bar appears, as shown on the previous page. Drag the slider right or left to enlarge or reduce the image.

7. **To reposition the image within the frame,** double-click on the photo, then press-and-drag the photo to reposition it within its frame (you can't reposition the frame itself).

You can change templates at any point. If there are fewer photos in the new template, some of your images will disappear. Your custom text will reappear in the new template.

Click the "Hide Stationery" button in the top-right corner of the window to put the row of templates away so you can see more of the template.

Save as Stationery

You can save a simple design of your own as stationery. You can't use the templates that Apple provides, but you can set up an email message with the fonts you like to use, as well as colors, links, and images that you want to appear in the message. When it looks the way you want it to, go to the File menu and choose "Save as Stationery."

A new category appears in the list of stationery, called "Custom." Click on that new category and you'll see a thumbnail of your customized stationery.

To delete stationery you made, position your mouse over its thumbnail in the "Custom" category. A little **X** appears in the top-left corner of the thumbnail. Click the **X** to delete the stationery.

Create Mailboxes to Organize Your Mail

Organize your mail with mailboxes in the same way that you make folders in a Finder window to organize all the files on your Mac. Most mailboxes look just like folders, and they're stored in Mail's sidebar.

To move messages into the mailboxes that you created, select a mailbox in the sidebar, then drag messages from the message list into one of the other mailboxes in the sidebar.

To create a new mailbox:

From the Mailbox menu, choose "New Mailbox...." **Or** click the Plus (**+**) button in the bottom-left corner, then choose "New Mailbox...." In the dialog that opens (right), choose a location from the pop-up menu, then name the folder.

To create a folder that contains another folder, type *folder name/ folder name 2,* as shown on the right.

Mail automatically groups mailboxes in the sidebar. The **Mailboxes** category on the left contains four different email accounts, all in the Inbox group.

Mailboxes with small disclosure triangles contain other folders. Click a triangle to show a folder's sub-folders. For example, the "Junk" folder contains two folders, one for each account that has collected some junk mail.

The **Reminders** category contains folders that store Notes and To Do items.

When you create **Smart Mailboxes,** they're automatically grouped together.

The **On My Mac** category is the location for most local mailboxes you create.

The **RSS** folder is automatically created when you set up the option to receive RSS feeds in Mail.

Blue folders can store both messages and other folders. **White folders** can store only other folders. To create a white folder that contains a blue folder, follow the instructions at the top of the page for creating a folder within another folder.

When you synchronize Mail with a .Mac email account (go to the Mailbox menu, then choose "Synchronize"), a new category group appears in the sidebar, named for your .Mac account. It contains all of the folders that exist in your online .Mac email account.

Filter Incoming Mail with Rules

Create rules (also known as filters) to **sort incoming mail** into the appropriate mailbox. First, create the mailboxes you want for organizing (see the opposite page), then:

1. From the Mail menu, choose "Preferences…."

2. Click the "Rules" icon in the toolbar, then click "Add Rule" button (right).

3. In the Rules dialog that opens (below-left), choose conditions for the mail coming in and what actions to perform. (If you haven't yet created a special mailbox location for this rule, you can actually do it while the Rules pane is open on your screen; from the Mailbox menu, choose "New Mailbox…." The new mailbox immediately appears in the "to mailbox" pop-up menu (shown below-left).

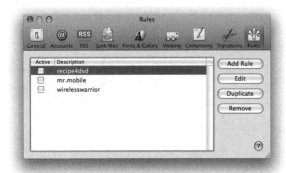

In the example below, we first made a new mailbox called "NancyD."

Then we created a new rule to find any incoming mail from Nancy Davis. The first (and only) *condition* tells Mail to look for messages that have "Nancy Davis" in the "From" field. The first *action* tells Mail to move those messages to the mailbox named "NancyD." The second action tells Mail to play an alert sound when messages arrive that meet the set condition.

4. Click OK. Now when email arrives from Nancy, the message moves directly into the "NancyD" folder and plays an alert sound so we know it has arrived.

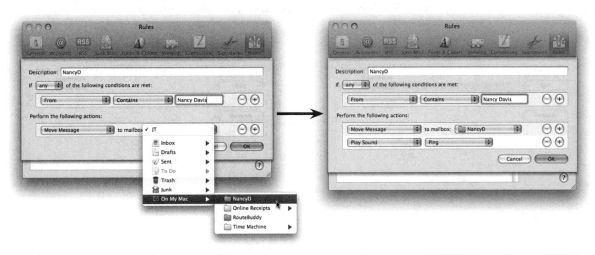

Add Signatures to Your Messages

An **email signature** is a little blurb you can automatically add to the bottom of your messages. A signature might include your contact information, promotion for your upcoming art show or book publication, your favorite quote, or even a small graphic. You can make more than one signature, then choose which one you want for an individual email message, set up a default signature that automatically appears, or you can let Mail randomly choose for you.

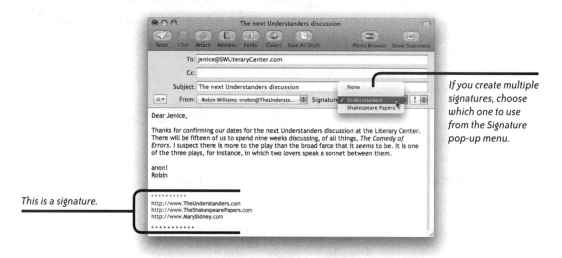

This is a signature.

If you create multiple signatures, choose which one to use from the Signature pop-up menu.

To create a signature:

1. From the Mail menu, choose "Preferences...."

2. Click the "Signatures" icon in the toolbar. The window shown on the opposite page opens.

3. At the top of the left column, click "All Signatures."

4. To create a new signature, click the plus sign (**+**) under the middle column. By default, the new signature file is named "Signature #1." Rename it something more relevant so you can identify it in a pop-up menu.

5. Click in the right column and type your signature. Use the Format menu at the top of the screen to choose a font, size, style, alignment, and color. Don't choose a font that your email recipients probably won't have. Use a font that came with your Mac.

6. If you want an **image** to appear in this signature, drag an image from the Finder and drop it into the right column. The image should be very small, both in file size and visually!

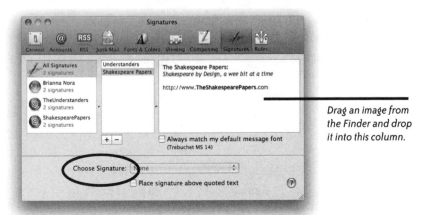

Drag an image from the Finder and drop it into this column.

7. Drag a signature from the middle column and drop it on top of an account name in the left column to add it to that email account. You can have lots of different signatures, and make only certain ones available for different email accounts.

8. Each email account can have its own **default signature** that automatically appears in each email message you write: select an email account in the left column, then from the "Choose Signature" pop-up menu (shown above), choose a signature.

TIP: To create a new signature that's similar to an existing signature, select the signature you want to use as a model, then click the **+** button. The duplicate shows up in the list of signatures. Edit its name and content.

To choose a signature for messages, you'll need to place the "Signature" pop-up menu in the New Message form:

1. Open a new message form (click the "New Message" button in Mail's toolbar).

2. Click the Menu button (right), then choose "Customize...."

3. In the Customize dialog that opens, checkmark the "Signature" box (shown on page 284).

4. Click OK. Now the Signature pop-up menu is in every new mail message (circled on the right). Choose a signature from this pop-up menu for each individual message you compose.

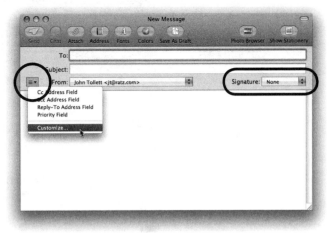

Search Your Mail

When you need to find information that's in an old email, a Note, or a To Do item, use Mail's powerful Spotlight search feature.

1. To limit the search to a particular mailbox (an email account, Notes, or the To Do mailbox), select that mailbox in the sidebar. If you've set up multiple email accounts, click the top-level Inbox to search all mail (and Notes) in all accounts.

2. Enter a word or phrase in the Spotlight search field (in the top-right corner). Search results immediately appear in the main viewing area.

   To narrow the search to certain types of documents, type "kind:" followed by one of these phrases: email message, mail message, mail mailbox, mail cached IMAP mailbox, or mail stationery.

3. A new search bar also appears, shown below. In this bar you can choose which mailbox to search, and which part of the email to search. Choose "Entire Message" to search the message and all of the data entry fields (From, To, and Subject).
   Or choose to search just one of those options by selecting "From," "To," or "Subject" in the bar.

4. **To display all messages again,** click the gray **X** on the right side of the search field to remove the search results and return to a normal view of your mail.

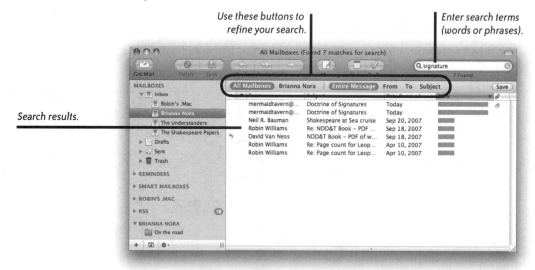

Use these buttons to refine your search.

Enter search terms (words or phrases).

Search results.

Smart Mailboxes

You can create **Smart Mailboxes** that store all the email messages that meet your chosen criteria. Smart Mailboxes are similar to Rules (filters), as explained on page 289, but there are a couple of differences between Rules and Smart Mailboxes.

- ▼ A Rule is an action that is applied to incoming messages, such as filtering certain email into a certain folder. The original email is moved into the folder.

- ▼ A Smart Mailbox contains messages that match certain criteria. No action is taken on the messages.

- ▼ A Smart Mailbox does not contain the original message, thus the same message can be "stored" in a number of Smart Mailboxes.

- ▼ A Smart Mailbox automatically updates itself as messages come in or are deleted.

- ▼ A Smart Mailbox applies the search conditions to mail that is already in your Inbox, not just on future incoming mail.

Below you see an example of several Smart Mailboxes in the sidebar. The ones named "Understanders" and "The Shakespeare Papers" are actually Smart **Folders** that each contain Smart **Mailboxes.** The folder is just for organizational purposes. Both are explained on the following page.

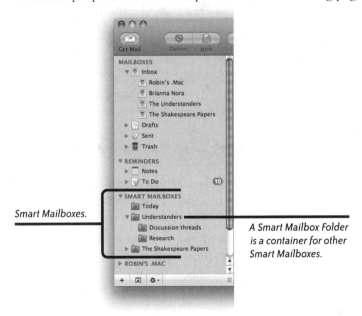

Smart Mailboxes.

A Smart Mailbox Folder is a container for other Smart Mailboxes.

Create a Smart Mailbox

There are several ways to **create a Smart Mailbox.** One is from the Mailbox menu, and another is with the Save button, explained on the opposite page.

To create a Smart Mailbox from the Mailbox menu:

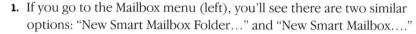

1. If you go to the Mailbox menu (left), you'll see there are two similar options: "New Smart Mailbox Folder…" and "New Smart Mailbox…."

   The **Smart Mailbox Folder** creates a folder with no search parameters; it is simply for organizing other **Smart Mailboxes** inside (as shown on the previous page). If you choose to make a Smart Mailbox Folder, you will only be asked to name the folder and click OK.

   If the command to make a Smart Mailbox Folder is gray (unavailable) in the Mailbox menu, it's probably because something is selected in the sidebar and Mail can't put a Smart Mailbox Folder inside of whatever is selected. Click on an empty space in the sidebar to clear all selections, and the option to create a Smart Mailbox Folder will become available.

   If you want your Smart Mailbox to be inside of an existing Smart Mailbox Folder, first select that Smart Mailbox Folder in the sidebar.

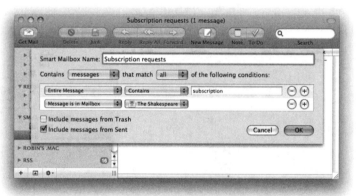

2. When you choose "New Smart Mailbox…" from the Mailbox menu, the edit dialog shown above opens. Choose the conditions you want from the pop-up menus and click OK.

3. If you need to edit the conditions of your new Smart Mailbox, select it in the sidebar, then from the Mailbox menu, choose "Edit Smart Mailbox…." The edit dialog shown above opens.

   Or Control-click on a Smart Mailbox in the sidebar, then choose "Edit Smart Mailbox…."

To create a Smart Mailbox from the Save button:

After a successful search, you can use the search results to create a Smart Mailbox that automatically collects messages matching the current search conditions.

1. Do a search as usual, as explained on the previous pages.

2. If the search provides the wanted results, click the "Save" button in the upper-right corner of the window (circled below).

3. A Smart Mailbox edit dialog opens, as shown on the previous page. You can refine your search, if you like, using the edit dialog's pop-up menus and text fields. Click OK to create a new Smart Mailbox in the sidebar. It is automatically named with the search phrase you used, unless you changed the name in the edit dialog.

4. If you want to change the conditions of your new Smart Mailbox, select it in the sidebar, then from the Mailbox menu, choose "Edit Smart Mailbox...." The edit dialog shown on the previous page opens for you to make changes.

    Or Control-click on the Smart Mailbox in the sidebar, then choose "Edit Smart Mailbox..." to open the edit dialog.

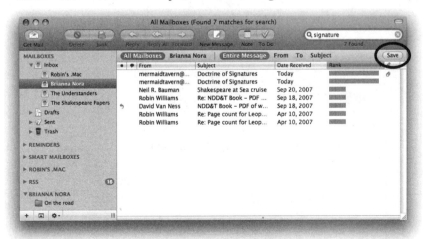

To Do Items

Mail is no longer just an email program—it's the message center for your digital lifestyle. When you use Mail to create To Do lists and Notes, you stay organized and can find all your information quickly and easily. Mail keeps track of everything and even integrates with iCal to make sure you never miss a date or event.

Create a To Do item from selected text in an email message:

Select the text in a message you've received, then click the "To Do" button in Mail's toolbar (circled below). **Or** Control-click selected text, then choose "New To Do." The selected text becomes a To Do item at the top of the message, as shown below.

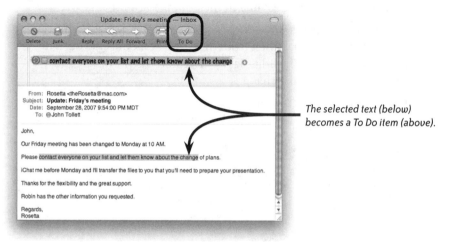

The selected text (below) becomes a To Do item (above).

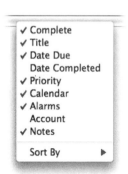

Click To Do folders in Mail's sidebar to show them in the viewing pane with their own **columns of information.** Control-click on any column heading to see a pop-up menu (left) of other columns you can add to the To Do view. In the example below we added a "Notes" column. Click in the "Notes" column to type a short note about the To Do item.

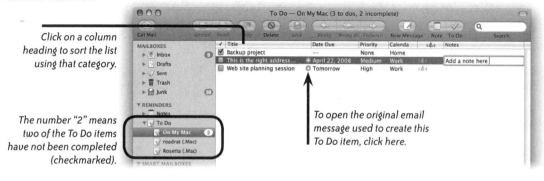

Click on a column heading to sort the list using that category.

The number "2" means two of the To Do items have not been completed (checkmarked).

To open the original email message used to create this To Do item, click here.

When you create a To Do item within a received email message, as shown on the right, it appears at the top of the email message. You can set a due date, an alarm, and a priority; and you can assign the item to the iCal calendar of your choice.

To set these options, click the red circled **arrow** to the left of the To Do item's check-box in the top of the email message window (circled, right). A yellow "To Do Options" window opens. Set the options you want, then click the small **x** in the top-left corner to close the window. **Or** click anywhere other than inside the To Do Options window.

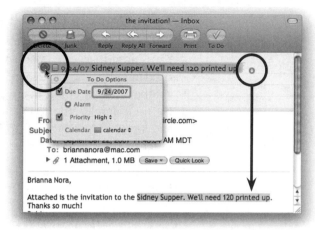

Click the small red arrow above to locate and highlight the original To Do reference in the email message.

*To delete a To Do item, click the red circle **X**.*

When a To Do task is completed, checkmark its box.

You can create multiple To Do items for a single email message.

Create a To Do item related to an email message:

Control-click in a blank area of the email message. From the pop-up menu that appears, choose "New To Do." A yellow To Do form slides down from the top of the window, similar to the examples above.

Create a To Do item without using an email message:

Just click the "To Do" icon in Mail's toolbar. Type your message in the field provided. Control-click on the message to show options for setting priorities, due date, etc. To Do items are created in the mailbox you choose in the Composing pane of Mail preferences, where a pop-up menu (right) lets you choose the location to store newly created To Do items—in the last viewed mailbox, or in an existing mailbox (right).

To Do Items in the Mail Window

To Do items have their own section in the sidebar, as shown below. If you have more than one .Mac email account, the To Do items are subcategorized into the different accounts. If you have just one .Mac email account and another email account that is not a .Mac account (a POP account from your ISP, for example), the To Do items are subcategorized into the .Mac account and into "On My Mac." All To Do items that are assigned to email accounts other than a .Mac account go into the subcategory called "On My Mac."

You won't see these subcategories in your sidebar until you create a To Do item, and then they appear automatically.

The title bar shows how many To Do tasks you have, and how many have not been marked as completed.

Add or remove columns: Control-click on any column header to see the options.

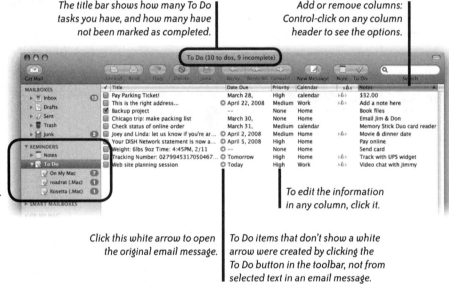

The numbers indicate how many To Do tasks in each mailbox have not been completed (checkmarked).

To edit the information in any column, click it.

Click this white arrow to open the original email message.

To Do items that don't show a white arrow were created by clicking the To Do button in the toolbar, not from selected text in an email message.

For instance, if you have a .Mac email account (which is an IMAP account, or a *remote* account), the To Do mailbox in the "Reminders" group (above) will be named whatever you named your .Mac email account (in the "Description" field, in the Accounts pane of Mail preferences). You won't see the "On My Mac" mailbox, shown in the sidebar above, unless you create a *local* email account (a POP account), or open iCal and create a new *local* calendar (click the Plus sign (+) in the bottom-left corner of the iCal window). If you do either of these things, Mail creates mailboxes in the sidebar called "On My Mac" to store local information—information that exists only on your Mac, and *not* on a remote server, as in the case of a .Mac account. You can have "On My Mac" mailboxes in the To Do mailbox, the Notes mailbox, and as a group category in the sidebar, to store folders you created to organize your messages.

The Data Detector

In Mail, your pointer has a built-in Data Detector that recognizes dates and addresses, and knows how to use that data in iCal and Address Book. If you hover your pointer over a day or date in an email message, the data highlights with a gray dotted outline and adds a menu button (right). Click the menu button to open a pop-up menu, then choose "Create New iCal Event…," or "Show This Date in iCal" (below). This does not create a To Do item, but an *Event* in iCal.

If you select "Create New iCal Event…," a dialog opens in which you can edit the Event information, set alarms, etc. When you're satisfied with the settings, click the "Add to iCal" button (below-right). The new Event automatically appears in iCal, placed in the matching date.

In the example below, even though a numerical date was not available (just the word "Monday"), iCal automatically assumed the message meant the next Monday following the date of the email.

The pointer's built-in Data Detector can recognize a date, month, address, or even relative dates like "tomorrow," "yesterday," "last Friday," "tonight," etc.

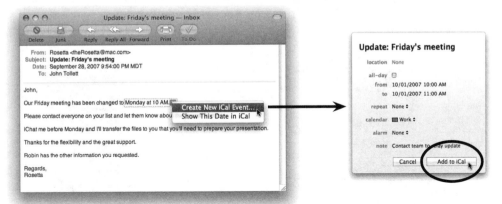

When you hover your pointer over an address in an email message, the Data Detector recognizes the data as information that can be used in Address Book. Click the menu button that appears, then choose one of the options in the pop-up menu (below). You can use the address to create a new contact, or add the address to an existing contact. Choose "Show Map…" to open a Google map of the location. To show the address on your screen large enough to be seen across the room, select "Large Type."

How Mail Works with iCal

To Do items are automatically sent to iCal where they're stored in the To Do list of one of iCal's calendars. If the iCal To Do list isn't visible, click the pushpin button in the bottom-right corner of the iCal window. **Or** from iCal's View menu, choose "Show To Do List." All To Do items from all calendars are displayed in the To Do list, *if* the calendars' checkbox (in iCal's sidebar) is checked. When you check iCal's To Do list, it doesn't matter which calender is currently selected, all To Do items are visible as long as the calendar it belongs to is marked as visible (checkmarked) in the sidebar.

To create a new iCal calendar while in Mail: Control-click on a To Do mailbox in Mail's sidebar. From the pop-up menu, choose "New Calendar…" (below-left). A new calendar instantly appears in **iCal's** sidebar, with the default name of "calendar." It is placed in a category group named the same as the mailbox you selected in Mail (below-left).

If, in Mail, you selected a To Do mailbox that's linked to a .Mac email account (such as "roadrat" in the example below-left), **iCal** creates a .Mac category in its sidebar, named for that .Mac email account. iCal also creates a new calendar with a default name of "calendar," and places it in the .Mac account group (as shown below-right).

Mail   iCal

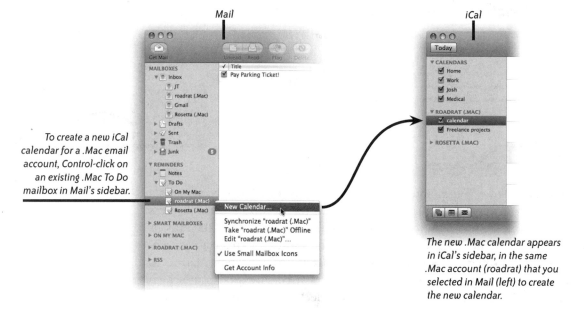

To create a new iCal calendar for a .Mac email account, Control-click on an existing .Mac To Do mailbox in Mail's sidebar.

The new .Mac calendar appears in iCal's sidebar, in the same .Mac account (roadrat) that you selected in Mail (left) to create the new calendar.

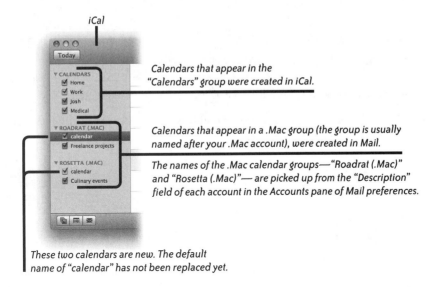

iCal

Calendars that appear in the "Calendars" group were created in iCal.

Calendars that appear in a .Mac group (the group is usually named after your .Mac account), were created in Mail.

The names of the .Mac calendar groups—"Roadrat (.Mac)" and "Rosetta (.Mac)"— are picked up from the "Description" field of each account in the Accounts pane of Mail preferences.

These two calendars are new. The default name of "calendar" has not been replaced yet.

If, in Mail's sidebar (see the previous page), you select the To Do mailbox named "On My Mac" to create a new calendar, iCal creates a new calendar in the "Calendars" group that appears in the top section of iCal's sidebar (above). Calendars in this group are *local,* they were created in iCal, and the To Do items from these calendars can be viewed in the "On My Mac" mailbox (in Mail's sidebar). And, of course, they're also viewable in iCal's To Do list.

To Do items you create in a .Mac mailbox (within Mail) are assigned to one of the calendars in that iCal *Mac* group only—*not* to any of the *local* calendars you may have created in iCal that appear in the "Calendars" group in iCal's sidebar. The To Do items in a .Mac mailbox are also available to you from anywhere in the world when you log in to your .Mac account and check your mail online.

To Do items created in mailboxes other than a .Mac mailbox can be assigned to any existing *local* calendar in iCal (the top group of calendars in iCal's sidebar, shown above).

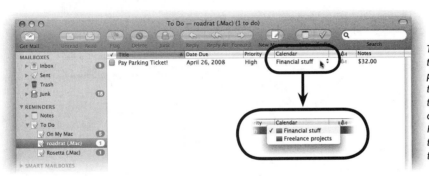

To reassign a To Do item to a different calendar, place the pointer over the "Calendar" column of the item. Click the small double-arrows that appear. From the pop-up menu that opens, choose one of the available calendars.

Notes

While the To Do items are great for tracking things that need to get done, Notes are a handy place to store ideas, thoughts, or any other information you want to keep track of. Mail truly becomes a central location for information—messages, Notes, and To Do lists. And RSS feeds (see page 304).

Notes, like To Do items, are listed as mailboxes (or folders) in the "Reminders" category in Mail's sidebar. They look like yellow note pads.

Create a new Note

To create a new Note, click the "Note" button in Mail's toolbar (left).

A "New Note" window opens (right) in which you can type brief or lengthy comments. Mail uses the first line of text as the subject of the note (keep that in mind as you write the note), and shows that first line in the Subject column of Mail's message list.

When finished, click the "Done" button in the Note toolbar. The Note is stored in the Notes mailbox in Mail's sidebar. If multiple Mail accounts are active, the note is added to the Mail account of the last viewed mailbox, unless you've specified otherwise in the Composing pane of Mail preferences.

To show *all* Notes, regardless of what account they belong to, click the main "Notes" mailbox, not one of the Notes sub-folders.

Create a formatted list

It's often useful to use a *list* in a Note (or in any message). To create an automatically bulleted or numbered list, go to the Format menu, choose "Lists," then choose the type of list you want—bulleted or numbered. Type your list, hitting a Return after each item. The text is automatically indented and numbered after each Return. To turn off the list formatting and type regular text, hit the Return key twice.

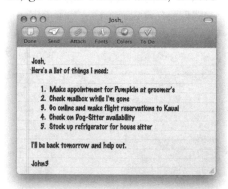

Format text in a Note

To format the text in a Note, select the text you want to format, then click one of the format buttons in the Note's toolbar (right). The "Fonts" button opens the Fonts palette in which you can choose a typeface, font size and color, and drop-shadow settings. The "Colors" button opens the same Colors palette that's accessible from the Fonts pallette. If the only formatting you want to do is color formatting, click the "Colors" button.

Add attachments to a Note

Click the "Attach" button to attach a photo or file to a Note. In the Finder window that opens, locate a file, then click "Choose File."

Add To Do items to a Note

Click the "To Do" button to add a To Do item to a Note.

Send a Note as an email message

Click the "Send" button. An email message form opens with the Note inserted (right).

View Notes in Mail

Mail's sidebar includes a Notes mailbox as shown below. Click the top-level Notes icon to show all notes (below-left). Click one of the second-level Note icons in the sidebar to show the Notes in that account only. Notes also appear in the message list as yellow note icons (below-right). If you have multiple email accounts, select the Inbox of the account you want to show. To see all Notes (and messages) for all Inboxes, select the top-level Inbox.

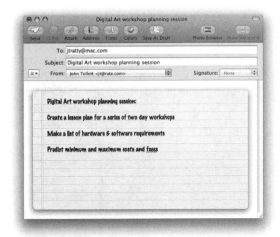

This notes contains text formatting, a To Do, a photo attachment, and a file attachment.

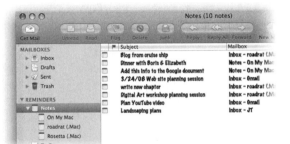

RSS News Feeds in Mail

To complete its mission as an all-in-one information center, Mail can even collect your favorite RSS news feeds so you can check on stories of interest when you check your mail. RSS is a subscription technology that many sites use, especially news-oriented sites whose content changes often.

Subscribe to an RSS news feed

Subscribing to an RSS feed is as simple as bookmarking it.

1. Use Safari to open a web page that includes RSS feeds. Look on the right side of the address field for an RSS icon (left, and circled below). Some sites also put an RSS link somewhere on their home page. If you see an XML icon (left), it's essentially the same thing, just slightly different technology.

2. Click the RSS icon in the address field (or on the web page). The site's RSS feed page opens (below). This page contains headlines and short excerpts from the articles that you'll find at that site.

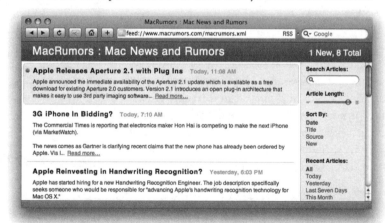

3. Bookmark this page by clicking the Plus (**+**) button in the Safari toolbar. In the dialog that opens (right), edit the bookmark name (if you want), then checkmark the "Mail" checkbox. Checkmark both "Mail" and "Safari" to make the RSS feed appear in both places. If you have other RSS readers installed, they appear in this dialog also. Click "Add."

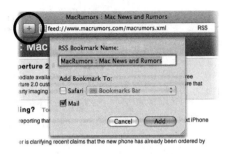

4. Look in Mail's sidebar for the new RSS mailbox, in the "RSS" group category (right-middle). The number to the right of the mailbox tells you how many articles have not been read yet.

   Click the upward-pointing arrow to show the RSS mailbox in your Inbox group at the top of the sidebar (the original RSS mailbox remains in the RSS group).

   To hide the RSS mailbox from the Inbox group, click the downward-facing arrow (lower-right).

Show in Inbox.

5. Click an RSS mailbox icon in the sidebar to show a list of the RSS headlines from that feed, in the message list area.

6. Double-click a headline in the list to open the article in its own window (below). Click the "Read more…" link to open Safari and show the entire article on its web site.

Hide from Inbox.

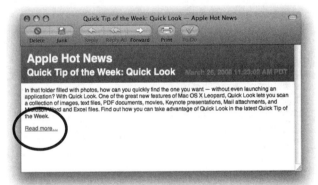

In the RSS pane of Mail preferences (right), you can choose to check for updates and remove articles manually, or set how often you want Mail to perform those tasks automatically.

Attachments

One of the most useful and fun things about email is the ability to send files and photos back and forth. Mail has some great features for attachments, making it easier than ever to share files.

To send an attachment:

1. Open a new message window.

2. To attach a file or photograph, click the "Attach" icon in the toolbar.

   This opens a standard Open dialog box. Find your file, select it, and click "Choose File." Hold down the Command key to select more than one file to attach.

   Or drag a file or photo from any Finder window, or from your Desktop, and drop it directly into the message window.

3. A file icon appears in your window. If it's a one-page PDF or a photo, the actual image will probably appear, as shown below, instead of a file icon.

4. If the file in the window appears as the actual image, you can change it into an icon if you like (but you don't have to): Control-click (or right-click) on the image. From the menu that pops up, choose "View as Icon." This does not determine how the person who receives the file will view it.

5. Click "Send" to send your message.

If the photograph is too large, you can choose to send a smaller version here.

To receive and download an attachment:

When you receive an attachment in a message, there are several ways to deal with the file:

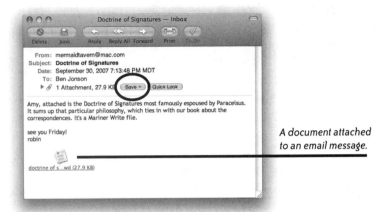

A document attached
to an email message.

If it's a photograph and you can see it in the window, then maybe that's all you want to do with it. So you're done.

Or if it's **one file or a photograph,** you can do any of the following things:

▼ Drag the file to the Desktop or directly into any window or folder on your Mac.

▼ Click the "Save" button in the header information area (circled above). The attachment is instantly added to the Downloads folder (see page 309).

▼ Save the image directly into **iPhoto** (if it's installed): Press (don't click) on the "Save" button and choose "Add to iPhoto" (see the following page).

▼ Control-click on the photo or file icon (as shown below), then choose any of the options shown below.

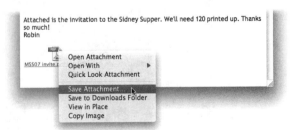

If you have **multiple photographs** in your email message, you have even more options. You can do everything mentioned on the previous page, plus:

Save only one file from a collection of files. Press (don't click) on the "Save" button to show a pop-up menu (below). From the menu, choose the file you want to save. It goes to the Downloads folder.
Or choose "Save All…" in the pop-up menu.
Or choose "Add to iPhoto."

To view a **full-screen slideshow** of multiple, attached photos, click the "Quick Look" button in the header area of the message.

Press the "Save" button to show this pop-up menu.

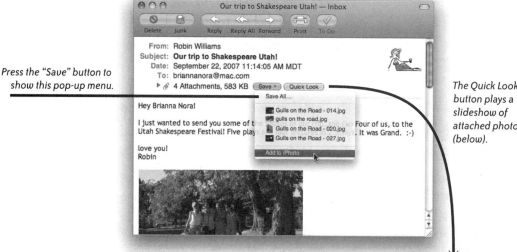

The Quick Look button plays a slideshow of attached photos (below).

Quick Look provides slideshow controls—Play, Pause, Back, Forward, Index Sheet view, Full Screen view, and "Add to iPhoto."

Show Index Sheet View (all photos in one window).

Play slideshow in Full Screen mode.

Add to iPhoto.

The Downloads Folder

When you click the "Save" button in an email to save the files that someone sent you, the files are automatically stored in the **Downloads folder.** The Downloads folder appears in the Dock, near the Trash (below-left). The same Downloads folder also appears in your Home folder (you can see it in the Finder window shown below). Open the folder in either location to access the files in it.

The Downloads folder in the Dock can have different appearances, based on settings you choose. Press on the Downloads folder to open a pop-up menu of options (right). Choose "Display as Folder" to show a *folder icon* in the Dock, as shown below-left. Choose "Display as Stack" to show the Documents folder as a *stack of file icons.* An icon of the most recent download appears on top (below-right). "Fan" and "Grid" views are also options.

Display as Folder.

Display as Stack.

Press on the folder to show a menu of options.

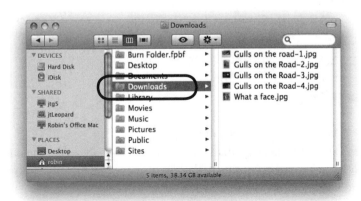

The Downloads folder shown in a Finder window.

View content as a Fan. Click on an image to open it. Click the arrow at the top to open the Downloads folder in a Finder window, as shown to the left.

The "Sort by" options in the pop-up menu let you choose how the contents of the Downloads folder are sorted when you click the Downloads folder in the Dock.

Mark Messages with Priority Settings

You can set one of three **priority** settings in Mail messages so your recipient understands how urgent a particular message is—provided the recipient's email program can display the priority marker. If someone sends you a message marked as high or low priority, Mail marks it as such.

To set a priority:

With a message window open (below), go to the Message menu in the menu bar, choose "Mark," then choose the priority option you want for this message (Low, Normal, or High priority).

Or click the priority pop-up menu in the compose window (circled below) and choose a priority. If the priority pop-up menu isn't present, you can customize the window's heading and add it (see page 284).

The priority pop-up menu.

To check the priority of an incoming message:

In the Flag column you will see two exclamation marks to denote a message that has been labeled **High Priority.** A dash indicates **Low Priority. Normal Priority** doesn't show any symbol.

If the Flag column is not visible, Control-click any heading, then from the pop-up menu, choose "Flag."

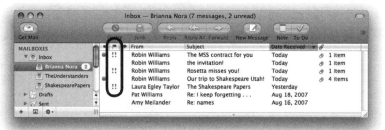

Let Mail Complete a Word for You

If you aren't sure of a word's spelling, or if you don't want to type an entire long word, Mail can help.

1. Type part of a word in an email message.

2. From the Edit menu, choose "Complete" (or press Option-Escape).
   A pop-up menu opens with a list of possible words that match what you've typed so far (right).

3. Select the word you want to use from the pop-up list, then hit Return (or double-click the word in the list).

   Mail automatically completes the word you partially typed in the message.

Create a Message Summary

To save a portion of a lengthy email message for use somewhere else later, you can create a "summary."

1. Select a range of text in a message.

2. From the Mail menu, choose "Services," then choose "Summary."

3. In the "Summary" dialog that opens (below), choose to adjust the summary size by "Sentences" or "Paragraphs." Adjust the "Summary Size" slider.

4. Save the file: From the File menu, choose "Save." In the "Save" dialog, name the file and choose a location where you want to store the file. The text is saved as a .rtf (Rich Text Format) file. You can open the .rtf file later, copy it, and paste it into an email or almost any other kind of document.

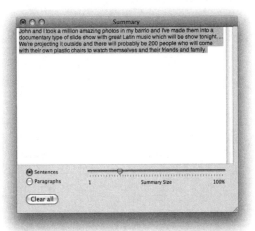

Archive Mailboxes

As a safeguard against accidentally losing important email messages, make an archive of your important mailboxes. It's a good idea to create a mailbox named something like "Important" (left), then drag important messages into it. It's also a good idea to create subfolders in the "Important" folder (as shown on the left), to better organize important messages. Archive the "Important" mailbox regularly and save the archives in a folder named something like "Archived Mailboxes."

To archive mailboxes:

1. Select one or more mailboxes to archive.

2. From the Mailbox menu, choose "Archive Mailbox...."
   Or choose "Archive Mailbox..." from the Action pop-up menu in the bottom-left corner of Mail's sidebar (circled, below-left).

3. In the dialog that opens (above-right), choose a location where you want to store the archive. If the mailbox you want to archive contains subfolders, checkmark "Export all subfolders."

4. Click "Choose." The archive is saved as a .mbox package.

Important.mbox

To recover messages from an archive:

1. Go to the File menu, then choose "Import Mailboxes…."

2. In the Import dialog (below-left), choose to import data from "Mail for Mac OS X." A Finder window opens for you to locate a mailbox archive, or a folder containing archives (below-right).

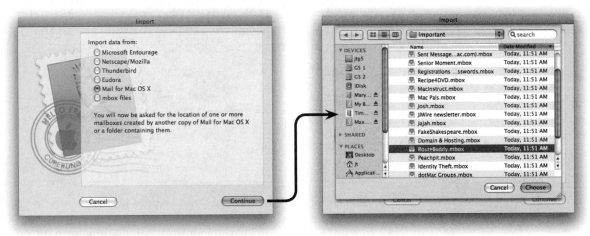

3. Select the mailboxes you want to restore (above-right), then click "Choose."

4. A final dialog appears (below) to tell you the imported mailboxes can be found in a folder in the mailboxes list (Mail's sidebar), named "Import" (right).

5. Click "Done."

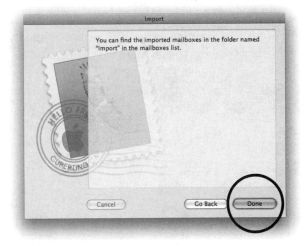

This example shows that we imported only the "RouteBuddy" mailbox, which was in an archived folder, named "Important," which contained multiple mailboxes (above-right).

Smart Addresses

A Smart Address is what appears in the "To" field when you start to type someone's email address. As you type, Mail looks inside your Address Book and in your Previous Recipients list (found in the Window menu) for matches to what you type. A drop-down list of matches appears (below-left). Click one of the contacts in the list to enter it in the "To" field. **Or** hit Return if the address you want is the one highlighted in the list. A Smart Address shows the contact's name, and hides the email address, as shown below-right.

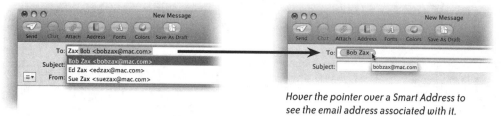

Hover the pointer over a Smart Address to see the email address associated with it.

bobzax@mac.com.mailloc

This is what a Smart Address file looks like on the Desktop.

A Smart Address is an "object" that you can drag and drop into other locations. You can drag a Smart Address object between the To, Cc, and Bcc fields. You can also drag a Smart Address to an email message, to a text document, or to your Desktop.

Double-click a Smart Address that's on your Desktop to open a new email message window addressed to that recipient.

To turn off Smart Addresses, go to the Mail menu and choose "Preferences...." In the "Viewing" pane (below-left), uncheck the box to "Use Smart Addresses." The address itself is still an object that you can drag and drop into other places, as described above, and Mail still provides a list of matches as you type. The difference is that the actual email address is visible in the "To" field, along with the contact's name (below-right).

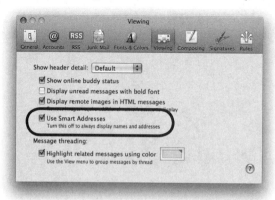

When "Use Smart Addresses" is unchecked, an address looks like this.

The Address Pane

Address a message using the Address Pane: Click the "New Message" button to open a new message window. In the toolbar, click the "Address" button (right) to open a limited version of your Address Book (below). Double-click a name or Group in your list to address your message to that person or group.

To send the same message to more than one person, hold down the Command key and *single*-click on names in the Address Pane; then let go of the Command key and click the "To" button in the Address pane toolbar. **Or** double-click on each person's name to add them one at a time.

You can also use this technique to add addresses to the "Cc" and "Bcc" fields of a message (the *carbon copy* and *blind carbon copy* fields.)

To Add the Address button to Mail's toolbar (so you don't have to open a new message first), customize the toolbar as explained on page 319.

Save a Draft

To finish a message later, click the "Save As Draft" button in the toolbar, (right). **Or** press Command S to save the message draft in the Drafts mailbox. Click the "Drafts" mailbox in Mail's sidebar to show a list of all saved message drafts.

Mail **automatically** creates a draft for you whenever you write a message— if something happens and your computer goes down, you won't lose the entire letter. But to make sure, save regularly (press Command S), as you would in any document.

To open the draft later for editing, select the "Drafts" icon in Mail's sidebar, then double-click the desired draft in the list.

Reply to a Message

1. Select or open a message you want to reply to, then click the "Reply" button in the toolbar (circled, left).

2. A message window opens that contains the original sender's address in the "To" field, with the original message formatted as a quote. Type your reply above the quote (or below, if you prefer), then click the "Send" button in the toolbar.

    Great tip: If you select a portion of the text before you click "Reply," just that portion of text will be copied into the new email message!

Reply to all recipients of a message

Mail that you receive may have been sent to multiple recipients, either directly as a "Cc" ("Carbon copy," or "Courtesy copy" since it's no longer on carbon paper), or privately as a Blind courtesy copy (Bcc). You can choose to reply to all recipients with one email (the reply will *not* go to anyone in the hidden Bcc list).

1. Select or open a message in the message list, then click the "Reply All" button in the toolbar (circled, left).

2. Type your reply above the original, quoted message, then click the "Send" button in the toolbar.

Forward a Message

1. Select or open a message, then click the "Forward" button in the toolbar (circled, left).

2. Type any comments above the original quoted message, then click the "Send" button in the toolbar.

    Please remove all the names and addresses of everyone else in the forwarded list before you send it! It's bad email etiquette to forward messages that contain long lists of email addresses. This happens a lot, and it makes the senders look like they don't know what they're doing. And sometimes they don't. You can look like you're an expert. Just remove any long list of email addresses that might be included in the message *before* you forward it to others.

Send a Cc (courtesy copy) to others

To send a copy of your message to other contacts that need to stay informed about your correspondence, put their addresses in the "Cc" field. This makes it obvious to all that the main recipient is the one in the "To" field. To add a Cc field, go to the View menu and choose "Cc Address Field." **Or** click the Action button (circled on the next page), then choose "Cc Address Field."

Send a Bcc (blind courtesy copy)

Any email address you put in the Bcc field will not be seen by any other recipients. That is, you might want to send a message to a coworker, but you want your boss to be aware of the issue and the response. So you create a Bcc field and put your boss's email address in it. The coworker does not know your boss received a copy of the message.

When the coworker replies, the reply does *not* go to anyone who was in the Bcc field of *your* message.

1. Address and write your message as usual.

2. From the View menu, choose "Bcc Address Field."
   Or click the Action button (circled below),
   then choose "Bcc Address Field."

   This puts a new field in the address area, labeled "Bcc."
   Addresses you type in this field will *not* be seen by anyone whose address is in the "To" or "Cc" field.

   To remove the "Bcc" field, go back to the View menu and choose "Bcc Address Field" again. Or uncheck it in the Action menu (circled below).

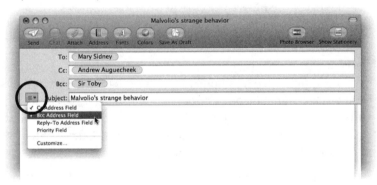

In the example above, Mary Sidney is the primary recipient of the message.

Andrew Aguecheek receives a copy of the message. Mary knows he received a copy because she can see who's listed in the "Cc" field.

Neither Mary nor Andrew know that Sir Toby also received a copy of the message because his address is in the private "Bcc" field.

When you send an email to a mailing list, such as a Group from Address Book, the name of the Group is put in the "To" field, and the individual Group member addresses are put in the "Bcc" field. This helps to protect the privacy of Group members.

Other Email Actions

The following actions are not as common for most of us, but can be very useful in certain circumstances. These commands can be found in the menus at the top of the screen. If you want to add them as buttons to Mail's toolbar, customize the toolbar, as explained on the next page.

Bounce To Sender

Bounce To Sender is meant to discourage unwanted email. Select an unwanted message, then from the Message menu, choose "Bounce." The sender receives a reply that says your email address is invalid and the message was not delivered. The recipient cannot tell if the message has been read. The unwanted message is moved to your Trash folder. Unfortunately, this does not work for most junk email because spam return addresses are usually stolen to prevent spammers from getting caught.

Redirect

Redirect is similar to "Forward," except that redirected mail shows the *original* sender's name in the "From" category instead of yours, and shows the time the message was originally composed. When you redirect mail, your name is at the top of the message so the new recipient knows you received the message and redirected it.

Go Offline

If you have a dial-up Internet connection, you probably don't want to stay online while you answer and compose email. You can log on to get your mail, then **go offline** (disconnect). While offline, you can read your mail and write replies. Mail will save each composed message in your Drafts folder. When you're ready, go online again and send your email messages.

To take all accounts offline, go to the Mailbox menu, then choose "Take All Accounts Offline."

To go back online, go the Mailbox menu, then choose "Take All Accounts Online."

If you have multiple email accounts, and want to take just one of them offline, go to the Mailbox menu, choose "Online Status," then choose the account you want to take offline.

You can also take accounts offline or online by Control-clicking the account mailbox in Mail's sidebar, then from the pop-up menu, choosing "Take *account name* Offline" or "Take *account name* Online."

Customize Mail's Toolbar

The buttons in Mail's toolbar are shortcuts for commands that are also available in the various menus at the top of the screen. You can customize the toolbar to add or remove command buttons.

To add buttons to the toolbar, go to the View menu and choose "Customize Toolbar…." **Or** Control-click the toolbar, then choose "Customize Toolbar…" from the pop-up menu.

A sheet of buttons slides down from the toolbar that represent various functions (shown below). Drag and drop any of these items onto the toolbar, then click "Done."

To remove a button at any time, Command-drag it off the toolbar.

Or Control-click on a button in the toolbar, then choose "Remove item" from the pop-up menu. To remove a button while the Customize sheet is open, just drag the item off the toobar.

To rearrange buttons, Command-drag them left or right to other positions in the toobar.

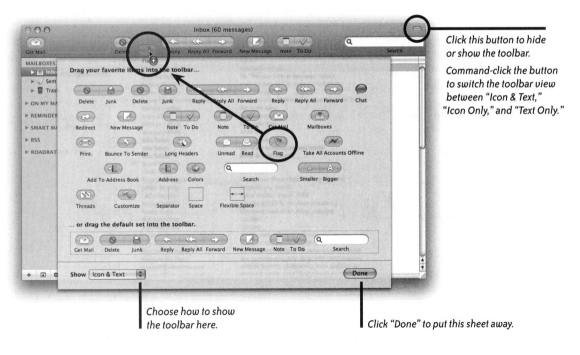

Click this button to hide or show the toolbar.

Command-click the button to switch the toolbar view between "Icon & Text," "Icon Only," and "Text Only."

Choose how to show the toolbar here.

Click "Done" to put this sheet away.

The Message Window

The **message window** displays all messages in the currently selected Mailbox. The list is divided into several columns and provides different organizational views, depending on which column is selected and whether or not you choose to organize by message thread (page 324).

The columns of information

In addition to the columns that automatically appear in your Viewer window, you can choose to show a number of other columns. From the View menu, slide down to "Columns," then in the flyout submenu, check or uncheck columns you want to show or hide. Or Control-click on a column heading, then check or uncheck one of the column headings in the pop-up menu.

To sort the message list according to the column heading, click the heading at the top of a column. The column heading that is blue is the one by which items are currently arranged. For instance, I like to keep my email organized by date received with the newest email at the top of the list, as shown below. But sometimes I want to find an old email from a particular *person,* so I click the "From" column to alphabetize the names. Then I can quickly skim through the collection of email from each person.

To move columns, position the pointer over a column heading, then press-and-drag the column left or right. As you drag a column on top of another column, the column underneath moves over to leave an empty area for you. Let go and the column snaps into the new position.

To change the column widths, position the pointer over the gray dividing line in the column headings. The pointer turns into a two-headed arrow (circled below). Press-and-drag the column edge left or right.

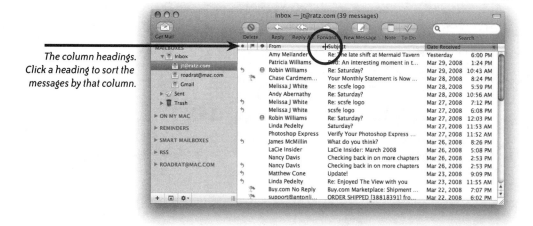

The column headings. Click a heading to sort the messages by that column.

Message Status column (●): This column displays different icons to indicate if you've read the message, replied to it, forwarded it, or redirected it. These icons show up automatically when one of those actions takes place.

Click the message status column heading (●) to group similar categories, such as unread or replied messages, together in the list. Click again in the column heading to reverse the order of the list.

The message status **icons** provide visual clues about the messages.

- ● Blue orb: Message has not been read.
- ↰ Curved arrow: Message was replied to.
- → Right arrow: Message was forwarded.
- ↯ Crooked arrow: Message was redirected.

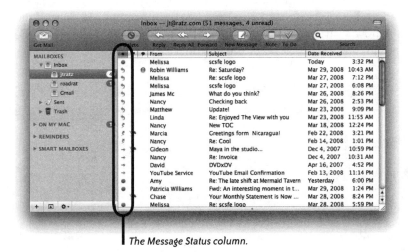

| The Message Status column.

Manually mark an email that you've already read as "unread." Use this as a reminder to go back and read a message again or to make a message stand out: Select one or more messages, then from the Message menu, choose "Mark," then choose "As Unread." The blue orb reappears in the status column, next to the message.

Manually mark an email that you haven't read as "read." Perhaps you don't want to read a message, but aren't ready to throw it away. But you don't want Mail to make you think you've got new mail by putting a red tag on the Mail icon in the Dock. To mark the message as read, go the Message menu, choose "Mark," then choose "As Read." The blue orb is removed from the status column.

Number column: In a series of email exchanges, it may be useful to know in what order messages were received. The Number column keeps track of the order for you. Click the **#** symbol in the column heading to arrange messages by order. Click again in the column heading to reverse the order of the list.

Subject column: The Subject column shows what the sender typed into the Subject field of his email message. Click the column heading to show the subjects in alphabetical order; click again to reverse the order of the list.

Date Received column: The Date Received column shows when you received a message. Click the heading of the column to show messages in the time sequence they were received. Click again to reverse the order of the list.

Flags column: Mark a message as flagged when you want it to stand out in the list or if you want to temporarily tag a group of related messages. **To see all flagged files** in a list, click the "Flag" column heading. All flagged messages will move to the top of the list. Click the heading again to reverse the order and put flagged messages at the bottom of the list.

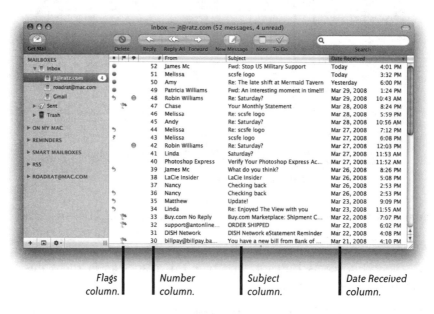

Flags column.   Number column.   Subject column.   Date Received column.

Buddy Availability column: If you have a Buddy List set up in iChat, and if this feature is turned on in the Viewing pane of Mail preferences, the Buddy Availability column displays a green orb when a Buddy is online. If the buddy is online but idle (perhaps his computer has gone to sleep), you'll see an amber orb.

When you see that a Buddy is online, you can double-click the green orb to open an iChat dialog (as shown below). Choose the type of chat you want, then click "Chat."

You can customize the toolbar (see page 319) to include a "Chat" button, shown below. Select an *online* Buddy in the message list, then click the "Chat" button in the toolbar to open the "New Chat" dialog shown below-right. Select the type of chat you want, then click "Chat."

Chat button.

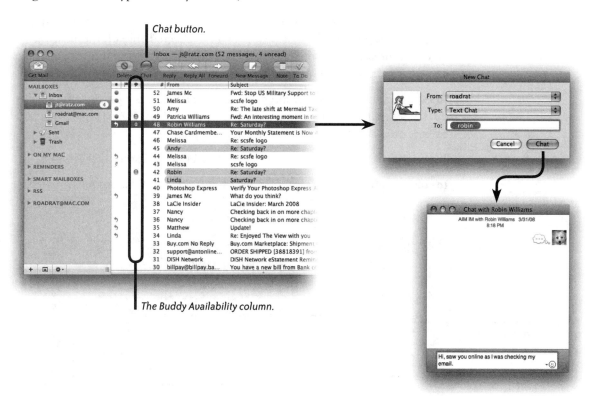

The Buddy Availability column.

View Message Threads

A collection of related messages and replies are called **message threads.** If you reply to an email whose subject field is labeled "Dogfood," the reply's subject field is automatically labeled "Re: Dogfood." Mail identifies messages that have identical subject fields as being in the *same thread* and highlights *all* of the messages in a thread when any related message is selected, as shown below. You can turn off this highlighting, or change the highlight color, in the Viewing pane of Mail's preferences.

To group all messages in a thread, from the View menu, choose "Organize by Thread." All related messages are now grouped together and highlighted in the message list, as shown below. This is a convenient and easy way to find all the correspondence related to a particular subject.

All of the messages in a thread are *highlighted* when you select any single related message. To select all messages in a selected thread, the next message in a thread, or the previous message in a thread, go to the View menu and use the "Select" command.

To expand a selected thread and *show* all its related messages, click the small disclosure triangle to the left of a message thread. Click the triangle again to **collapse** the thread and *hide* the related messages.

To expand all threads: From the View menu, choose "Expand All Threads."

To collapse all threads: From the View menu, choose "Collapse All Threads."

Threads column.

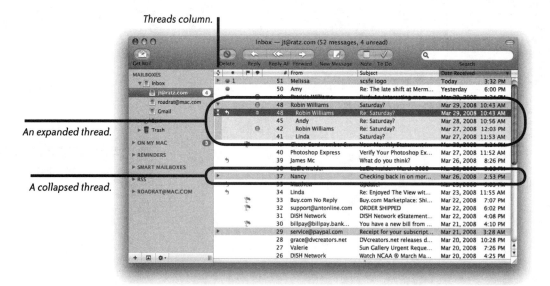

An expanded thread.

A collapsed thread.

Parental Controls

If you're concerned about young children being exposed to inappropriate email, there are built-in parental controls that can limit email and Internet access for a specific user account. The first step is to set up a new user account for the child. The new account can use an existing email account.

1. Open System Preferences, then open the Accounts pane. Click the Add (+) button in the bottom-left corner. If the padlock in the bottom-left corner is locked, click it, then enter an admin password, in order to make changes.

2. In the new account pane (top-right), name the account, then checkmark "Enable Parental Controls."

3. Click the "Open Parental Controls" button. The Parental Controls pane shown below-right opens. In the "Mail & iChat" tab, checkmark "Limit Mail" and "Limit iChat." The child will be able to email and iChat only addresses you add to the list below. Click the Add (+) button to add email addresses and iChat buddy names.

4. To receive an email notification when the little brat attempts to email or iChat with someone not in your list, checkmark "Send permission requests to:," then type your own email address into the text field. The little darling will see a dialog that gives the options of "Cancel" or "Ask Permission." The email you receive shows the child's message and includes an "Always Allow" button.

Word Search through Spotlight, Google, or the Dictionary

This is a very fun feature. Select any word or phrase in any email message. Control-click on the selection (or right-click). From the pop-up menu (below-right), choose to send that word or phrase to Google as a web search! **Or** choose "Search in Spotlight" to search your computer for all other references to the selected word or phrase. **Or** look it up in the built-in Dictionary. This feature also works on web pages and in TextEdit.

Control-click a selected word or phrase.

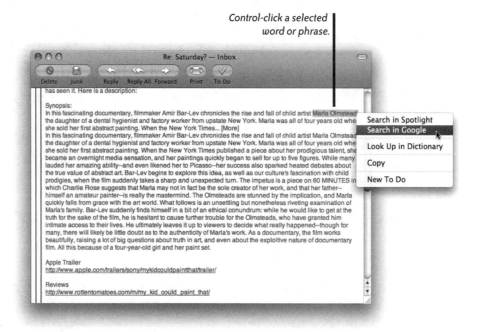

Contextual Menus

Mail makes extensive use of **contextual menus:** Control-click on a message, the toolbar, or an item in the Mailbox Sidebar to open a pop-up menu that offers various commands, as shown below. If you have a two-button mouse, you can also right-click on an item to show a contextual menu.

Using contextual menus is just a convenient way to access menu commands—there is usually nothing in a contextual menu that you can't find in the main menu bar across the top of your screen.

The Junk Mail Filter

Mail automatically deletes junk mail without you ever having to see it. If you want to be a little more cautious, you can have junk mail sent to a "Junk" folder in the sidebar, where you check it in case something you want mistakenly gets marked as junk.

To turn the Junk Mail feature on or off:

1. Go to the Mail menu and choose "Preferences…."
2. Click the "Junk Mail" icon in the toolbar (below).
3. Check (or uncheck) the box, "Enable junk mail filtering."

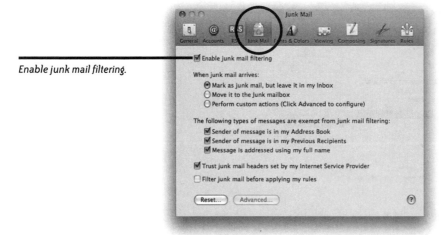

Enable junk mail filtering.

Mail analyzes incoming messages and identifies what it thinks is **junk mail** by highlighting the message in brown (below). If the "Flags" column is showing, you'll see a junk mail icon (a brown mail bag) in that column.

To show the Flags column, from the View menu, choose "Columns," then from the submenu, choose "Flags." **Or** Control-click a column heading, then from the pop-up menu, choose "Flags."

Train Mail to find junk more accurately

You can **train Mail to be more accurate** in identifying junk:

1. From the Mail menu, choose "Preferences…."

2. Check the box to "Enable Junk Mail filtering."

3. From the options titled "When junk mail arrives," choose "Leave it in my Inbox, but indicate it is junk mail."

4. When you receive a new email message, check to see if Mail has correctly identified it.

   ▼ If the new message is **unwanted junk mail, but Mail did not mark it** as such: Select the message, then click the "Junk" icon in the toolbar (right) to mark it as junk mail.

   Or from the Message menu, choose "Mark," then from the submenu, choose "As Junk Mail."

   Or press Command Shift J.

   ▼ **If Mail *incorrectly* identifies** a message as junk mail, correct it: Select the incorrectly marked message and notice the "Junk" icon in the toolbar has changed to "Not Junk" (right). Click the "Not Junk" icon to correctly identify the message.

5. Continue training Mail in this way for a couple of weeks, or until most incoming messages seem to be correctly identified.

   If Mail seems to be doing a good job of identifying junk mail, you can switch from "training" mode to "automatic" mode. Automatic mode prevents junk mail from entering your message list and puts it in a "Junk" folder in the sidebar instead (see the next page). If you go for a while without marking any messages as "Not Junk," Mail eventually assumes that its junk mail detection is working just fine, and opens a dialog (below) that lets you "Stay in Traning" mode, or "Switch to Automatic." But you don't have to wait for this dialog to appear to switch to automatic mode. You can do that at any time, as explained on the next page.

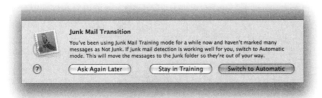

Continued…

When you're ready to **let Mail automatically handle junk mail,** go to the Mail preferences, click the "Junk Mail" button in the toolbar, then choose "Move it to the Junk mailbox." Mail creates a Junk mailbox in the sidebar to store the unwanted mail. You should occasionally review the messages in this mailbox to make sure messages are being correctly identified.

If you would like to **adjust the junk mail settings yourself,** choose the option to "Perform custom actions (Click Advanced to configure)." Then click the "Advanced…" button at the bottom of the window.

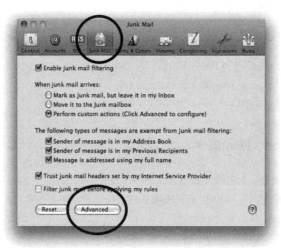

When you click the "Advanced…" button, a sheet drops down, as shown below. This shows you the rules that Mail is using to filter the junk mail. If you find it's too restrictive or not restrictive enough, you can change these. See page 289 for more information about Rules.

Instantly delete junk mail

When you're satisfied that Mail is accurately identifying junk mail, you may want to change your setting so **Junk mail is instantly deleted.** Be careful with this! If you choose this option, you will never see the mail, and you can't undo the action or find it in any "Trash" mailbox—it's gone.

To delete junk mail before it ever appears in your box:

1. From the Mail menu, choose "Preferences…," then click the "Junk Mail" button in the toolbar.

2. As shown on the opposite page, checkmark the box to "Enable junk mail filtering."

3. Select "Perform custom actions (Click Advanced to configure)."

4. Click the "Advanced…" button to open the sheet shown below.

5. At the bottom of the sheet, under the section, "Perform the following actions," set the pop-up menu to "Delete Message" (circled below).

6. Click OK. Messages that meet these conditions are instantly deleted.

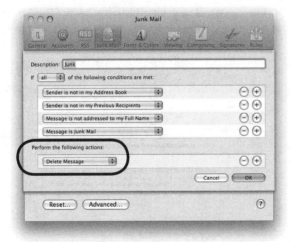

Remember, you have to be very confident that you're not getting any real mail mixed up in your junk mail! (Personally, if something gets accidentally labeled as junk and disappears, that's too bad—it's not worth it to sort through hundreds of pieces of junk mail to see if there's one good message. Sorry.)

Empty the Trash

When you delete messages, they're not gone. They're just in the Trash folder that's in the sidebar. Click the Trash mailbox and you'll see all the stuff you've been throwing away.

If your Trash mailbox shows a small disclosure triangle to the left of it, click the triangle to expand the mailbox and show the different Trash mailboxes for individual accounts. Click the top-level Trash mailbox to show deleted messages from all accounts.

To *really* get rid of deleted items (and reclaim some disk storage space), you need to empty the Trash. There are several ways to do that:

▼ Control-click on a Trash mailbox, then choose
"Erase Deleted Messages…."

▼ Select one or more messages in a Trash mailbox, then press Delete.

▼ Select one or more messages in a Trash mailbox, then from the Edit menu, choose "Delete."

▼ From the Mailbox menu, choose "Erase Deleted Messages," then from the submenu, choose "In All Accounts," or choose a specific account.

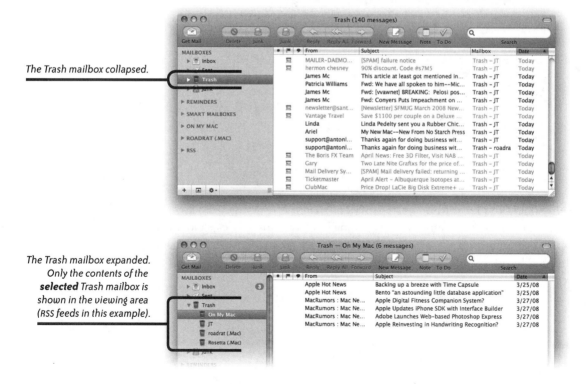

The Trash mailbox collapsed.

The Trash mailbox expanded. Only the contents of the selected Trash mailbox is shown in the viewing area (RSS feeds in this example).

Remove Deleted Messages from the Server

When you set up a POP type of email account, you have the option (in the Accounts pane of Mail preferences) to "Remove copy from server after retrieving a message." As shown below, you can set how often to remove messages from the server, or you can choose "Remove now." If messages aren't occasionally removed from the server, your allotted storage space eventually fills up, preventing email delivery.

Even when you choose the correct settings, sometimes it just doesn't work. Or perhaps I should say, *often* it just doesn't work. But there's an alternate method to delete the messages that always works.

To delete messages from the server:

1. Select a mail account in Mail's sidebar.

2. Press Command I to open the "Account Info" window shown on the right.

3. Click the "Messages on Server" tab. A list of messages that are being stored appears on the POP server.
Press Command A to select all of the messages (or make a partial selection).

4. Click the "Remove From Server" button in the bottom-right corner. This does not affect the local copies of messages that might be stored on your computer.

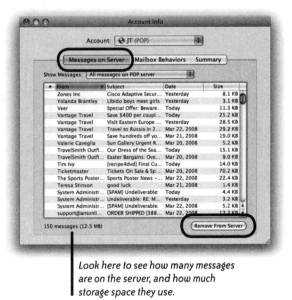

Look here to see how many messages are on the server, and how much storage space they use.

Mail Preferences

As usual in a Mac application, you have a lot of preferences that you can set in Mail to suit how you like to work. Go to the Mail menu, then choose "Preferences...." Each button in the toolbar opens a different pane of settings.

General

Default Email Reader: Choose "Mail.app (3.2)" in this pop-up menu so when you go to a web page or a PDF and click an email link, it will open a pre-addressed message window for you.

Check for new mail: Set how often you want to check for new mail. This only works if Mail is open. If you don't have a full-time, always-on connection to the Internet (such as DSL or cable modem), you'll probably want to select "Manually" from this pop-up menu to avoid having your modem dialing and trying to connect when you least expect it.

New mail sound: Choose a sound (or "None") to alert you when new mail appears in your Inbox. If you create rules that filter your mail, you can have different sounds for each of the rules so you know exactly when junk mail has been deleted, a letter from your sweetheart has arrived, or an important message from your boss has been delivered.

Play sounds for other mail actions: Plays the sound of an airplane taking off when mail has been sent, and plays other tiny sounds when it checks for mail and there isn't any, or when there's a problem fetching mail.

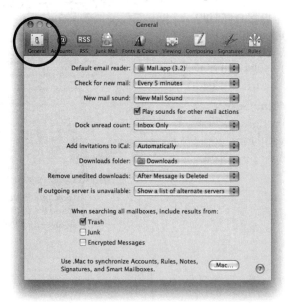

Dock unread count: Select which mailboxes are included in Mail's count of unread messages that appears as a red tag on the Mail icon in the Dock.

Add invitations to iCal: When a Mac user sends you an iCal invitation via email, this option tells Mail to automatically send it to iCal. You'll see the invitation in the Notifications pane and an event will be automatically created. You can respond to the person either through Mail or through iCal. The other option in this menu is "Never."

Downloads folder: When an email message to you includes an attachment and you open that attachment to view it, Mail temporarily stores the attachment in the folder you designate here. The default setting is the Downloads folder in your Dock. You can choose "Other…" to set any location on your computer that you prefer.

Remove unedited downloads: This option tells Mail when to delete the downloads that came as email attachments. The default is to delete them "After Message is Deleted," but you can choose "When Mail Quits" or "Never." This does not affect any attachments you have saved into custom folders in Mail's sidebar.

If outgoing server is unavailable: This default setting tells Mail what to do if the outgoing mail server (the SMTP server) of an email account is unavailable. Choose to have Mail show you a list of alternate servers that you may have access to, or try again later.

When searching all maiboxes, include results from: Checkmark the items you want to include in searches (Trash, Junk, and Encrypted Messages).

Use .Mac to synchronize Accounts, Rules, Notes, Signatures, and Smart Mailboxes. If you want to synchronize these items between Macs, or with your online .Mac account, click the ".Mac…" button.

Accounts preferences

Account Information. From this tab you create new email accounts, or edit existing ones. See page 278 for detailed information about how to create an email account.

Mailbox Behaviors. The options in this tab can change, depending on the type of email account that's selected in the Accounts column on the left. Choose settings for Notes, Sent messages, Junk messages, Drafts, and what to do with Trash messages.

Advanced. The options in this tab can change, depending on the type of email account that's selected in the Accounts column on the left. Choose settings to enable or disable the selected account, incude the selected account when checking for new mail, or remove messages from the server.

Accounts preferences.

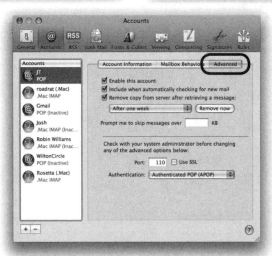

RSS preferences

Default RSS Reader: Choose a default reader for RSS feeds. Safari and Mail are the two readers that come with every Mac. If you've installed a third-party reader, you can select it to show in this pop-up menu.

Check for updates: Choose how often your RSS reader checks RSS feeds you've subscribed to for unread articles.

Remove articles: Choose how often articles are removed from the reader.

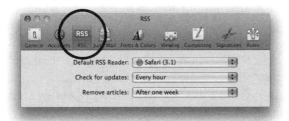

Junk Mail preferences

Enable junk mail filtering: Check this box to turn on junk mail filtering. If you use a third-party software to filter junk mail, you'll probably be instructed to uncheck this box so it won't interfere with the other software.

When junk mail arrives: Choose what Mail should do with junk mail.

Choose what types of messages you want exempted from junk mail filtering. All three of these options are good to choose.

Trust junk mail headers set by my Internet Service Provider: Select this option to include your ISP's junk mail detection in the filtering process.

Reset...: Return your junk mail database to its original information. All training you've done, marking what is junk and what is not, is removed.

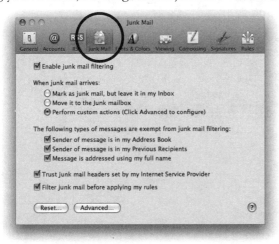

Fonts & Colors preferences

Mailbox font: Click "Select…" to choose a font and size for the mailboxes that appear in Mail's sidebar.

Message list font: Click "Select…" to choose a font and size for the list of messages in the viewing area of Mail's window.

Message font: Click "Select…" to choose a font and size for your email messages. If you choose a font that your recipients don't have installed on their computers, your font choice turns into the default font on their computer.

Note font: Click "Select…" to choose a font and size for the Notes feature.

Fixed-width font: Click "Select…" to choose a fixed-width font and size for when you write messages in "plain text," which is totally without formatting. In the "Collections" column of the Fonts dialog that opens, choose "Fixed Width," then choose one of the font options that appears.

Use fixed-width font for plain text messages: Checkmark this option if you want to write plain text messages (no formatting).

Color quoted text: Email replies often contain quotes from previous emails. Color coding and indenting the quotes helps visually organize the message in a hierarchy of responses. To apply color to quoted messages, checkmark the box. To change the default colors, click the color pop-up menus.

Viewing preferences

The **Viewing** preferences affect the information you see in the main Viewer pane and in the body of email messages.

Show header detail: This menu lets you choose how much, if any, header information (all that to/from/date stuff) appears at the top of emails. This can be handy when you want to check for fraudulent emails, like those from spammers pretending to need your eBay account information.

Choose "All" to show all header information when you want to look for suspicious data, like a return address that is different from the one that appears elsewhere.

Select "Custom..." to choose what information appears in the headers. "Default" shows the basic stuff you usually see.

Show online buddy status: This option puts a Buddy Availability column in the messsage list so you can see if a buddy is online. When a buddy from your iChat buddy list is available, a green orb appears next to his name, in the Buddy Availability column (identified by a small speech balloon icon).

Display unread messages with bold font: This makes unread messages in the message list appear in a bold font so it is very clear which ones you haven't read yet.

Display remote images in HTML messages: HTML messages are those fancy ones that look like web pages with graphics. Some junk mailers use these to embed graphics that have to be downloaded from a remote server. When you open this junk mail, the server can tell the junk mailer your computer's address, that your email address is valid. To protect your privacy, you can uncheck this box. Keep in mind this will also prevent legitimate HTML messages that contain remote images from loading the images.

Use Smart Addresses: Smart Addresses show only a person's name in the message address fields (not the actual email address). Uncheck this option to always show both the name and the email address in the address fields.

Highlight related messages using color: Turn message threading on or off, and customize the threading highlight color. Learn about message threading on page 324.

Composing

Message Format: "Rich Text" allows you to style messages with fonts and formatting, but not everyone will be able to see these features, depending on his computer and mail program. The other option in this pop-up menu, "Plain Text," can be seen by everyone but does not show any color and style formatting. Choose "Rich Text." You can change individual messages to "Plain Text" when necessary (from the Format menu, choose "Make Plain Text").

Check spelling: Choose "as I type" to highlight and catch spelling errors immediately. If you choose "when I click Send," Mail runs a spell check as soon as you click the Send button. If there are spelling errors, the message won't go out until you've had a chance to fix them.

If you choose "never," spell checking is turned off. Even then, you can do an individual spell check. From the Edit menu, choose "Spelling and Grammar," then choose "Check Spelling," then choose "While Typing" or "Before Sending." Your choice becomes the setting in the pane shown below.

If you need help with the correct spelling, Control-click on a misspelled word to open a pop-up menu with alternate spellings.

Automatically Cc myself: Checkmark this option and choose "Cc" from the pop-up menu to send a copy of outgoing messages to yourself. From this same pop-up menu, you can also choose "Bcc" to send yourself a copy without the recipient knowing it (a blind carbon copy).

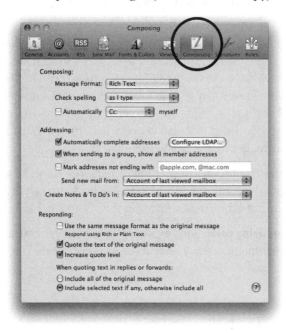

Automatically complete addresses: As you type a few letters in an address field, Mail will add the rest of the address for you. If there is more than one possible match, you'll get a list to choose from. If the correct one is the one in the Address field, just hit Return. If you get a list of possible addresses, you can use the DownArrow to move down the list. Hit Return or Enter when the proper address is selected.

If you don't like this feature, uncheck the box.

Configure LDAP…: If your workplace uses an LDAP Directory, ask your System or Network administrator for instructions on how to configure your LDAP server when you click this button.

When sending to a group, show all member addresses: When you send a message to a Group, Mail displays everyone's address in every message. Unless you have a specific reason to do this, uncheck this box so the actual addresses are hidden and group members' individual privacy is protected.

Mark addresses not ending with: If you want to create a "safe list" of addresses or email domains ("@mac.com" for example), enter the email addresses (or just the domains) here. When you address a message with an email address or domain name that is not in your safe list, the email address appears in red to alert you. This is useful when Mail is set to automatically complete addresses, and you accidentally select the wrong one when a list of possible matches pops up.

Send new mail from: If you have more than one email account, or if you use aliases with your Mac.com account, each address will be listed in this menu. Choose which one you want to use as a default return address.

Create Notes & To Do's in: Choose a location where you want these items to be stored.

The "Responding" options in this pane are mostly self-explanatory. It's a good idea to **quote the text of the original message** so the person you are responding to knows what you're talking about. **Increase quote level** makes each successive response a different color and indented a little more.

Checkmark **Include selected text if any, otherwise include all**. This means you can select just a few words or lines in a message to include in your reply. The message you send back includes only the text you selected.

Signatures preferences

A **signature** is a blurb of prepared information about you or your company that can be added to the end of a message. You can create different signatures that include different types of information or images, to be used in different situations.

This pane is where you actually create signatures, designate a default signature, and assign certain signatures to certain email accounts.

To apply a signature to an account, drag it from the middle pane and drop it on the account name in the left-hand pane, shown below. You can drag a signature to multiple accounts. See pages 290–291 for more information about creating signatures.

Always match my default message font: Checkmark this box to make sure your signature font matches the text in your message. However, if you have chosen a certain font, size, or color for your signature, uncheck this box so your formatting and styling appears in the message. You can turn this option on or off for each individual signature.

Choose Signature: To choose a default signature, select an account name in the far-left pane. Then select a signature from the "Choose Signature" pop-up menu. The chosen signature will be used in all messages from that account *unless* you override it with another choice from the pop-up menu that's available when you compose a new message.

Place signature above quoted text: This puts your signature at the end of *your message,* not at the end of all the quoted information from other emails that might already be in the message. This is a good thing.

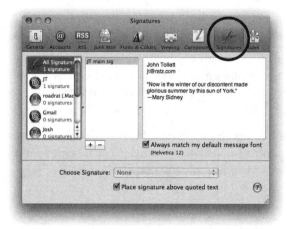

Rules preferences

The Rules preferences pane is really more a creation pane than a preferences pane. This is where you create Rules for filtering email, edit Rules, activate or disable them, and remove the ones you don't want. See page 289 to learn how to add and manage Rules.

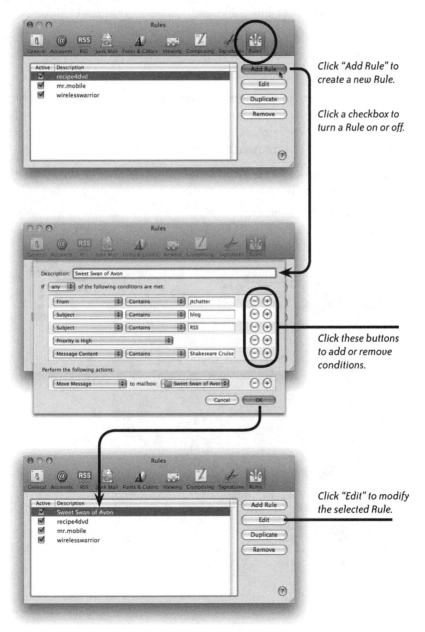

Click "Add Rule" to create a new Rule.

Click a checkbox to turn a Rule on or off.

Click these buttons to add or remove conditions.

Click "Edit" to modify the selected Rule.

Menu Commands

Following are a few items in the **menus** that aren't explained elsewhere.

File menu

New Viewer Window: If you've closed the main Viewer window and realize that you need it back, use this command, or press Command Option N.

Save Attachment: Select a message that has attachments, then choose "Save Attachment...." In the dialog that opens, you can choose a location where you want the files saved.

Print...: To print an email message, open a message, then from the File menu choose "Print...." In the dialog that opens (shown below), choose a printer, then click "Print." In the Print dialog you can also choose to save the email as a PDF. Click the "PDF" button, then choose "Save as PDF...."

To see a preview before you print, click the "Preview" button. The preview is a PDF file that also includes a "Print" button.

To print *multiple* email messages, select multiple messages in the message list, then from the File menu, choose "Print...." All selected messages are sent to the printer as separate files.

Edit menu

Paste As Quotation: Use this command when you want to paste text copied from another document into an email message as a quotation. In Mail, quotations are styled with indentation, a vertical bar, and a text color.

Paste and Match Style: When you copy and paste text from another message or another document, it drops in with its own font and size which usually doesn't match your chosen font in the message you're writing. But if you copy text and then choose this command, the text pastes in matching the font style of the message you paste it into.

Append Selected Messages: This adds an entire email message you have received onto the end of a new message you compose. Compose your message, then go to the message list and select the message you want to append. Click on the message you composed, then choose "Append Selected Messages" from the Edit menu.

Attachments: The option to "Include Original Attachments in Reply" does just what it says—when you reply, any photos or other files that came to you will be sent back to that person. Only do this if you have a reason to do so.

"Always Send Windows Friendly Attachments" tries to make sure your attachments can be read by people using Windows machines. However, this can mess up files for Mac users, so only use it if you need it for every file you send. You can always choose to make *individual files* Windows friendly: click the Attach button in a message window to show a Finder dialog. At the bottom of that dialog box is a checkbox to "Send Windows Friendly Attachments." This will apply only to the attachment you select.

"Always Insert Attachments at End of Message" ensures that attachments appear *after* your message text. However, if you want to send just a photo, without a message, the photo (or any attachment) won't attach because there's no message to attach it to. You're probably better off not selecting this item.

View menu

Display Selected Messages Only: Select messages (Command click to select more than one), then choose this option so *only* those messages will be visible in the message list. To show all of the messages again, go back to the View menu and choose "Display All Messages."

Mailbox menu

Online Status: If you have a dial-up account that ties up your phone line while you're connected to the Internet, you can "Go Offline." This disconnects you from the Internet, but leaves Mail open so you can read your downloaded email, compose messages, print them, etc. Messages you compose while offline are stored in the Drafts mailbox in the sidebar, where you can open and edit them at any time. When you're ready to send mail, from the Mailbox menu, choose "Online Status" and then select an account to take online.

Get New Mail: If you have more than one account in Mail, go to this menu to selectively check the mail in a single account.

Rebuild: If messages arrive garbled or with some strange font, try using the Rebuild command. If your hard disk is really full, clear some room before you try this because it needs hard disk space to do its rebuilding.

Window menu

Activity Viewer: To the right of the Inbox icons, you've probably seen little revolving wheels when checking your mail. If you want to see the actual activity represented by the wheels, go to the Window menu and choose "Activity." The "Activity" window opens (below-left) and shows the progress as Mail fetches or sends messages.

Or click the "Show Mail Activity" button beneath the sidebar (circled, below-right). The "Activity" pane appears at the bottom of the sidebar.

Click a "stop sign" icon to stop that particular activity.

Show Mail activity.

Format menu

The **Alignment** submenu lets you set text alignment with "Align Left, Center, Justify," and "Align Right." The submenu also contains some alignment commands for images. Select an image that you've placed in a message, then choose "Float Left" or "Float Right."

Make Plain Text changes messages from "Rich Text" format to "Plain Text" format, which will strip out all of the formatting, different fonts, colors, etc. If the message is already in Plain Text, this command appears as "Make Rich Text." This will *not* restore any formatting that was removed.

Quote Level: To format text as a Mail-style quote or to increase the existing quote level, click within a line of text, choose "Quote Level" from the Format menu, then choose "Increase." Choose the command again to further increase the quote level, as shown below. Choose "Decrease" to take the text back towards normal.

The operation is much easier and faster if you learn the keyboard shortcuts. Click within the appropriate text, then type Command ' (that's the typewriter apostrophe, just to the left of the Return key) to increase the quote level, or type Option Command ' to decrease the quote level.

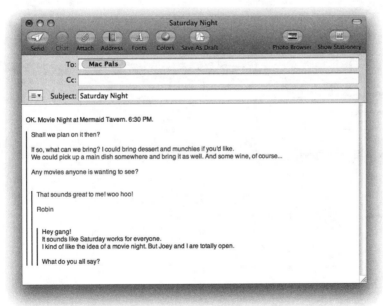

Each of the quoted sections in this message has been increased one level more than the one above it.
The oldest message is at the bottom.
The most recent message is at the top.

Script menu

An **AppleScript** is a small piece of code that makes something happen. If you know how to write scripts or how to use Automator, you can do all kinds of great things. Mail provides you with a list of several useful and useless scripts in the Scripts menu. You won't see the word "Scripts" in the menu bar. Instead, look for an icon that looks like a parchment scroll (circled below).

If the Script icon isn't in the menu bar, you can add it. Open the Applications folder, then open the AppleScript folder. Double-click the AppleScript Utility. In the window that opens (below-left), check the box to "Show Script menu in menu bar." The script icon now appears on the right side of the menu bar, at the top of the screen. Quit AppleScript Utility.

Click the Script menu, choose "Mail Scripts," then choose one of the scripts in the list. Experiment with these scripts—just choose one and let it run. Check out the "Crazy Message Text" script.

For more information about AppleScript, go to the website at **www.apple.com/applescript**.

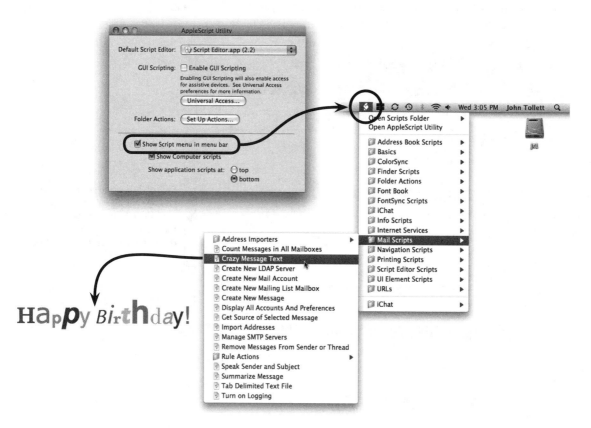

@ Address Book

Address Book keeps track of all your contact information—names, street addresses, telephone numbers, email addresses, and more—on individual address cards known as **vCards.** Address Book works closely with both Mail and iCal, making it easier than ever to keep in touch with friends and business associates.

Create **Groups** to organize contacts and use as a mailing list so you can email everyone in the Group with one click. All of your Address Book contacts will be available from within Mail. You can add an "Address" icon to the Mail toolbar that opens an Address Book contact list. And when you start to type an address or name in the "To" field of an email message form, Mail searches for matches in Address Book and autofills the address information for you.

You can customize your address cards and add new information fields to a card. For instance, you can add a "birthday" field or a "nickname" field. You can change a card's labels, add a photo, or add a URL (a web address). And you can add any comments or information about the contact in the Note field at the bottom of a card.

You can create **Smart Groups** that add contacts automatically when designated conditions are met.

.Mac members can publish their Address Book online, providing access to their contacts from almost any computer connected to the Internet, anywhere in the world.

Address Book's ability to work with other applications on your Mac makes it more than just a list of addresses:

iChat uses the buddy names and photos in Address Book.

Mail looks in Address Book for email addresses and to identify email messages as coming from a trusted source (not spam).

iCal can grab birthday information from Address Book, send email invitations to an event, and respond to email invitations.

The Address Book Window

Use **Address Book** to create an address card (also known as **vCards**) for each of your important contacts.

Address Book can be shown in Column view (below-top) or Card-only view (below-bottom). To show multiple cards at once, choose a card, then from the Card menu, choose "Open in Separate Window." Repeat this for each card you want to open.

Column view.

Search for contacts.

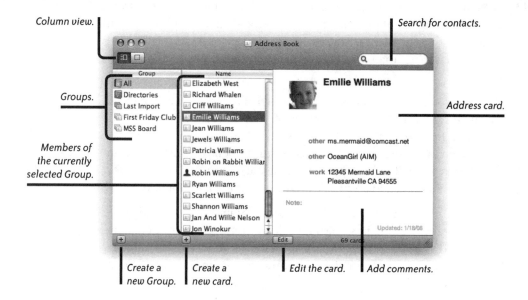

Groups.

Members of the currently selected Group.

Address card.

Create a new Group.

Create a new card.

Edit the card.

Add comments.

Card-only view.

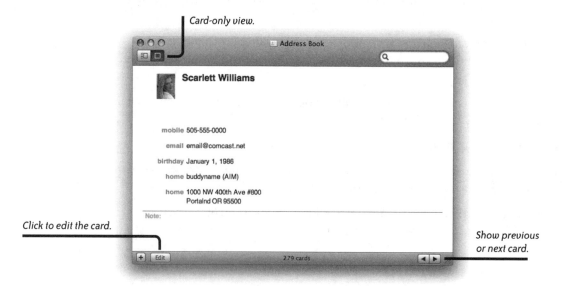

Click to edit the card.

Show previous or next card.

Add New Address Cards

Add as many cards as you need. You can create more than one card per person if necessary.

To add a new card:

1. Select a Group, then click the **+** sign at the bottom of the "Name" column. If Address Book is in Card-only view (previous page, bottom), Click the **+** sign in the bottom-left corner of the card.

2. A new card appears on the right side of the window.
   Type a person's first name in the highlighted field, then hit the Tab key to select the last name field.

   Type the last name, then hit Tab to select the next field.

   Continue in this way and enter all the information you can.

3. You can change the label names of the items on the card. Click a label name to open a pop-up menu (shown below-right). Choose one of the label names in the pop-up menu, or choose "Custom…" then type a label name.

4. To add another item to a particular category, click the green Add symbol (**+**) that appears on the left side of the category label. To remove an existing item from the card, click the red Delete symbol (**−**) that appears to the left of the label.

➕ Add item.

➖ Delete item.

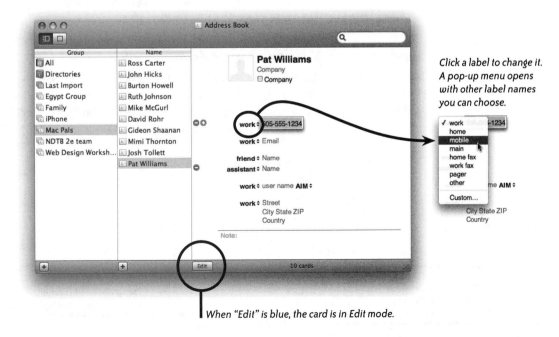

Click a label to change it. A pop-up menu opens with other label names you can choose.

When "Edit" is blue, the card is in Edit mode.

Start a Chat from Address Book

A green orb next to a contact name means that person's iChat buddy name is in your Address Book, he's online and available for a chat.

1. Click the green orb to open a "New iChat" dialog (below-right).

2. From the "Type" pop-up menu, select the type of chat to use (Text, Audio, or Video).

   If both you and the other person have enabled Screen Sharing in the Sharing pane of System Preferences, you'll also be able to choose "Share My Screen" or "Share *Other Person's* Screen."

3. Click "Chat."

If the other person doesn't have a microphone or camera connected that enables an audio or video chat, a basic Text Chat window opens, bypassing the "New Chat" dialog shown below.

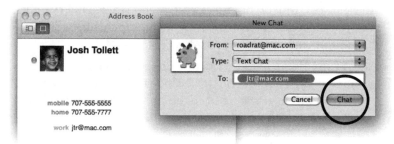

Send an Email Message from Address Book

Make sure Address Book is *not* in Edit mode. Click the gray label next to the contact's email address. In the pop-up menu, choose "Send Email." A new Mail message window opens with that person's address in the "To" field. The pop-up menu also provides other actions, as shown below.

Click the label next to the contact's email address to open this pop-up menu.

Search for files that reference this email address (email messages, iCal events, etc.).

Click "Send Update..." to send this contact an email with your vCard attached.

The "Me" Card

When you first set up your Mac, it made a card for you in Address Book and automatically labeled it as "me." This is very important! Safari uses the information in this card to AutoFill web page forms for you. iChat uses the photo from this card and the AIM address. If you choose to send automatic updates of your contact information (page 367), this is the vCard that's sent.

Tip: To find your "Me" card quickly, from the Card menu, choose "Go to My Card."

You can have more than one card for yourself, but be sure to designate the appropriate one as "me."

1. Select your card in Address Book.
2. From the Card menu, choose "Make This My Card."

   Address Book adds a silhouette icon next to your name in the "Name" column (below), and the photo on the card is tagged with "me."

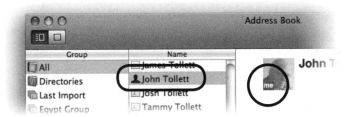

Editing the "Me" Card

You can choose to keep certain information on your "me" card private when you export a copy of it and send to others.

1. From Address Book's application menu, choose "Preferences…."
2. Select the "vCard" icon in the Preferences window toolbar (right).
3. Checkmark "Enable private me card" (right).
4. In Address Book, select your "me" card and click the "Edit" button.
5. Checkboxes appear next to each item on the card (below). Uncheck items you don't want to include when you export a vCard for others.

Explore the Other Label Options!

Make sure the card is *not* in Edit mode. Click on any gray label and check out the options available for each item.

Open a Google map for an address.

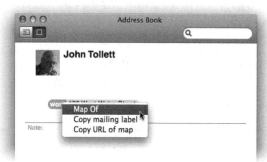

Click on an address item, then choose "Map Of" to open a Google map to this address.

Choose "Copy mailing label" to copy the address to your Clipboard, then paste the address into a document.

Choose "Copy URL of map" to copy the Google map's web address to your Clipboard, then paste the address into a document, such as an email.

See a phone number from across the room.

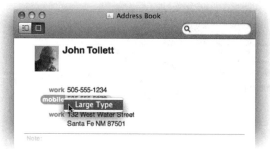

Click a phone number, then choose "Large Type." The number displays in full screen size.

Open a .Mac member's iDisk Public Folder (and other options).

You will see more options if the person is a .Mac member.

Click the "email" label, then choose "Send Email."

Choose "Visit HomePage" to open the person's .Mac HomePage (if one exists).

Choose "Open iDisk" to access the person's iDisk Public Folder.

Choose "Send Update…" to send the person a vCard that contains your updated contact information.

Choose "Perform search with Spotlight" to find documents on your computer that reference this contact.

Edit the Card Template

You can add more information fields to an individual card, or to all the cards.

To add new fields to an *individual* card:

1. Select a card in Address Book.

2. From the Card menu, choose "Add Field," then choose the field you want to add (below).

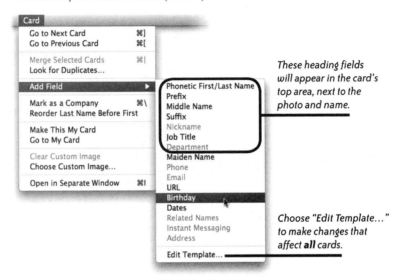

These heading fields will appear in the card's top area, next to the photo and name.

*Choose "Edit Template..." to make changes that affect **all** cards.*

Tip: Make a Sticky note out of the text in any field.

Select the text in a field.

From the Address Book menu, choose "Services," then choose "Make New Sticky Note."

Or press Command Shift Y instead of going to the menu.

To add a new field to *all* cards:

Change the card *template* (instead of an *individual* card) to add a new field to *all* address cards.

1. From the Card menu, choose "Add Field," then "Edit Template..." as shown above.

   Or open Address Book Preferences, then click the "Template" icon in the Preferences toolbar (right).

2. From the "Add Field" pop-up menu (circled, right), choose a field type to add. The options are the same as those shown above.

To remove a field from *all* cards:

1. To remove a *heading* field (circled in the top example), open the "Add Field" pop-up menu, then click a field name to remove its checkmark.

2. To remove one of the other item fields, click the red minus symbol (–) next to it.

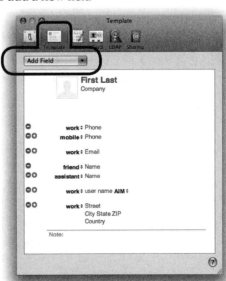

Add an Image to a Card

When you add an image to a card, it will appear in that person's messages when he sends email to you. It will also appear in your Buddy List and in iChat sessions with that person.

To add an image to a card:

1. Select a card in Address Book, then click the "Edit" button.

2. Double-click the small picture box on the card.
   An image editor opens (below).

3. Drag an image from anywhere on your computer and drop it in the empty image box (below). Almost any type of graphic image file works. JPEG is the most common format to use.

   Or if you have an iSight or video camera connected, click the camera icon to take a video snapshot (shown below).

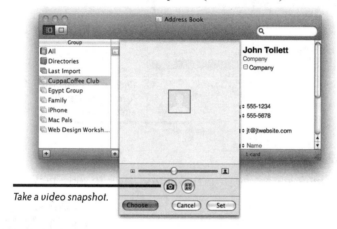

Take a video snapshot.

Or click the "Choose…" button. In the Finder window that opens (below), select an image, then click "Open." To search for an image, click in the search field and type a keyword.

Search for an image.

4. Adjust the selected image. Use the size slider (below) to enlarge or reduce the image size. Press and drag the image to change its position within the frame.

Size slider.   *Apply effects.*

5. To apply a visual effect to the image, click the Effects button (above). Click an effect (below) to preview it. To remove an effect, click the "Original" thumbnail in the middle of the effects pane.

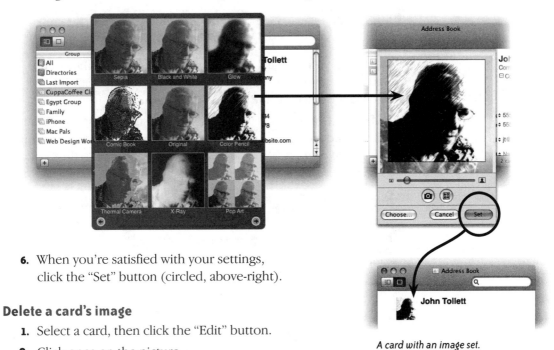

6. When you're satisfied with your settings, click the "Set" button (circled, above-right).

Delete a card's image

1. Select a card, then click the "Edit" button.

2. Click once on the picture.

3. Hit the Delete key.

A card with an image set.

Create a Group Mailing List

Create **Groups** in Address Book to help organize your contacts, and to use as **mailing lists.** When you send an email message to a Group name, the message is sent to everyone in the Group who has an email address on his card. The same contact name can be placed in more than one Group.

To make a Group mailing list:

1. Open Address Book and make sure the "Group" and "Name" columns are visible, as shown below. If you only see a card, switch views to show the Group and Name columns (click the Column-view button).

Column view button.

Select a Group to see its members in the "Name" column.

2. Create a new Group: click the **+** sign located beneath the Group column. A new Group appears in the Group column (above). Replace the default name with a custom name.

3. Add contacts to the new Group: click the **+** sign beneath the "Name" column and create a new address card. Fill out the contact information on the new card. The new address card is added to the Group you just created, and to the "All" Group.

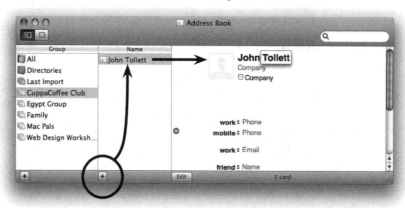

Or drag an existing card into the new Group. Select any Group to show its members in the "Name" column, then drag members from the "Name" column onto the new Group in the "Group" column (below). This does not remove the contact from its original Group.

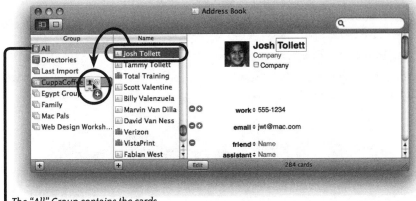

The "All" Group contains the cards of every person in every Group.

Shortcut to make a new Group

If you already have contacts entered in Address Book, there's an **even faster way** to make a new Group.

1. Make a mulitple selection of contacts by holding down the Command key as you click on names in the "Name" columm.

2. From the File menu, choose "New Group From Selection." A new Group is automatically created that contains the selected contacts.

3. Replace the default name of "Group Name" with a more appropriate name that describes the group.

Delete a name from a Group

Select a Group in the "Group" column, then select a contact name in the "Name" column. Tap the Delete key. A dialog opens (right). You can choose to delete the contact from Address Book completely, remove the card from the Group, or cancel the operation.

Delete a Group

Select a Group, then tap the Delete key. **Or** from the Edit menu, choose "Delete Group."

Send email to an entire Group

Groups can act as mailing lists. Send a message to everyone in a Group by addressing the email to the Group name.

To send an email message to every person in a Group:

1. In **Mail,** open a new email message form. Address Book does not have to be open.

2. In the "To" box, type the name of the Group.

Write a message, then click "Send." It will go to everyone in the Group who has an email address included on his card.

Enter the name of the Group here.

If individual names or email addresses of Group members are visible instead of the Group name, follow the instructions below.

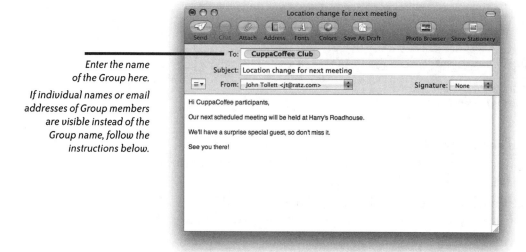

Hide the address list when sending mail to a Group

It's polite to **hide the address list** when sending email to a Group. For one thing, it's *really* annoying to have to scroll through a long list of addresses to get to the message. For another, some people don't want their private email address broadcast to everyone else on the list.

To hide the Group's list of email addresses:

1. Open Mail's Preferences (from the Mail menu, choose "Preferences…").

2. Click the "Composing" icon in the toolbar.

3. Uncheck (if it's checked) "When sending to a group, show all member addresses" (shown below).

☐ When sending to a group, show all member addresses

Create Smart Groups

A Smart Group is a Group that automatically adds contacts to itself according to conditions you set. Contacts can come and go from a Group if you change the conditions for membership to the Group.

To create a Smart Group:

1. From Address Book's File menu, choose "New Smart Group...." The dialog shown below-left opens.

   Or hold down the Option key to change the **+** sign beneath the "Group" column into a Smart Group button (a gear icon, shown on the right). Option-click the Smart Group button to open the dialog shown below-left.

   Smart Group button.

2. Name the new Smart Group, then use the pop-up menus to choose conditions that contacts must meet in order to be included in the Group. Experiment with the settings to understand the possibilities.

3. Click the **+** button, circled below, to add more conditions. Click the **−** button to remove an existing condition.

4. To create a visual alert when a new contact has been added to the Smart Group, checkmark the "Highlight group when updated" box. Click OK. Recently added contacts in the "Name" column appear bold and in color (below-right).

When you use the Search field in Address Book, search results can be used to create a new Smart Group. Do a search, then from the File menu, choose "New Smart Group from Current Search."

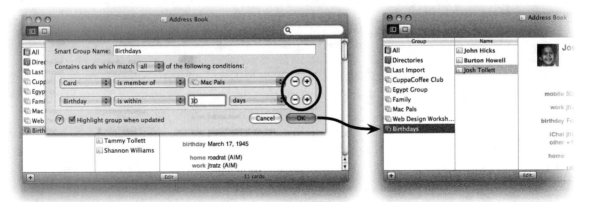

To change a Smart Group's conditions, Control-click the Group name in the "Group" column, then choose "Edit Smart Group...." **Or** select a Smart Group, then from the Edit menu, choose "Edit Smart Group." The dialog shown above-left opens for editing.

Add a Group to iCal

Use an Address Group to create an event in iCal. All members of the Group are automatically listed in the new Event as an attendee. With the click of a button, iCal sends the attendees an email invitation that contains a vCard (an iCal data file) with details of the Event. Attendees can then respond to the email, as explained in the iCal chapter. iCal tracks the responses and keeps you notified. See the iCal chapter for more details about Event invitations and notifications.

1. Open both Address Book and iCal.

2. Select a Group in the "Group" column, then drag the Group name from Address Book to a date or time in iCal (below).

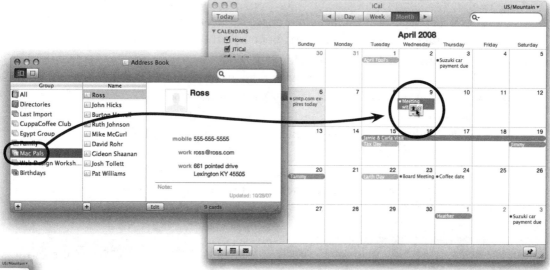

3. Double-click the new Event in iCal to open its Event editor (left). All members of the Group are in the Attendees list. Edit the Event details, such as Event name, location, time, alarms and notes.

4. When you've finished editing the Event, click the "Send" button in the bottom-right corner of the Event editor (left).

iCal automatically opens Mail and sends a vCard to each attendee. When the attendee clicks the vCard in the email, it is automatically placed in his iCal and it appears in iCal's Notifications pane. The Notifications pane contains response buttons of "Maybe," "Decline," and "Accept." When the attendee clicks one of the response buttons, an email containing the response is automatically sent back to the Event's organizer.

Export an Address or a Group of Addresses

You can **export** a single address, a collection of selected addresses, or a Group. Once exported, other Address Book users can import the addresses into their applications. There are several simple ways to export:

▼ Drag a Group, a name, or a collection of names from Address Book and drop them on the Desktop or inside any Finder window or folder. vCard icons like the ones shown below are created.

Elizabeth Thornton and 2
others.vcf

*This vCard contains the contact
information for three individuals.*

Mac Pals.vcf

*This vCard contains the contact
information for every member
of the Mac Pals Group.*

▼ To create a separate vCard for each person in the Group, Option-drag a Group name to the Desktop, or to any location on your computer.

▼ Select a Group, a name, or a collection of names in the Address Book. From the File menu, choose "Export card…" or "Export Group card…." You will be asked to name the exported vCard and choose where you want to save it. An icon like the ones shown above appears in the location you choose.

When someone with a fairly recent version of Address Book double-clicks a vCard, the contact information in the card appears in his Address Book. You can send a vCard to someone who uses a contact application other than Address Book, even if he uses a PC instead of a Mac.

If someone double-clicks a vCard, and a name in the vCard is already in his Address Book, a dialog appears, stating that a duplicate card exists, and asking for permission to update the existing card.

*A shared
Address Book.*

Share Your Address Book

If you are a .Mac member, you can share your Address Book with selected .Mac members. Your *entire* Address Book will have its own space in the "Group" column of the other person's Address Book (the contacts are not merged), as shown on the left. When you add or update contacts on your Mac, those updates appear in the other person's shared version.

In Address Book's Sharing Preferences, if you check the box to "Allow Editing" (below), the other person can make changes to your Address Book on *his* computer, and those changes are automatically sent to *your* Address Book on *your* computer. At any time, you can go back and uncheck the "Allow Editing" box to stop that behavior. The other person will still be able to edit the cards on his own Mac, but his changes will not be sent to your Mac.

To share your Address Book:

1. The person with whom you want to share must be in your Address Book, and a working email address must be on the card.

2. From the Address Book menu, choose "Preferences...."

3. Click the "Sharing" icon in the Preferences toolbar (below).

4. Checkmark the "Share your address book" box.

5. To create a list of .Mac members with whom you want to share your Address Book, click the **+** sign in the bottom-left corner of the "Sharing" window. Another window opens that contains your Address Book contacts. Double-click a contact's name to add that person to the sharing list.

6. To allow someone in the list to **edit** your Address Book (the edits will appear in Address Book on your Mac), checkmark the "Allow Editing" box in the far-right column (circled below).

7. Select a name in the list, then click "Send Invitation."

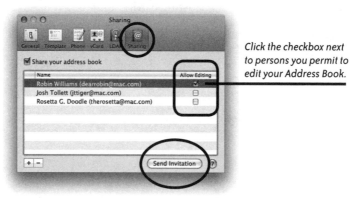

Click the checkbox next to persons you permit to edit your Address Book.

8. The recipient receives an email invitation to subscribe to the Address Book, as shown on the right. If the recipient of the email chooses to accept the invitation and subscribe to the Address Book, he clicks the link in the email message that says "Click here to automatically subscribe now."

9. Address Book opens and a dialog asks "Would you like to subscribe to *.Mac member name's* address book?" If the recipient clicks the "Subscribe" button, Address Book starts to sync with the shared Address Book through the .Mac account of the owner of the shared Address Book.

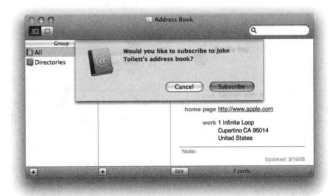

10. The shared Address Book appears in the subscriber's Group column (right-bottom). The shared Address Book icon is tagged with an **@** symbol. To show all shared contacts in the "Name" column, select the shared icon in the "Group" column. To show all shared Groups, click the disclosure triangle next to the shared Address Book.

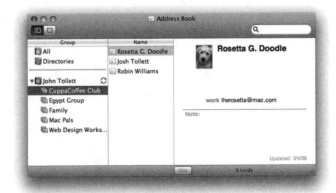

Subscribe to an Address Book without an invitation

You can only subscribe to someone's Address Book if he has already set you up in Address Book Preferences as a person who has permission to share, as explained on the previous page. If you know someone who has done that, go to Address Book's File menu and choose "Subscribe to Address Book...." A dialog opens from your Address Book title bar and asks you to enter the email address of a .Mac member whose Address Book you have permission to share.

Back Up Your Address Book

**Address Book
2008-03-04.abbu**

If you depend on your Address Book, be sure to back it up. From the File menu, choose "Export," then choose "Address Book Archive...." A dialog opens from your Address Book title bar for you to choose a location to save the archive and name it. By default the archive is named the current year, month, and date (left). Copy this file to another location for safekeeping.

Restore your Address Book

To restore your Address Book as it was the last time you backed it up, go to the File menu and choose "Import," then choose "Address Book Archive...." In the Finder window that opens, locate the file you backed up earlier, select it, then click "Open." **Or** locate the backup file and double-click it.

Send Updates

Whenever you change the information in your own personal address card (the "Me Card" described on page 353), you can send the new contact information to the email contacts in a Group manually or automatically.

If there's certain information on your card that you don't want to share, you can make some of the card information private. Any comments you add to the "Notes" field of a card will *not* be sent out with updates unless you choose to send them. See page 370 to learn about privacy options.

To send updates of your card *manually:*

1. From the File menu, choose "Send Updates...."

2. In the "Send Updates" dialog (below-left), select the Groups you want to send updates to. To modify the email's "Subject" or message, type new copy in the fields shown.

3. Click "Send." The Group's members receive a message that includes your vCard as an attachment (below-right).

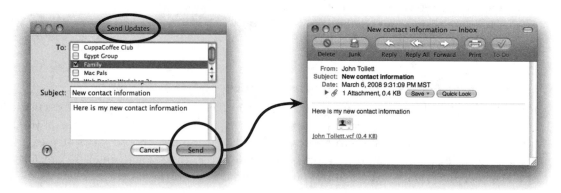

4. When a Group member clicks the vCard link in the email message (if he uses a Mac running some version of OS X), your vCard information is automatically added to his Address Book.

If he already has a card for you in his Address Book, a "Reviewing Card" window opens (below) with a bar of import options at the bottom. He can choose to keep the old card, keep the new card, keep both, or update the old card by adding the new information to it. After he chooses an import action, he clicks "Import."

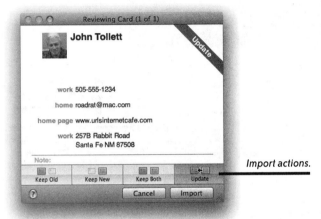

Import actions.

To send updates of your card *automatically:*

You must have at least one Group created before you choose this option.

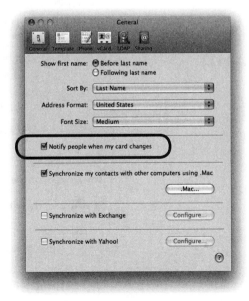

1. From the Address Book menu, choose "Preferences…."

2. Click the "General" pane.

3. Checkmark "Notify people when my card changes" (right).

Now when you change your "Me Card," an alert dialog will ask if you want to notify people of the changes. If you click "Notify," the "Send Updates" window opens (shown on the opposite page). Choose the Groups you want to notify, then click "Send." Address Book opens Mail, composes an update message, attaches your revised vCard, and sends the email to the Group members.

Address Book Preferences

Two of the preference panes, "Template" (page 355) and "Sharing" (pages 364–365), have already been explained in this chapter. The other preferences are described here.

General preferences

Most items are self-explanatory. Others are explained below.

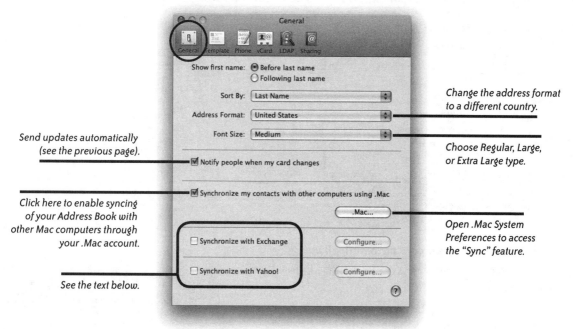

Send updates automatically
(see the previous page).

Click here to enable syncing
of your Address Book with
other Mac computers through
your .Mac account.

See the text below.

Change the address format
to a different country.

Choose Regular, Large,
or Extra Large type.

Open .Mac System
Preferences to access
the "Sync" feature.

If you're on a network that supports **Exchange 2000,** you can synchronize your address book using Outlook Web Access, a web service that provides access to your email messages and contacts. Your network administrator will give you an Exchange user name, password, and the Outlook Web Access server address. The Outlook Web Access server URL will be similar to **www.myserver.com/exchange/UserName**.

If you use **Yahoo! Address Book,** you can synchronize it to Address Book.

1. Click "Synchronize with Yahoo!," enter your Yahoo! ID and password, then click OK.

2. Click the Sync status icon in the menu bar, then choose "Sync Now." If you need to add sync status to your menu bar, open iSync (in the Applications folder). From the iSync menu, choose "Preferences…," then select "Show status in menu bar."

Template preferences

Add fields to card templates that are not included in the default layout, such as "Middle Name," or "Birthday." See page 355 for details.

Phone Preferences

When typing phone numbers into your Address Book, you don't have to enter all the parentheses and hyphens yourself—just type the numbers. Address Book displays them according to the formats in this window.

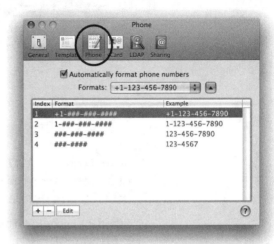

Checkmark "Automatically format phone numbers," then from the "Formats" pop-up menu, choose a format. The examples in the lower pane show how different types of phone numbers will appear. Choose "Custom..." from the pop-up menu to enter a different format altogether.

To add or remove formats from the list of examples, select a format, then click the Add (+) or Remove (–) button.

To edit existing formats, select one of the examples, then click the "Edit" button.

LDAP Preferences

Lightweight Directory Access Protocol (LDAP) is an Internet protocol, or set of rules, to look up contact information in directories stored on servers on a network or on the Internet. If you have access to an LDAP directory through your workplace, you can have Address Book search the directory. Many large companies with large networks use LDAP directories.

Ask the network administrator for details about how to use LDAP.

vCard preferences

This pane provides options for the vCards that you might export and send to others.

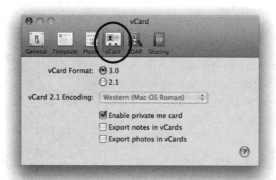

vCard Format: If you need to send vCards to people using older computers or older software, you can choose to save your vCards in version 2.1 instead of the current version of 3.0.

vCard 2.1 Encoding: This pop-up menu is available if you choose vCard format 2.1 (above). Leave this setting as it is, unless you *know* you need different encoding so you can create vCards in another language.

Enable private me card: Checkmark this box to make certain information on your card private when you send your vCard to others.

1. Checkmark "Enable private me card" (above).

2. In Address Book, select your "Me" card, then click the "Edit" button. Checkboxes appear next to the data entry fields (below).

3. Checkmark the items you want to include when you export the card or send updates.

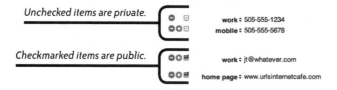

Export notes in vCards: Checkmark this option to include your notes and comments in the "Note" field when you export the card or send vCard updates to others.

Export photos in vCards: Checkmark this option to include the photo used on a card when you export cards and send photos to others.

Print Your Contact Information

Address Book can print contact information as mailing labels, envelopes, lists, and as a pocket address book.

1. In Address Book, select the names or the Group (or Groups) whose information you want to print.

2. Press Command P to open the Print dialog (below). **Or** from the File menu, choose "Print." If you don't see the full "Print" window shown below, click the small blue disclosure triangle to the right of the "Printer" pop-up menu.

3. From the "Style" pop-up menu, choose what you want to print—lists, envelopes, mailing labels, or pocket address book pages. Each "style" provides different settings to experiment with. Whatever you choose is shown in the preview pane on the left side of the window.

4. Make choices for the options that are presented with each "Style" choice (Mailing Labels, Envelopes, Lists, Pocket Address Book).

5. Click "Print."

While the Print dialog is open, you can save the print job as a PDF. PDFs can be opened and printed by almost anyone on any computer.

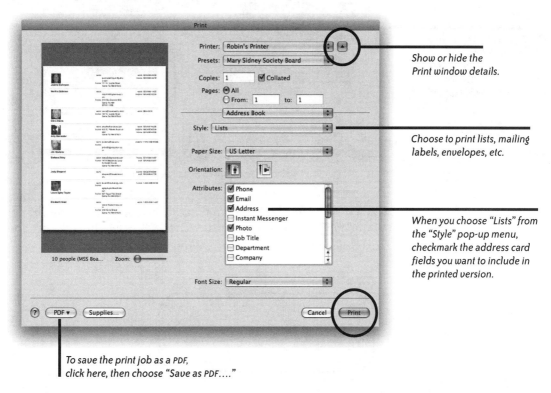

Show or hide the Print window details.

Choose to print lists, mailing labels, envelopes, etc.

When you choose "Lists" from the "Style" pop-up menu, checkmark the address card fields you want to include in the printed version.

To save the print job as a PDF, click here, then choose "Save as PDF...."

Spend some time poking around the print dialog so you know what all your options are. As you can see below, you can add an image to the return address of envelopes, choose different fonts and colors for the text, choose different envelope sizes, and so much more.

Address Book automatically uses your "Me" card for the return address. If you want it to use another card, go back to the Address Book, choose another card, then go to the Card menu and choose "Make This My Card." You can switch it back when you're done printing. Of course, you can uncheck the box so it doesn't print any return address at all.

Choose "Envelopes" to print envelopes.

To add an image to your return address, click the "Label" tab, then click the "Set…" button (circled, bottom-right corner).

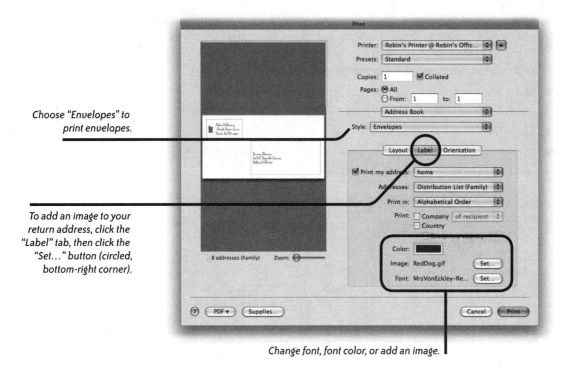

Change font, font color, or add an image.

To print a *sheet of mailing labels,* choose "Mailing Labels" from the "Style" pop-up menu. The pop-up menus under the "Layout" tab (below) contain standard mailing label templates from Avery and DYMO.

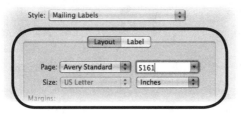

iChat AV and Bonjour

7

What is iChat? It's an app that makes it incredibly easy to chat in real time with your buddies. Chats can be in the form of instant text messaging, audio chats, or video conferences. An Internet connection enables you to chat for free with buddies anywhere in the world. You can even have multi-person audio and video chats—as many as ten people in an audio chat, and up to four people in a video chat (if your computer and Internet connection are fast enough).

Create Groups for organizing your iChat buddies; show iTunes' currently playing song in your iChat Status (your buddies can preview the track with a single click); take advantage of iChat's multiple platform support and chat with friends who use other popular chat clients, such as AOL Instant Messenger, the Jabber IM network, and Google Talk.

What is Bonjour? Bonjour makes it easy to chat and share files with others on your local area network (LAN) by automatically detecting other computers on the network that have iChat installed and connecting to them.

Both iChat and Bonjour provide a great new feature called Screen Sharing. If you've ever tried to give or receive computer instructions over the phone, you'll love being able to see a Buddy's computer on your own screen—or just watch and listen as your Buddy manipulates your computer from his. See page 404 for details.

iChat requires a Buddy name—your .Mac account name. Or you can use an AIM (AOL Instant Messaging) Buddy name, a Jabber user name, or a Google Talk user name. If you sign up for a .Mac membership, your .Mac member name becomes your Buddy name. If you don't want a .Mac membership, you can sign up for a free 60-day trial membership. When the free trial is over, you can keep and use your .Mac Buddy name.

Text messaging needs only a low bandwidth connection, such as a dial-up modem. Video chats and audio chats require broadband connections. Minimum requirements for initiating or participating in audio and video chats are listed on pages 396 and 400.

Robin chats with friends at home from the steps of an Internet cafe in London.

To sign up for a .Mac account, go to:
www.mac.com

To sign up for an AIM account, go to:
www.aim.com

To sign up for a Google Talk account, go to:
www.google.com/talk

To sign up for a Jabber account, go to:
www.jabber.org

Note: You must
be connected to the
Internet to use iChat!

Bonjour does not require
an Internet connection,
just a local network.

*Use the pop-up
menu to choose
a .Mac, AIM (AOL),
Jabber, or Google
Talk account.*

Set Up iChat

The first time you click the **iChat** icon in the Dock, a Welcome window opens. Click the "Continue" button to proceed to the next window where you enter information to set up a new iChat account (shown below). In the "Account Type" pop-up menu, choose to use your .Mac account, an existing AOL Instant Messenger account, a Jabber account, or a Google Talk account.

If you have a .Mac account, enter your information, and click OK. If you don't have a .Mac account, you can click the "Get an iChat Account" button to sign up for one right now.

Your iChat Buddy name is the same as your member name. Online buddies will use that name to chat with you. You can create separate iChat accounts for AOL Instant Messenger, Jabber, or Google Talk, if you've registered with those services, and switch between them in the Accounts pane of iChat Preferences (only one account can be active at a time).

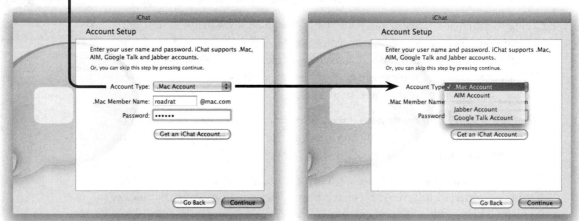

*From the Account Type pop-up menu, choose the
account type you want to create.*

After you enter the information to set up a new iChat account, click the "Continue" button.

The next window contains a checkbox to "Enable iChat encryption." Checkmark this item to enable iChat encryption, an extra security measure that protects your information during chats with other .Mac members who have also enabled encryption in their iChat application.

☑ Enable iChat encryption

Create an iChat Buddy List

No matter what kind of iChat you want to do (text, audio, video, or screen sharing), the first thing you must do is create a Buddy List. If you plan to chat often with certain people, **add them to your Buddy List** so you can easily see if they're online and start a chat session.

*A **green orb** means the buddies are online and you can start a chat with them.*

*A **red orb** means the Buddy is away or doesn't want to be disturbed, but is online. You can send a message, but you may not get a response.*

*An **amber orb** means the Buddy is away and the computer has been idle for a while and may not respond.*

*A **dimmed** (gray) orb or Buddy name indicates the Buddy is offline and unavailable.*

In this example, the two offline Buddy entries are mobile phone numbers, indicated by the wireless signal icon attached.

Add people to your Buddy List

1. Open iChat. If you don't see your Buddy List, press Command 1, **or** go to the Window menu and choose "Buddy List."

2. In the Buddy List window, click the **+** button (circled below-left). Enter an account name (a Buddy name), then from the pop-up menu, choose the type of account the Buddy uses—AIM (AOL) or .Mac.

3. To add someone from your Address Book, click the blue disclosure triangle button (shown below). The sheet expands to show the contacts in your Address Book. Select a contact, then click the Add button (circled, below-right).

To remove a Buddy from the Buddy List, select the Buddy, then press Delete.

Offline buddies appear dimmed in the Buddy List. To hide offline buddies, in the View menu, uncheck "Show Offline Buddies."

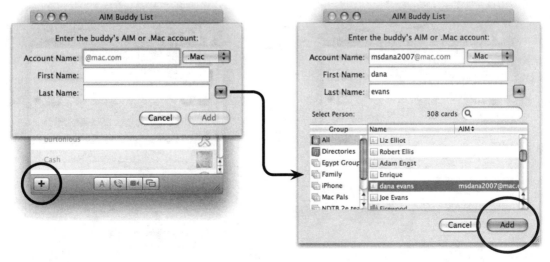

Show Information About a Buddy

1. To show information you have about a Buddy, select the Buddy name in the Buddy List, then from the Buddies menu, choose "Show Info."

2. Click the Profile tab to show information about a Buddy, including a descriptive profile—if the Buddy has created one. The Profile panel also includes a notes field so you can add your own notes about the Buddy.

3. Click the Alerts tab (below-left) to set alerts for iChat events, such as when a Buddy becomes available.

4. Click the Address Card tab (below-right) to show information that is supplied by your Address Book. To change the Buddy picture, drag an image on top of the Picture well. The image format can be JPEG, GIF, TIFF or Photoshop file.

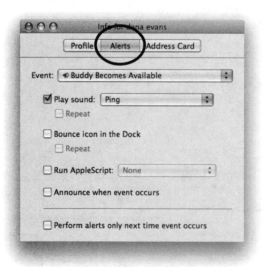

Status Messages In Your Buddy List

Your name, as it appears in your Address Book, shows in the top-left corner of the Buddy List. If you click on the name, a pop-up menu lets you choose to "View as Name" or "View as Handle." Your handle is the same as your Buddy name.

A **status message** appears below your name to indicate your online availablility. Other iChat users that have you listed as a Buddy can see your status message in their iChat window. Choose one of the preset messages, or create a custom message.

To create a *custom* status message, click the existing status message, then from the pop-up menu, choose "Custom Available…" or "Custom Away…." Type your message in the text field that appears, then hit "Return" or "Enter" to set the new message.

Tip: If you're colorblind to red and green, you can set the status buttons to display as squares, circles, and triangles.

In the General pane of iChat Preferences, choose "Use shapes to indicate status."

A circle means "Available." A square means "Away." A triangle means "Idle."

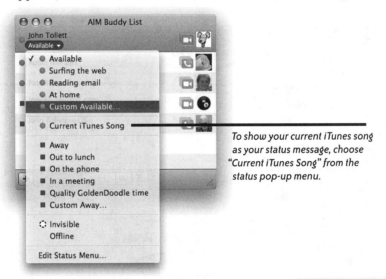

To show your current iTunes song as your status message, choose "Current iTunes Song" from the status pop-up menu.

To edit the Status Menu, click the existing message beneath your name to open a pop-up menu (above), then choose "Edit Status Menu…." In the dialog that opens (right), click the Add (+)button beneath either category ("Available" or "Away") to add new messages. To remove a status message, select it, then click the minus (−) button. When finished, click OK.

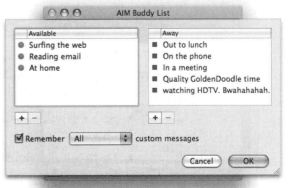

Buddy Pictures

When you place a picture of a Buddy in your Address Book, it appears in your Buddy List and iChat windows. If a Buddy places a different picture in his own chat application, it will appear instead of the one you placed.

If you want to use an image other than the one your Address Book uses, or if you want to replace the default icon provided by AOL or .Mac, you can change the Buddy picture and override the existing image choice.

Change a Buddy picture

1. Select a Buddy name in the Buddy List, then from the Buddies menu, choose "Get Info."

2. The Info window opens (shown below-left). Click the "Address Card" tab. Drag an image into the Picture well.

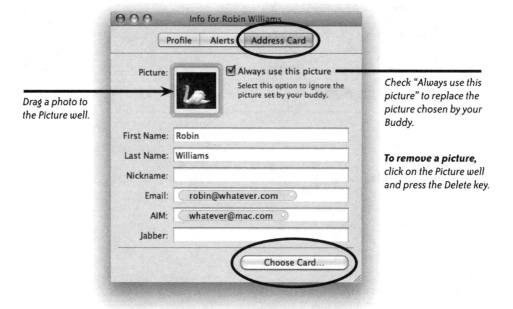

Drag a photo to the Picture well.

Check "Always use this picture" to replace the picture chosen by your Buddy.

To remove a picture, click on the Picture well and press the Delete key.

Put a Buddy's iChat picture in Address Book

You can easily copy a Buddy photo from iChat's Info window to an address card in your Address Book.

1. Select a Buddy name in the Buddy List, then from the Buddies menu, choose "Get Info."

2. Open Address Book and choose the card for the selected Buddy. Create a new card for the Buddy if necessary.

3. Click the "Edit" button beneath the card (circled, below-right).
Drag the picture from the iChat Info window to the address card's
Picture well.

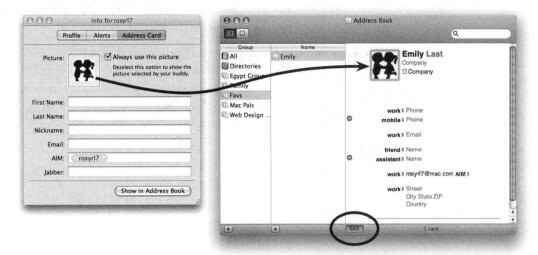

Crop or resize Buddy pictures

1. To edit a Buddy picture, select a Buddy name in the Buddy
List, then from the Buddies menu choose "Get Info."

2. In the Info window, click the "Show in Address Book" button
(above-left). When Address Book opens, double-click the
Buddy picture on the Buddy's address card. In the edit sheet
that opens, use the slider to zoom the photo in or out. Drag
the image to reposition it. Click "Set" after making changes.
Both Address Book and iChat update to show your changes.

Collect pictures for your Buddy picture

You can keep a collection of Buddy pictures in a pop-up menu and change
your visual identity as often as you like. Drag and drop multiple images
into the picture well in the top-right corner of the Buddy List window.
When you're ready for a new look, click on your Buddy picture to open a
pop-up menu containing your stored pictures. Click a picture to instantly
apply it, even if you're in the middle of a chat. Choose "Edit Picture…" in
the pop-up menu to open the edit window (shown above) and change
its size and cropping. To clear the menu of all existing photos except the
current selection, choose "Clear Recent Pictures."

Message views

The appearance of text messages can be customized, even during a chat. The Messages pane of iChat Preferences lets you set the color of balloons and text for outgoing and incoming messages (see page 415). To have even more control over message appearance, go to iChat's View menu.

From the View menu (shown below), choose "Messages," then choose an appearance style in both the middle and bottom sections of the Messages submenu. The combination of selections from these two areas determine if a Buddy's name or picture is shown, and the graphic style of the speech balloons. The following page shows some of the style combinations.

Or, Control-click anywhere *in a chat window,* then from the pop-up menu (below), choose chat appearance styles.

This page shows various View settings as described on the previous page. The examples on the right show how screen space can be optimized with different settings. The top-right example uses View settings of "Show Balloons" and "Show Pictures." The bottom-right example uses View settings of "Show as Compact" and "Show Pictures."

The earth can yield me but a common grave,
When you entombed in men's eyes shall lie.
Your monument shall be my gentle verse,
Which eyes not yet created shall o'er-read

Shown as "Balloons" and "Show Pictures."

Robin Williams
Now is the winter of our discontent
Made glorious summer by this sun of York;
And all the clouds that lour'd upon our house
In the deep bosom of the ocean buried.

Shown as "Boxes" and "Show Pictures."

 John Tollett Life's but a walking shadow; a poor player,
That struts and frets his hour upon the stage,
And then is heard no more: it is a tale
Told by an idiot, full of sound and fury,
Signifying nothing.

Shown as "Compact" and "Show Pictures."

 Robin Williams : Be not afraid of greatness: some are born great, some achieve greatness, and some have greatness thrust upon 'em.

Shown as "Text" and "Show Pictures."

All the world's a stage,
And all the men and women merely players.
They have their exits and their entrances,
And one man in his time plays many parts,
His acts being seven ages.
Robin Williams

Shown as "Balloons" and "Show Names and Pictures."

The earth can yield me but a common grave,
When you entombed in men's eyes shall lie.
Your monument shall be my gentle verse,
Which eyes not yet created shall o'er-read

Shown as "Boxes" and "Show Pictures."

John Tollett : A Mac! A Mac! My kingdom for a Mac!

Shown as "Text" and "Show Names."

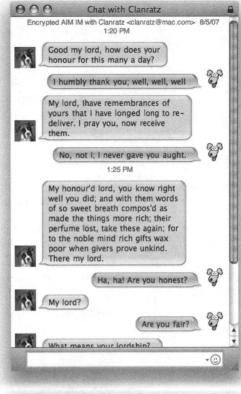

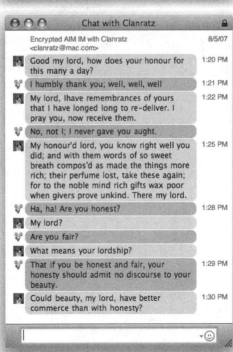

Types of Chats

iChat provides three general types of communication that work over both the Internet and over a local network—text, audio, and video.

After you create a Buddy List (page 375), select a Buddy name that's online. If a green orb appears next to the Buddy name, the Buddy is online and you can start chatting. You can chat using text-based instant messaging, audio, or video—depending on the connection speed and the hardware being used.

The icon next to a Buddy photo indicates what kind of chat is possible. If no icons are showing, go to the View menu and make sure these two menu items are checked: "Show Audio Status" and "Show Video Status."

A *camera icon* means the Buddy has a video camera attached and can use text, audio, or video to chat. A *multiple-camera icon* shows that a multiple-Buddy video chat is possible (based on the connection speed and hardware being used). A *phone icon* means the Buddy's computer has a microphone and can use text or audio to chat. *No icon* means the Buddy can use only text messages to chat.

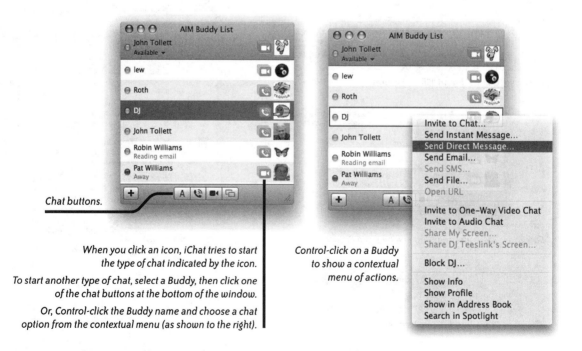

Chat buttons.

When you click an icon, iChat tries to start the type of chat indicated by the icon.

To start another type of chat, select a Buddy, then click one of the chat buttons at the bottom of the window.

Or, Control-click the Buddy name and choose a chat option from the contextual menu (as shown to the right).

Control-click on a Buddy to show a contextual menu of actions.

Text messages

iChat provides several different types of text messaging. This includes Instant Messages, also known as IMs, Direct Instant Messages (even more secure than IMs), SMS (text messages sent to mobile phones), Chat Rooms, and Group IM chats.

Text messaging sounds low-tech, but it has some advantages. It's more private and less intrusive to others than talking aloud, as you would during an audio or video chat. It allows sending files to others as you chat, including HTML web addresses. And you can chat with whole groups of people.

An **Instant Message** is a two-way text chat with *one other person*. Your talk is private, but it can be made even more secure by enabling iChat encryption, available when both parties use iChat.

A **Direct Instant Message** looks just like an Instant Message, but it's even more private. Ordinary IMs go through a central messaging server on the Internet, while a Direct Message goes directly to the other person's computer, bypassing the central server. If you send a file during an Instant Message chat, iChat automatically switches to a Direct Instant Message session.

A Direct Instant Message is between two people. Sometimes network or firewall security settings will not allow Direct Messages to be sent or delivered.

A **Chat Room** is a public "room" that you create and name. Anyone who knows the chat room name can join in. Any number of people can join in and they can come and go as they please. The room stays open until the last person leaves.

A **Group Chat** is similar, but instead of allowing anyone who knows the chat room name to join, group chat participants must be invited by someone in the current group.

An **SMS** message (Short Message Service) is a technology for sending text messages to mobile phones.

Audio chats

Audio chats are like free phone calls to almost anywhere in the world. Or like an automatic intercom system for your home or office. They require participants to have a microphone built-in or connected to their computers.

Video chats

Video chats require a fast broadband Internet connection (page 400). iChat video includes **Screen Sharing** that allows two Buddies to share each others' screens and share files (page 404). **iChat Theater** enables you to show *streaming* versions of photos, movies, and files to a Buddy in the iChat window (page 408).

Instant Messages

To start an Instant Message:

1. Select a Buddy in the Buddy List.
   Or, double-click a name in the Buddy List, then skip to Step 3.

2. Click the Text button (the letter "A") to open a message window.

3. Type a message in the text field, then press Return.

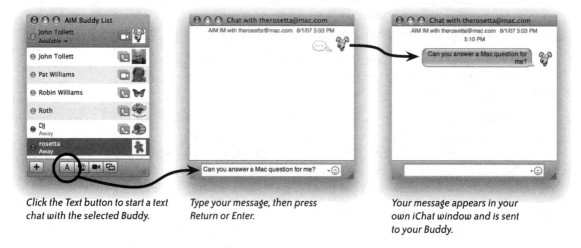

Click the Text button to start a text chat with the selected Buddy.

Type your message, then press Return or Enter.

Your message appears in your own iChat window and is sent to your Buddy.

Or, start a new chat of any kind from the File menu.

1. From the File menu, choose "New Chat…" to open a New Chat window (shown below).

2. From the "Type" pop-up menu, choose a type of chat— "Text Chat," "Audio Chat," "Video Chat," "Share My Screen," or "Share (Buddy Name's) Screen."

3. In the "To" field, type a Buddy name.

4. Click the "Chat" button.

To receive an Instant Message:

1. When you're invited to a chat, a message alert opens on your Desktop (below-left). The sender is identified at the top of the alert. Click on the window to expand it (below-right).

2. Type a response in the text field, then click "Accept."
    Or, click "Accept" first, to expand the window again, then continue the chat in the larger window.

The iChat icon in the Dock shows how many unread messages you've received.

Click on the message alert to open it (shown on the right).

Click "Accept" to expand the window and continue the chat.

To decline or block an Instant Message:

Click the "Decline" button if you don't want to accept the invitation.

To block this and all future messages from the sender, click "Block" (shown above-right). An alert dialog opens to ask if you really want to block all future messages from this Buddy (right). Click the blue "Block" button to apply a block. You can remove a block at any time in the Security pane of iChat Preferences.

Direct Instant Messages

For extra security, Direct Instant Messages go directly to the other person's computer, instead of through a central server. A Direct Instant Message session is automatically started when you send a file (a photo, for example) to a Buddy. Files cannot be sent in group chats.

iChat alerts you when a Direct Instant Message session starts.

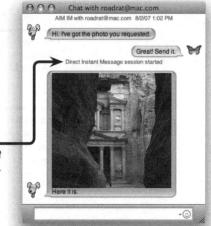

Collect Multiple Instant Messages in One Window

When you have chats with several different buddies all at once, you can collect all of the chats into one tabbed window, as shown below, then easily switch back and forth between them. This is called tabbed chatting.

To collect chats into a single window:

1. From the iChat menu, choose "Preferences...."

2. Click "Messages" to show the Messages options.

3. Click the checkbox "Collect chats into a single window" (page 415).

   When you accept an invitation from more than one Buddy, the iChat window changes to a tabbed window as shown below. Each chat is represented by a tab in the left sidebar that includes the Buddy's name and Buddy icon.

4. Select one of the Buddy tabs to show that conversation in the main message pane on the right.

   When you're chatting with a Buddy and a new message arrives from another Buddy in the sidebar, a white speech balloon appears under the Buddy's name to alert that a new message has arrived in another chat. Click on the tab with the alert to see the current message.

5. To exit a chat with one of the buddies, hover your pointer over the Buddy name to show a circled-X icon. Click the icon to end that chat.

You have to choose this option in iChat Preferences before you need it. If a chat or two is already in progress when you decide to switch to a tabbed chat window, iChat won't be able to turn the separate chats into a collection.

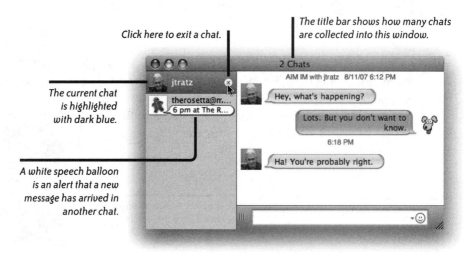

Click here to exit a chat.

The title bar shows how many chats are collected into this window.

The current chat is highlighted with dark blue.

A white speech balloon is an alert that a new message has arrived in another chat.

Customize the Chat Background

You can **customize the background** of any chat window by adding a picture or graphic. This could be useful if you've got several chats going on and don't want to get confused about who is in which window. Mostly, it's just fun.

This image will appear only on *your* computer—the person you are chatting with will not see it. As soon as you close this chat window, the background disappears and does not automatically reappear anywhere.

To customize a chat window:

1. Click anywhere in a chat window to activate the window.

2. From the View menu, choose "Set Chat Background...."

   Or Control-click on an empty area of the chat window, then choose "Set Chat Background..." from the pop-up menu.

3. In the Finder sheet that opens, select an image file, then click "Open."

Small images tile (repeat over and over) to fill the chat window space. Large images display full-sized, cropping the image if necessary.

To remove a background, go to the View menu (or Control-click on the window background), then choose "Clear Background."

View Your Account as Name or Handle

If you have multiple chat accounts, and you're not sure which one you're using, click your name above the Status menu. Choose to "View as Handle" instead of "Name." Your chat Buddy name displays at the top of the Buddy List instead of your real name.

Show a Message Date and Time

Someday you may need to prove what was said and exactly when it was said. If you've set iChat to save transcripts of your chats (page 394), just open the chat, then hover your pointer over a message balloon until a yellow text box pops open that contains the date and time the message was sent, down to the second. This also works on chats that are live.

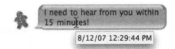

Send or Receive Files through iChat

You may want to **send a photo or some other file** to a Buddy in your list. This technique only works if your Buddy is also an iChat user.

Send a file to a Buddy in your list:

1. If you're *not* currently chatting with the Buddy, drag and drop a file on top of a Buddy's name in the Buddy List.

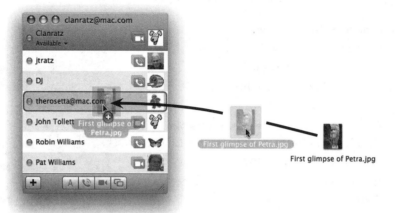

First glimpse of Petra.jpg

2. An alert appears **on the recipient's computer,** warning of an incoming file (below-left).

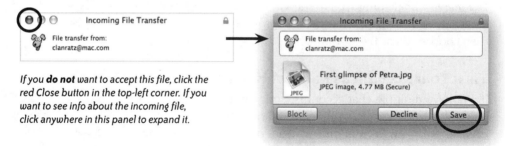

*If you **do not** want to accept this file, click the red Close button in the top-left corner. If you want to see info about the incoming file, click anywhere in this panel to expand it.*

Click anywhere in the white alert panel (above-left) to expand it into the "Incoming File Transfer" window (above-right). This window identifies the sender, the file name, the file type, and the file size.

You can choose to "Decline" the transfer, or click the "Save" button to download it. The saved file appears in your Downloads folder (Leopard) or on your Desktop (Tiger). You can specify another location in the General pane of iChat Preferences to save received files.

3. If you *are* currently chatting with the Buddy, you can drag a file to the iChat message window, to the Buddy List, or to the text-entry field of your iChat window. Depending on where you drag the file, and if the file is an image or not, it appears in the recipient's message window as either an image that can be dragged to the Desktop, or as a text link that can be clicked to download.

 *When a transferred file appears as a link, click the link to download it.*

When you receive a photo in a message balloon, you can drag it from the message window to your Desktop, or to any folder.

Send HTML web addresses to others

During a chat you might want to send a clickable web address link to your Buddy. To transfer a web link, type a web address in the text entry field.

Or open a web page in a browser, then drag the web address from the browser's location field to the iChat message window, or to the iChat text-entry field.

When a transferred web address appears as a link, click the link to open it in your browser.

Send SMS messages to a mobile phone

SMS (Short Message Service) is a form of text messaging on mobile phones. You can enter someone's mobile phone number in iChat instead of a Buddy name, then type a message that's sent to her mobile phone.

1. From iChat's File menu, choose "Send SMS...."

2. In the "Send SMS" window (right-top), type the mobile phone number you want to access.

3. Click OK. In the message window that opens, type your message, then hit the Return key to send the message. An auto-reply message appears in iChat, as shown on the right.

SMS messages can only be sent to US mobile phones.

Chat Rooms and Group Chats

A **Chat Room** allows any number of different people in the same chat window, all chatting at once. You create a name for the Chat Room, then invite others to join the chat. Anyone who knows the chat room name can join the chat. If you have a regular group of people that chat with each other often, create a chat room that participants can check for online at any time.

A **Group Chat** is similar to a Chat Room, but instead of a *named* room that can be entered by anyone who knows the room name, a participant must be invited by the originator of the chat or by one of its invited participants. This is a good way to have an invitation-only chat with multiple people.

Create a Chat Room

You can create a chat room with a unique name and invite any number of people to join you. .Mac members, AOL members, AIM users, and Jabber users can all be invited into the chat.

To create a Chat Room:

1. From iChat's File menu, choose "Go to Chat Room…."

2. In the "Room Name" field, type a name for the chat room, then click "Go."

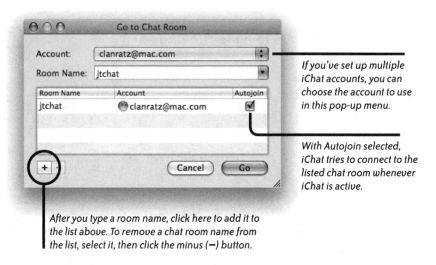

If you've set up multiple iChat accounts, you can choose the account to use in this pop-up menu.

With Autojoin selected, iChat tries to connect to the listed chat room whenever iChat is active.

After you type a room name, click here to add it to the list above. To remove a chat room name from the list, select it, then click the minus (—) button.

Anyone who knows the chat room name can join the chat, and any participant can invite any of their own buddies.

If you plan to use this chat room again, and would like to make it easily accessible in the future, click the **+** button to add the chat room to the "Room Name" list shown above.

Join an existing Chat Room

You can **join an existing Chat Room** that another Mac.com member started if
you know the chat room name.

1. From the File menu, choose "Go to Chat Room…."

2. In the "Go to Chat Room" window (shown on the previous page),
   type the name of the chat room you want to join, then click "Go." If a
   chat room with this name exists, it will open on your screen. Existing
   participants appear in the participants drawer.

Invite others to the Chat Room

Once in the chat room, you can invite others to join in. Click the Add (+)
button in the bottom-right corner of the participants drawer, then choose a
Buddy from the pop-up menu (shown below-right).

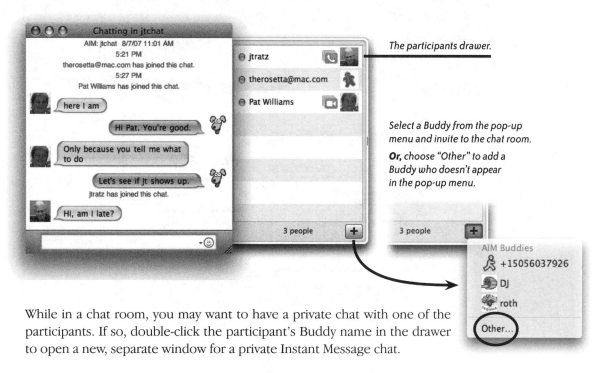

The participants drawer.

*Select a Buddy from the pop-up
menu and invite to the chat room.*

Or, *choose "Other" to add a
Buddy who doesn't appear
in the pop-up menu.*

While in a chat room, you may want to have a private chat with one of the
participants. If so, double-click the participant's Buddy name in the drawer
to open a new, separate window for a private Instant Message chat.

To invite someone who is not in your Buddy List:

If the Participant's Drawer is not visible, from the View menu, choose "Show Chat Participants."

1. Click the Add (+) button at the bottom of the Participants Drawer, then choose "Other…" (shown on the previous page).

2. Type a Buddy name in the sheet that slides down from the top of the message window (below-left), then click OK.

3. In the invitation sheet that slides down, customize the message if you want, then click "Invite" (below-right).

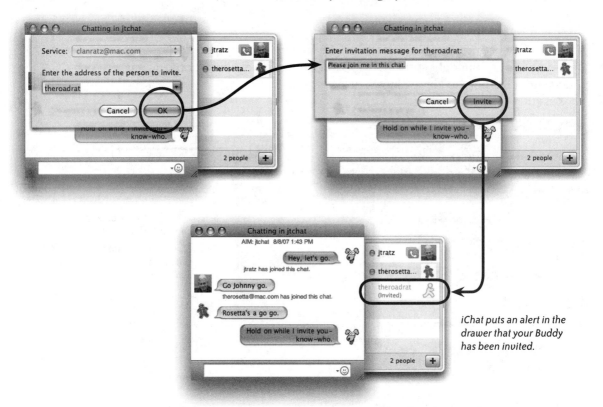

iChat puts an alert in the drawer that your Buddy has been invited.

After you've invited participants to the Chat Room, type a message into the text field at the bottom of the chat room window, hit Return, and that message goes out to everyone in the list.

You can add more participants at any time, and anyone who knows the Chat Room name can drop in. If some buddies are not yet online when you send out invitations, you can send emails asking them to join you in that particular chat room as soon as they are online.

Create a Group Chat

In addition to Instant Messages (a *private* chat between two participants) and Chat Rooms (a *public* chat between multiple participants), you can also start a *Group Chat* that enables a *private* chat between multiple participants, but does not require the creation of a named public chat room.

1. To select multiple buddies in the Buddy List, Command-click on their names (right).

2. Click the Text Chat button (the letter "A") to open a new Group Chat window.
   Or, Control-click on one of the selected Buddies, then choose "Invite to Chat…" to open a new group chat window.
   Or, double-click one of the selected Buddy names to open a new group chat window.

3. In the new Group Chat window (right), type an invitation message, then hit Return. Your invitation is sent to all selected Buddies.

To add additional buddies during a group chat, select them from the Participants Drawer (below). To show the Participants Drawer, from the View menu, choose "Show Chat Participants."

Click here to access a menu of Smiley icons.

1. Click the Add (**+**) button in the bottom corner of the Participants Drawer.

2. From the pop-up menu, select a Buddy. If the person you want to invite isn't in the menu, choose "Other…," then type the Buddy name you want to invite.

Or, drag a Buddy from your Buddy List into the Group Chat window.

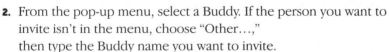

Participants of a Group Chat appear in the Participants Drawer.

Click here to see a pop-up list of online buddies.

Save a copy of Chats

You can save a transcript of any text chat—Instant Messages, Direct Messages, and Group Chats—to document a conversation, to read later, or to store important information contained in a chat.

jtratz on 2007-08-09 at 08.59.ichat

A saved chat transcript looks like this. The default file name includes time and date information.

To save an individual chat:

1. Make sure the chat you want to save is the active window on the screen.
2. From the File menu, choose "Save a Copy As...."
3. In the sheet that opens (right), name the document, choose where to store it, and click "Save."

To automatically save all iChat transcripts:

1. From the iChat menu, choose "Preferences...."
2. Click the "Messages" button in the Preferences toolbar.
3. Check "Automatically save chat transcripts to:" (see page 415). This creates a new folder inside your Documents folder called "iChats." Every conversation you have in iChat will automatically be recorded and stored in this folder. To save chats in some other location, click the pop-up menu and choose where to save your chats.

To open the most recently saved iChat transcripts:

From the File menu choose "Recent Items," then choose a file from the "Saved Chats" section of the submenu. **Or,** go to the location where you save iChats, then double-click a saved iChat file.

To print a chat:

1. Open a saved iChat transcript.
2. From the iChat File menu, choose "Print...."
3. In the Print dialog box, click the "Print" button. **Or,** click the "Preview" button to preview your document as it will look like when printed, then click the "Print" button in the Preview window.

To email a saved iChat transcript:

It could be helpful at some point to provide an iChat conversation to another Mac user. Just drag the iChat transcript's file icon into the body of an email message and send it.

Show Your Buddy List as Groups

If you have lots of buddies, it can be helpful to organize them into *Groups*. When you tell iChat to "Use Groups," your Buddies are grouped in the Buddy List in categories such as "Buddies," "Recent Buddies," etc.

To use Groups:

1. From the View menu, choose "Use Groups" (right).

2. A default group named "Buddies" appears in the list as a gray bar with a black disclosure triangle on the left side. Click the bar to hide or show Buddies in the group (bottom example).

   Select the "Use Offline Group" item in the View menu to place offline Buddies in their own Group.

To create a new Group:

1. Click the Add button in the bottom-left corner of the Buddy List, then choose "Add Group…" (shown on the right).

2. In the dialog that opens (shown on the right, next to bottom), type a name for the group, then click the "Add" button. The new group appears in the list as a gray bar (shown bottom-right).

Add a new Buddy to a Group: Click the Add (+) button, then choose "Add Buddy…." In the sheet that drops down, type a Buddy name, then from the "Add to Group" pop-up menu, choose a Group.

Move a Buddy to another Group: Drag an online or offline Buddy from its current group to another group. The Buddy is *removed* from the original group. To keep the Buddy in the original group, *Option-drag* to *copy* the Buddy to the new group.

Delete a Buddy from a Group: Select the Buddy, then press Delete. A Buddy that you delete from one group remains in other groups.

Delete an entire Group: Control-click on a Group, then from the pop-up menu, choose "Delete Group…." An alert asks you to confirm your decision. This deletes all buddies in that group. Before you delete the Group, drag buddies you want to keep into another Group.

Hide Groups: From the View menu, *uncheck* "Use Groups."

Start a group chat with members of a Group: Control-click the Group name, then choose "Invite Members to Chat…."

Send individual Instant Messages to members of a Group: Control-click the Group name, then choose "Send Instant Message to Members…."

Audio Chats

Tip: You need a broadband connection (not a dial-up modem connection) to audio or video chat. Many hotels and coffee shops around the world provide broadband connections. Broadband wireless connections (Wi-Fi) can be found almost anywhere.

You can audio chat with other iChat users who have a microphone connected or built into to their computer. Audio chats with buddies anywhere in the world are free. If your computer meets the minimum requirements (listed below), you can audio chat with up to ten people at a time.

Setup for audio chats

Audio chats require almost no setup. The settings below are automatic and you don't need to change them unless you have a problem connecting.

1. Make sure you have a microphone connected or built into your Mac.
2. Open iChat. From the iChat menu choose "Preferences...."
   Click the "Video" icon in the toolbar to open the Audio/Video Preferences pane.
3. From the "Microphone" pop-up menu, choose a source for audio.
   Choose **"Internal microphone"** if you have a built-in microphone or a built-in Apple iSight camera. If you have a USB external microphone connected (or a FireWire enabled video camera), the device name or model number appears in this pop-up menu.
   Choose "Line In" if you have an external microphone connected to your computer through the Line In port.

Minimum requirements for audio chats

If you're not sure what your Internet connection speed is, do a Google search for "speed test." You'll find many web sites that provide free tests and all you have to do is click a button.

Look for a test page that provides results for both download and upload speeds, such as *www.speedtest.net*

It takes a more powerful computer and a faster Internet connection to initiate a multi-person audio chat than it does to participate in one.

To *initiate* an audio chat, this is what you need:

▼ **1-to-1 chat:**
   Any G3, G4, G5, or Intel Mac computer
   56 Kbps Internet connection (this could be a dial-up modem)

▼ **Multi-person chat (up to ten people):**
   1 GHz G4, a dual 800 MHz G4, any G5, or any Intel Mac computer
   128 Kbps Internet connection, both ways (upload and download)

To *participate in* an audio chat, this is what you need:

▼ **1-to-1 chat:**
   Any G3, G4, G5, or Intel Mac computer
   56 Kbps Internet connection (this could be a dial-up modem)

▼ **Multi-person chat (up to ten people):**
   Any G3, G4, G5, or Intel Mac computer
   56 Kbps Internet connection (this could be a dial-up modem)

Start a 1-to-1 audio chat

1. Open iChat.

2. Select a Buddy in your Buddy List that shows a video camera icon or an audio icon (a telephone icon) to the right of the Buddy name.

3. To start an audio chat, click the telephone icon next to the Buddy name. **Or** click the telephone button at the bottom of the window. **Or** from the Buddies menu, choose "Invite to Audio Chat." **Or** Control-click on a Buddy, then choose "Invite to Audio Chat" from the shortcut menu.

4. An audio panel opens on your Desktop, waiting for your Buddy to reply, as shown below.

The icon to the right of a Buddy name indicates what kind of chat is possible.

5. On the Buddy's Desktop, an Audio chat invitation appears (below-left). When the invitation is clicked, it opens into the audio chat panel shown below-right. The Buddy can choose to "Decline" or "Accept" the invitation. The Buddy can also choose a "Text Reply" if an audible reply is inappropriate at the moment.

A multi-layered chat icon means the connection is fast enough to support a multi-person audio chat.

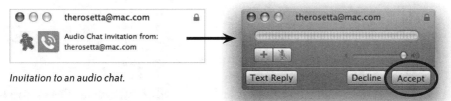

Invitation to an audio chat.

6. When the invitation is accepted, you can talk back and forth just as if you were using a telephone. The audio chat panel shows an animated sound level meter and provides a volume slider so you can adjust the chat volume. To stop sending audio, click the microphone icon.

Click here to stop sending audio.

End a 1-to-1 audio chat

To end an audio chat, just click the red Close button in the top-left corner of the audio panel. Either party can end an audio chat at any time.

Start a group audio chat

Once you've started an audio chat with one person, you're just a click away from audio conferencing with up to ten Buddies at a time.

1. Start a 1-to-1 audio chat, as described on the previous page.

2. To add another Buddy to the chat, click the Add (+) button in the bottom-left corner (below-left), then choose a Buddy from the pop-up list (below-right). **Or,** Control-click on another Buddy in the Buddy List. From the shortcut menu, choose "Invite to Audio Chat."

3. The audio chat window expands (below-left) to show that you're waiting for a response. When the invited Buddy accepts your invitation, he appears in your chat window as another sound level meter (below-right). To invite another Buddy to the chat, click the plus button (+), then choose a Buddy from the pop-up menu. **Or,** Control-click on a Buddy in the Buddy List, then from the shortcut menu, choose "Invite to Audio Chat."

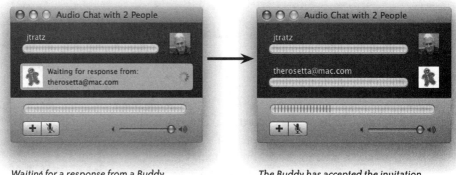

Waiting for a response from a Buddy.   *The Buddy has accepted the invitation.*

When you receive an invitation to a group audio chat, the icon changes back and forth between a telephone icon and a number that tells you how many people are currently in the chat.

Remove someone from a group audio chat

Participants in audio chats can choose to leave the discussion at any time by closing their chat window (just click the red Close button in the upper-left corner). The person who *initiates* a group audio chat is the host of the chat and is the only one who can remove other participants.

To remove a Buddy from a group audio chat:

1. Hover your pointer over the Buddy until a red circled-X appears (right).

2. Click on the red circled-X to remove the Buddy. The removed Buddy is alerted that all the participants have left the audio chat.

Invite multiple buddies to a group audio chat

If everyone you want to chat with is online and visible in the Buddy List, you can invite everyone all at once to a group audio chat.

1. To select multiple buddies, Command-click the Buddy names you want to invite. The selected Buddies are highlighted in blue (below-left).

2. Click the audio chat button (the telephone icon) to send an invitation out to all selected Buddies.

    Or, from the Buddies menu, choose "Invite to Audio Chat."
    Or, Control-click one of the selected Buddies, then from the pop-up menu, choose "Invite to Audio Chat."

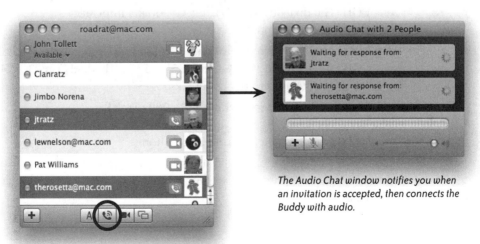

The Audio Chat window notifies you when an invitation is accepted, then connects the Buddy with audio.

Video Chats

iChat makes video conferencing so easy and fun. If your computer and your Internet connection meet certain minimum requirements, you can video chat with one, two, or three other Buddies at the same time.

Minimum requirements for Video Chats

It takes a more powerful computer and a faster Internet connection to *initiate* a video chat than it does to *participate* in one.

To *initiate* or *participate in* a 1-to-1 video conference:

▼ You need at least a 600 MHz G3, any G4, any G5, or any Intel Mac
56 Kbps Internet connection (up/down)

To *initiate* 4-way video conference:

▼ **Good quality (video resolution: 80 x 60 pixels)**
Dual 1 GHz G4, any G5, or any Intel Mac
384 Kbps Internet connection (up/down)

▼ **Better quality (video resolution: 160 x 120 pixels)**
Dual 1 GHz G4, 1.8 GHz G5, or 1.66 GHz Intel Core Duo Mac
600 Kbps Internet connection (up/down)

▼ **Best quality (video resolution: 320 x 240 pixels)**
Dual 2 GHz G5 or 1.83 GHz Intel Core Duo Mac
1500 Kbps Internet connection (up/down)

To *participate in* a 4-way video conference:

▼ **Good quality (video resolution: 80 x 60 pixels)**
1 GHz G4, dual 800 MHz G4, any G5, or any Intel Mac
100 Kbps dial-up Internet connection

▼ **Better quality (video resolution: 160 x 120 pixels)**
1 GHz G4, dual 800 MHz G4, any G5, or 1.66 GHz Intel Core Duo Mac
200 Kbps dial-up Internet connection

▼ **Best quality (video resolution: 320 x 240 pixels)**
Any G5 or 1.83 GHz Intel Core Duo Mac
500 Kbps broadband Internet connection

Video quality settings are automatically optimized based on the available bandwidth and your computer's processing power. You can't manually change video quality settings.

Set up a video conference

If your Mac doesn't have a built-in iSight video camera, connect some other FireWire-enabled video camera to your Mac and turn it on. Make sure the video camera is in *Camera* or *Record* mode instead of *Play* mode.

This icon means you can have a 1-to-1 video chat with a Buddy.

1-to-1 Video Chats

1. Before you start a Video Chat, it's a good idea to check your Audio/ Video Preferences. From the iChat menu, choose "Preferences…," then click the "Video" button in the Preferences toolbar. Check your settings, as described on page 417.

This multi-layered icon means you can have a multi-person video chat with a Buddy.

2. Select a Buddy in your Buddy List who has a Video Chat icon (a video camera) showing. If the icon is a *multi-layered* Video Chat icon, that's OK—you can still have a 1-to-1 video chat instead of a multi-person chat.

3. Click the Video Chat icon next to the Buddy name.

   Or click the Video button at the bottom of the Buddy List window.

   Or Control-click on the Buddy name, then from the shortcut menu, choose "Invite to Video Chat."

   Or from the Buddies menu, choose "Invite to Video Chat."

4. An iChat preview window opens on your Desktop (below-left). This preview shows you what your Buddy will see. When the Buddy accepts the invitation, the chat begins (below-right).

Drag this corner to manually resize the chat window.

Click here to show the video chat full screen.

The inset thumbnail image shows what your Buddy can see. To reposition it to another corner, click any other corner of the main video window. To resize the thumbnail, drag the corner stripes that appear when you mouse over the thumbnail.

Continued…

5. When you *receive* a video chat invitation, click on the invitation to open a video window. Choose "Decline" or "Accept." Or, choose "Text Reply" if a video/audio response is not appropriate at the current time or place.

Click on an invitation (above) to open a video chat window (right), then click the Accept button.

One-way Video Chats

Tip: Take a snapshot of a Buddy as you chat. From the Video menu, choose "Take Snapshot." The snapshot is placed on your Desktop.

Or, Command-click on the window and drag the image to your Desktop.

Or, while in a Video Chat, press Command C, open Preview, then from the File menu choose "New from Pasteboard."

If your Mac has a video camera built-in or connected, but your Buddy doesn't, you can have a *one-way* video chat. Your Buddy will see you, but you won't see your Buddy.

1. Select a Buddy in the Buddy List (or the Bonjour List) that doesn't have a camera-enabled computer—a Buddy that does not have a Video Chat icon next to her Buddy name.

2. From the Buddies menu, choose "Invite to One-Way Video Chat."

Or click the icon next to the Buddy name. **Or** click the icon button at the bottom of the Buddy List. iChat automatically knows to start a one-way video chat.

3. The Buddy receives an invitation (below-left). When the invitation is accepted, you appear in a video window on the Buddy's Desktop (below-right).

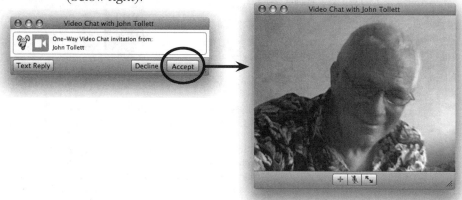

Multi-person Video Chats

The computer hardware and bandwidth requirements shown on page 400 determine the video quality of a multi-person Video Chat. Adding more than one Buddy to a Video Chat often degrades the video quality.

1. Start a 1-to-1 Video Chat, as explained on pages 401–402.

2. To add another Buddy, click the Add (**+**) button at the bottom of the video window. From the Add pop-up menu, choose an online Buddy. If the newly invited Buddy doesn't have a camera-enabled computer, she joins the chat as an *audio* participant (right). To add a third Buddy (below), click the Add button again.

Click the Add (+) button to invite additonal buddies to the chat.

The person that *initiates* a Video Chat is the only one who can invite additional participants or remove a participant from the chat.

To remove a participant from a multi-person video chat, hover your pointer over a Buddy until a red circled-X appears in the top-right corner of the Buddy picture (above). Click the circled-X to remove the Buddy.

Any participant can voluntarily leave a multi-person chat by closing his chat window.

Screen Sharing

iChat Screen Sharing enables you to share a screen, and your entire computer, with a Buddy. When you choose a Buddy from the Buddy List, you can share your own screen and computer, or share your Buddy's screen and computer.

This is really great for anyone who has experienced the frusration of trying to give Mac support and instruction with a telephone call or email. Now you can just activate Screen Sharing and watch as you give instructions. Or, control the Buddy's computer while she watches and listens. When Screen Sharing is activated, iChat automatically starts an audio chat so the two buddies can discuss whatever matter is at hand.

You can also use Screen Sharing with computers on your local network that are running the Tiger operating system. In the Tiger computer's Sharing Preferences, turn on "Apple Remote Desktop."

Screen Sharing can be used over a local network using Bonjour or the Finder (see page 406–407), or over the Internet using iChat. Both computers must be running the Leopard operating system to use Screen Sharing.

Screen Sharing through Bonjour and iChat

Before you start Screen Sharing, make sure both computers have "Screen Sharing" selected in the Sharing pane of System Preferences.

1. Select a Buddy in the **Bonjour List** or the **Buddy List.** If the Screen Sharing icon at the bottom of the Buddy List (left) is black (instead of gray), you can use Screen Sharing with that Buddy.

2. Click the Screen Sharing button at the bottom of the list (shown to the left). Then, from the pop-up menu, choose "Share My Screen…" or "Share (Buddy Name's) Screen…."

   Or from the Buddies menu choose "Share My Screen…" or "Share (Buddy Name's) Screen…."

When you receive an invitation to share your screen, you can decline, accept, or respond with a text reply.

In this example, Robin chooses to share her own screen instead of the Buddy's screen.

3. When you accept the invitation to share someone's screen, the remote screen (the flower in this example) appears full-size, while your own screen appears as a miniature. When you mouse over the miniature screen, a "Switch to My Computer" message pops up. Click anywhere on the miniature screen to enlarge it to full screen size and miniaturize the remote screen. Meanwhile, the Buddy that initiated Screen Sharing doesn't see any change on his own screen, even though his Buddy can now control his computer, grab files, open applications, or do anything a normal user can do.

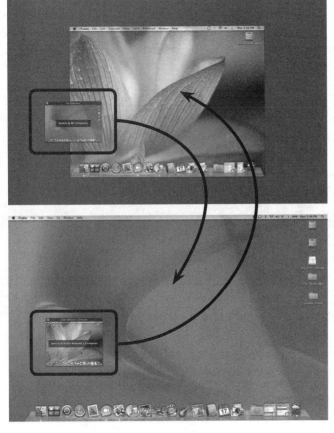

Click the miniature version of your screen to switch to your own computer (shown below).

Click the miniature version of the remote screen to switch back to the remote computer (shown above).

To copy files between computers: Drag a file from the large screen to the miniature screen. As you press and drag, hover over the miniature screen for a few seconds until it enlarges to full-size, then drop the file to any location you want on that computer.

To end a Screen Sharing session: Click the circled-X in the top left corner of the miniaturized screen. **Or** from the iChat Screen Sharing icon in the top menu bar, choose "End Screen Sharing."

Screen Sharing through the Finder (on your local network)

You can also go through the Finder to connect to other computers that are connected to your local network. This technique provides a slightly different presentation of the other computer's screen than that provided by going through Bonjour or iChat, explained on the previous two pages.

Remember, both screen sharing Macs must have "Screen Sharing" selected in the Sharing pane of System Preferences.

1. Open a Finder window, then select a computer on your network from the "Shared" section of the sidebar (below-left).

2. Click the "Share Screen…" button under the selected computer's icon in the column to the right.

3. In the dialog box that opens (below-right), enter the administrator name and password for the remote computer. Click the checkbox for "Remember this password in my keychain" to make future connections even faster.

4. Click "Connect" (below-right). The remote computer screen opens on your Desktop in its own window, as shown on the next page.

Choose a shared computer on your network.

Column View.

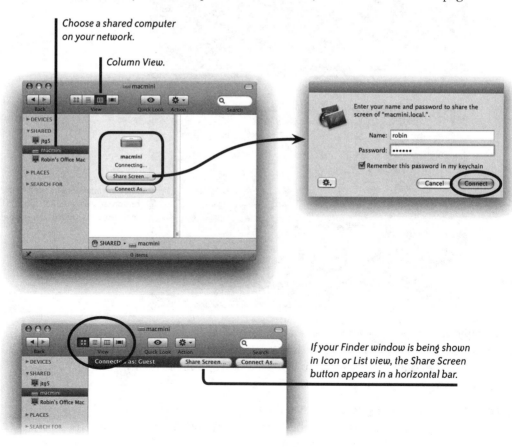

If your Finder window is being shown in Icon or List view, the Share Screen button appears in a horizontal bar.

The remote computer's screen floats in your screen.

To resize it, drag the bottom-right corner. **Or** change the size option in the Screen Sharing Preferences window (below).

Control the remote computer by working in the floating window.

To move the remote screen out of the way, double-click its title bar and send it to the Dock.

The toolbar at the top of the floating shared sceen contains buttons to "Fit screen in window," "Get the remote clipboard contents," and "Send clipboard contents to the remote clipboard." If you don't see the buttons, click the white, pill-shaped button in the top-right corner to expand the toolbar.

Get the remote clipboard contents.

Hide or show the Screen Sharing toolbar.

Fit screen in window.

Send clipboard contents to the remote clipboard.

Screen Sharing Preferences

To open the Screen Sharing Preferences (shown on the right), start Screen Sharing with a remote computer, then from the Screen Sharing menu, choose "Preferences…." **Or** during a sharing session, click the Screen Sharing icon that appears in the menu (circled, below-right), then choose "Screen Sharing Preferences…" (below-right).

End a Finder Screen Sharing session

Click the red Close button in the top-left corner of the floating window. **Or** from the Screen Sharing menu, choose "Quit Screen Sharing." If you're sitting at the remote Mac, click the Screen Sharing icon in the top menu bar, choose "Screen Sharing Preferences…," then deselect the "Screen Sharing" checkbox.

Disconnect 192.168.0.191
Screen Sharing Preferences…

iChat Theater

Once you've initiated a Video Chat with a Buddy, you can use iChat Theater to show files, photos, slideshows, or movies while you continue your chat.

Share a File with iChat Theater

Share a visual presentation of one or more files in your video chat.

To share a file with iChat Theater:

1. Start a Video Chat with a Buddy.

2. From the File menu, choose "Share a File With iChat Theater…."

3. In the Finder window that opens, select a file, photo, or movie you want to share, then click "Share."

   Or, simply drag and drop any file, photo, or movie from its location onto the Video Chat window.

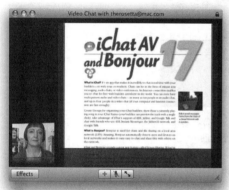

When you drag a file to the Video Chat window, the Buddy's image minimizes to the bottom-left corner to make room for an *image* of the file (left). Your Buddy sees you as a thumbnail video, and also sees the file image.

iChat Theater also opens a *file window* on your screen (below-left). It allows you to scroll through a shared multiple page document as your Buddy watches, play or pause a movie, and show previous or next files in the chat window.

If the shared file is a movie, the file window displays a Play/Pause button and a scrub bar (below-middle).

To share *multiple* files of the same or different types, Command-click to select the files, then drag the files to the Video Chat window. Multiple files will automatically play as a slideshow unless you click the Play/Pause button. Use the arrow buttons to manually show previous and next files (below-right).

The file window for a PDF in iChat Theater.

The file window for a movie.

The file window for multiple files.

Click here to end an iChat Theater session.

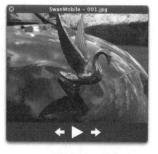

Share iPhoto With iChat Theater

iChat Theater works with iPhoto so you can share iPhoto albums as a slide-show, very similar to the feature shown on the previous page.

1. Start a Video Chat with a Buddy.
2. From the File menu, choose "Share iPhoto With iChat Theater…."
3. In the iPhoto window that opens (below-left), select an album, then click "Share."

iChat Theater also opens a separate window (below-right) on your screen so you can control the slideshow with the Play/Pause, Previous, and Next buttons.

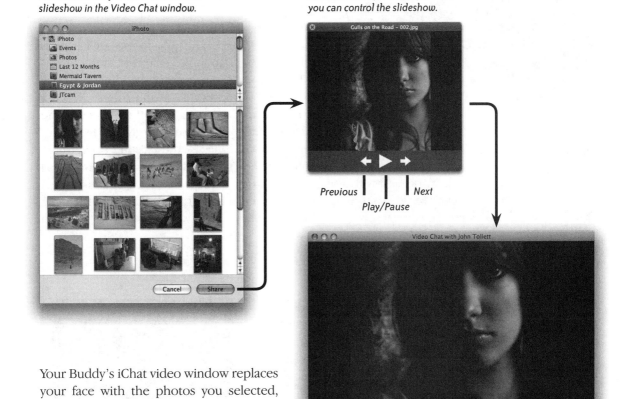

Select an album you want to show as a slideshow in the Video Chat window.

iChat Theater opens this window so you can control the slideshow.

Previous *Next*

Play/Pause

Your Buddy's iChat video window replaces your face with the photos you selected, played in an automatic slideshow (right). To stop the slideshow and control the slides manually, click the Pause button (above-right), then use the Arrows to show the previous or next photo.

iChat Effects

Video Chats are a great way to keep in touch. Now you can also entertain (or annoy) your chat buddies with Effects. To preview the various effects before you use them in a Video Chat, from the Video menu, choose "Video Preview," then from the same menu, choose "Show Video Effects." Select an effect from the Effects palette (shown below).

Amaze your buddies with how long you can hold your breath under water. In this Video Preview, we selected the "Fish" Effect.

To apply an effect during a Video Chat, click the "Effects" button in the bottom-left corner of the chat window. The Video Effects palette opens. The original video (without effects) appears in the middle of the palette. Click an effect to apply it as you chat. To return to the original video, click the "Original" image in the center of the palette.

In addition to distorting your video image with various effects, you can add photo or movie backgrounds to your image. Select an image or movie in the Effects palette. To add your own background photos or movies, just drag them to empty wells in the palette. When a text prompt appears on the screen, move yourself out of the video frame. The prompt notifies you a few seconds later with "Background Detected." Move back into the picture, and iChat replaces the existing background with the photo or movie you selected. This background replacement feature works best with a simple, uncluttered, single-color background. You get better results (but not perfect) by using a background that's smooth and a solid color.

Choose an effect from the Video Effects palette. Click one of the effects, or use the keyboard arrow keys to cycle through the effects.

Click the Previous or Next arrows to access more effects.

Drag photos or movies of your own into blank palette wells for easy access in iChat.

Record Chats

You can record an Audio Chat or Video Chat that is in progress.

1. Start an Audio or Video Chat with a Buddy.

2. From the Video menu, choose "Record Chat."

3. The Buddy's Audio or Video chat window opens a "Recording Request" alert (top-left and bottom-left). When the Buddy clicks "Allow," the chat continues.

4. A red Record light alerts both participants that recording is in progress.

Recorded video iChat files require a lot of storage space, approximately 1 megabyte for every 5 seconds of video.

This light means the video chat is being recorded.

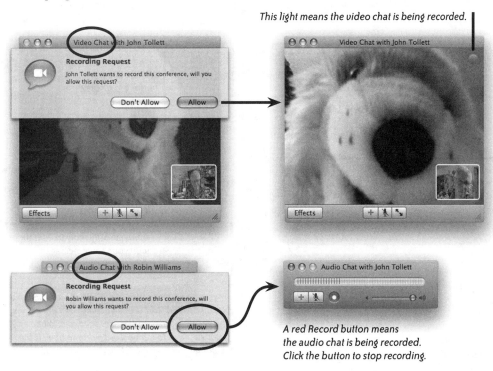

A red Record button means the audio chat is being recorded. Click the button to stop recording.

To stop a video recording, from the Video menu, choose "Stop Recording."
To stop an audio recording, click the red Record button (above-right).

Locate recorded chats on your computer

To locate the recorded video or audio file, go to your Home folder, open the Documents folder, then look in the iChats folder. The files can also be found in iTunes. Look in the iTunes sidebar for a playlist named "iChat Chats." Click that playlist to show any recorded iChats.

Look for this playlist in the iTunes sidebar.

iChat Preferences

To open iChat Preferences, from the iChat menu, choose "Preferences…." Click one of the buttons at the top of the Preferences window to show the options for that particular iChat category.

Many of the preferences don't need explanations. The next several pages provide comments and explanations for those that may not be obvious.

General preferences

Use the General preferences to customize some of iChat's behaviors. Most of the General preferences are self explanatory; others are explained below.

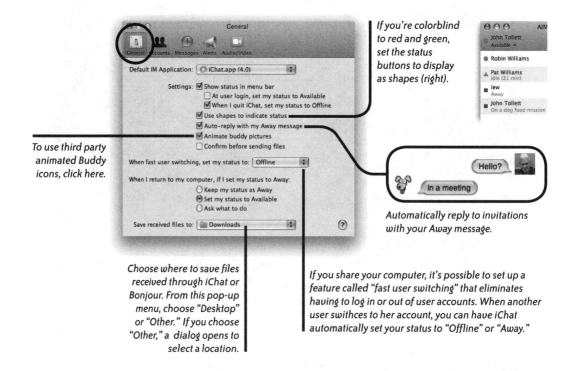

If you're colorblind to red and green, set the status buttons to display as shapes (right).

To use third party animated Buddy icons, click here.

Automatically reply to invitations with your Away message.

Choose where to save files received through iChat or Bonjour. From this pop-up menu, choose "Desktop" or "Other." If you choose "Other," a dialog opens to select a location.

If you share your computer, it's possible to set up a feature called "fast user switching" that eliminates having to log in or out of user accounts. When another user swithces to her account, you can have iChat automatically set your status to "Offline" or "Away."

The Accounts preferences

The Accounts pane is where you add, delete, and manage accounts. The Accounts preferences are separated into three tabs on the right side of the window: Account Information, Security, and Server Settings.

Account Information settings (top-right):

Your chat accounts are listed in the "Accounts" pane on the left side of the window. Bonjour is automatically listed here (see pages 418–420 for more information about Bonjour).

To add another chat account, click the plus button in the bottom-left corner (see page 414 for details). **To delete** an account in the list, select it, then click the minus button.

Check "Use this account" (top-right) to activate the selected account in the Accounts pane.

Security settings (middle-right):

Checkmark "Block others from seeing that I am Idle" if you don't want your online status to show as "Idle" when you've been away from your computer for a while. An Idle status message also shows how long the computer has been idle, and you may not want others to know this information.

In the Privacy Level section, choose who you want to allow to see you online and who you want to block. If you choose "Allow specific people" or "Block specific people," click the "Edit List…" button to open a dialog (shown bottom-right) in which you enter the chat names of specific buddies to allow or block.

Server settings:

This tab contains server settings for the selected chat service. If you don't know what these settings are all about, you shouldn't try to change them.

To add a name to the Block list, click the plus (+) button, type a Buddy chat name, then click "Done."
To remove a name from the list, select it, click the minus (−) button, then click "Done."

Create Additional Accounts

In addition to your .Mac account, you can also set up iChat accounts using existing accounts you may have with other popular chat clients (AIM, Jabber, or Google Talk). No matter how many different accounts you have, though, only *one* can be *active* at a time. Each account you create has its own Buddy List. You can switch between accounts whenever you want.

Set up iChat to use another chat account:

1. From the iChat menu, choose "Preferences...."

2. Click the "Accounts" icon in the toolbar.

3. Click the **+** button beneath the "Accounts" pane.

4. In the sheet that opens (below-left):

   ▼ From the "Account Type" pop-up menu, choose .Mac Account, AIM Account, Jabber Account, or Google Talk Acccount.

   ▼ Enter your account or member name.

   ▼ Enter the password for that account.

   If you don't have a chat account, click "Get an iChat Account...." A web page opens so you can sign up for a 60-day free trial .Mac membership. After 60 days, pay for a full membership ($99.95/year), or let the membership expire and keep the membership name to use with iChat.

5. Click the "Done" button.

6. Select "Use this account" to make it the active account (below-right).

7. Your new account is added to the Accounts pane (below-right). To turn an account on or off, click "Use this account" in the "Account Information" tab (below-right).

To delete a chat account, select the account in the list, then click the minus button in the bottom-left corner.

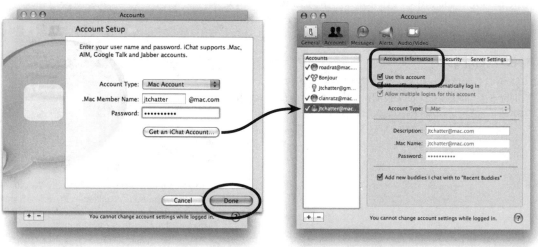

Messages preferences

Use the the pop-up menus in the top section of the Messages pane to customize the appearance of both your messages and incoming messages. Customize the color of speech balloons, the fonts used, and font colors. As you change settings, your choices are displayed in the preview pane at the top of the window.

The bottom section of the Messages pane lets you choose the formats and behavior options listed below.

Use keyboard shortcut to bring iChat to the front: When you have a lot of windows open, a keyboard shortcut to bring iChat to the front is helpful. Click the checkbox, then from the pop-up menu choose a pre-set keyboard shortcut. **Or** type a shortcut of your own in the text field.

Automatically save chat transcripts to: If you want to keep a copy of text chats, click this checkbox, then from the pop-up menu choose where to save them. The default location is a folder named "iChats" in the Documents folder located in your Home folder.

Collect chats into a single window: When you have an Instant Message chat with several different buddies at once (not a Group Chat or Chat Room), switching between chat windows is confusing and messy. Click this checkbox to collect all chats into one tabbed window, as shown on the right. For details about using a tabbed chat window, see page 386.

Remember my open chats across launch: With this option chosen, iChat remembers open chats, even when you quit iChat. When you launch iChat again, the same chat window opens, ready to continue the conversation without sending an invitation. If both chat buddies choose this option, both can quit iChat while a chat is in progress, and when they launch iChat again the original message window opens, ready to continue without the need to send or accept an invitation.

Watch for my name in incoming messages: This option provides an alert that a message refers to you. When someone types your name in a message, it's graphically highlighted, as shown on the right. This is helpful in a Chat Room when you don't read every message. Instead, you can quickly scan for messages that have your name in them.

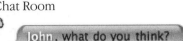

Alerts preferences

Set *global* iChat alerts to get your attention when buddies log in or out, when you receive a chat invitation, etc. This is also where you enable the computer to speak your received messages aloud. To set *custom* alerts for individual buddies, select the Buddy, then from the Buddies menu, choose "Show Info." In the "Alerts" tab, make customized settings.

To set iChat alerts:

1. From the "Event" pop-up menu, choose an event (below-left).

2. Set alerts for that event (below-right).

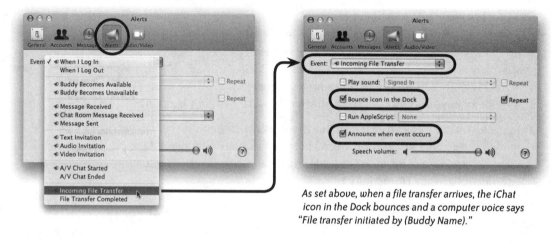

As set above, when a file transfer arrives, the iChat icon in the Dock bounces and a computer voice says "File transfer initiated by (Buddy Name)."

For the computer voice to speak incoming messages, set the "Event" pop-up menu (above-left) to "Message Received," then checkmark "Announce when event occurs" (above-right).

Choose "Run AppleScript" to automate certain tasks using scripts. From the pop-up menu, choose from three default scripts: Auto Accept, Auto Decline, and iTunes Remote Control.

- ▼ **Auto Accept.applescript** initiates an automatic acceptance of an iChat invitation. Set this option on a camera-equipped Mac that you want to use as a security camera. From a Mac in another location, invite the remote computer to a video chat. The AppleScript automatically accepts the invitation and starts the video feed, even though no one's there. Check to see if the dogs are having a party.

- ▼ **Auto Decline.applescript** automatically declines iChat invitations.

- ▼ **iTunes Remote Control.applescript** lets you remotely control iTunes from another computer (Why? I don't know.) Set this script on the computer you want to control remotely.

Audio/Video preferences

This pane lets you preview your video camera picture, set the audio source, and set a bandwidth limit for your connection.

The large **preview pane** confirms that your camera is working and lets you check the lighting and video quality. The horizontal Audio Levels bar below the preview pane gives an indication of the audio activity and volume.

Use the **Microphone** pop-up menu to choose a source for audio. The options that appear in the "Microphone" pop-up menu vary depending on the computer you use and if an external microphone is connected.

> ▼ **Choose "iSight Built-in"** if you have an iSight camera built-in or connected. If you have some other FireWire video camera connected, or a USB mircrophone, the device name or model number appears in this pop-up menu.

> ▼ **Choose "Internal microphone"** to use a built-in internal microphone.

> ▼ **Choose "Line In"** if you have an external microphone connected to your computer through the Line In port.

The Line In port is a small round hole labeled with this icon.

To use a wireless **Bluetooth headset,** click the "Set Up Bluetooth Headset…" button. A Bluetooth Setup Assistant walks you through the steps of pairing the device with your computer.

Use the **Bandwidth Limit** pop-up menu to set limits for how much bandwidth to use when having a video chat. Lower bandwidth limits are best for slower connections.

> ▼ **Choose 100 Kbps** or **200 Kbps** (kilobits per second) when you have a slow broadband connection.

> ▼ **Choose 500 Kbps** for an average broadband connection.

> ▼ **Choose None** or **1 Mbps** or **2 Mbps** (Megabits per second) if you have a fast broadband connection.

Click the bottom two checkboxes if you want iChat to open automatically when an external camera is turned on, or if you want iChat to make a ringing sound when you've been invited to a video chat.

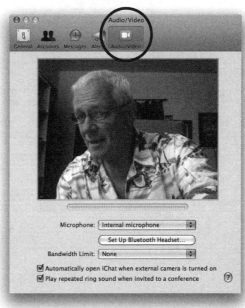

Bonjour

Bonjour is an integrated component of **iChat**. If you have two or more Macs connected through a local area network (an ethernet network, wireless network, or a combination of both), Bonjour automatically detects and connects all of the computers (or other Bonjour-smart devices, such as a printer) on the network. You can send Instant Messages or files to Bonjour buddies on your local network. You can have audio or video chats with others on the local network if a microphone or digital video camera is connected to your computer. And you can use *screen sharing* to share your computer with others or to access another Buddy's computer.

To use Bonjour, you don't need a .Mac account, or some other messaging service account, as required to use iChat. Any computer that you want to connect through Bonjour must have iChat installed (which automatically includes Bonjour), and the computers must be connected through some sort of network (ethernet, wireless, or a combination of the two).

To set up Bonjour:

1. Open iChat, then from the iChat application menu, choose "Preferences."

2. Click the "Accounts" button, then click "Bonjour" in the Accounts pane on the left side of the window.

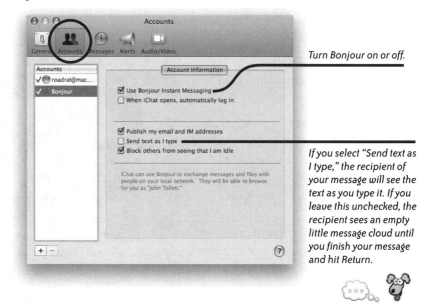

Turn Bonjour on or off.

If you select "Send text as I type," the recipient of your message will see the text as you type it. If you leave this unchecked, the recipient sees an empty little message cloud until you finish your message and hit Return.

Another way to enable Bonjour

After you've opened iChat, you can enable Bonjour from the Window menu.

1. Open iChat, then from the Window menu, choose "Bonjour List" (shown on the right).

2. A message window opens that asks if you would like to login. Click the "Login" button (below).

3. The Bonjour List window opens immediately. If you check the iChat Preferences window, you'll see that a checkmark has been added to the item "Use Bonjour Instant Messaging" (shown on the previous page).

Just about everything that applies to **iChat** also applies to **Bonjour.** Read the other pages in this chapter about iChat to learn how to chat or share files using Bonjour. Remember, iChat connects to buddies through the Internet, and Bonjour connects to buddies who are on your local network—otherwise, text chats, audio chats, video chats, and file sharing look and work the same as in iChat. In fact, it's easy to lose track of which application you're using, iChat or Bonjour. Look at the top of a message window for a line of gray type that tells you if you're using Bonjour or iChat (below).

Bonjour automatically detects a local network and connects you to it. If you're in a public space, such as an Internet cafe, you should quit iChat and turn off Bonjour when you're not using it to ensure privacy and security. Bonjour can be turned off (or on) in the Accounts pane of iChat Preferences.

Use Bonjour to send a file to someone on your local network

1. Open iChat.

2. To open Bonjour, press Command 2, **or** go to iChat's Window menu and choose "Bonjour List." Other users on your local network who also have iChat installed will appear in the Bonjour List window (right).

3. Locate a file on your computer you want to send, then drag and drop the file icon on top of a name in your Bonjour List.

4. An Incoming File Transfer window opens on your Buddy's computer. It identifies the file and asks the Buddy to accept or decline the transfer.

Drag and drop a file on top of a name in your Bonjour list.

Send a file during a chat

1. Start a chat by selecting a Buddy in Bonjour (or iChat), then click the Text Chat button ("A") at the bottom of the Bonjour List to open a chat window. Type a message, then hit the Return key to send it.

2. Locate a file you want to send, then drag the file icon into the main iChat window. You can also drag the file into the text field.

3. Hit the Return key to send the file. On the Buddy's computer, the file appears as a link in a speech bubble (left). The Buddy can click the link to download the file to his computer.

Final iChat Tip

In the event of a lost or stolen computer, revoke your Secure iChat Certificate. Log in to your .Mac account online, then click the "Account" button. On your Account Settings web page, click the "Secure Certificates" button, then click the "Revoke" button next to "Secure iChat Certificate."

Safari

8

Safari is Apple's beautiful web browser for viewing web pages on the Internet. You've probably already used it, but you might be surprised at the tips and tricks it offers that you haven't taken advantage of yet.

Safari includes its own "news reader" that brings in RSS feeds. RSS stands for Really Simple Syndication. It's an Internet technology that "feeds" you news and information of your choice from a huge variety of sources. Safari can gather the RSS feeds you are interested in and display the headlines from many sources in one place—a web page. You'll have access to them with one click of a button, and you can organize the information, filter the feeds, automatically update them, and more.

Safari Web Browser

Below is a brief overview of the main features of the Safari window. Although it looks simple, it holds a lot of power in subtle ways.

Customize what shows in the toolbar. Choose "Customize Toolbar…" from the View menu, or Control-click the toolbar.

Enter a web address here, then hit the Return or Enter key to go to that page.

Start a Google search here!

The Bookmarks Bar is a convenient place for your most visited links. Type Command B to show or hide the bar.

The Status Bar shows the address of the link your pointer is over. If you don't see it, go to the View menu and choose "Show Status Bar."

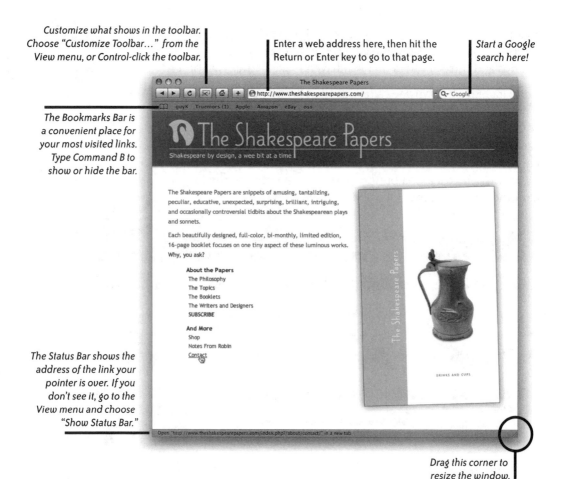

Drag this corner to resize the window.

Enter a new web address quickly

When you double-click between "www" and ".com," it selects just the domain name so you can change it. This means you don't have to accurately drag the mouse across a bunch of small type to select it and change the address.

And you never need to type "http://" when you enter an address. If it's a .com address, all you need to type is the main word. For instance, to go to **www.apple.com**, just select everything in the location bar (Command L), type "apple," then hit Return.

Find a Word or Phrase on the Current Page

To find a word or phrase on the web page you are looking at (as opposed to searching the Internet for it), press Command F. Then just type—Safari knows to put the search term in the search field (shown below).

To make it easy for you to see the found word or phrase, Safari dims the rest of the page and highlights every instance of what you're looking for, as you can see below. Just click on the page to un-dim it.

To make Safari put the strong yellow highlight on successive results, press Command G. Each time you hit that shortcut, Safari puts the yellow highlight on the next search result.

Safari holds onto that search. You can go to another page and hit Command G again—Safari will search for the last word or phrase you requested. In fact, you can close or even quit Safari and the next time you open it, Command G will find results of the last word or phrase you were looking for.

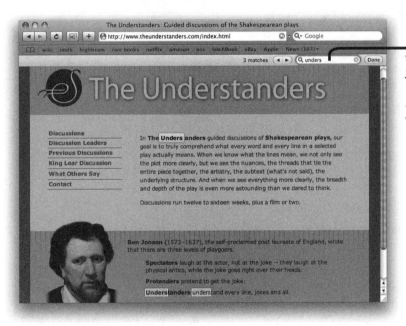

This field appears when you press Command F to search for something.

It will stay there until you click the "Done" button.

Fill in Forms and Passwords Automatically

Safari will **fill in online forms** with the information you have entered into your Address Book; it takes the data from the card you have designated as "My Card." You can also tell Safari to remember your **user ID and password** for specific sites, which is great if no one else uses your Mac or if you have set up individual accounts for different users.

To enable Safari to fill in forms and passwords, go to the Safari Preferences and click the "AutoFill" icon in the toolbar. Check the appropriate boxes.

Click one of the "edit" buttons to review or edit that item's information.

The next time you start to fill in a form, Safari will fill it in for you. The next time you go to a page that needs an **ID and password,** go ahead and fill them in, then Safari will ask if you want to save that information.

To delete saved user names, passwords, or forms, go back to the AutoFill preferences. Click the "Edit…" button. Select and remove items.

AutoFill is turned off when you turn on private browsing, as explained on page 432.

Block Pop-Up Windows!

Go to the Safari menu and choose "Block Pop-Up Windows." Only pop-up windows that you click on will appear—none of those obnoxious ads.

Occasionally, however, this can cause a problem. You might run across a web site where you click on a link for extra information and nothing happens. This might be because the extra information appears in a pop-up window. If so, go back to the Safari menu and choose "Block Pop-Up Windows" again to take the checkmark off.

SnapBack to a Results Page or Other Page

Do you see a little **orange arrow** icon in the web address field, or in the Google search field below? This icon (above-left) indicates "SnapBack" pages.

When you do a search in Google, either at Google.com or through the Google search field in the upper-right corner of Safari, you get a page of results. As soon as you click on a link on that page, the SnapBack arrow appears. Wherever you surf, you can always click the SnapBack arrow **to return to the original results page.**

You can **mark any page** you want as a SnapBack page: Go to the History menu and choose "Mark Page for SnapBack." As soon as you leave that page, the arrow appears in the location field, ready for you to click to return. You'll also see the SnapBack arrow anytime you type in a web address yourself (as opposed to getting there from a link or bookmark).

Quickly Enlarge or Reduce Text

Make the **text on a web page** larger or smaller with Command **+** (larger) or Command **–** (smaller). You don't have to select anything first.

Tabbed Browsing

When you click on a link, of course, Safari takes you to another page and thus you lose track of the one you were on. Besides taking advantage of the SnapBack feature described on the previous page, you can also choose to open web pages in **tabs.**

Instead of losing your original page, a tabbed page gets loaded and displays as a tab, as shown below. **To open any link into a tabbed page,** Command-click the link (hold down the Command key and click on the link).

Command-click on lots of links and they will all load themselves into individual tabs. Then when you're ready, click any tab to display that page, while leaving your original page still available.

Click a tab to display that page.

*Click the **X** to close that page.*

*Option-click the **X** to close all open tabs.*

To use tabbed browsing, go to the Safari preferences and click the "Tabs" icon. Take a few minutes to check out the options. For instance, if you check "Select tabs and windows as they are created," (shown below), the tabbed window will immediately come to the front instead of lining up behind the current page.

Bookmarks

The **Bookmarks Menu,** shown below, drops down from the menu bar across the top of your screen.

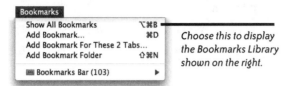

Choose this to display the Bookmarks Library shown on the right.

The **Bookmarks Bar** is that strip in the browser window just below the address field, shown on the opposite page. To show it (if it isn't already showing), go to the View menu and choose "Show Bookmarks Bar." **Or** type Command B to toggle back and forth between hiding and showing the bar.

The **Bookmarks Library** (right) lets you organize hundreds of bookmarks in a sidebar so you don't have to put them all in the Bookmarks Menu, which would make your list too long to navigate. Click the "Show all bookmarks" button ( ) at the far left of the Bookmarks Bar when you want to open the Bookmarks Library and make new folders for organizing your bookmarks.

When you hit Command D to **create a bookmark,** a sheet drops down and asks you where to store it. You can rename the bookmark at that point and choose to store it in any folder you have already created in this Bookmarks Library in the sidebar.

Organize your bookmarks with folders

You can organize all of your bookmarks in the Bookmarks Library.

1. From the Bookmarks menu, choose "Show All Bookmarks," or click the bookmarks icon on the far left of the Bookmarks Bar.

2. In the bottom-left corner of the window, click the **+** sign. This puts a new bookmark *folder*, called a Collection, in the left-hand pane.

   When you create bookmarks, as mentioned above, you can choose the folder in which to store the bookmark.

3. To put this folder in the Bookmarks Menu so you can access it in that menu, first click on the "Bookmarks Menu" item in the Library. Now drag the folder from the left pane and drop it into the large right pane, which is the list that will appear in the Bookmarks Menu. You can drag the items into the order you want them listed. You can also drag folders or bookmarks directly into the Bookmarks Bar.

Click here to create a new folder to store bookmarks. Select a folder to show its bookmarks in the pane on the right.

*Click the Add (**+**) button to the right to create a folder in the pane on the right, to organize those bookmarks.*

Email the Contents of, or a Link to, a Web Page

Safari makes it especially easy to **email an entire web page** to someone, complete with images and links.

1. Open the web page in Safari.

2. From the File menu, choose "Mail Contents of This Page."

3. The Mail application opens with the name of the web page as the subject (below). The entire web page is in the body of the email. Just add the recipient's address and click the "Send" button.

Or you can **email just the link.** Follow the steps above, but choose "Mail Link to This Page."

View PDF Documents

To view a PDF document right in Safari, just drag the PDF file and drop it into the middle of any Safari page.

To enlarge or reduce the size of the PDF on the screen, Control-click (or right-click) anywhere on the PDF page. From the menu that appears, choose "Zoom In" to enlarge or "Zoom Out" to reduce.

If the PDF has **more than one page,** but all you see in Safari is one page, Control-click (or right-click) and choose "Continuous."

Save a Page and Everything on It

Safari lets you save a web page and all the images and links and text on the page. It creates one file, an archive, that you can open at any time. All the links will work, as long as the destination pages haven't changed. This is particularly handy for pages that you know aren't going to last long, such as online newspaper articles or purchase receipts. Keep in mind that some web pages can prevent you from saving items on the page.

1. Open the web page you want to save.
2. From the File menu, choose "Save As...."
3. In the Format menu in the dialog box, choose "Web Archive," as shown below.
4. Choose the folder you want to save into, then click "Save."

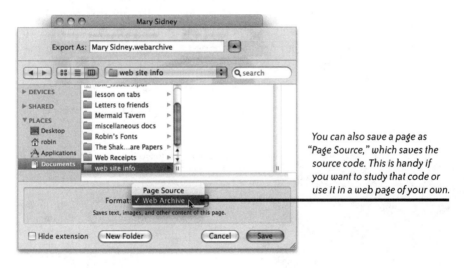

You can also save a page as "Page Source," which saves the source code. This is handy if you want to study that code or use it in a web page of your own.

To save a frame of a web page, Control-click (or right-click) on the frame. From the menu that pops up, choose "Save Frame As...."

Make a Web Clip Widget

This is pretty cool. There's a button in the Safari toolbar that lets you make a Dashboard widget of any section of any web page. Any buttons, fields, or links that are captured in that widget will work in Dashboard. If you delete this widget, you'll have to remake it from scratch to get it back.

To make a web clip widget:

1. Go to any web page in Safari.

2. Click the Web Clip Widget button in the toolbar (left and circled, below-left). If this button is missing, Control-click on the toolbar, choose "Customize Toolbar," then drag the Web Clip button into the toolbar.

3. The page grays out, except for a clear box that follows your mouse around. Click in the area that you want to capture as a widget. Immediately eight handles appear on the clear box. You can drag any of these handles to reshape the box. Press and drag inside the box to move it.

4. When it's positioned where you want, click the "Add" button.

5. Immediately Dashboard opens, displaying the new widget.

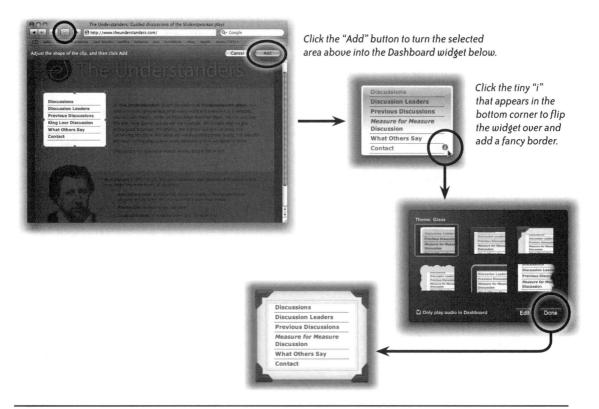

Click the "Add" button to turn the selected area above into the Dashboard widget below.

Click the tiny "i" that appears in the bottom corner to flip the widget over and add a fancy border.

Print Web Pages

When you need to print a web page, you have more control of how it prints than you may think. You can see a preview of how your web page will print, you can tell the background not to print, and you can make sure the web address and date appear on the page.

To print a web page:

1. Just go to the web page you want to print, then press Command P to access the Print dialog box, as shown below (or go to the File menu and choose "Print...").

2. If you don't see the expanded box shown below, click the blue disclosure button.

3. Make sure the "Safari" option is chosen in the menu in the middle of the pane, shown below. You'll see the preview on the left.

4. Check or uncheck the boxes to print the background or the headers and footers, circled below.

5. If the web page needs more than one sheet of paper to print, the preview will show you every page; use the arrows under the preview to navigate through the pages.

6. Click "Print."

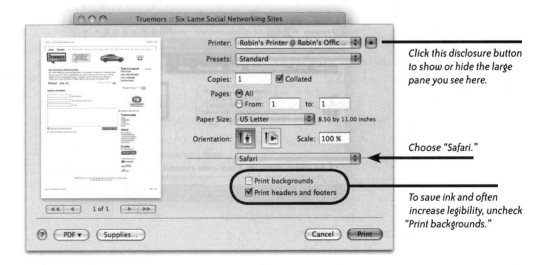

Click this disclosure button to show or hide the large pane you see here.

Choose "Safari."

To save ink and often increase legibility, uncheck "Print backgrounds."

Private Browsing

You may have noticed that Safari keeps track of where you've been and what you've entered into search fields and what web pages you've asked to see. Safari's AutoFill feature even keeps track of user names and contact information you've entered on sites, as well as passwords and credit card numbers. If there are other people who use your computer, or if you are using Safari on someone else's Mac or at a school or an Internet cafe, you probably don't want Safari keeping track of all that information. To protect your privacy, use Safari's **private browsing** feature.

When you turn on private browsing:

▼ None of the information you enter on any page is saved.

▼ Any searches you do will not be added to the pop-up menu in the Google search field.

▼ Web pages you visit are not added to the History menu. However, you can still go back and forward to pages you've viewed.

▼ If you downloaded anything, those items are automatically removed from the Download window when you quit Safari or turn off private browsing.

▼ Cookies are automatically deleted when you turn off private browsing or quit Safari.

To turn on private browsing, go to the Safari menu, then choose "Private Browsing."

To turn off private browsing, first close all Safari windows. Then go to the Safari menu and choose "Private Browsing" again to remove the checkmark.

When you **quit Safari,** private browsing is automatically **turned off,** even if you left it on before you quit. Each time you open Safari, you need to turn private browsing on again if you want to use it.

To further secure your privacy, when you are finished, go to the Safari menu and choose "Reset Safari...." You can eliminate any trace of your whereabouts from the options you see listed here. This, however, will remove everything from that feature in Safari, not just the ones you used today!

Parental Controls

If you have a young child (or anyone acting like a young child), you can set up some serious parental controls to limit access to web sites. You'll need an admin user (you) to set up another user account for the child. The child will be able to view only web sites you have placed in the Bookmarks Bar. The little darling won't be able to enter web addresses in the Address field, modify any bookmarks, or use the Google search field in the toolbar.

To limit web access:

1. Using the Account preferences, set up another user. In the "New Accounts" menu, choose "Managed with Parental Controls."

2. In the next pane, click the button to "Open Parental Controls...."

3. Choose the account to which you want to add parental controls.

4. Click the tab labeled "Content."

5. Click the button to "Allow access to only these websites."

6. Select any site listed in that pane and delete it with the – button.

    Click the + button to type in web addresses of your choice.

7. Log in to that user's account, open Safari, and make sure it's what you expect. Safari puts the web sites chosen in Step 6 into the Book-marks Bar (below). The user will not be allowed to go anywhere else.

Note: This does not prevent the user from surfing the web with any other browser. To limit the *applications* this user can use, do so in the Parental Controls, as above.

Bookmarks Bar.

What Is RSS?

All major news organizations, as well as thousands of personal web logs (blogs) and individual web sites, offer article summaries and headlines in the form of RSS feeds. Below is a sample of what an RSS feed from Apple looks like in Safari.

You can drag the "Article Length" slider (circled below) to display more or less of an article. Use the categories to organize the information.

At any time you can add more feeds to Safari, delete ones you don't want to view, search through feeds for particular information, and even bookmark searches to which you want to return.

You can separate the various feeds into your own folders so with the click of a button, you can view all the headlines from each particular area of your life. For instance, you might want to see just the technology headlines or just the screenwriting headlines or just the personal blog headlines.

View the existing feeds in Safari

Apple has provided an RSS feed to get you started. Experiment with it for a while and then start building your own collection of RSS bookmarks, as described on the following pages.

To see the RSS feed(s):

1. Open Safari, your web browser.

2. If the Bookmarks Bar is not showing, press Command Shift B, or go to the View menu and choose "Show Bookmarks Bar."

3. Open the Bookmarks Library: single-click on the little book icon at the far-left end of the Bookmarks Bar (circled below).

4. In the Collections pane, which appears on the left side of the Bookmarks Library, single-click on "All RSS Feeds." A list appears on the right. Each item shows a blue **RSS** icon to indicate this address is an RSS feed.

5. Double-click any link in the list to open its RSS feed page.

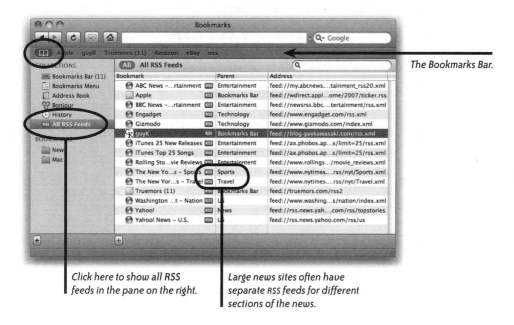

The Bookmarks Bar.

Click here to show all RSS feeds in the pane on the right.

Large news sites often have separate RSS feeds for different sections of the news.

View the RSS Collections Apple has made for you

Apple has placed a number of folders, or Collections, of bookmarks in the Bookmarks Bar for you, including an RSS "News" folder, as shown below.

Click on a folder in the Bookmarks Bar (it doesn't look like a folder, just text) and choose **View All RSS Articles** from the pop-up menu that appears (shown below). Every headline from every feed in this folder appears on a web page in Safari. You can sort the information as explained on the next page.

If you choose **Open in Tabs** from the pop-up menu (below), each bookmark in the list opens as a separate tab and each page displays the RSS headlines from that source.

The number tells you how many unread articles are in this Collection.

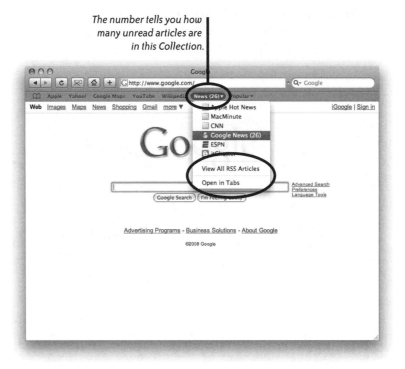

Customize the information display

Once you display an RSS feed page, you can adjust how information is shown. Use the options on the right side of the window to sort the headlines by date or by title, by the source of the headline, or whether it's unread. You can view headlines by relative time; for instance, you can view all articles from yesterday or from last month.

In the example below, notice that the "Article Length" slider is almost all the way to the left so only the main headline and a blurb for each article shows.

To display an entire article, click on any headline.
Or click the "Read more…" link.

To sort the order of articles, click one of the options in the "Sort By" section of the right-hand sidebar.

To choose which articles to show, choose an option from the "Recent Articles" section in the sidebar.

In the "Actions" category of the sidebar, click **"Subscribe in Mail"** to have this RSS feed appear in Mail's Source list.

To mark unread articles with a blue highlight color (as shown below), go to the Safari menu, choose "Preferences…," then click the RSS button in the preferences toolbar. Click the "Highlight unread articles" box (right).

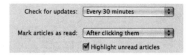

Adjust how much of the article shows.

Click one of these links to sort the articles.

Choose which articles to show.

Click here to have this RSS feed appear in Mail.

Find other feeds

When you come across a web site that has an RSS feed, Safari will display an RSS icon in the address field, as shown below.

To view the actual RSS feed, click the icon in the address field.

This little menu may or may not appear, and it might have different items in it. If "RSS 2.0" is an option, select it. Otherwise, most any choice will work.

To find a directory of RSS feeds, go to your favorite search tool, such as Google.com. Search for **directory rss feeds** or **directory XML feeds.**

Bookmark your favorite feeds

There are at least three ways to bookmark a feed you want to keep track of.

If you plan to categorize your bookmarks, first make folders in the Collections pane in the Bookmarks Library (click the plus sign at the bottom of the pane, then rename the folder). You can create a folder for an eclectic collection of headlines in a number of your favorite interests so you will have your own customized "newspaper."

To bookmark a feed, do one of the following:

▼ Click the RSS icon in the address field, as shown on the opposite page. This takes you to the news feed page. Bookmark that page; in the little sheet that drops down, choose the folder (one you previously created in the Bookmarks Library) in which to save the bookmark, or choose "Bookmarks Bar" to put that RSS feed bookmark directly into the Bookmarks Bar.

▼ Look on the web site for a little **RSS** or **XML** logo, icon, or note (or also check for "Atom"). Click it, which takes you to the news feed web page. Bookmark that page and choose the folder in which to save the bookmark.

▼ If you find a link to **RSS** or **XML** (Atom) on a web page, Control-click on it (or right-click). From the menu that appears, choose "Add Link to Bookmarks…" (shown below). Be sure to name the bookmark something that describes the content.

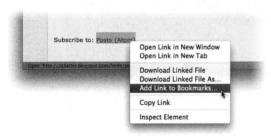

Auto-Click to view all pages or feeds in tabs

Safari has a nifty little feature called "Auto-Click" that lets you load all the pages in a Collection into different tabs with the click of a button. Instead of going to each individual page one at a time and then losing the previous page, you can peruse them all while they are all open, each in its own tab.

To view all pages in tabs automatically:

1. In the Bookmarks Library, single-click on "Bookmarks Bar" in the Collections pane, as circled below.

2. Check one of the "Auto-Click" checkboxes that you see next to each folder. (Of course, if there are no folders, you won't see any checkboxes!)

3. As soon as you check the "Auto-Click" box, you'll notice that the tiny triangle in the Bookmarks Bar has changed to a tiny square.

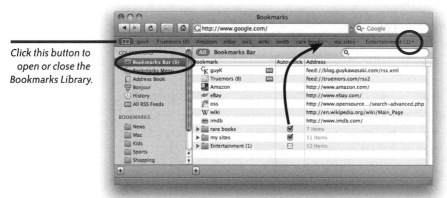

Click this button to open or close the Bookmarks Library.

Note the visual clues:

A triangle indicates a folder of bookmarks.

A square indicates a folder of bookmarks that will all open as tabs.

A number indicates unread RSS articles.

4. When you click on a folder in the Bookmarks Bar that has the tiny square, every page in that folder opens, each with a different tab (which indicates a different page), as shown below. Click a tab to go to that page.

Tabs.

View RSS feeds in Mail

To make it even easier to get your info fix, you can send the RSS feeds directly to Mail so whenever you check your email, you can see if you have news articles waiting to be read.

To send an RSS feed to Mail, make a bookmark (press Command D) of an RSS feed. In the dialog that opens, check "Mail" to add the bookmark to Mail.

Change the RSS preferences

In the Safari preferences, you can tell Safari RSS how often to check for updates, what color to highlight new articles, when to get rid of old articles, and more.

To open the RSS preferences, go to the Safari menu and choose "Preferences…." Then click the "RSS" tab to show the RSS options.

If you choose to "Automatically update articles," Safari will put a number after the feed (or folder of feeds) to tell you how many new and unread articles there are.

Send an RSS feed to a friend

If you want to share a feed with someone, simply open that RSS feed page in Safari. On the right-hand side of the Safari window, at the bottom of the sidebar, is a link called, "Mail Link to This Page." Click on it, and your Mail program will open with the link to the page already in the message area and a subject line already written. Just add an address and send.

Use RSS Feeds as a screen saver

Ha! This is very clever. You can let the current headlines from your favorite RSS feed become your screen saver.

1. From the Apple menu, choose "System Preferences…."
2. Click on "Desktop & Screen Saver," then click the "Screen Saver" tab.
3. In the left-hand pane, choose "RSS Visualizer."
4. Click the "Options…" button to choose your favorite feed.
   After you have made all the setting changes, close the window.

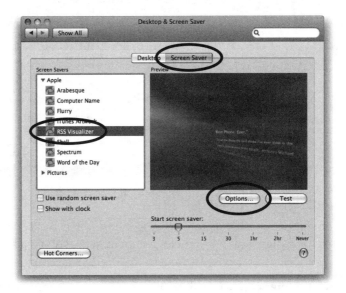

Add a Web Page Image to iPhoto

Safari makes it easy to place web page photos (or graphics) in iPhoto. Since you wouldn't dream of doing anything with images that would violate copyrights, here's how you can do it.

1. Control-click on a web page image to open a contextual menu.

2. From the pop-up menu, choose "Add Image to iPhoto Library." iPhoto opens automatically and imports the photo.

As you can see, the pop-up menu also provides other choices of things you can do with a web page image.

The iPhoto window.

Safari Preferences

Go to the Safari menu, then choose "Preferences…." The toolbar at the top of the Preferences window (below-left) contains buttons that open eight different panes of settings for you to customize. Most of the options are self-explanatory. If you're not sure exactly what an option means in one of the panes, click the purple question mark button in the bottom-right corner of the pane (circled, below-left). A "Safari Help" window opens (below-right) with explanations for every item in the current preference pane.

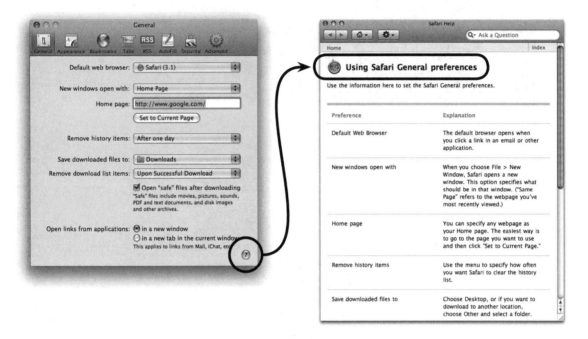

iCal

iCal is a personal calendar, organizer, and scheduler built around the idea that you need more than one calendar to manage the different aspects of your life. You can create as many specialized calendars as you want—one for work, one for family, another for school, etc. You can choose to display just one calendar at a time, all calendars, or any collection of calendars.

Use iCal's **To Do list** to remind you of events, errands, and tasks. Add **events** and let iCal automatically email invitations to selected people in your Address Book. Let iCal **notify** you of upcoming events and appointments with an alarm sound, an email alert, or a Desktop message. iCal's **search** feature lets you easily find any event or To Do item that you've added to your calendar.

If you travel with a Mac laptop, iCal's **time zone** features let you set all (or just specific) events and appointments to another time zone.

You can **publish** your calendar online so you or others can check it from any computer, anywhere in the world. The number of calendars you create is limited only by the amount of free disk space on your computer. All kinds of published calendars are available online that you can subscribe to and have them appear in iCal. Many organizations, music groups, sports teams, schools, and entertainment companies post calendars on their web sites.

iCal does all this and more with style and simplicity. Your Mac can even make it fun to be organized!

The iCal Window

iCal's window provides access to all calendars, views, events, and To Do lists. Color-coding makes it easy to glance at multiple calendars in the window and instantly see if there are any overlapping events (left). Each person in your family can have her own color-coded calendar. And you can create separate calendars for special projects, events, or interests.

The Calendars list

The top-left pane of the iCal window shows the **Calendars** list. The list contains calendars that you've created or to which you've subscribed. Click the checkbox of one or more calendars in the list to show the events and To Do items assigned to them. To *select* all calendars in the Calendars list with one click, Command-click an *unselected* calendar. To *unselect* all calendars with one click, Command-click a *selected* calendar.

When you click an event in Day or Week view, the event is brought forward and shown as a solid color shape (above-left), while other events are made semi-transparent. In Month view (below), events are shown as text, with the exception of all-day and multi-day events, which are shown as horizontal bars that stretch across the grid for the duration of the event.

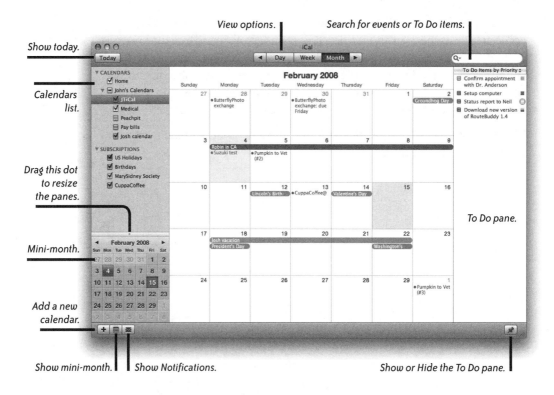

View options.

Search for events or To Do items.

Show today.

Calendars list.

Drag this dot to resize the panes.

Mini-month.

Add a new calendar.

To Do pane.

Show mini-month. | Show Notifications.

Show or Hide the To Do pane.

Choose a calendar view

The appearance of the iCal window changes according to the view option you choose—Day, Week, or Month.

To change the number of days that display in the weekly calendar view, press Command Option and any number from 1 through 7 (e.g., Command Option 3 shows three days instead of seven days). **Or** change the "Days per week" setting in iCal Preferences.

▼ **To choose a view,** click one of the View buttons at the top-center of the iCal window—Day, Week, or Month (shown below).

▼ **To show a different Day, Week, or Month,**
click the Previous or Next arrows on either side of the View buttons.

Or, from the View menu, choose "Go to Date…" **or** "Go to Today."

Or, click the "Today" button in the top-left corner of the iCal window.

Previous ┃   ┃ *Next*

The mini-month pane

The mini-month pane lets you jump to any day, week, or month of any year.

▼ **To show a specific month,** click the Previous or Next triangle (right).

▼ **To show more than one mini-month,** drag the small dot at the top of the pane upward (circled on the right).

Previous   *Next*

┃ *Show mini-month.*

Return to today's date

There are a couple of ways to **return to the current date** after jumping to future or past dates in iCal. Do one of the following:

▼ From the View menu, choose "Go to Today."

▼ Press Command T.

▼ Click the "Today" button in the top-left corner of the iCal window.

The Notifications box

The Notifications box (right) lets you know when you've received email with an iCal invitation to an event. This is also where you'll get a notification that you've received an email reply to an iCal event invitation that you sent. Learn more about iCal invitations on pages 454–455.

A red badge on the iCal icon in the Dock shows how many notifications have been received.

A red badge on the Notifications button alerts you that a notification has been received. Click the button to see the notification (above).

Create a New Calendar

Create a new calendar for someone who shares your user account, for a special project, or for any reason you want. When iCal gets crowded with events and appointments, you can turn off the visibility of any calendar by clicking its checkbox in the Calendars list.

To create a new calendar, click the Add button (+) in iCal's bottom-left corner. Type a name for the new, untitled calendar (left). From the File menu, select "Get Info" to reveal a calendar info dialog (below-left). Add a calendar description if you want.

To change a calendar name, double-click the calendar in the list, then type a new name.

To change the color of a calendar, select a calendar in the Calendars list, then from the File menu, select "Get Info." In the Calendar dialog, choose a calendar color from the color pop-up menu (below-right).

Calendar Groups.

*Press the Shift key to change the Add button to the **Add a new calendar group** button (circled).*

Make a Calendar Group

Organize calendars by *grouping* certain calendars together, as shown on the left with the "Kids" group. Each sibling has her own calendar. When the kids aren't around, you can click the small disclosure triangle and hide the grouped calendars in the list. Or you can uncheck the Group checkbox to turn off visibility of all the calendars in the Group with a single click.

From the File menu, choose "New Calendar Group." A new group named "untitled" appears in the Calendars pane. Name the new group, then drag individual calendars into the group by dropping them on top of the new group name. If you click the Add (+) button while a Calendar Group is selected, a new, untitled calendar is added to the selected group.

Or Shift-click the Add (+) button. The Shift key changes the Add button into the "Add new calendar group" button (circled on the left). Name the new group, then drag calendars from the list into the new group.

Create a New Event

Items that you enter into a calendar are called **events.** An event can be an appointment, a party, a reminder, an all-day class, or any other kind of information you want to keep a record of. I like to create a new event whenever I pay a credit card bill. In the event notes I add information such as card name, amount, check number, online confirmation number, etc. Later, if necessary, I can search for the card name and quickly find all the information I need.

To create an event:

1. Select one of the calendars in the Calendars list. If none of the existing calendars seems appropriate for the new event you want to add, create a new calendar as explained on the previous page.

2. Double-click in the calendar grid where you want to place an event.

   Or click in the grid, then from the File menu, choose "New Event."

   Or Control-click anywhere in a calendar's grid, then choose "New Event" from the contextual pop-up menu.

A new event, shown in Week view.

3. Replace the highlighted text in the new event with a custom description, such as "lunch date" (right-above).

   Or double-click the event shape to open the event editor (right), then select the text at the top of the event editor and type a custom description.

4. **To set event details,** such as alarms or invitations to the event, click the Edit button (circled, right). The event editor expands to show more settings, shown on the following page.

After you create an event, drag it to any position in the calendar grid to automatically change its date or time.

If the calendar is shown in *Day* or *Week* view, you can click and drag downward in the calendar grid to create an event and set a duration at the same time. At any time after the event is created, you can drag the top and bottom edges of the event up or down in the grid to change its start and end times.

The event editor

To open the event editor, double-click an event in the iCal window. In the event editor that opens (below-left), click the Edit button to open an expanded window that contains event settings (below-right).

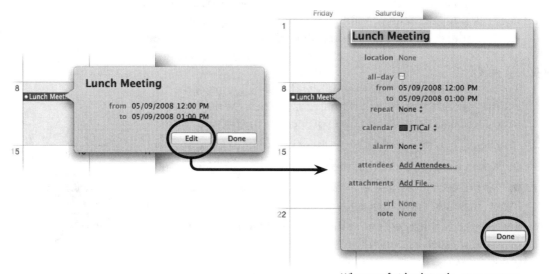

When you finish editing the event settings, click "Done" to leave edit mode and close the event editor.

Click an item in this window to select it for editing. Edit only the information you need. If the "lunch date" event is just a simple reminder, you can choose not to type a location, add attendees, or include a URL (web address). The following is a description of the items and settings shown in the event editor.

location: Type the location of the event. If you use iCal to invite attendees, this information is included in the invitation.

all-day: Click this checkbox to designate an event as an *all-day* event. The event will appear in iCal as a horizontal bar with round corners (left). To make it a *multiple-day* event (such as a conference or a vacation), click the checkbox, then set the **from** and **to** dates to match the event's duration. See page 344 for information about all-day events.

from/to: To set (or change) the start or end date of an event, select and change the day, month, or year. Then select and change the hour, minutes, and AM/PM settings. Type the changes, or use the Up and Down arrows on your keyboard to change the settings. To move from one number setting to the next, click the Tab key.

repeat: If the event recurs on a regular basis, set it to repeat. Click the default setting ("None") to open a pop-up menu (below-left). Choose how often to repeat the event. For more options, from the pop-up menu, choose "Custom…" A small pop-up window provides settings for frequency, duration of weeks, and day of week options (below-right).

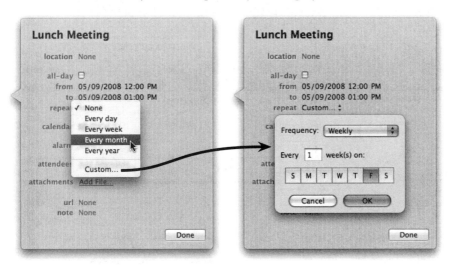

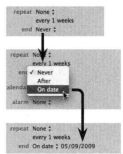

When you set an event to repeat, an "end" option appears so you can set when to stop repeating the event.

calendar: The calendar that appears here is the calendar to which the selected event is assigned. To switch the event to another calendar, click the calendar name, then from the pop-up menu, choose another calendar in the list.

alarm: iCal can remind you of upcoming events. Click "None" to see a pop-up menu of alarm options. See page 456 for more information about alarms.

attendees: iCal can automatically invite attendees to your event, place the event in their iCal, then notify you when they respond to your invitation. Click "Add Attendees…" (right), then type an email address, or type the name of someone in your Address Book. Click "Send" (lower-right) to automatically send an email invitation to the attendees list. See page 454 to learn more about event invitations.

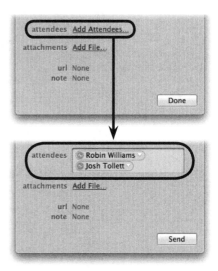

attachments: Click "Add File…" to attach a document for reference, such as a travel itinerary or brochure PDF.

url: If the event has a web site associated with it, click "None" to show a text entry field, then type the web address.

note: Click "None" to select the notes area, then type any comments you want to add about the event.

All-day events

All-day events are represented by horizontal bars that stretch the width of the event duration. In Day and Week View, all-day events appear in an *all-day row* at the top of the calendar (the lower example). This leaves more room in the calendar grid and minimizes visual overlapping of events. In Month View (the top example), all-day events stretch across the duration of the event.

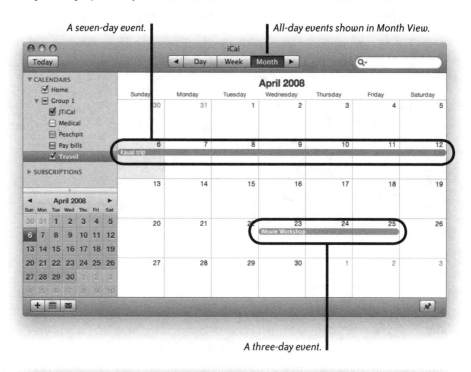

A seven-day event.

All-day events shown in Month View.

A three-day event.

*If you don't see the **all-day** row in your calendar, from the View menu, choose "Show All-Day Events."*

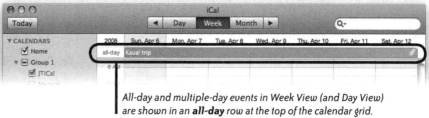

*All-day and multiple-day events in Week View (and Day View) are shown in an **all-day** row at the top of the calendar grid.*

To create an all-day event, double-click an event. In the event editor, click the **all-day** checkbox. To make an event span multiple days, change the **from** and **to** dates in the event editor.

Or Control-click on an event. From the pop-up shortcut menu, choose "Make All Day Event."

Delete an event

To manually delete an event, select it, then press the Delete key on your keyboard. To delete multiple events at once, Shift-select two or more events, then press Delete. **Or** from the Edit menu, choose Delete.

To automatically delete events that have passed:

1. From the iCal menu, choose "Preferences…," then click the "Advanced" button (shown below).

2. Checkmark "Delete events" (circled below).

3. Type a number in the text field to set how many days are to pass after events before iCal automatically deletes them.

   An alert message (below-right) opens to alert you that this option automatically deletes older events. If you're sure you want to do this, click "Yes."

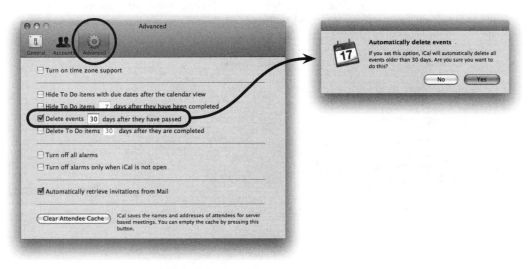

Send iCal Invitations

iCal uses Mail and your Address Book to invite people to an event. If you have more than one email account, Mail uses the *default* email account.

Invite someone to an event

1. Double-click an iCal event to open the event editor (below-left).

2. Click the default setting ("None") to the right of the "attendees" label, then enter email addresses to which you want invitations sent. As you type, iCal automatically matches the name with email addresses in your Address Book and displays all the matching names in a pop-up window.
   Select the address you want to use, then press Return. If a contact in your Address Book has several email addresses listed, they all appear in a pop-up dialog (below-right) from which you can choose one. An invitee who isn't in your Addess Book appears in the attendees list as an email address.

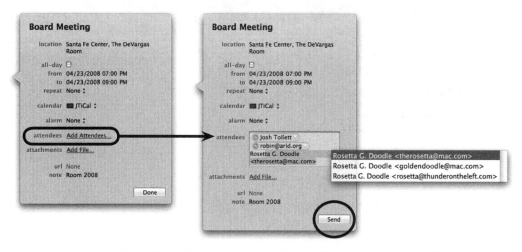

3. Click "Send." iCal automatically emails an invitation as a file attachment to each of the attendees.

You can also Control-click on an event, then from the pop-up shortcut menu, choose "Mail Event." A new message form opens in Mail with the event as a file attachment. Enter an email address in the "To:" field of the email form, then click "Send. "The event is sent to the recipient.

If you later make changes to the event details in the event editor, such as the time or location, the "Send" button changes to an "Update" button. Click "Update" to send the attendees a new, updated email invitation.

Reply to an iCal invitation

1. When you *receive* an iCal email invitation, the event is automatically placed in iCal's Notifications pane. The Notifications icon is tagged with a red arrow (right).

2. Click on the Notificatiion icon to show the invitation in the Notification pane (right). Choose one of the responses (Maybe, Decline, or Accept) in the pane. iCal creates a new email message and sends your response as an email attachment to the event organizer.

3. When the event organizer receives your email response, iCal automatically puts your response in his Notifications pane (below-left) and updates his iCal event editor (below-middle).

   If you delete an invitation from iCal, the sender is automatically notified through email that you've declined the invitation.

   The attendee's event editor (below-right) shows the status of everyone who has been invited. An attendee can change his status by clicking the current status (circled, below-right) and choosing another status from the pop-up menu.

Update iCal invitations

If you make changes to the details of an event in the event editor (such as its date, time, or place), iCal changes the "Done" button into an "Update" button. Click "Update" and iCal automatically sends the attendees a new email (right) with an attached iCal file that contains the updated event information. When the email recipient clicks the attachment in the email message, the event in his iCal is updated, and his Notification pane lets him respond again.

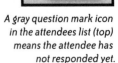

A gray question mark icon in the attendees list (top) means the attendee has not responded yet.

If the organizer removes someone from the attendees list, that person receives an automatic email notification that the event has been canceled.

Set an iCal event alarm

There's no need to worry that you'll forget an important event. iCal can notify you of upcoming events with different alarm types, even if the iCal application is not open.

To set an Event alarm:

1. Double-click an iCal event, then click "Edit" in the event editor (below-left).

2. Click the "alarm" item (below-middle), then from the pop-up menu, choose the type of alarm you want to set (below-right).

3. Depending on the alarm type you choose, set the other options that appear in the alarm field, such as sound effect, email address, etc.

   Enter the number of minutes, hours, or days before or after an event that you want to be notified.

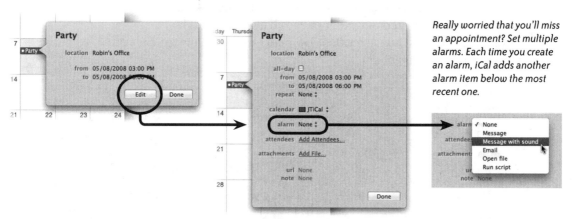

Really worried that you'll miss an appointment? Set multiple alarms. Each time you create an alarm, iCal adds another alarm item below the most recent one.

A "Message" alarm opens an "iCal Alarm" window at the set time (below-left). A "Message with sound" alarm adds a sound of your choice. An "Email" alarm sends you an email message. "Open file" automatically opens a file that you designate. "Run script" lets you assign an AppleScript to some other automated action.

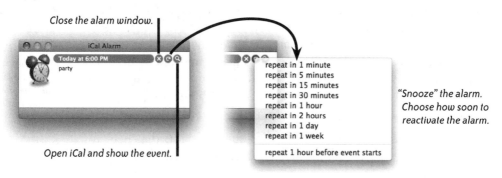

Close the alarm window.

Open iCal and show the event.

"Snooze" the alarm. Choose how soon to reactivate the alarm.

Set a To Do alarm

You can set an alarm (or multiple alarms) for To Do items to remind you of pending tasks and errands. Learn about To Do items on the next page.

Show or hide To Do items.

1. Double-click an existing To Do item (see the next page) in the To Do pane to open its To Do editor (below). If the To Do pane isn't visible, click the pushpin icon in the bottom-right corner of the iCal window (shown on the right).

   To create a new To Do item, double-click in the To Do pane.
   Or from the File menu, choose "New To Do."
   Or drag an event from the calendar grid to the To Do pane.
   Or Control-click in the To Do pane, then choose "New To Do."

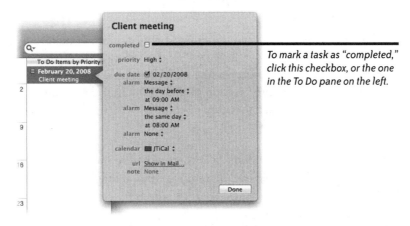

To mark a task as "completed," click this checkbox, or the one in the To Do pane on the left.

2. In the To Do editor (above), make sure the checkbox next to "due date" is selected and that a due date is filled in.

3. Click the word "None" next to the "alarm" item to show a pop-up menu of alarm types. Choose the alarm type you want, then set any other information required by the alarm type you choose, such as date and time, or the alert sound you want the computer to play if you choose "Message with sound."

4. When you set an alarm, iCal adds another alarm item under the existing alarm, in case you want to add multiple alarms. You can set up to five alarms for each To Do item.

5. From the "calendar" pop-up menu, choose the calendar to which you want to assign the To Do item.

6. Click "Show in Mail…" to add the To Do item to the "Reminders" category in Mail's sidebar (shown on the right).

7. Click the "note" item to add comments or detailed information.

8. Click "Done."

To Do items in Mail's sidebar.

Create a To Do List

Use iCal to keep a reminder list of things you need to do.

1. Select a calendar in the Calendars list to which you want to assign the To Do item.

2. Click the To Do button in the bottom-right corner of the iCal window (the pushpin) to open the To Do pane (left).

3. To create a new To Do, double-click inside the To Do pane. A new item named "New To Do" is added to the list (left).
   Or Control-click in the To Do pane, then select "New To Do" from the pop-up menu.
   Or from the File menu, choose "New To Do."
   Or drag an event from the calendar grid to the To Do pane.

4. To add information (or an alarm) to a To Do item, double-click it in the To Do pane. In the To Do editor that opens, you can set a priority, a due date, one or more alarms, or switch the To Do item to another calendar. In the notes section of the To Do editor, you can type a description, notes, comments, directions, instructions, or anything you need for the task.

Hide or show the To Do list.

After a To Do task is completed, click its checkbox in the To Do pane to mark it as completed. **Or** double-click the To Do item, then click the "completed" checkbox in the item's To Do editor.

Select how you want to **sort the To Do list.** Click the pop-up menu in the pane's title bar (below-middle), then select a sorting option (below-right).

Control-click a To Do item to show a shortcut menu of commands and options.

*Choose "Hide items After the Calendar View" to hide To Do items that have **due dates** that are not shown in the current Calendar view.*

To Do items that don't have due dates assigned are always visible.

Rate the priority of To Do items

You can **assign priorities** to To Do items, rating them as "Low," "Medium," or "High." You can also choose "None" as the priority setting. A "High" priority item is marked with a small icon of three horizontal bars. A "Medium" priority item shows two horizontal bars. A "Low" priority item shows one horizontal bar. Multiple items with the same priority are listed alphabetically within that priority group.

1. Click a To Do item to select it.

2. Click the priority icon on the right side of the To Do item to show the priority pop-up menu (above-right).
   Or Control-click a To Do item to show a shortcut menu.

3. From the pop-up menu, choose a priority.

   Or you can double-click a To Do item, then set a priority in the To Do editor that opens. (below-right).

A To Do item's priority is indicated by the number of horizontal bars in the icon next to it.

The To Do editor

Double-click a To Do item to show its To Do editor (right). This is where you set a due date, switch the item to a different calendar, set one or more alarms, add notes and comments, or tell iCal to show the To Do item in Mail's sidebar.

Hide To Do items

When you uncheck a calendar in the Calendars list, all of the To Do items associated with that calendar are hidden. If you have a lot of items in your To Do list, hiding some of them can make finding others easier.

*To set an alarm for a To Do item, it must have a **due date** set.*

Convert events and To Do items

Drag an event to the To Do pane to convert it to a To Do item.
Or drag a To Do item into the calendar grid to convert it to an event.

iCal Search

Use iCal's **search** feature to find events or To Do items.

To search for an event or To Do:

1. Click the magnifying glass icon in the iCal search field (circled below). From the pop-up menu that opens, choose the type of items you want to search for, then type a word or phrase to look for.

Make sure the calendars you want to search are checkmarked in the Calendars list.

All matches for your search appear in the search results list at the bottom of the window (below).

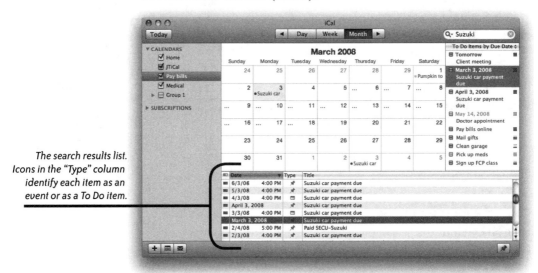

The search results list. Icons in the "Type" column identify each item as an event or as a To Do item.

2. To show or modify an item's information, double-click the item in the search results list (or in the main calendar grid) to open its To Do editor. In the To Do editor you can add notes, set alarms, or mark the item as "completed." This is a great way to keep a record of bill payments or any other information you may need later.

Sort your search results

Your search results can be sorted by date, type, or title. Click one of the column headers in the search results list to sort the items using the criteria of that column.

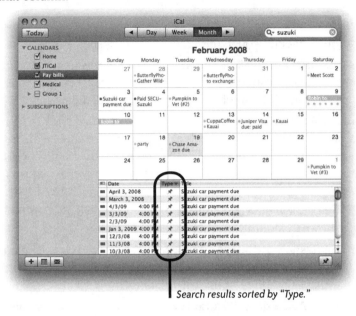

Search results sorted by "Type."

Hide the search results list

To hide the search results list, click the gray circle "X" icon in the search field. **Or** delete the text in the search field. **Or** click any event in the main window.

Search iCal from the Finder

You can use your Mac's powerful Spotlight search feature to search your calendars for events and To Do items even when iCal is not open. Click the Spotlight magnifying glass icon in the top-right corner of your screen, then type a search term in the Spotlight text field (right). Spotlight searches your computer and shows the results in a pop-up menu. Click a found item to open it in iCal.

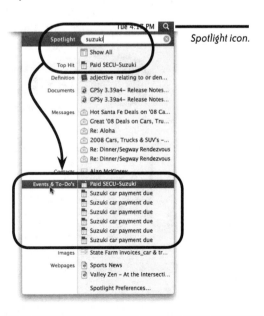

Spotlight icon.

iCal Preferences

Open iCal Preferences to customize the appearance and behavior of your calendars. From the iCal application menu, choose "Preferences...."

General Preferences

1. Click the "General" icon in the Preferences toolbar.

2. From the **Days per week** pop-up menu, choose how many days are shown in the iCal window. From the **Start week on** pop-up menu, choose the day of the week you want to start a calendar.

3. From the **Day starts at** pop-up menu, choose the first hour to show on a calendar. From the **Day ends at** pop-up menu, choose the last hour to show on a calendar. From the **Show** pop-up menu, choose how many hours are visible in a calendar when shown in Day or Week view.

4. Checkmark **Show time in month view** to show an event's start time when shown in Month view (below-left).

5. Checkmark **Show Birthdays calendar** to add a Birthdays calendar to the Calendars list. Address Book contacts that include a birthday date are automatically added to this calendar.

6. Checkmark **Add a default alarm to all new events and invitations** to automatically create alarms. Set **how many minutes before the start time** of an event the alarm will activate.

7. Select **Synchronize my calendars with other computers using .Mac** to enable syncing. If you have a .Mac membership, you can easily synchronize your iCal calendars to multiple computers.

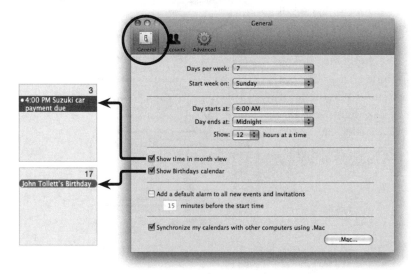

Accounts Preferences

The Accounts pane lets you set up an account that can share information with a CalDAV server that your workplace uses for server based meetings. For more information about working with a CalDAV server accounts, see your workplace server administrator.

Advanced Preferences

1. Click the "Advanced" icon in the Preferences toolbar (circled below).

2. **Turn on time zone support:** Change iCal time zones in two different ways—for an individual event, or for iCal in general. Learn more about setting iCal time zones on pages 470–471.

3. **Hide To Do items with due dates after the calendar view:** Limit the number of items in the To Do list by not showing items with a *due date* not visible in the current calendar view.

4. **Hide To Do items (number) days after they have been completed:** Choose how many days you want to pass before To Do items are hidden. Don't checkmark this option if you want old To Do items to be visible.

5. **Delete events (number) days after they have passed:** Choose how many days you want to pass before iCal deletes old events.

6. **Delete To Do items (number) days after they are completed:** Choose how many days you want to pass before completed To Do items are deleted.

7. **Turn off all alarms:** Click here to switch all alarms off.

8. **Turn off alarms when iCal is not open:** If you share a computer, you may not want your alarms to bother other users. Otherwise it's helpful to have alarms working, even when iCal is not open.

9. **Automatically retrieve invitations from Mail:** Choose this option to enable iCal's notifications feature when you receive an invitation. See page 455.

10. **Clear Attendee Cache:** For calendars administered by a CalDAV server and administrator.

Publish an iCal Calendar

To make your calendar available to others, you can *publish* it on the Internet. Anyone who knows the calendar address can view a published calendar from any computer with an Internet connection, anywhere in the world.

To publish your calendar:

1. Select a calendar in the Calendars list.

2. From the Calendar menu, choose "Publish...."
   The "Publish calendar" dialog opens (below).

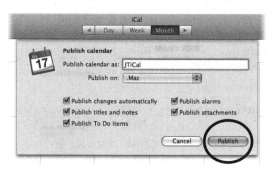

*A **broadcast** symbol in the Calendars list indicates a published calendar.*

3. Type a name for your published calendar, then select a server option from the "Publish on" pop-up menu:

   ▼ Choose ".Mac" to publish your calendar to the Apple server that's provided with a .Mac account.

   ▼ Choose "a Private Server" if you plan to publish to a WebDAV server other than your .Mac account.

   ▼ Checkmark other items you want to include.

4. Click the "Publish" button (above).

5. When your calendar has uploaded to the server, the "Calendar Published" window opens (below) to show the address where you or others can go to view or subscribe to the published calendar.

   To see your calendar online, click "Visit Page" (below).
   To notify others that you've published a calendar, click "Send Mail."

If you choose not to send email at this time announcing your published calendar, you can do it later. From the Calendar menu, choose "Send Publish Email...."

Click OK to return to iCal.

Publish to a private server

If you have access to a private WebDAV server, you can publish calendars to it. WebDAV (Web Distributed Authoring and Versioning) servers enable sharing of calendars that have been created using the industry-standard .ics format.

1. From the Calendar menu, choose "Publish…" to open the dialog shown on the right.

2. From the "Publish on:" pop-up menu, choose "a Private Server." Enter a WebDAV server address, a login name and password. Checkmark the options you want, such as "Publish changes automatically" and "Publish titles and notes."

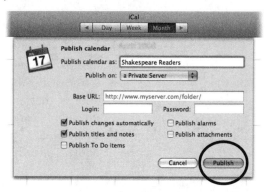

Make changes to a published calendar

You can update a published calendar in several ways.

▼ Make changes, then from the Calendar menu choose "Refresh."

▼ **Or** make changes, then click the Publish icon (right) next to the calendar name in the Calendars list.

▼ **Or** make changes, then from the Calendar menu, choose "Publish." Name the calendar the same as the existing published one. The updated calendar replaces the older one.

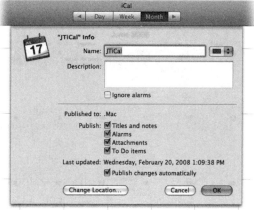

▼ **Or** set iCal to automatically publish changes. When you first publish a calendar, select "Publish changes automatically" in the "Publish calendar" dialog (see the previous page). **Or** after you publish a calendar, Control-click on it in the Calendars list, then from the shortcut menu choose "Get Info." In the Get Info window (right), select "Publish changes automatically."

Unpublish an iCal calendar

It's easy to unpublish a published calendar. Make sure you're connected to the Internet, select a published calendar in the Calendars list, then from the Calendar menu choose "Unpublish."

The original copy of the calendar is still on your computer, but it's no longer available for viewing by others.

Subscribe to Calendars

You can **subscribe to calendars** that have been published by others. You do not have to have a .Mac account to subscribe to a calendar that's hosted on .Mac or other WebDAV servers.

To subscribe to a calendar:

1. From the Calendar menu at the top of your screen, choose "Subscribe...."

2. In the dialog that appears (below-left), enter a calendar's web address that was given to you by someone. If you received an iCal email notification of a published calendar, click the web address link in the email. The dialog shown below-left appears, with the web address already filled in.

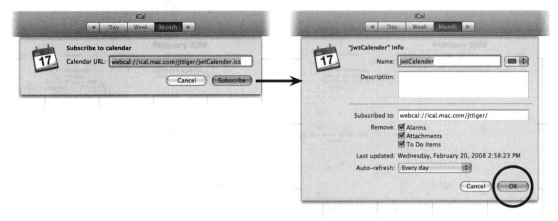

Or if you know the web address of a web site that provides calendars for subscription (such as **http://apple.com/ical/library**), visit the site and select one of the calendar links. A dialog opens (above-left) with that calendar's web address in the "Calendar URL:" field.

If a subscription to the chosen calendar requires a password, an "Authentication" dialog opens. Enter the required user name and password, then click OK to continue.

3. Click the "Subscribe" button (above-left). A second dialog opens (above-right) where you can modify settings: choose a calendar color, remove certain calendar items, and choose how often to check for calendar updates ("Auto-refresh").

4. Click OK. Subscribed calendars appear in your Calendars list under the heading "Subscriptions" (shown on the left). Click a subscribed calendar's checkbox to show its events in the main calendar grid.

Refresh calendars

To make sure that you have the most current version of a subscribed calendar, you can manually *refresh* it. Refresh downloads the current calendar from the server, ensuring that you have the latest published information. If you don't have a full-time Internet connection, make sure you connect to the Internet before you choose to refresh.

1. Select a subscribed calendar in the Calendars list.
2. From the Calendar menu at the top of your screen, choose "Refresh."

Other calendars available for subscription

In addition to subscribing to the calendars of friends, family, and colleagues, there are many special interest calendars available online to which you can subscribe. You'll find calendars that list special events, sports teams, school calendars, religious events, new movie releases, new DVD releases, television programming, Mac User Groups, and many more. From the Calendar menu, choose "Find Shared Calendars…" to visit Apple's web site of published calendars (below). Also, visit **www.iCalshare.com** to browse another large collection of published calendars.

Apple's collection of published calendars. Choose how you want to sort the calendars and browse for some you think will be useful.
"Most popular" is a good place to start.

Pay bills.ics

Import Calendars

An iCal file is actually a text file format (.ics) that can be sent as an email attachment. iCal can import iCal files or vCal files (an older calendar data format) that you may have received from someone.

To import a calendar file:

1. From the File menu, choose "Import…" to open the Import window shown below-left.

2. Click the "Import" button to open the "iCal: Import" window (below-right). Find and select the calendar file you want to import.

3. Click "Import." **Or** simply drag a calendar file (an iCal file or a vCal file) from the Finder to the Calendars list.

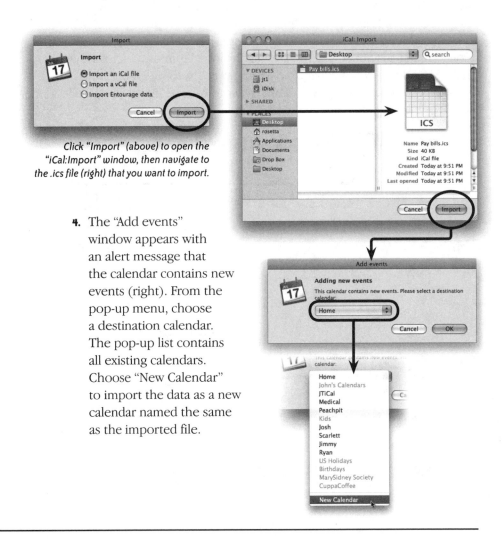

Click "Import" (above) to open the "iCal:Import" window, then navigate to the .ics file (right) that you want to import.

4. The "Add events" window appears with an alert message that the calendar contains new events (right). From the pop-up menu, choose a destination calendar. The pop-up list contains all existing calendars. Choose "New Calendar" to import the data as a new calendar named the same as the imported file.

Export Calendars

You can export a calendar as an ".ics" file, a standard calendar format. The exported .ics file can then be imported by iCal on another computer (see the previous page). Exported iCal files are small, so they're easy to send as email attachments, as network file transfers, or through iChat text messages.

To export a calendar:

1. Select a calendar in the Calendars list.

2. From the File menu, choose "Export…" to open the export dialog shown below.

3. The name of the selected calendar is automatically placed in the "Save As:" text field. If you want to change the name of the imported calendar, type a new name in the field.

4. From the "Where:" pop-up menu, choose a location to save the exported .ics file.

5. Click "Export."

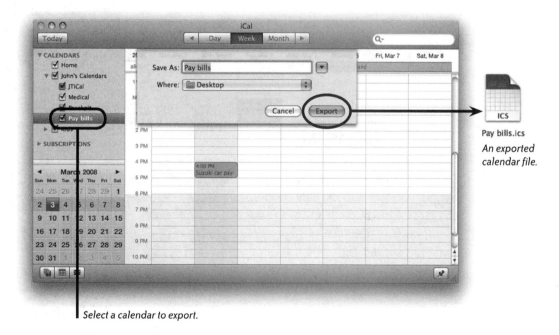

Pay bills.ics

An exported calendar file.

Select a calendar to export.

Change iCal's Time Zone Setting

iCal uses the time zone setting in your Date and Time System Preferences to set the time zone for your calendars. You can change the time zone setting for *all of iCal,* **or** you can change the time zone setting for *a single event,* without changing your computer's System Preference settings.

If, for instance, you create an iCal event to call someone at a certain time in another time zone, you can set that *specific event* to the other person's time zone. iCal automatically moves the event forward or back in time in your calendar to compensate for the time zone difference.

Or if you take a trip and want to change *all calendars and events* in iCal to your current time zone, you can do that with a click or two.

Change the time zone setting for iCal

1. Open iCal Preferences. Click the "Advanced" tab, then select "Turn on time zone support." The time zone setting appears in the top-right corner of the iCal window (below-left).

2. Click the time zone text in the upper-right corner (above-left) to open the time zone pop-up menu (above-right). Choose "Other…" to open the map shown below.

3. Click on a map location closest to you, then from the "Closest City" pop-up menu, select the city closest to you.

4. Click OK.

Change the time zone setting for a single event

You can change the time zone for a specific event *if* it's not set as an all-day or multi-day event.

1. Open iCal Preferences and select "Turn on time zone support." The time zone setting appears in the top-right corner of the iCal window (see the previous page).

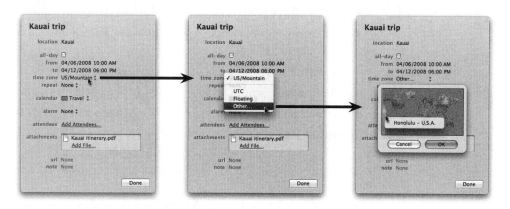

2. Double-click an event to open its event editor.

3. In the event editor (above-left), click to the right of the *time zone* label and choose one of the options in the pop-up menu (above-middle).

   If you previously selected other time zones, they remain listed in the top section of the pop-up menu.

   UTC sets the time zone to Universal Time—a standard used as a basis for calculating time throughout most of the world.

   Choose **Floating** if you want to create events that stay at the same time, no matter what time zone you're in. For instance, a lunch event scheduled for noon will always appear in the noon time slot, no matter where you are. If you've changed the iCal time zone (as explained on the previous page) or the time zone setting in Date and Time System Preferences, the event stays in the same position.

   Select **Other...** to show a small world map (above-right). Click on the map near a time zone you want. A pop-up menu of cities in that time zone appears. Select a city that's closest to where you are (or plan to be), then click OK in the bottom-right corner of the map.

4. Click "Done."

An event's time zone setting affects its location in the calendar. If the iCal time zone is set to San Francisco and you create a lunch event and change its time zone to New York, the event will move three hours back in the calendar.

Print Your iCal Calendar

No matter how digital your lifestyle may be, sometimes you need an old-fashioned paper printout of your schedule.

1. Select a calendar in the Calendars list that you want to print.

2. From the File menu, choose "Print…."

3. The Print window opens (below). The left side shows a preview of how the calendar will look when printed.

4. From the **View** pop-up menu, choose the view you want to print—Day, Week, Month, or List.

5. From the **Paper** pop-up menu, choose a paper size.

6. In the **Time range** section, choose a calendar start and stop time.

7. In the **Calendars** section, checkmark the calendars to include.

8. In the **Options** section, checkmark the items you want to include in the printing. This section changes slightly depending on the view you've selected in the "View" pop-up menu. Month view is shown in the example below.

    In the Options section, **Calendar Keys** refers to the color legend in the top-left corner of the document that helps to identify calendars. Checkmark "Black and White" if you want to print in black and white.

9. Pick a **text size** from the "Text size" pop-up menu. Choose Big, Medium, or Small. If your calendar is crowded, choose small.

10. Click "Continue" to open a standard Print dialog box.

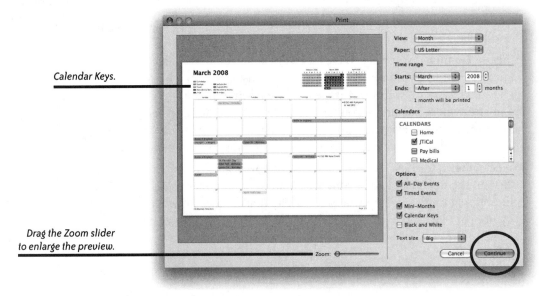

Calendar Keys.

Drag the Zoom slider to enlarge the preview.

11. In the Print dialog box that opens (below), select a printer and other options. If the other options are hidden in your Print dialog, click the blue disclosure triangle (circled).

12. Click "Print."

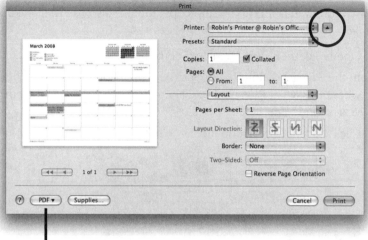

| Click here to save the calendar as a PDF.

Save a calendar as a PDF

An easy way to share your calendar is to save it as a PDF, a cross-platform file format that almost anyone can open.

1. From the File menu, choose "Print...." The Print dialog shown on the previous page opens.

2. Select settings described on the previous page, then click "Continue."

3. In the next window that opens (above), select a location to save the PDF, then click the PDF button in the bottom-left corner to open a pop-up menu of PDF options. Choose "Save as PDF..." to open a "Save As" dialog (right). Click the "Security Options..." button to set a required password for certain operations— to open the file, to copy elements in the file, or to print the file.

4. Click "Save."

Back Up iCal

If you use iCal to keep a permanent record of your activities, schedules, and appointments, you certainly don't want to lose that information accidentally. Make regular backup copies of all your iCal data and store it in a safe place—on another hard disk or on a removable disc. Later, if necessary, you can completely restore iCal from the backup copy. You can also use the backup copy to duplicate your iCal data in another Mac's iCal.

An iCal backup file.

iCal 2008-02-21.icbu

1. Open iCal, then from the File menu, choose "Back up iCal...."

2. In the Save As dialog that opens (below), name the file and choose where to save it. By default, iCal names the backup with the current year, month, and date.

3. Click "Save." The backup file name has an extension of .icbu (left).

Restore iCal

Restoring iCal from a previous backup copy is quick and easy.

1. Locate an iCal backup file, and double-click it.

2. In the alert that opens (right), click "Restore."

   Or from the iCal File menu, choose "Restore iCal...."

   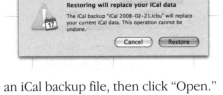

   In the dialog that opens, locate an iCal backup file, then click "Open." The alert shown above opens and warns you that this operation cannot be undone.

3. Click "Restore."

Dashboard 10

Important Information at Your Fingertips

Ever want to know what time it is right now in London? Or what the weather is like where you mother lives? Do you need to track the plane your daughter is taking to Istanbul—including whether it's going to leave on time and from what terminal—and then follow the flight path across the world in real time?

These are just a few of the many things you can do with literally the click of one button, using Dashboard. The information appears to you in the form of widgets. Some widgets are already on your Mac, but many others are being created by people and developers. Widgets are not only useful, they're fun!

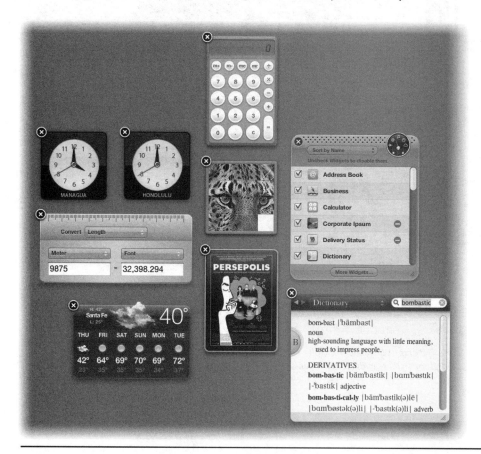

Take a Look at Dashboard

Dashboard provides quick access to information customized just for you, displayed in the form of **widgets.** Dashboard pops up in a split second, but only when you want it. With the click of a button, it goes away just as quickly. Below is an example of a **Dashboard,** with the **Widget Bar** showing (the Widget Bar doesn't appear until you ask for it; see page 478).

When you activate Dashboard, the widgets instantly appear on top of a grayed-out Desktop, on top of any windows or applications you have open. After you get the information you need, click in any blank area of the screen to put them all away.

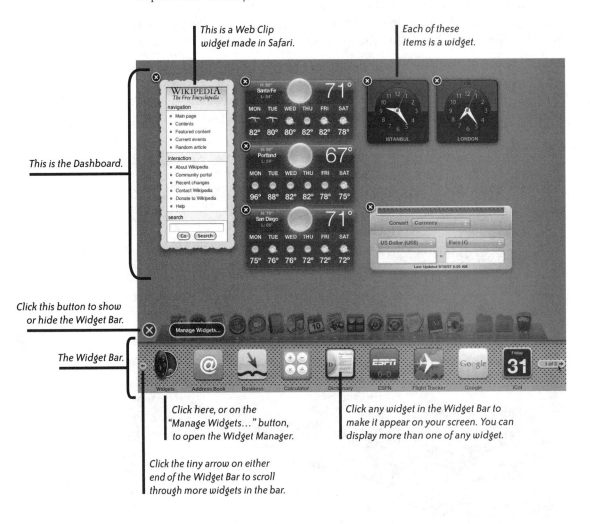

This is a Web Clip widget made in Safari.

Each of these items is a widget.

This is the Dashboard.

Click this button to show or hide the Widget Bar.

The Widget Bar.

Click here, or on the "Manage Widgets..." button, to open the Widget Manager.

Click any widget in the Widget Bar to make it appear on your screen. You can display more than one of any widget.

Click the tiny arrow on either end of the Widget Bar to scroll through more widgets in the bar.

Discover Different Kinds of Widgets

There are three different kinds of widgets, although they are all so interesting and easy to work with, you won't really care which is which!

Information widgets work with data from the Internet. You can check external events such as the weather anywhere in the world, the flight status of any plane, or current prices of your favorite stocks. You must be connected to the Internet to get the information for these widgets.

Application widgets work with applications on your Mac. They typically provide a small and easy way of displaying the critical features of the main application. For instance, the iTunes widget is a small controller that gives you buttons—start, stop, play songs, and more—to listen to your Playlists or Internet radio without having the iTunes interface take up your whole screen. If the main application requires the Internet to function, so will its widget.

Accessory widgets are self-contained little utilities that provide a variety of features. Widgets such as clocks, calculators, notes, or timers are accessories. Some of these do need Internet access, but they are not dependent on any application on your Mac.

Activate Dashboard and the Widgets

Dashboard is built into your Mac—just click the Dashboard icon in your Dock to make it appear (below).

The Dashboard icon in the Dock.

Add Widgets to Your Dashboard

To add widgets to your onscreen Dashboard, open Dashboard, then open the **Widget Bar:** click the Plus sign (left) in the bottom-left corner of your screen. The Widget Bar displays icons for all installed widgets. The Plus sign turns into an **X** to close the Widget Bar.

The Widget Bar.

To add a widget, click on it. The widget opens on your screen.

To see other widgets that are already installed, click one of the small arrows that appear at either end of the Widget Bar.

Organize widgets on the screen in any arrangement you like—simply press anywhere in a widget and drag it around. They will stay where you put them, even after you close Dashboard.

Remove Widgets from Your Dashboard

To close a widget and remove it from the Dashboard screen, hold down the Option key and click the **X** that appears on the upper-left corner of the widget. The widget disappears and is stored in the Widget Bar.

When the Widget Bar is visible, an **X** appears in the upper-left corner of each widget. **To close a widget,** click that **X**. The widget stays in your Widget Bar until you want it again.

Put Dashboard Away

To put Dashboard away, click on the Desktop, outside of any widget. When you reopen Dashboard, your widgets are right where you left them.

Work with Widgets

Different types of widgets have different features. Experiment with them all. For instance, open the Unit Converter and check all the different kinds of conversions you can make.

Most widgets have a tiny "i" in a corner, the **info button.** It's not in the same corner for all widgets, and it won't even appear until your pointer gets close to it. So hover over the corners of a widget to see if an "i" appears, then click on it—the widget flips over so you can change its settings.

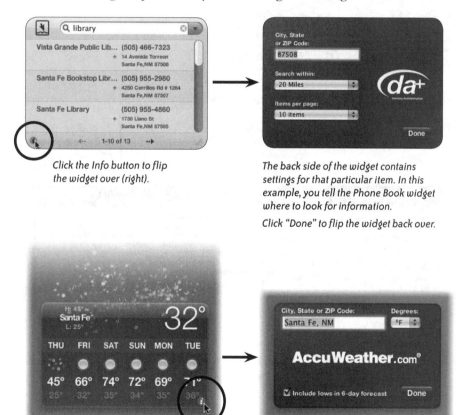

Click the Info button to flip the widget over (right).

The back side of the widget contains settings for that particular item. In this example, you tell the Phone Book widget where to look for information.

Click "Done" to flip the widget back over.

Experiment with Your Widgets!

Lots of different people create widgets, and they're designed to do a lot of different things. Be sure to pay attention to the sometimes-subtle visual clues that are built into widgets.

In the iTunes widget shown below, notice the tiny dot in the outer circle. That's a clue! Drag that tiny dot around to change the volume.

Also notice the Info button that appears (the "i")—click on it to flip the widget over and see the options that are available on the other side. This widget lets you choose which iTunes Playlist to play.

In the Dictionary widget below, there are several visual clues, as shown.

Back and forward arrows indicate you can return to panes you previously viewed.

The double-arrows indicate a pop-up menu. Click to see the options (left).

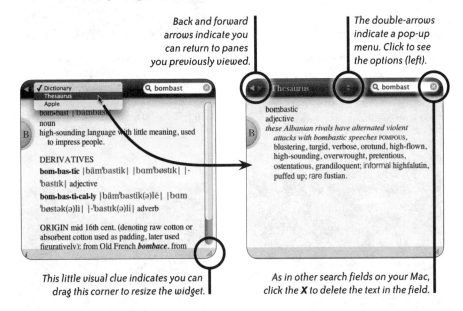

This little visual clue indicates you can drag this corner to resize the widget.

*As in other search fields on your Mac, click the **X** to delete the text in the field.*

Display More Than One of a Widget

You can display multiple copies of any kind of widget. For instance, you might like to know the time or weather in several different places, view the flight paths of a number of different flights, open several different dictionary widgets to compare words, or view a number of different conversions at the same time.

To display more than one of any kind of widget, open the Widget Bar (when Dashboard is open, click the **+** sign in the bottom-left corner of your screen). Then just single-click the widget as many times as you want, one for each display on your screen. Each new widget shows up in the center of the screen. Just drag each one to any position on the screen and it will stay there.

See at a glance what the weather is like (and whether it's day or night) in any number of cities at once.

To change the picture in the Tile Game widget:

1. Open Dashboard, then open the Tile Game widget on your screen.

2. Close Dashboard (click anywhere on the Desktop, except on a widget).

3. In the Finder, find a photo you want to use in the widget. Drag the photo to nowhere in particular. While you're dragging (keep pressing on the mouse), press the keyboard shortcut to show Dashboard (see the following page).

4. Drop the photo on top of the Tile Game widget. The widget instantly changes to your photo.

Use any photo in the Tile Game widget.

Change Dashboard's Keyboard Shortcut

If you want to change the keyboard shortcut that opens Dashboard, or if you just need to know what shortcut is assigned, do this:

Exposé & Spaces

1. At the Finder, when Dashboard is not active, go to the Apple menu and choose "System Preferences...."

2. Click the "Exposé & Spaces" icon shown on the left.

3. In the pane that opens, select the "Exposé" tab (circled below).

    Choose an Fkey from the "Hide and show" pop-up menu (circled below) to use as your shortcut.

    To add one or more of the modifier keys to your shortcut, just press that key(s) while the menu is open. The menu will change to reflect the key combination you are pressing. For instance, you might want to use Control F1 to activate Dashboard. So hold down the Control key and click the Dashboard pop-up menu, then choose this option in the menu: **^F1** (**^** indicates the Control key).

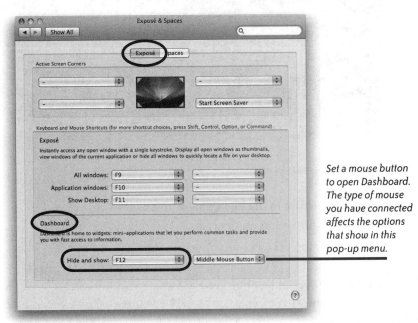

Set a mouse button to open Dashboard. The type of mouse you have connected affects the options that show in this pop-up menu.

If you have a **multi-button mouse** attached to your Mac, a second pop-up menu lets you choose which mouse button hides and shows Dashboard. This is great for laptop users—you can't always use a shortcut like F12 without holding down the **fn** key also. This means it takes two hands to open Dashboard. But with a secondary mouse button assigned to Dashboard, you can click the assigned mouse button just once to open Dashboard instantly.

Manage Your Widgets

If you become a widget junkie and start collecting lots of them, you'll want some way to manage them. Use the **Widget Manager** to enable or disable widgets, or find new widgets. If you install third-party widgets downloaded from the Internet, you can use the Widget Manager to delete them (see the next page).

1. Click the Dashboard icon in the Dock.

2. Click the Plus button in the bottom-left corner of your screen (right) to open the Widget Bar, shown below-left (notice that the Plus button (**+**) turns into an **X** button for closing the Widget Bar).

3. Click the "Manage Widgets…" button to open the Widget Manager (below-right). This list shows all widgets that are installed.

4. To enable or disable a widget, click its checkbox (to add or remove the checkmark).

5. When you disable a widget, it's removed from the Widget Bar, but still hidden away on the Mac somewhere so you can always turn it back on.

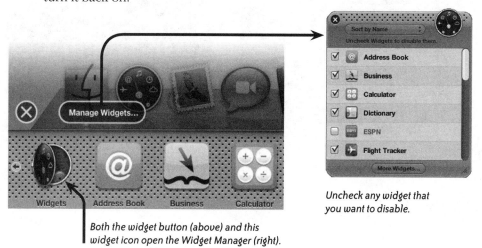

Uncheck any widget that you want to disable.

Both the widget button (above) and this widget icon open the Widget Manager (right).

To get more widgets, click the "More Widgets…" button at the bottom of the Widget Manager. This takes you to the Apple web site where you can download lots of cool, free widgets from third-party developers.

To create your own widget from a portion of a web page, see page 430.

Remove Widgets

You can't remove widgets that came packaged with your Mac's operating system. But you may have installed other third-party widgets that you found by clicking the "More Widgets…" button in the Widget Manager, or by searching the Internet for "widgets."

Any third-party widgets that you may have downloaded and installed will show a red Delete icon to the right of their name in the Widget Manager list, as shown below-left.

To remove one of these widgets, click the Delete icon. The widget displays a message (below-right) that lets you cancel or confirm the action.

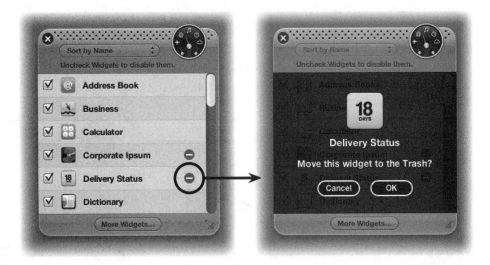

Photo Booth

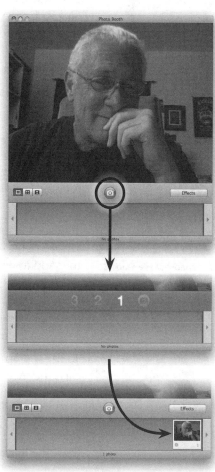

Photo Booth works with an iSight camera (built-in or external), or with a FireWire-enabled digital video camera.

Photo Booth is a convenient and fun way to take snapshots or movies of yourself for use as an iChat buddy picture or as your user account picture. You can email the photos or movie clips to friends, upload them to a web page, open them in Preview to save in other formats, or view them as a slideshow.

Make a Snapshot

Photo Booth can make three differenct kinds of snapshots: a still picture, a "4-up" movie, and a full-motion movie clip.

Still picture

To take a still picture, click the still picture button (shown highlighted in the row of three buttons), then click the red camera button. A red timer replaces the toolbar (right-middle) and starts a countdown, including audible beeps, for the picture to be taken. Your display flashes when the photo is taken.

A thumbnail version of the photo is placed at the bottom of the window (right-bottom). Click the thumbnail to show it in the main viewing area. A new toolbar replaces the original one (below).

To delete a snapshot, click the circled "x" on a thumbnail.
***Or,** select a thumbnail, then hit the Delete key.*

Click the icons in the toolbar (above) to choose how to share your photos—as an attachment in an email message, placed in iPhoto, as your Account picture, or used as an iChat buddy picture.

"4-up" movies

A "4-up" movie is an animated GIF movie made of four frames (four different photos). An animated GIF can be placed on a web page, used as your iChat buddy picture, or emailed to a friend so she can view it in a web browser. Each individual photo in the 4-up collection can also be used alone as a single snapshot.

To make a "4-up" snapshot, click the "4-up" button (shown on the left), then click the red camera button to start a timer countdown. Photo Booth shoots 4 pictures in a row, then displays the four shots in the window, as shown below-right.

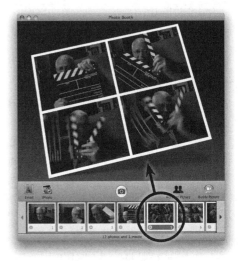

To export the "4-up" snapshot as an animated GIF movie, from the File menu, choose "Export." The saved file is an animated GIF. When you view the file in a web browser, or on a web page, the image animates, switching among the four frames. To test the effect, drag the GIF into a web browser window.

Using the tools in the toolbar, choose how to share the animated GIF.

The snapshot as a 4-up JPEG.

To email the picture as a JPEG 4-up still photo, click "Email" in the toolbar (above-right). Mail opens a New Message form, with the picture attached.

To place the 4-up picture into **iPhoto** (as a JPEG), click "iPhoto" in the toolbar (above-right). **Or,** from the View menu, choose "Start Slideshow," then click the "Add to iPhoto" button in the on-screen slideshow controls (below).

On-screen slideshow controls.

To use a 4-up snapshot for your **Account picture** or as your **Buddy picture,** click the "Account Picture" icon or the "Buddy Picture" icon located on the right side of the Photo Booth toolbar.

To use a single image from a 4-up collection, click one image of the four to select it. Use the toolbar icons to choose how you want to use the picture. Click the image again to return to the 4-up view.

Movie clips

To make a movie clip, click the movie clip button (the film strip icon, circled on the right). The camera button in the center of the toolbar changes to a red video button (right). Click it to begin recording. While recording, the toolbar shows a timer, and the red video button changes to a Stop Recording button (below). When you stop recording, a video thumbnail appears at the bottom of the window, tagged with a movie camera icon.

When you've finished recording, select the movie clip thumbnail that appears at the bottom of the window, then use the toolbar to choose how to use the movie clip. Photo Booth provides the following options:

- ▾ In the toolbar, click "Email" to attach a QuickTime version of the clip to a New Message window in Mail. Movie files are large, about 1MB per second of video, so strive to keep your movie clips short.

- ▾ To save the movie clip as a QuickTime movie, drag the video thumbnail to your Desktop or to any folder on your computer.

- ▾ To use a single frame of the movie clip for your Account picture or Buddy picture, select the movie thumbnail in the toolbar. Next, use the scrubber bar under the video (shown on the right) to select the frame you want, then click "Account Picture" or "Buddy Picture" in the toolbar.

- ▾ You can export the movie clip as an animated GIF file for use on a website or as your iChat buddy picture. From the File menu, choose "Export." The animated GIF file contains one frame per second of video. A ten second video contains 10 frames. It's not smooth animation, but the file size is a much smaller download than a QuickTime version which is saved at approximately 15 frames per second.

A video clip is tagged with a small movie camera icon in the bottom-left corner of the thumbnail.

Create a Slideshow

To preview all of your snapshots, from the View menu, choose "Start Slideshow." Use the on-screen slideshow controls to choose Play, Pause, Back, Next, Index Sheet (a full-screen display of all snapshots), Fit to Screen, Add to iPhoto, and Close (exit Slideshow). You can also press the Escape key to exit a Photo Booth Slideshow.

Add Effects to Snapshots

Photo Booth includes a gallery of special effects that you can apply as you take a snapshot or record a movie clip.

1. Click the Effects button to show a pane of effects (below-left). The center image always shows a Normal preview without effects.

2. Click the arrows on either side of the "Effects" button to see all three Effects panes. The fourth Effects pane contains empty spaces to which you can add your own photo or movie clip to be used as a special effect backdrop for a still photo or movie clip.

3. Click on the effect you want. A full-size preview of the effect displays in the window (below-right).

4. Click one of the three snapshot buttons to choose the type of snapshot you want (still picture, 4-up, or movie clip), then click the red camera button. The special effect snapshot appears in the row of thumbnails. Select it, then use the tools in the toolbar to share it.

Click one of the four gray squares in the toolbar to show another pane of effects.

Or, click the arrows on either side of the "Effects" button to cycle through all of the Effects panes.

Create a custom special effects backdrop

Click the extreme-right gray square to show a pane of blank image wells. Drag one of your own photos or movies into a blank space, then select it to use as a special effects backdrop. When you take a snapshot, a message instructs you to move out of the view so Photo Booth can patch the image into the background.

Print a Proof Sheet of Your Snapshot

From the File menu, choose "Print...." In the drop-down sheet, select a page layout, click "Preview" to preview your selection, then click "Print."

Time Machine

We know we should back up important files every day, but really it's just too much trouble. Surely everything will be OK for a couple of days until we have time to make backups. Months later we still haven't had time to backup and one of our applications crashes, damaging an important file. Or an earlier version of a file has been overwritten by a newer version with changes, and now you need the original version. Oh, if only we had a time machine that could go back in time and grab earlier versions of files. And, wouldn't it be nice if the time machine did this automatically, without us doing anything.

Wait… there is such a thing! And, surprisingly, it's called Time Machine. After you set it up, it backs up your computer regularly. For the initial backup, Time Machine backs up everything, including system files, applications, etc. After that, only files that have changed are backed up. Hourly backups are stored for the past 24 hours, daily backups are stored for the past month, then weekly backups are stored until the backup disk is full. Because backups are stored by date, you can restore files or folders (or your entire system) exactly as they were at specific points in time.

When the backup disk fills up, Time Machine deletes the oldest backups to make room for new ones. It could take a long time to reach this point, but be prepared either to replace the Time Machine disk with another one, or let Time Machine delete older files when necessary. While Time Machine is a good solution for temporary storage of backups, and a great way to restore files that have been thrown away, lost, or changed, it isn't a final solution for creating permanent archives of your files. If you plan to replace the full Time Machine disk with an empty one, you can use the full disk for permanent storage of your backups. But if you plan to keep using the same disk and let Time Machine delete the oldest files to make room for new backups, be sure to use other backup methods to create permanent backups of important files and folders (such as burning items to CDs or DVDs, copying items to your .Mac iDisk, or copying items to other external drives). Remember, it's safest to create *multiple* backups of items that you absolutely cannot afford to lose.

Starting Time Machine

For best results, you should use an external disk dedicated only to Time Machine backups. If you use the backup drive to store other files, you lose that storage space for backups. It should have enough capacity to backup the entire drive that it's assigned to backup.

Both FireWire and USB disks work with Time Machine, including most disks that might be available on your local network. Disks used for Time Machine backups must be formatted as Mac OS Extended (Journaled), and have Access Control Lists (ACLs) enabled. Time Machine will erase and reformat the disk if necessary, if you OK the procedure.

To set up Time Machine backups:

1. Connect an external disk to your Mac. A dialog opens and asks, "Do you want to use 'disk name' to back up with Time Machine?" Click the "Use as Backup Disk" button.

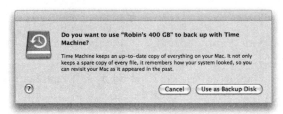

2. The Time Machine pane of System Preferences opens and shows information about the connected external disk (disk name, available space, date of oldest backup, and date of latest backup).

3. Click the Options button (shown below) to open a dialog (shown on the next page) in which you can designate any items you want to exclude from Time Machine backups.

To pause a Time Machine backup, slide the switch to OFF.

See the next page.

To add items to the "Do not back up" list, click the Add (**+**) button. A Finder sheet slides down from the title bar. Select the items (drives, volumes, files, or folders) you want to exclude. To remove items from the list, select them and click the Remove (**–**) button.

4. Click "Done." Time Machine makes an initial backup that includes everything on your computer (below). This backup can be time consuming, depending on how many folders, files, and applications are on your computer. Subsequent backups are faster since only changed files are backed up.

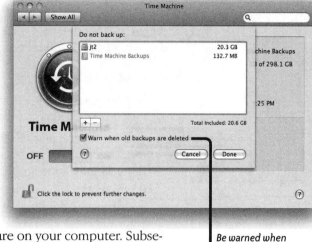

Be warned when Time Machine deletes the oldest backups.

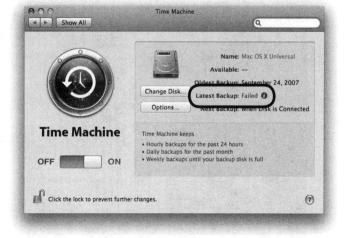

Click the gray circle-x to stop a backup.
Or, slide the ON button to OFF (shown below).

If an alert says the latest backup failed (circled, right), click the red Info button for an explanation—the disk may be too small. To change to another disk, click the "Change Disk…" button, then select another connected disk. If Time Machine alerts you that the new disk must be erased (below), Click "Erase." If you don't want to lose information on the disk, click "Choose Another Disk."

How To Use Time Machine

There are several different ways you might choose to use Time Machine to find earlier versions of files, or to find missing files.

To find and restore a file:

1. Single-click a file (or folder) in a Finder window to highlight it.

2. Click the Time Machine icon in the Dock. The Time Machine star field is revealed in the background, showing the current Finder window on top of a stack of windows, with earlier versions of that same window receding into the past. The selected text file is shown prominently in the upper section of the Cover Flow view, and it's also shown highlighted in the list view in the bottom section.

   The bar located at the bottom of the star field is labeled "Today (Now)" to indicate the files shown in the Finder window on top of the stack are the most current, up-to-date versions.

3. To go back in time and find previous versions of the selected file, click the back-in-time arrow (circled, below).

In the example below, the Finder window is set to Cover Flow view, but you can use any of the other views (Icon view, List view, or Column view).

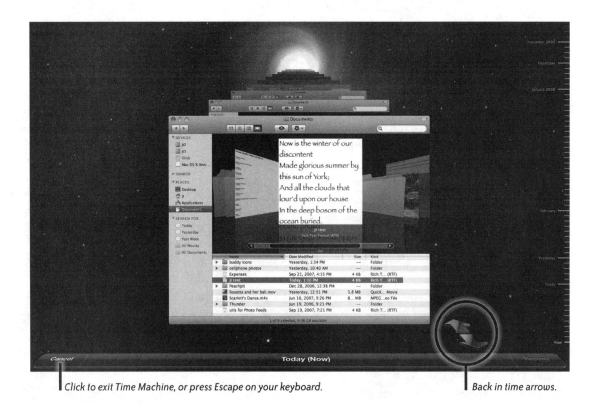

| Click to exit Time Machine, or press Escape on your keyboard. | Back in time arrows. |

The star field view zooms back in time through the stack of windows until it reaches a window where an earlier version of the selected file exists. The file is already selected, and, in the example below, it's displayed in the Cover Flow view. Notice that the bar at the bottom of the window now says "Today at 8:50 AM," which is about 12 hours earlier than the current time. And you can see that the file had different formatting in this earlier version.

If this isn't the version of the file you're looking for, click the back-in-time arrow again to find earlier versions. You can also drag your pointer over the timeline on the right edge of the screen to select a specific backup time or date.

4. To restore an earlier version of the file, make sure it's selected, then click "Restore" in the bottom-right corner. A dialog (right) asks if you want to keep the *original* version of the file (not the backup), keep *both* files, or replace the original with the Time Machine version. If you choose "Keep Both," a restored copy of the backed up file is made and put on your computer (right-top). The word "original" is added to the original's file name (right-bottom).

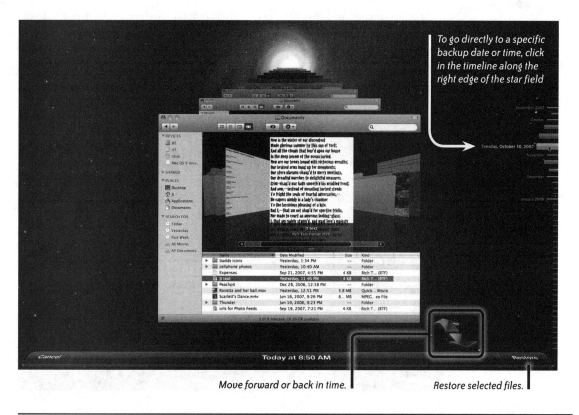

To go directly to a specific backup date or time, click in the timeline along the right edge of the star field

Move forward or back in time.

Restore selected files.

Spotlight searches in Time Machine

When you use Spotlight to search for a file, the search takes place in the "Now" time frame. In other words, you find the current version of the file. Time Machine extends your search into the past to find the same file as it was in earlier versions. If you've lost or deleted a file, Time Machine can zoom into the past and find the various versions of the file that were automatically saved for you.

Search, then switch to Time Machine:

1. Start a Spotlight search in the Finder. If Spotlight doesn't find the item you're looking for, click the Time Machine icon in the Dock.

   The Time Machine star field screen is revealed, with Finder windows receding into the past. The window in the foreground is labeled "Today (Now)." Your search term is still in the Spotlight text field.

2. Click the back-in-time arrow. Time Machine zooms back in time until it finds the item. To look for an even earlier version of the item, click the back-in-time arrow again. Or, click in the timeline along the right edge of the screen. Notice that the time label in the bar at the bottom of the screen shows when the item was backed up.

3. When you find the item you want, click "Restore" on the right side of the bar at the bottom of the Time Machine screen.

You can also go straight to Time Machine (click Time Machine in the Dock) and initiate a Spotlight search from there—enter a search term in the Spotlight text field of the foreground window.

To show a "Quick Look" view of the item (an instant preview), make sure the item is highlighted, then tap the spacebar.

To close the Quick Look preview, tap the space bar again, or click the Close button in the top-left corner of the Quick Look window.

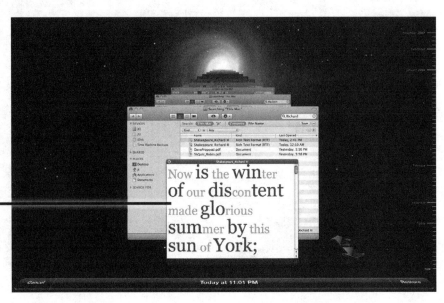

Index

YouTube